THE REIGN OF
EDWARD III

THE REIGN OF
EDWARD III

TEMPUS

Updated edition first published 2000

PUBLISHED IN THE UNITED KINGDOM BY:

Tempus Publishing Ltd
The Mill, Brimscombe Port
Stroud, Gloucestershire GL5 2QG

PUBLISHED IN THE UNITED STATES OF AMERICA BY:

Tempus Publishing Inc.
2A Cumberland Street
Charleston, SC 29401

Tempus books are available in France, Germany and Belgium
from the following addresses:

Tempus Publishing Group	Tempus Publishing Group	Tempus Publishing Group
21 Avenue de la République	Gustav-Adolf-Straße 3	Place de L'Alma 4/5
37300 Joué-lès-Tours	99084 Erfurt	1200 Brussels
FRANCE	GERMANY	BELGIUM

British Library Cataloguing in Publication Data.
A catalogue record for this book is available from the British Library.

ISBN 0 7524 1434 8

Typesetting and origination by Tempus Publishing.
PRINTED AND BOUND IN GREAT BRITAIN.

Contents

Illustrations

Colour plates (between pp. 128-129)

Preface

This book was first published in 1990; the text as set out here is the same as that found in the 1990 edition and its 1993 paperback version (with minor corrections and stylistic changes), but the book has been re-designed and includes many new illustrations. I am grateful to Jonathan Reeve of Tempus for offering me the opportunity to re-issue the work, and to Kate Adams and Anne Phipps for their assistance.

The 1990s has been a fruitful decade for Edward III studies and much new material has become available for the study of the reign. That work, and my own continued interest in the subject, has led me to recast some of my thoughts on both the achievements and the shortcomings of the Edwardian regime: were I writing this book in 1999, it would undoubtedly be different. However, I also hold firm to my original thesis that the long period of domestic political stability during the middle decades of the fourteenth century cannot be accounted for merely in terms of successful foreign war and can only satisfactorily be explained by examining the nature and achievements of Edward's government in England. While recent work (including my own) has tended to place much greater stress on the theme of justice than is evident in this study, I nevertheless remain convinced that the fiscal accomplishments of the mid-fourteenth century also represent the outcome of sound political management and effective administrative control.

There is still no definitive modern biography of Edward III: in spite of (or rather, perhaps, because of) the recent spate of specialised studies of the reign, it seems that the task becomes more, rather than less, challenging with the passing of time. This is inevitably a somewhat unmanageable reign, too long, too disparate, too eventful (as it were) for its own good. To write it from the perspective of 1327 is to acknowledge Edward III's extraordinary transformation of a monarchy brought low by the personal and political ineptitude of his father into one of the most respected regimes in fourteenth-century Europe; yet to write it from the vantage point of 1377 is to emphasise the defects and weaknesses of the regime exposed to bitter public criticism in the Good Parliament and the Peasants' Revolt. Above all, perhaps, Edward himself remains an enigma. Lacking the vividness of contemporary sources that open windows on the characters of a Henry II, a Henry V or a Henry VIII, we are left with mere fragments and constructions that are strong on the king's attitude to fighting, less certain on his commitment to culture, decidedly shadowy on his personal vision of governance. It may be that new techniques in textual analysis may yet fill some of the holes in our understanding. In the meantime, however, the subject (both human and thematic) remains an abiding interest precisely because it is so uncertain and so fluid.

I have never liked the notion of intellectual monopolisation that lies behind the claim that Edward III is 'my' king; rather, I offer this book as representing something of 'my' personal interpretation of that king and of his reign. It is in the contrasts that emerge between this and other, less sympathetic, studies that we will begin to find if not the definitive Edward III then at least a new, more vivid and more dynamic picture of political life in fourteenth-century England.

Mark Ormrod
November 1999

Introduction

> ...the Lord Edward, lately king of England, of his good will, and by the common counsel and consent of the prelates, earls, and barons, and other nobles, and all the community of the realm, has given up the government of the realm, and has granted and wishes that the government of the said realm should fall upon the Lord Edward, his eldest son and heir, and that he should reign and be crowned king ...[1]

It was in these words, proclaimed in public places throughout the realm, that most of the inhabitants of England heard of the change of ruler effected in the winter of 1326–7. Few knew the details or understood the implications of this event. The abdication, or deposition, of Edward II was arranged by Queen Isabella and her lover Roger Mortimer during an extraordinary parliament held at Westminster in January 1327. The prelates and peers, knights and burgesses present at this meeting were closely in touch with events, as were some of the citizens of London, who put strong pressure on the assembly to deliver the realm from the ineptitude of the king. The people who knew most of all were the members of the deputation sent to Edward at Kenilworth to present the demands of his subjects that he renounce his title. Some of those who attended this meeting later told their stories, and the events were reported in the chronicles.[2] It is doubtful, however, whether many were interested in the theoretical significance of the revolution which had taken place. Within the limits of legal memory no king had been deprived of his authority in this way. Edward II had simply lost the right to rule by his own blatant incapacity, and by allowing his henchmen the Despensers to exercise a quite arbitrary authority during the last years of his reign. Somehow (and the details are by no means clear) a satisfactory compromise was reached, by which the king was held to have given up the throne freely and to have bestowed it on his eldest son. Events in 1326–7 could therefore be conveniently interpreted as a simple speeding up of the natural succession. Those who best understood what had happened at Westminster and Kenilworth were precisely those in whose interests it was to draw a discreet veil over the proceedings. The majority of the new king's subjects in the provinces were in any case more than content to know that a highly unpopular ruler had been removed, and to hope for better things from his successor.

Fifty years later, when Edward III died, the image of the monarchy was very different. Edward was to be remembered as a victorious and honourable king who had won respect abroad and popularity at home. A poem written several years after his death presented him as the minister of God, a scourge to his enemies, and a kind and just ruler to his people: one who indeed deserved the society of the angels.[3] At the end of the fourteenth century the St Albans chronicler Thomas Walsingham wrote thus:

> Without doubt this king had been among all the kings and princes of the world renowned, beneficent, merciful, and august; given the epithet 'the Favoured One' on account of the remarkable favour through which he distinguished himself . . . Certainly his fame spread so far abroad amongst foreign and remote nations that they considered themselves fortunate who were either subject to his lordship or were partly allied with him. Indeed, they did not believe that there could be any kingdom under the heavens which produced so noble, so high-minded, or so fortunate a king, or could in the future produce such another after his decease.[4]

Walsingham was not blind to Edward's failings, and attributed the political problems of the 1370s directly to the old king's moral depravity. But his eulogy left a lasting impression. Edward III was remembered as a great leader in the wars with France, a king who 'brought back victory in triumphant glory from all encounters on land and sea'. He had ruled his kingdom 'actively, wisely, and nobly', showing due devotion to God, generosity to the great, and compassion to the weak.[5] As the years passed, the failure of most of his successors to live up to such achievements gave further encouragement to the flourishing cult of Edward III. By the fifteenth century the most popular chronicle of the day, the *Brut*, claimed that this king had 'passed and shone by virtue and grace, given to him from God, above all his predecessors that were noble men and worthy.[6] Edward III had become the very prototype of the successful king.

No modern reader could seriously accept all these compliments at face value. Since the nineteenth century, indeed, historians have become a good deal more circumspect about the supposed accomplishments of this king. Edward III is now often seen as a rather second-rate ruler, stubborn and selfish in his foreign ambitions, weak and yielding in his domestic policies. He lacked the forcefulness of Henry II, the statesmanship of Edward I, the charisma of Henry V, or the application of Henry VII. He was prepared to accept short-term compromises and to ignore the wider implications of his actions. Far from providing a model of successful kingship, Edward ultimately damaged the power of the monarchy and contributed to the political difficulties of his successors.[7] The adulation of the chronicles has therefore given way to the critical judgements of the textbooks. But in their determination to destroy the myth of Edward III, historians may well have gone too far. To measure his achievements by the failures of later kings is to write history backwards, and to forget the formidable problems which Edward himself faced and overcame. The prestige of the English monarchy had never sunk so low as in 1327. Yet in the course of the next generation Edward III successfully rebuilt public confidence in the crown. The result was one of the longest periods of political calm in the whole of the later Middle Ages.

That achievement was all the greater considering the number and variety of men that had to be accommodated in the new dispensation. The structure of politics had undergone a fundamental change since the thirteenth century as a result of the unprecedented and often outrageous pressures applied by the crown on its subjects. The disputes which had led to the issue of Magna Carta in 1215 and the subsequent attempt to reform royal government in 1258 were chiefly the concern of the barons, who in the name of the 'community of the realm' had sought to defend their own interests against the intrusions of King John and the inadequacies of Henry III. By 1259 the so-called 'gentry', the middling land-holders in the shires, were also taking part in political debate, though for the next half-century they were usually content to work through the magnates.[8] It was Edward I's wars in Wales, Scotland and France that really transformed the structure of politics. From the 1290s representatives both of the shires and the towns were summoned to meet with the king and his great lords in parliament and authorize universal taxes to subsidize military expenditure. At the same time Edward began to impose extremely heavy charges on the English clergy, and to negotiate special taxes on overseas trade with native and foreign merchants. In return for such financial support, these groups naturally expected some recognition and respect. If the crown asked too much and gave too little in return, then it ran the risk of confrontation. Edward I's bitter quarrel with Archbishop Winchelsey and his struggle with the barons in 1297 were a dramatic indication of the new forces at work in English politics.[9] By 1300 the crown had obtruded itself on to the lives of its subjects in a manner unthinkable in the twelfth century. If Edward I's successors were to continue with his policies, it was essential that they should also come to terms with the new political society that had grown up in response.

Edward II failed not only in this respect, but also in almost every other of the challenges left him by his father. His clash with the nobility indicated a complete disregard for the interests of any but a handful of his personal followers. In 1311, as in 1258, the great lords took it upon themselves to remove royal favourites and to force on the king ordinances for the better governance of the realm. Had Edward subsequently come to terms with the magnates, he might yet have re-established his credibility with the wider community. But the 1320s witnessed the complete breakdown of co-operation. In 1322 the king defeated and killed his cousin, Thomas of Lancaster, at the battle of Boroughbridge, and began to persecute all those who had supported the Ordinances of 1311. For a while, political society was left leaderless and powerless. Edward II's deposition was really a palace revolution, the work of Isabella and Mortimer. But the delegation sent to Kenilworth to secure the king's abdication included a complete cross-section of the community: bishops, monks and friars; earls, lords, barons of the Cinque Ports, provincial knights, Londoners, and possibly representatives from other lesser towns.[10] Under exceptional circumstances it was found necessary to mobilize the whole realm against its common enemy, a perverse and grossly incapable king. The lessons for the future were plain enough. Any ruler who so obstinately refused the wise counsels of his great subjects and so consistently failed to provide good governance for the realm was not worthy to hold the title of king. This lesson was not lost on Edward's successor.

It was in the reign of Edward III that the crown finally came to terms with the new political conditions which had emerged since the later thirteenth century. Realizing the dangers of perpetual conflict and the positive advantages to be gained from consensus, Edward III acknowledged the influence not only of the magnates but also of the other politically active classes — the clergy, the county landholders and the prosperous townsmen — and tried to win their active support for his domestic and foreign policies. It would obviously be a mistake to exaggerate this development. The process of reconciliation was gradual and often painful, and the compromise eventually struck in the middle years of the reign benefited only a small number of men. In many ways it was the nobles who continued to dominate politics and to dictate the fortunes of the crown. The great mass of the king's subjects remained powerless, and were increasingly resentful of the way in which the ruling classes manipulated power for their own ends. Indeed, certain sections of the rural and urban population felt sufficiently betrayed by their betters to take the only form of political action open to them and launch the Peasants' Revolt within four years of Edward's death. Nevertheless, it is clear that by the mid-fourteenth century the 'community of the realm' incorporated a larger cross-section of the population than ever before.[11] By the end of Edward III's reign a new political society had emerged in England, one that was to remain substantially unaltered for the rest of the Middle Ages and beyond. The principal purpose of this book is to examine that society and to explore the political implications of its relationship with the crown. But in order to appreciate these developments, it is first necessary to give a brief outline of Edward III's long reign. The period divides itself naturally into three phases. The years until the parliamentary crisis of 1341 form a postlude to the reign of Edward II and indicate the formidable problems inherited by Edward III. The middle period from 1341 to 1360 was, by contrast, one of extraordinary good fortune, during which military success abroad and political harmony at home helped to re-establish the prestige and power of the monarchy. After the high point of the early 1360s, however, Edward's last years witnessed the gradual disintegration of royal authority. Finally, diplomatic and military failures combined with domestic mismanagement to produce a serious political confrontation in the Good Parliament of 1376.

1 The early years: 1327–41

The forcible removal of Edward II made an inauspicious start to the new reign. Edward III was a boy of fourteen when he was set prematurely on the throne of England. At his coronation, which took place just a few days after the publication of his succession, he was asked whether he would take the additional oath made by his father in 1308 to observe the just laws chosen by the community of the realm. He was reputedly told that if he did not so swear, he would not be crowned.[1] Those who took part in the coronation, however, were well aware that the real political problem lay not with the young king but with Queen Isabella and Roger Mortimer. They had put Edward on the throne, and they clearly intended to control his government.[2] In their rush to establish some form of legitimate and workable regime, the queen and her lover won the initiative. The parliament of February-March 1327 was preoccupied with efforts to undo the evils of the previous reign, securing the posthumous rehabilitation of Thomas of Lancaster, acknowledging the succession of Thomas's brother Henry to most of the family titles, and guaranteeing an amnesty for those of Lancaster's followers victimized by the Despensers.[3] The assembly lacked the authority and missed the opportunity to dictate the form of a regency government, and merely asked that suitable wise men be chosen by the magnates to advise the king.[4] A council of sorts was set up, led by Henry of Lancaster, and including some of the leading opponents of the Despenser regime such as the old king's brothers, the Earls of Norfolk and Kent, and Bishops Stratford of Winchester and Orleton of Hereford.[5] This was in no sense a regency council, however, for it enjoyed no executive power. It was Mortimer, through his intimacy with the queen and his influence over the boy king, who actually held the reins of government.

For a while, popular measures helped to disguise the self-seeking ambitions of Isabella and her paramour. The popular cult of Thomas of Lancaster, which had been repressed by Edward II, now received some degree of official support. In 1327 the commons actually demanded that the Ordinances of 1311, for which Lancaster had fought and lost his life, should be added to the list of great and solemn charters observed by the crown.[6] Although the government balked at this idea, it did take up the commons' proposals for the canonization of Lancaster and began to negotiate with the Curia for the making of a new St Thomas.[7] The liberality of the new regime also won the queen some powerful allies. Sympathies for Edward II remained, especially in the Welsh Marches, where the Despenser stronghold of Caerphilly held out well into 1327. Even those who had welcomed the queen's invasion in 1326 might be ambivalent unless rewarded for their support. Erstwhile servants of the Despensers were therefore left at their government posts; and important figures such as the new king's uncles, who might have expected a greater share of power, were bought off with large grants of money and land. None the less, it was soon obvious who were the real beneficiaries of the coup. The queen and Mortimer helped themselves greedily to the large financial resources left by Edward II, and made free with the possessions of his followers. The Despenser estates in South Wales and the lands of Edward II's partisan the Earl of Arundel in the northern march now fell under Mortimer's control. Despite his formal acceptance of the revived Lancastrian inheritance, Mortimer also insisted on seizing Thomas of Lancaster's former lordship of Denbigh. By snatching marcher lands from Edward II's supporters and opponents alike, Mortimer consolidated an enormous block of territories on the Welsh borders.[8] Before long, he was king in all but name. He held ostentatious tournaments, and married his daughters off to the heirs of the great earldoms of Norfolk and Pembroke. The climax came late in 1328 at the parliament of Salisbury, when Mortimer assumed the title of Earl of March. Within two years of the collapse of the Despensers, an overmighty marcher principality was once again threatening to upset the political balance. The political community braced itself for another confrontation.

The first opportunity for criticism came with the failure of Mortimer's foreign policy. Edward II had been humiliated by the Scottish leader Robert Bruce at Bannockburn in 1314 and defeated by the French in Gascony during the war of St Sardos of 1323–5. Military or diplomatic victories were much needed in order to re-establish the political credibility of the crown. But Queen Isabella had already tarnished her reputation by working out a humiliating truce with her brother, Charles IV, in 1325. This had required the English king to pay £60,000 as a relief for his duchy of Gascony, and an additional 50,000 marks (£33,333 6s.8d.) by way of a war indemnity. Moreover, in 1326 the French and Scottish kings had made a treaty at Corbeil, guaranteeing the integrity of their alliance irrespective of any English approaches to either side. The diplomatic and military situation was therefore unpromising in 1327. On the very night of Edward III's coronation a Scottish force crossed the northern border and laid siege to Norham Castle. When news reached the court of Bruce's plan to launch a combined Irish, Welsh and Scottish attack against Edward, preparations for a campaign were immediately put in hand. But Mortimer proved less than adequate as a war leader. When the two armies eventually drew up at Stanhope Park near Durham in early August, the Scots were able to launch a surprise night attack on Edward III's quarters and then withdrew before battle could be joined. The whole affair proved a fiasco, and an expensive one at that. All that was left of Edward II's considerable financial reserve was now used up, and the government had to pawn the crown jewels to pay for the campaign. There was no alternative but to sue for peace. By the treaty of Northampton of 1328 the English renounced all claims to feudal suzerainty and to lands in Scotland. The queen and her lover salvaged some personal satisfaction from the treaty by securing the promise of £20,000 from the Scots, most of which found its way into their own treasuries. But for the young king, and for many of his subjects, the terms were an unmitigated disaster.

It was in the wake of the treaty of Northampton that the first signs of active opposition to Mortimer began to emerge.[9] Although the treaty was presented to parliament in 1328 for ratification, a number of the barons, including the Earl of Lancaster, declined to give their assent. In the summer, Lancaster refused to support a projected campaign in Gascony; and later in the year he absented himself from the parliament of Salisbury, returning to his estates in the midlands with the intention of raising rebellion. He was joined by the Earls of Norfolk and Kent and by his son-in-law Sir Thomas Wake. In the event, the uprising was short-lived. The king's uncles rapidly made peace with the court, and in January 1329 Lancaster was forced to surrender. He and most of his followers were treated leniently: their forfeited estates were restored and the fines imposed on them were pardoned. But Lancaster was now permanently alienated from the court. Others soon followed. Bishop Orleton, who had acted as treasurer for a short while after the deposition, had already fallen out with the queen and her lover by the end of 1328; and Bishop Stratford gave public support to Lancaster in 1328–9, firmly establishing himself as one of Mortimer's bitterest enemies.[10] Several of those implicated in Lancaster's rebellion, including Henry Beaumont and Thomas Wake, were excepted from the general pardon and forced into exile on the continent, where they plotted Mortimer's downfall. Those who remained in favour at court hoped that Mortimer's magnanimous treatment of the rebels would revive public respect for the regime. But such expectations were dashed early in 1330, when the Earl of Kent was arrested and executed. There were rumours that Edward II was still alive, and Kent was charged with the highly unlikely crime of conspiring to put his brother back on the throne.[11] The accusation of treason conjured up memories of the very worst moments of Despenser rule. The government's arbitrary methods now made it plain that the whole revolution of 1326–7 had been redundant.

Mortimer's influence in government depended entirely on his ability to dominate a puppet king, and for three years he did not miss a single opportunity to humiliate his young charge. Edward III's father had intended that he should marry a French or Aragonese princess, but his mother had forced him into a hasty marriage with the young Philippa of Hainault in order to secure military backing for the invasion of 1326. Edward and his bride then found their precedence flouted by Isabella and her lover, who blocked Philippa's coronation until February 1330 and consistently kept the king's household short of cash. Mortimer quite obviously distrusted Edward from the very start, and set spies in the royal household to track his every move.[12] By the summer of 1330 the king was seventeen years old and had just become a father to a healthy boy child. But his efforts to involve himself in government were getting nowhere. A letter to the Pope revealed that he was unable even to secure patronage for his clerical servants and followers.[13] He could however depend on two close associates: Master Richard Bury, the keeper of the privy seal, who had served Edward since his earliest years; and William Montagu, the son of one of Edward II's personal favourites, who had ingratiated himself with the new regime and won the confidence of the young king. With their connivance, Edward managed to inform the Pope that the only royal letters sent to Avignon which really reflected his personal wishes would be those bearing the words *pater sancte* (holy father) written in the king's own hand. By such clandestine means did Edward serve out his apprenticeship as king and count the days to Mortimer's downfall.

His chance finally came late in 1330. Mortimer was increasingly suspicious of Edward's actions, and insisted on interrogating him and his followers before a great council at Nottingham in October. The king was infuriated at this insult to his title. In the company of Montagu and a small band of young men, he entered Nottingham Castle secretly on the night of 19 October, took the Earl of March unawares, and dragged him off to London

1 *The young king receives the arms of England from St George*

to face trial and execution. The enormous earldom which Mortimer had created fell forfeit to the crown, and Edward eagerly carved it up to reward his own supporters. The events at Nottingham confirmed the popular opinion of the Earl of March as an unscrupulous usurper of the king's rightful power. Few had mourned for Edward II; and although Queen Isabella probably shed more tears for her lover than for her husband, fewer still can have regretted the passing of Roger Mortimer.

On the morrow of the Nottingham coup Edward III issued a proclamation to be read by the sheriffs in public places throughout his realm.

> ... the king's affairs and the affairs of his realm have been directed until now to the damage and dishonour of him and his realm and to the impoverishment of his people..., wherefore he has, of his own knowledge and will, caused certain persons to be arrested, to wit the earl of March [etc.], and he wills that all men shall know that he will henceforth govern his people according to right and reason, as befits his royal dignity, and that the affairs that concern him and the estate of his realm shall be directed by the common counsel of the magnates of his realm and in no other wise ....[14]

These were fine words, by which Edward was able to deflect criticism from himself and lay the blame for the misrule of the previous three years firmly on the shoulders of his enemy, Mortimer. It was less easy to live up to such pious declarations of good intent. Historians have tended to see the assumption of personal rule by Edward III as the start of a new period in English politics, when the disagreements and factions of the previous twenty years gradually broke down. But the ineptitude of Edward II and the discord within the ruling elite had left a deep and lasting impression on political society. The fiscal demands of the government, combined with the famines of the early 1320s, had also left the economy, and especially the lower levels of the population, materially weakened.[15] The king's laws were flouted as bands of thugs set up local protection rackets and terrorized their neighbours with complete impunity.[16] Edward III therefore had to do much more than win a few noble allies. He had to re-establish some respect for himself and some sense of order in the society over which he theoretically ruled. In the long term, he achieved these ends by diverting the latent hostilities within his realm towards a common external enemy. The wars against Scotland and France helped to unite the realm in a series of national military adventures. But this political transformation did not come about quickly or easily. The campaigns of the 1330s were costly and unproductive, and only temporarily disguised the serious divisions still remaining in political society — divisions which appeared again, and as wide as ever, in the crisis of 1340–1.

WAR AND POLITICAL STRIFE

The single most important reason for the outbreak of the Hundred Years War was the long-standing dispute over the feudal status of Gascony. Since the treaty of Paris of 1259, the kings of England had been forced to acknowledge that they held this duchy as a fief of the French crown. The reluctance of both Edward I and Edward II to accept this personal and political subjugation had already provoked seizures of their French lands in 1294 and 1324. So from his earliest years, Edward III was conditioned to the idea of an Anglo-French struggle. He was also well aware of the many reasons for holding on to the English possessions in Gascony. The duchy was the last remnant of the once enormous Plantagenet empire that had sprawled across western France from the Channel to the Pyrenees. To withdraw without a fight would be to betray those Gascon lords such as the Captal de Buch and the Sire d'Albret whose families had given long and honourable service to their English rulers. Gascony was also rich: in 1324 it was said to yield £13,000 a year for the crown,[17] and it was the source of most of the wine consumed in fourteenth-century England. Finally, any losses on the continent would inevitably produce criticism at home. Edward II's failure to defend his possessions in France, Scotland and Ireland was cited as one of the principal reasons for his deposition in 1327.[18] The interplay of long-standing points of feudal principle with more pragmatic concerns made it inevitable that Edward III would one day have to defend his titles and lands in France by force of arms.

In the early 1330s, however, the king could hardly afford to take an aggressive stance towards the French. It was Scotland which occupied most of his energy and time during these years. Robert Bruce had died in 1329, leaving the throne to his infant son, David II.

This inevitably reopened the long-standing dispute over the Scottish succession, and encouraged the English king to give public support to his own preferred candidate, Edward Balliol. It also offered an opportunity to placate a group of powerful English lords, led by Henry Beaumont, who had been deprived of their possessions in the Lowlands in 1328 and been alienated from the regime of Mortimer and Isabella.[19] When these northern magnates defeated the Scots at Dupplin Moor in 1332, Edward III agreed to give his official backing to the new Scottish pretender. He moved his administrative resources to York, won control of Berwick, and launched a long campaign which culminated in a battle at Halidon Hill on 19 July 1333. Employing the mixed formation of archers and dismounted men-at-arms later to be used to such good effect against the French, Edward won a great victory. David Bruce was forced into exile, and Balliol seized his throne. Edward pushed a hard bargain with his new royal ally, gaining full sovereign control over eight Lowland shires and securing the homage of Balliol at Newcastle upon Tyne in June 1334.

The English king therefore had every reason to consider his first Scottish adventure a resounding success. Unfortunately, he had reckoned without the strength of the Franco-Scottish alliance. He had already been forced to make diplomatic compromises with the new French king, Philip VI. Indeed, in 1331 he had actually declared himself willing to perform liege homage for the duchy of Gascony and had made an incognito trip across the Channel to discuss his continental possessions and a possible marriage alliance with France.[20] But the deposition of David II inevitably changed the situation. In the spring of 1334 Philip VI took David into his protection and announced that the Scottish succession must be included on the agenda in any future Anglo-French talks. Every warlike move made by Edward III towards Scotland now brought his country one step closer to open hostility with France. The king and his advisers were acutely aware of this danger, and were anxious not to go to war until they were adequately prepared. Wiser and more modest men might indeed have left Scotland to its own devices. But the English intervention there had become a matter of personal pride for Edward III. For a brief while an enormous show of military strength in the summer of 1335 gave Balliol some semblance of authority and allowed the English king to hold control of the Lowland shires. But from 1334 there were frequent threats of French reprisals, and in August and September 1335 it was rumoured that a great armada amassed by Philip VI was about to attack the south coast of England. Edward was forced to deflect attention and resources away from the north, and the Scottish war rapidly settled into an uneasy series of border raids from which neither side secured much advantage.

Philip VI's public support for the Bruce family partly reflected his growing frustration over the question of Gascony. Despite their overtures of peace in 1331, the English showed no sign of capitulating in the protracted talks over the Agenais, the land between the Dordogne and the Garonne which had been ceded to the French after the war of St Sardos of 1323–5 but was now being claimed as a part of the duchy of Gascony by Edward's negotiators.[21] By the end of 1335, with things going badly in the north, Edward was briefly prepared to respond to papal requests for an Anglo-French settlement, and later in 1338 he patched up a truce with Scotland. But in 1336 the signs of impending war with France were plain enough. When Philip VI moved his fleet from the Mediterranean to the Norman ports in the summer of that year, he was not only abandoning the crusading project to which both he and Edward had earlier given dilatory support,[22] but was also making a clear declaration of hostile intent. Both the Scottish war and the French negotiations had foundered. It was time for a larger and more decisive confrontation between Edward and the Valois king.

On 24 May 1337 Philip VI formally confiscated the duchy of Aquitaine and the county of Ponthieu. It was claimed that Edward III, who owed liege homage for those lands, had broken his feudal bond by giving sanctuary and aid to Robert of Artois, the cousin, brother-in-law and mortal enemy of the French king. In the normal course of events, this would have been followed by a brief show of English military strength in northern France and Gascony and a diplomatic compromise allowing Edward to repossess his lands on condition that he acknowledge the suzerainty of Philip VI. What made the dispute so different after 1337 was the decision of Edward III to break free of the subordinate status imposed on him by the treaty of Paris. Through his mother, Edward was the grandson of Philip IV of France and the nephew of the last Capetian king, Charles IV. When Charles had died without a direct male heir in 1328, some attempt had been made to forward Edward's claim to the French throne. But the comparative weakness of his case, depending on descent through the female line, and the acute problems of his own kingdom meant that the claim had been ignored, and the crown had passed to Charles IV's cousin, Philip VI. It was almost inevitable, then, that Edward would respond to his opponent's hostility by reasserting his own title to the French throne. He came very close to making a public declaration of that claim in 1337, and in 1340 he formally assumed the title 'King of England and France'.[23] The dual monarchy which was to cause so many diplomatic and military problems for Edward's successors had thus come into being.

Whether Edward III had any intention of making this title a reality is, of course, quite another matter. The claim was useful primarily because it allowed him to escape his feudal obligations and assert full sovereign control over the English lands in France. It was also a clever publicity stunt designed to attract allies. In the initial stages of the war Edward relied much on promises of assistance from the princes of the Netherlands. Flanders also fell under his influence when the pro-French count was forced into exile and the cloth-producing towns sought to maintain their trade links with England. He even won the support of the Emperor Louis IV, who in 1338 created Edward his imperial vicar-general and gave him extensive authority over Germany and the Low Countries. For a while, indeed, it seemed that most of north-western Europe was falling within Edward's grasp. His formal assumption of the French royal title in 1340, representing a characteristic mixture of personal vanity and political opportunism, was the inevitable climax to this diplomatic success story. But the inconsistencies and inadequacies of military policy in 1337–40 speak more of Edward's aims than do any empty titles. There was virtually nothing in the first phase of hostilities that could possibly justify the pretentious claims of the English king.

The early years of the French war were later to be remembered chiefly for the naval victory at Sluys in 1340. But contemporaries saw the war in different terms. The two factors that conditioned English politics in this period were the enormous fiscal pressures applied on the country to subsidize the war, and the king's almost complete failure to

2 & 3 The fourth great seal of Edward III, the first to be made after Edward claimed the throne of France

justify his huge expenditure with any military or diplomatic gains. The Scottish war had already witnessed a considerable outlay of manpower and money, and after 1336 the scale of such demands increased considerably.[24] In 1337 a great council was induced to grant three successive fifteenths and tenths, each estimated at just over £38,000, and the clergy were cajoled into granting three tenths valued at about £19,000 each (see Tables 1-2). This was only the start of an extraordinary bout of public taxation. Successive impositions on wool exports raised the customs duties to new and unprecedented levels. In 1337 the king attempted to make a compulsory seizure of 30,000 sacks of English wool; and when this plan collapsed in 1338, a great council was persuaded to grant the remaining 17,500 sacks as a tax. Finally, in 1340 the king was allowed to take every ninth lamb, wool-fleece and sheaf of corn produced from the year's crop. The total value of the money and the agricultural produce collected towards these various taxes and forced loans was well over £500,000. The only previous occasion on which royal taxation had approached these levels was during Edward I's French war of 1294–8, when the crown raised something in excess of £450,000 from a comparable series of levies. There is every indication that other wartime exactions also reached unprecedented peaks in the late 1330s. Undoubtedly the most controversial and oppressive of these was purveyance, the compulsory purchase of foodstuffs for the king's troops at prices which, if paid at all, were usually well below the market value. Coinciding as they did with a period of economic recession, these various fiscal burdens were bound to create real hardship and widespread resentment among Edward III's English subjects.

What really provoked criticism, however, was the king's failure to make productive use of such resources. Although Edward left for the continent in the summer of 1338, he spent his whole time in the Low Countries, and the promised offensive into northern

France had still not been attempted when he returned home to plead for more funds in March 1340. Such inactivity was highly unpopular, and after the initial euphoria of 1337 a substantial section of the English population quickly became disillusioned by the war effort. Much of the protest literature of this period concentrated on the iniquities of royal taxation and the corruption of the king's agents. Official and unofficial sources alike stated that the country was ripe for revolt by 1340, and attached the blame for this situation to the wilful and obstinate king.[25] Many politically active men felt that Edward III was abrogating his true responsibilities by pursuing reckless ambitions abroad and ignoring the tribulations of his subjects at home. Parliaments and convocations were more or less obliged by the state of war to respond to the king's requests for supplies; but this did not prevent such assemblies from making heart-felt pleas for the alleviation of onerous taxes and outright condemnations of the king's domestic and foreign policies.

THE GOVERNMENT OF THE REALM

If any sense of common purpose had been created after the fall of Edward II and the demise of Roger Mortimer, it was therefore wearing very thin by the late 1330s. The crisis of 1340–1 was to make it clear that the king had done little to resolve the political problems inherited from earlier regimes. Even the appearance of stability in the government was deceptive.[26] Bishop Stratford took over as chancellor after the Nottingham coup, and he and his family dominated the civil service for the next decade. But their ascendancy did not go unchallenged. In 1334–5 Stratford, now Archbishop of Canterbury, was temporarily replaced as chancellor by the royal confidant Richard Bury, who had recently been made Bishop of Durham. In 1338, before leaving for France in the company of the archbishop, Edward likewise removed Stratford's brother Robert from the chancellorship and put in Richard Bentworth, the new Bishop of London and an influential member of the royal household. These reshuffles suggest that the king was somewhat suspicious of the older generation of political bishops and entertained hopes of creating his own following in the civil service. But his efforts were too erratic to have much effect. In his preoccupation with warfare, Edward was content to leave the more mundane aspects of administration to others. The potential threat posed by this arrangement was to become acutely obvious when a rift developed between Edward and his chief ministers in 1340–1.

A similar lack of positive action characterized the king's treatment of the nobility during the early 1330s. Edward III's generosity towards the victims of earlier regimes is well known.[27] One of his first actions on assuming power in 1330, for instance, was to secure the restoration of Richard Fitzalan to the earldom of Arundel. What has not been sufficiently recognized is Edward's tendency to create political factions among the nobility by promoting a small group of personal friends. Indeed, the royal clique of the 1330s was almost as exclusive as those which had dominated the court of Edward II. The principal beneficiary of the new regime was undoubtedly William Montagu, who remained the chief influence behind the throne from Mortimer's downfall in 1330 until his own death in 1344. His faithful service in the Scottish campaigns won him many honours, culminating in the title of Earl of Salisbury in 1337. After 1335, admittedly, Edward III attempted to spread his patronage more widely. He revived the lapsed earldoms of Devon and Pembroke, and he cultivated the support of his Lancastrian cousins by bestowing on Henry of Grosmont the title of Earl of Derby. This was one of six earldoms created in March 1337 in an obvious attempt to strengthen the baronial ranks on the eve of a major war.[28] But although Henry of Grosmont and the new Earl of Northampton, William Bohun, were drawn from the greatest noble houses, there was still a worrying tendency to promote relatively humble men purely because of their intimacy with the king. One such was William Clinton, an obscure household knight, who now received the earldom of Huntingdon and, like Montagu, secured a generous allowance worthy of his new dignity. On the eve of the French war, then, Edward's relations with the nobility were still uncertain. Much would depend on his ability to unite the baronage in support of his great offensive against France.

In the event, the opening stages of the Hundred Years War proved not only a military disappointment but also a political disaster. In July 1338 when Edward embarked for the continent, he left behind a regency council staffed by the Earls of Arundel and Huntingdon, and Lord Neville. A series of instructions, the so-called Walton Ordinances, set out the administrative procedures to be used during Edward's absence.[29] These ordinances were quite straightforward, and caused no conflict at the time. They were simply intended, like similar orders issued during the Scottish campaign of 1333,[30] to establish the primacy of the war over all other administrative and political concerns. Problems only emerged when the king began to make totally unreasonable financial demands on the home government. In September 1339 Edward tried to resolve his differences with the regency council by granting it greater initiative and sending home Archbishop Stratford to take charge of the administration.[31] But in practice this simply meant that military policy became the exclusive preserve of the Earl of Salisbury and a number of other household officials including William Kilsby, keeper of the privy seal, and the steward, John Darcy. Back in England, Stratford found that his new authority was no solution to the basic problem of war finance. The requests made to parliament in 1339–40 for more supplies received grudging responses, and the commons refused to concede a tax until they had referred back to their constituencies. The king returned home to press his case, and his presence in the parliament of March–April 1340 was sufficient to secure the grant of the ninth. In return, however, Edward was forced to make royal tax collectors accountable to parliament, and to grant legislation which restricted the worst abuses of his purveyors and reserved the ninth solely for the costs of war.[32] The king returned to the continent resentful of such serious concessions but hopeful that the new tax would solve his financial problems and allow the war to continue.

Such confidence proved ill-founded. The crown issued assignments totalling approximately £100,000 on the income from the ninth, but by January 1341 this tax had yielded only about £15,000.[33] Edward was now effectively bankrupt, and had little hope of securing more money from his beleaguered subjects. With the failure of the siege of Tournai, he was forced into an ignominious truce at Esplechin in September. The king's refusal to respond to the advice of his ministers and barons had left him in an untenable position. The regency council reappointed in 1340 was led by Stratford and Huntingdon and included the Earls of Lancaster and Surrey and the northern lords, Percy, Wake and Neville. They were joined after July by Arundel and Gloucester. Warwick, Derby and Northampton had already given themselves up as hostages for the king's debts in the Low Countries.[34] A significant number of the earls and great barons were therefore removed from the war, and were becoming increasingly annoyed by the actions of Salisbury and his associates. Edward now conceived the notion that Stratford had poisoned the minds of the lords, and wrote in hysterical terms to the Pope of the archbishop's deceptions and treachery. Taking ship from Sluys, the king landed unannounced at the watergate of the Tower of London early on the morning of 1 December.[35] In scenes reminiscent of the Nottingham coup, he dismissed the chancellor and treasurer, arrested five of the royal judges, imprisoned several prominent financiers, and even seized one member of the regency council, Sir Thomas Wake. As in 1330, a spontaneous decision carried through in secret by the king and a small band of followers had given Edward the opportunity to wreak vengeance on his enemies. But whereas the arrests at Nottingham had been a welcome relief from the rule of Mortimer, the dismissals of 1340 served merely to intensify political divisions, and provoked a major political crisis.

THE PARLIAMENT OF 1341

As soon as Edward appeared back in the capital, Stratford retired to Canterbury. He remained there through the winter months of 1340–1, refusing summonses to the court and writing vitriolic letters of protest to the king. On 29 December, the feast of St Thomas the Martyr, he preached a sermon in the cathedral declaring his intention to stand as a worthy successor to Becket.[36] A public war of words ensued. Edward accused Stratford of advocating extravagant policies and failing to supply funds, making the king the scorn of his enemies both at home and abroad. The archbishop indicated several times that he would only answer such charges before the king, prelates and peers in parliament. When parliament met in Westminster Palace at the end of April 1341, however, Edward set his henchmen John Darcy and Ralph Stafford at the door of the Painted Chamber and stubbornly refused to allow Stratford access for over a week. The king attempted to carry on as normal, and asked the assembly to authorize a second instalment of the ninth. Such a demand was hardly designed to appease the already outraged assembly. Finally, the Earl of Surrey declared his contempt for Edward's actions:

> Sir king, how goes this parliament? Parliaments were not wont to be like this. For here those who should be foremost are shut out, while there sit other men of low rank who have no business to be here. Such right belongs only to the peers of the land. Sir king, think of this.[37]

Finding that Surrey's appeal was supported by Arundel and other members of the regency council, Edward had no option but to admit the archbishop and make his peace with him. The events of the previous months had struck a tender nerve among the lords, who now declared that none of their rank should be arrested, tried or imprisoned except in full parliament and before his peers. The commons also seized the opportunity to voice their grievances. They combined with the lords to demand a detailed public audit of the king's finances, and requested that the great officers of the realm should be appointed by the king in parliament and be sworn therein to obey the law. Edward had no choice but to give his hasty, if qualified, assent to all these demands, and solemn legislation was duly composed and written up on the statute roll.[38] Stratford's opposition had left Edward dangerously isolated and soundly defeated.

The crisis of 1340–1 was a serious blow to the crown, and evoked uneasy memories of earlier political confrontations. Historians have often pointed out the parallels between the legislation of 1340–1 and the aims of the baronial ordainers of 1311. The connections are not surprising given Stratford's earlier involvement in the opposition to Edward II. Moreover, the circumstances in 1311 and 1341 were in many ways very similar. On both occasions the king had shown himself unwilling to accept the advice of his great men, and had followed evil counsels which brought shame on the throne and danger to the realm. In some respects, indeed, the opposition of 1341 was even more ominous. Although Edward II's misrule had touched the lives of many and produced widespread disaffection, the only effective challenge to his policies had been mounted by a baronial elite. During the Despenser regime when the magnates had been cowed into submission, the commons had tried to maintain the pressure for reform, but had been unable to make any real headway.[39] By 1340–1, however, the pressures of war had given each section of the community, from the greatest nobleman to the humblest peasant, ample grounds for complaint against the monarchy. The hostility shown by the commons and clergy in 1340, and mobilized by Stratford and the lords in the crisis of 1341, had become a conditioning force in English politics. Edward III's disregard for the welfare and rights of his subjects had produced a powerful coalition of disaffected parties drawing strength and inspiration from their support in the country. If the dynastic upheavals of 1326–30 and the military pressures of 1337–40 had altered political conditions in England, it looked very much as though the balance would weigh increasingly heavily against the crown.

2 The middle years: 1341–60

The parliamentary crisis of 1341 had been a severe blow to Edward III, and for a short while it put a stop to his controversial foreign policies. Yet in the months and years that followed, the king staged one of the most remarkable political recoveries ever witnessed in medieval England.[1] On 1 October 1341 Edward announced that he had annulled the statute passed earlier that year on the grounds that it was contrary to the law of the realm and had been forced on him against his will. He was using a prerogative exercised by several of his predecessors, and most recently by Edward II in 1322: namely, the right to dispense with any legislation which the king believed to have compromised his authority. Even if concerted resistance continued, there was very little that the political community could do to challenge this principle. The renunciation of the statute demonstrated vividly that the medieval monarchy almost always had right on its side.

It also exposed the weaknesses in the political opposition. Edward quickly dismantled the temporary coalition that had gathered under Stratford's leadership. He showed no sign of restoring the archbishop or his followers to their positions in the government departments, and for the moment filled the offices of state with laymen who would be answerable for their actions before the royal courts. He also won over a sufficient number of the magnates to be able to claim that he had renounced the statute with their consent. Within weeks of this declaration, Stratford acknowledged his political isolation and made his final peace with the king. Two years elapsed before another parliament met in April 1343, and this assembly formally accepted the abolition of the earlier legislation. Although the commons expressed their annoyance at the king's actions, they could achieve little without the support of the great lay and ecclesiastical lords. The remaining opposition to the crown had therefore lost its effective bargaining position. In the decade that followed, the commons too were eventually won over to a working compromise with the crown. The scale of Edward's achievement in the middle years of his reign has not always been fully appreciated, because it has often been felt that he merely sought popularity at the expense of power. But such arguments give little consideration either to the seriousness of the conflicts that had divided political society for three decades before 1341 or to the enduring qualities of the new dispensation, which prevented any further confrontation for another generation. The period from the Stratford crisis to the treaty of Brétigny of 1360 witnessed one of the greatest royal success stories of the later Middle Ages.

The single most important reason for Edward's political recovery after 1341 was the lucky change in his military fortunes. At first, the situation looked depressing. The allies in the Low Countries fell away and Edward was deprived of his imperial vicariate. The return of David Bruce to Scotland in 1341 meant a renewal of cross-border raids, and forced the English king to undertake a northern campaign in the winter of 1341–2. But in 1341 new and more promising prospects emerged in France when the duchy of Brittany fell vacant. Edward decided to support the claim of John de Montfort against the French-backed Charles of Blois in the Breton war of succession. Thus emerged his so-called 'provincial strategy',[2] a technique already attempted in Flanders and soon to be extended into many other areas of France. The idea was simple, but effective. The English king sought to intervene in private disputes between the Valois and their feudal vassals, thus creating new allies, challenging Philip VI's rights as suzerain, and dissipating French military resources. Edward's claim to the throne of France was an essential part of this strategy, since it could be used to create alternative feudal relationships with the dukes and counts. Indeed, it was not long before the military situation encouraged Edward to believe that his somewhat empty dynastic claim might one day become a reality.

After an inconclusive campaign in Brittany in 1342, the king decided to launch a major continental offensive involving simultaneous attacks on several different fronts. In 1345 Henry of Grosmont and the Earl of Northampton were sent with expeditionary forces to Aquitaine and Brittany, and the king himself led a short campaign in Flanders. In the following year a Norman baron, Geoffrey de Harcourt, appealed for Edward III's assistance in his private dispute with the Valois regime. The king immediately sailed for Normandy with a substantial army of 15,000 men. After marching into the Ile de France, he turned north to Ponthieu and met the French in pitched battle at Crécy on 26 August 1346. Philip VI's forces were roundly defeated by the English mixed formation. Meanwhile David Bruce, encouraged by Edward's absence and prompted by his French ally, had invaded the north of England. In October his army met an English force led by the northern lords, and suffered a devastating defeat at Neville's Cross near Durham, where David himself was taken prisoner. His home defences thus secure, Edward III collected a huge army of 32,000 men — the largest English force ever raised during the Hundred Years War — and laid siege to the town of Calais, which eventually fell in the summer of 1347. Heavy with honours, Edward returned home to indulge his vanity and celebrate the valour of his warriors in a great series of feasts and tournaments.

NOBLEMEN AND MINISTERS

The military advances of the 1340s had far-reaching effects on the relationship between the king and the English nobility. The upturn in English fortunes helped dispel earlier misgivings about the king's abilities as a war leader and encouraged the earls and barons to give active support to a series of great military adventures. Edward very quickly realized the shortcomings of his earlier policies, and worked hard to bridge the dangerous divide between a narrow clique of household advisers and the rest of his great men. Throughout the summer and autumn of 1341 he discussed his new military plans with the magnates. Although few of those who had recently opposed him in parliament played any part in the Scottish campaign of 1341–2, most were prepared to serve or at least to supply troops by the time Edward launched his first expedition to Brittany at the end of 1342.[3] The new strategy of the 1340s also gave the magnates the outlet they needed for their energies.

Long-term fighting on several different fronts in northern France, Brittany, Aquitaine and Scotland prevented Edward from leading all his armies in person, and necessitated the appointment of lieutenants who would pursue his interests on the battlefield and at the negotiating table. The most important lieutenancies inevitably tended to be reserved for the earls: the king's cousin Henry of Grosmont was not only the greatest lord in England but also the busiest of all Edward's commanders, serving throughout the 1340s and 1350s in Aquitaine, Brittany and Normandy. Men such as Arundel and Northampton, who had earlier sat at home and criticized the campaigns of 1338–40, now had ample opportunity to prove their worth, and quickly established themselves as Edward's loyal and enthusiastic supporters. Indeed, with the exception of the elderly and infirm, all the earls and great lords served on one or other of the military campaigns of 1346–7.

Within five years of the Stratford crisis, Edward had redeemed his reputation with the magnates and made them his companions in arms. The process of reconciliation was facilitated by changes in the ruling elite. The Earl of Salisbury was killed in a tournament in 1344, and the elderly Earls of Lancaster and Surrey died in 1345 and 1347. Their replacements were younger men, less preoccupied with earlier controversies and more disposed by age and outlook to support the policies of Edward III. Royal patronage also began to follow a more consistent and predictable pattern. Outside the king's family there were very few wholly new titles: Ralph Stratford was the only royal confidant raised to an earldom in this period. Instead, old titles were revived for descendants of former comital families, and lapsed earldoms passed to existing members of the baronage. Thus Roger Mortimer, grandson and namesake of Queen Isabella's paramour, was created Earl of March in 1354. The real focus of Edward's patronage was his cousin Henry of Grosmont, who succeeded to the earldom of Lancaster in 1345 and gained the old earldom of Lincoln in 1349. Finally, in 1351, Henry was elevated to the rank of duke and given palatine control over the county of Lancaster. The Lancastrian family, which had led the opposition to the crown during the 1310s and 1320s, had now emerged as the very pillar of Edward III's monarchy.

Undoubtedly the most important symbol of Edward's new alliance with the nobility was the Order of the Garter.[4] This knightly confraternity was founded in 1348 specifically to celebrate the achievements of the king's most trusted companions in arms. Honour was the only real criterion for election to the order, and the original twenty-six members included some relatively obscure English and foreign knights such as Sir Walter Paveley and Sir Sanchet d'Abrichecourt. But a certain number of places were inevitably reserved for the greatest men in the realm. The Earls of Derby, Warwick and Salisbury were among the founder members of the order, together with Lords Stafford, Mortimer and Burghersh; and by 1350 they had been joined by the Earls of Suffolk and Northampton. It was a particular sign of Edward's new astuteness that he was able to play on the chivalric pretensions of the nobility and use membership of the order as a supplement to other more costly forms of patronage.

Just as important to the king's political fortunes were the changes in the central administration.[5] The chancellors and treasurers of the 1340s and 1350s were men of very different experience and outlook to those who had controlled the civil service in the previous decade. William Cusance, treasurer from 1341 to 1344, and the successive chancellors John Offord (1345–9) and John Thoresby (1349–56) had all served in Edward's continental administration of 1338–40 and had been closely identified with the king's party in the political disputes of 1340–1. The most influential of all these ministers was William Edington, who had first entered royal service as receiver of the much-hated ninth in 1340, and who went on to be keeper of the wardrobe (1341–4), treasurer of the exchequer (1344–56) and chancellor (1356–63). The long and uninterrupted tenure enjoyed by these officials suggests that Edward III had at last found ministers who were agreeable to him and supportive of his policies. The most conspicuous of all their achievements was in the financial sphere. Edington inherited a huge debt from his predecessors in the exchequer, and the king's demands for cash continued to provide him with numerous problems in the later 1340s. But as campaigns proved less costly and revenues from taxation increased, the situation gradually began to improve. Indeed, by the end of the 1350s Edington had transformed Edward III from an embarrassed bankrupt into a wealthy man. The king's political recovery clearly owed much to this new generation of capable and loyal ministers.

Changes were also under way in the ecclesiastical hierarchy.[6] Two of the older generation of political prelates, Henry Burghersh of Lincoln and Adam Orleton of Winchester, died in the 1340s, closely followed by John Stratford himself. Edward had little trouble in filling the episcopal bench with amenable and obedient men. Indeed, many of the prelates of this period were drawn from the ranks of the civil service: Thomas Hatfield of Durham, John Offord and Simon Islip of Canterbury, John Thoresby of York and Michael Northborough of London had all enjoyed distinguished careers in the king's government before going on to run the English church. The promotion of royal administrators to the episcopate was nothing new, and certainly did not prevent the prelates from taking stands against the king. But none of the squabbles that broke out between the crown and the bishops in the 1340s and 1350s bore comparison with the Stratford controversy of 1340–1. Indeed, the victories of Crécy, Neville's Cross and Poitiers persuaded the higher clergy that the king was fighting a just war, and turned them into enthusiastic supporters of the crown. Rarely had the English church been so unstinting in its praise of the monarchy and so convinced of the rightness of its cause as in the middle years of Edward III's reign.

THE PLAGUE AND ITS AFTERMATH

The victories won and honours bestowed during the 1340s and 1350s therefore created a powerful and enduring bond between the crown and the upper ranks of political society. But there were still many men who remained distinctly unimpressed by Edward's achievements. The campaigns of the 1340s entailed considerable pressures, which were inevitably resented in the country.[7] The parliament of 1341 refused to concede the ninth for a second year, but substituted a tax of 30,000 sacks of wool. Meanwhile, traditional forms of taxation became more frequent than ever before. Seven clerical tenths were collected between 1342 and 1353, and nine fifteenths and tenths were imposed on the laity between 1344 and 1354. The extra wartime subsidy on wool exports was fixed at the rate of £2 per sack in 1342, and was maintained at this level for the next twenty years (see Table 3). As if this was not enough, the government also stepped up its efforts to levy manpower and provisions. In 1344 it tried to assess all those holding land valued at over £5 a year to contribute troops. The compulsory array of infantry soldiers, which was normally used only for local defence, was greatly extended in 1346–7 in order to fill the ranks of Edward's continental army. Purveyance continued to be a major charge, especially after 1347 when the new garrison at Calais added considerably to existing pressures for food and other supplies. In its desperate search for funds, the government also imposed a controversial feudal aid in 1346 and a forced loan of 20,000 sacks of wool in 1347. These various exactions affected a wide cross-section of society, and precipitated an angry response from the commons in the parliaments of 1346 and 1348. Twenty years after his accession, and with several major victories to his credit, Edward III had still evidently failed to win the confidence and support of all his subjects.

As if these problems were not enough, the king and the country had also to contend with the first outbreak of the Black Death in 1348–9. This epidemic, usually diagnosed as a combination of bubonic and pneumonic plagues, came as a severe shock to a society and economy already weakened by the famines of the 1320s and the wars of the 1330s and 1340s. We do not know the number of people in England on the eve of the plague: estimates vary at anything between four and six million. But it seems plausible that the pestilence of 1348–9 killed off at least 30 per cent of the population.[8] The immediate results were dramatic. A high death rate combined with the sudden panic movement of survivors created an acute shortage of tenants and manpower on estates all across the country, and left many lands almost completely uncultivated. Overseas trade slumped with the drop in wool production and the collapse of foreign markets. Some landholders, like the Bishop of Winchester and the monks of Croyland Abbey, were able to compensate for declining yields by raising large sums in death duties and entry fines. But others found it impossible to prevent a serious reduction in profits: on the estates of the duchy of Cornwall, for instance, revenues fell by 40 per cent between 1347–8 and 1350–1. The sudden demographic change also disrupted market forces. Prices for agricultural produce fell in 1348–50, while wages soared. Some landholders had to take drastic action, and began to lease out their demesnes in the hope that rents might provide a more stable form of income.

Ultimately, however, the decade after the first outbreak of the Black Death was characterized not by far-reaching economic change but by a remarkably swift return to normality. A big increase in the money supply after 1351, together with a series of relatively poor harvests, helped to inflate prices and disguise the decline in profit margins.[9] Changes in the customs regulations after 1353 brought a boom in the wool trade and a rapid increase in the production of English cloth for foreign markets. The landholders seem to have had little trouble in filling vacant holdings on their estates and maintaining the traditional labour services demanded from their tenants. Most, like the monks of Christ Church, Canterbury, and the administrators of the great East Anglian honour of Clare, did not find it necessary as yet to give up the old demesne system of farming in favour of leases and rents. While chroniclers and churchmen bemoaned the visitation of the 'brute beast' as the judgment of God on a promiscuous people,[10] estate managers had set about the formidable task of restoring and maintaining their lords' proprietary rights.

The government proved a powerful ally in this respect. The king was naturally perturbed by the deaths of his local officials and the difficulties of raising revenues, and he adopted an uncompromising stance admired and emulated by many.[11] He generally refused to allow any formal reduction in the fee farms charged on the sheriffs or in the taxes being levied from his lay subjects. He also took full advantage of the deaths of his tenants-in-chief in order to increase the short-term profits of feudalism. This had the effect of identifying the king with other men of property and substance, and proved that the government was determined to uphold the interests of that class. The most important product of this new alliance was the attempt to prevent a further escalation of wage demands. In June 1349 the government issued the Ordinance of Labourers, which set maximum wage limits and required workers to serve out their contracts before seeking employment elsewhere. In the long term, this legislation was bound to be defeated by economic forces. But during the 1350s the special measures taken by the government to enforce the ordinance, and the determined reaction of the landholders against the 'malice of servants',[12] ensured that wage rates only really kept pace with inflation. The labour legislation convinced a large number of influential men that the king was concerned not simply with his own foreign ambitions, but also with the economic problems of his natural supporters in the country. The political implications were to be far-reaching.

If at first it seemed an unparalleled and unmitigated disaster, the plague therefore proved fortuitous for the crown. In particular, it necessitated a temporary cessation of the war. The pestilence had struck the continent with equal if not greater ferocity, and both sides were thankful for the series of truces patched together between 1347 and 1355. Edward called off a planned campaign late in 1348, and although sporadic fighting continued in Brittany and Aquitaine, the level of military activity was much reduced for several years. The lull saved England from an embarrassing diplomatic situation, for the victories of 1346–7 had done little to change the attitudes of Edward's opponents. The Scots were reluctant to offer a ransom for David II; and the new Count of Flanders, Louis de Mâle, was proving hostile towards England. An attempted marriage alliance with Castile came to nothing when Edward's daughter Princess Joan died of the plague on her way to Spain. In 1350 Edward defeated a Castilian merchant fleet off Winchelsea, in an engagement known as Les Espagnols sur Mer. But elsewhere the English achieved little, and for a short while after 1352 Edward gave his French enemies and his own subjects good reason to hope that a permanent peace might soon be arranged.

It was in these circumstances that the king and the commons drew together to resolve some of the long-standing political issues left over from the 1330s. The parliament of 1352 granted a three-year subsidy on the understanding that full-scale hostilities might be necessary to bring the war to a successful conclusion. After eight years of almost continuous direct taxation, the knights and burgesses naturally expected some concessions in return, and they presented the council with a long and varied list of grievances. The king was in generous mood, and a large number of the commons' petitions were allowed and made up into statutes. Three of the most important clauses of the new legislation settled recent disputes over military levies. The king agreed that in future feudal aids would only be raised with parliamentary consent. He also guaranteed that royal purveyors would abide by the existing legislation regulating the provision of supplies for the king's

4 *The imagery of death: the plague provoked a new preoccupation with the macabre*

armies and household. Finally, he promised to give up his earlier attempts to raise troops on the basis of landed wealth, and guaranteed that none except his own feudal tenants should be required to provide soldiers without the assent of parliament.[13] These statutes signified the king's willingness to give up controversial prerogatives and to depend instead on generous public funding for his campaigns. They also symbolized the re-emergence of parliament as an effective political force, working in co-operation with the crown. The years immediately after the plague therefore witnessed the completion of that alliance between the crown and the political community which was to endure until the 1370s.

Of all the developments in the early 1350s which helped to reconcile the political community to the king's policies, perhaps the most significant were the changes in the administration of justice. Public order had become a major political issue in the 1320s and 1330s, and Edward III stood little chance of winning support until he answered some of the many demands for judicial reform. The principal problem was to find a satisfactory alternative to the commissions known variously as the eyre, trailbaston and oyer and terminer which had been sent out by the crown in the thirteenth and early fourteenth centuries to hear civil and criminal cases. These roving courts had always been regarded as a threat to the tradition of self-government in the shires, and because of their irregularity they were ill-fitted to the task of maintaining the peace. The last national eyre was mounted in 1329 by Chief Justice Scrope, but only four shires had actually been visited by the time these extraordinary sessions were called off late in 1330.[14] Their place was taken mainly by the assize and gaol delivery sessions, held in theory three times a year in the county towns and larger boroughs, and presided over by royal judges. But these courts also proved inadequate, and there was a serious breakdown of law and order during Edward III's early campaigns in Scotland and France.[15] During one such interlude in the 1330s the county community of Wiltshire complained that the whole area had fallen prey to robbers and thugs, and that no one dared move around the county any more unless he could find safe lodgings in castles and fortified houses.[16] The clear impression is of a judicial system, and a whole society, severely threatened by a major deterioration in public order.

The greatest pressure for reform came from the landholders in the shires.[17] As keepers of the peace, these men had responsibility for accepting indictments and holding prisoners until the king's judges arrived to try cases in the relevant shire. By the 1340s at least, the commons were arguing that the law would be better kept if local men were allowed to try and convict offenders. In other words, the landed classes wished to act not simply as keepers, but as justices of the peace. In some ways the Stratford crisis hardened Edward's resolve not to bow to such pressure, and the following decade witnessed several attempts to revive the older system of central regulation. On his return from the continent late in 1340, the king issued general commissions of oyer and terminer to investigate the misdeeds of his agents and subjects.[18] From 1348 the court of king's bench also began roaming the country hearing assizes, delivering gaols, and using the contentious charge of treason to prosecute petty offenders.[19] It seemed to many that the eyre itself was now being reinstated. However, the special machinery created to implement the labour legislation seems finally to have convinced the government of the positive advantages to be derived from the delegation of judicial responsibility. In 1349 the enforcement of the Ordinance of Labourers was entrusted not to the king's hard-pressed judges but to the landholders in the shires. When the government issued the supplementary Statute of Labourers in 1351, it briefly handed over responsibility for the legislation to the commissioners of the peace, thus extending their powers considerably. In order to counteract suggestions that the king had renounced his judicial authority, the council took care to ensure that each peace commission now included a quorum of royal justices, who were required to be present with the provincial amateurs when serious cases of felony were brought to trial. Nevertheless, the developments of 1349–51 set an important precedent. In future, the administration of criminal justice would lie increasingly with the gentry in the shires. And the political implications were profound. The king and the country had at last come to a satisfactory compromise which allowed greater initiative to Edward's natural supporters in the shires and at the same time considerably enhanced the popularity of the crown.

THE WAR RENEWED

By the mid-1350s the reputation of the English monarchy was higher than at any point since the 1280s. Free from difficulties at home, it was inevitable that Edward III would turn his attention once more to France. For some time in 1352–4 it seemed that the king was prepared to accept his existing gains rather than risk further unproductive fighting. On several occasions he indicated his willingness to give up the claim to the throne of France, and in 1353 he came close to accepting Charles of Blois as the rightful Duke of Brittany in order to placate the French negotiators. But it remains unclear whether Edward's intentions were honourable or whether he was simply playing for time. There were certainly many arguments in favour of a continuation of hostilities. Philip VI had died in 1350, and although there had been no dispute over the succession of his son John II, other political problems within the kingdom of France may well have persuaded Edward that his own dynastic claims still stood some chance of success. The English king also had the next generation to think of. The Prince of Wales and his three teenage brothers Lionel, John and Edmund were naturally eager to reopen the war, not only to indulge their chivalric fantasies but also to secure foreign titles and territories to which they might one day succeed. In the end, it was Edward's unscrupulous cousin Charles, King of Navarre, who was responsible for reopening the war. Charles was locked in his own private dispute with John II, and naturally appealed to the English for help. Edward was persuaded to renege on the peace proposals put forward at Guînes in 1354, and to prepare for a great campaign. The Prince of Wales was appointed lieutenant in Aquitaine, and promptly set about a series of plundering expeditions which caused much distress to the already hard-pressed inhabitants of southern France. Consecutive campaigns were then planned for Brittany and Normandy. In the event, Edward was diverted by problems in Scotland, and had to march north in the winter of 1355–6 to recover control of Berwick. The Duke of Lancaster made a successful raid through Normandy in 1356, but failed to meet up with the other English forces. Consequently, the Black Prince had only a small band of 6,000 men when he met John II's army at Poitiers on 19 September. The ensuing battle was hard-fought, and ended in a disorganized mêlée. Yet out of this chaos the English plucked one of the greatest successes of the Hundred Years War. The victors eagerly helped themselves to booty and snatched up prisoners in the hope of securing ransoms. The greatest captive of all, King John, was delivered to the prince and despatched to England, where he was greeted with due honours by the delighted Edward III.

England now enjoyed by far the most powerful bargaining position since the start of Edward III's Scottish and French wars. The long-awaited agreement with Scotland came in the treaty of Berwick of October 1357. This left silent the intractable problems of the Scottish succession and the English claims in the Lowlands, but offered a valuable ransom of 100,000 marks (£66,666 13s. 4d.) for David II. Negotiations with the French also centred on the release of their king, but were complicated by the dispute over English possessions and rights on the continent.[20] Edward III tried to take advantage of the weakness of the enemy to press his claims, and arguably overplayed his hand. France was economically exhausted by the plague and the actions of the free-booting mercenary bands which now roamed the continent selling their services to the highest bidder. The absence of John II and disagreements within his regency government created political chaos, and precipitated an uprising in the Ile de France in 1358 known as the Jacquerie. Edward responded with a series of demands more daring than anything previously dreamed up by the English negotiators. The so-called second treaty of London of May 1359 sought to impose an enormous ransom of almost £700,000 for the return of John II. Edward promised to renounce his claim to the French throne, but in return demanded feudal suzerainty over Brittany and full sovereign control of a huge block of territory stretching uninterrupted from Calais to the Pyrenees. This would have created a new Plantagenet dominion reminiscent of the great empire of Henry II. The dauphin and the French estates general obviously could not countenance such a plan, and rejected the proposals outright.

Edward may well have expected such a response, for he quickly set about a further show of force. Late in 1359 he landed at Calais with a large army and headed for Rheims, the traditional coronation place of the French kings. For a while it seemed that his dynastic claim was about to become a reality. But the city did not give him the welcome he had expected, and shut its gates against the English. Abandoning the siege, Edward quickly accepted the dauphin's request for a negotiated settlement. At Brétigny in May 1360 it was agreed that the English king would give up his claim to the throne of France and be granted full sovereign control over an enlarged duchy of Aquitaine, together with Calais and some other small territories in the north. The ransom of John II was now reduced to £500,000. These new terms, confirmed at Calais in October 1360, were a good deal less generous than the proposals contained in the second treaty of London. But they still amounted to a major diplomatic victory, and offered Edward III everything for which his predecessors had fought since 1259. They also served to vindicate the long war and to reaffirm public pride and confidence in the monarchy. Edward's return to England was greeted with general rejoicing. The treaty marked the greatest achievement of a great king; and his subjects were duly thankful.[21]

3 The later years: 1360–77

The nine years following the treaty of Brétigny marked by far the longest period of uninterrupted peace since the opening of hostilities between England and France in 1337. Edward III's enemies quickly seized this opportunity to settle domestic problems and prepare for possible future military action. When John II died in 1364 he was succeeded by his son, Charles V, a man of considerable vision and talent, who in the course of the next few years effected a remarkable change in his wretched kingdom. Gathering around him a group of able administrators, Charles 'the Wise' greatly improved the financial resources of the French crown; and with the help of his outstanding lieutenant Bertrand du Guesclin he transformed his inadequate army into a formidable fighting force. Ironically, Edward III failed to follow the French lead. He became increasingly complacent during the years of peace, and was poorly prepared when war broke out again. The military reversals and the political tensions of the 1370s made a disappointing and undignified end to an otherwise remarkable reign. Edward III outlived his own generation and his own usefulness, and became a considerable liability to the throne during his last years.

The treaty of Brétigny was intended to provide a permanent settlement to the Anglo-French dispute, but its specifications were never fully implemented. In fact, it seems that neither side had any real intention of honouring the agreement, and they simply used it as a welcome respite before the inevitable renewal of war. Both were eager to withdraw from the main treaty the special clauses requiring Edward's repudiation of the French royal title and the handing over by the Valois of those territories now to be recognized as English possessions. This allowed the two sides to maintain a truce but to delay the final implementation of the peace. At first, Edward III may have had honourable intentions, and he stopped using the title of King of France. But within a short time new issues had arisen which made it evident that the renunciation clauses would never be put into effect. The picture of the 1360s as a time of peace and stability is therefore rather misleading. In fact, the decade witnessed a series of protracted and often tense negotiations which at any time might have dissolved into full-scale war.

One of the principal reasons for the failure of the treaty of Brétigny was Edward III's continued intervention in the French principalities. But this policy, which had earlier been so effective against Philip VI, now proved positively damaging to English interests. Edward's only success came in Brittany. He gave his daughter in marriage to John de Montfort, son of his earlier ally, and helped him defeat Charles of Blois at Auray in 1364. Elsewhere, however, Edward found little comfort. He may have hoped to re-establish links with Charles of Navarre, who had carried on his own quarrel with the Valois on the border between Normandy and the Ile de France after the withdrawal of English troops. But in 1364 Charles was defeated by du Guesclin, and eventually came to terms with the French king in 1371. An even bigger diplomatic setback occurred in Flanders. Louis de Mâle spent the 1360s negotiating the marriage of his daughter and heiress, Margaret. Edward hoped to secure this valuable match for his fourth son, Edmund of Langley. But in 1369 Margaret was betrothed to Philip of Burgundy, brother of Charles V. Although Louis himself remained theoretically bound to an earlier agreement with England, the prospects of any long-term support from Flanders were dashed. By the end of the 1360s, Edward's influence in the principalities had been severely compromised.

Ironically, however, the greatest threat to English security came from Edward's own continental possessions. The failure of the French to cede all the territories agreed at Brétigny meant that the much enlarged duchy of Aquitaine planned in 1360 never became a complete reality. But in 1363 Edward acted as though the renunciations had already taken place, and bestowed on his eldest son the title of Prince of Aquitaine. Dispatched to Bordeaux to take up duties as a resident lord, the Black Prince soon found that many of his new subjects were at best indifferent and at worst positively hostile to the new regime. He made matters worse by trying to improve the efficiency of local administration and to increase his revenues. The independent lords of Aquitaine resented this threat to their traditional privileges, and troublesome characters such as Gaston Phoebus, Count of Foix, began to intrigue with Charles V. Others followed the example of the Count of Armagnac, accepting the prince as their token suzerain but refusing to allow his tax collectors into their own lordships. The Black Prince's attempts to copy his father's achievement in England and to set up a strong, centralized regime indicated a complete misunderstanding of local political traditions and ultimately brought about the collapse of English rule in southern France.

Nor was Prince Edward content with his considerable responsibilities in Aquitaine. In 1362 Edward III made a treaty with Peter I of Castile and offered to support him against the pretender to his throne, the French-backed Henry of Trastamara. When Peter was deposed in 1365, the Black Prince eagerly seized the opportunity to escape the boredom of administration and to re-establish his military reputation. In the short term, the Spanish war was very successful. The great victory at Nájera in 1367 put Peter I back on his throne and provided the English with a valuable new ally. But the involvement in Castile ultimately weakened Edward III's position in a number of ways. By 1369 Henry of Trastamara had murdered Peter I and resumed control of the kingdom. The Black Prince had also contracted a disease in Spain which was to remove him from military and political leadership. Most seriously of all, the war had to be paid for by the inhabitants of Aquitaine, who bitterly resented the unprecedented financial charges made by their prince. The oppressive *fouages* (hearth taxes) imposed on their tenants provided certain of the lords of Aquitaine with the opportunity they had long sought to challenge English lordship. It was this dispute that ultimately led to the renewal of hostilities between England and France.

There were difficulties, too, in the British Isles. David II's subjects refused to pay any further instalments of his ransom between 1360 and 1366. Although they were forced in 1365 to raise the promised total from £66,666 13s. 4d. to £100,000, they had still paid only a small proportion of this sum by the time the Anglo-French war broke out again in 1369.

The absence of any reference to the Franco-Scottish alliance in the treaty of Berwick was also to create problems for Edward after 1369, and forced the English government to divert considerable resources to the defence of the northern march. Up to 1369, however, Edward III's major problem was Ireland. In the first half of his reign he had been content to leave the lordship in the hands of the great Anglo-Irish families. But in 1361 he appointed his second son, Lionel of Antwerp, as royal lieutenant in Ireland, and attempted to subdue the magnates by a large and expensive show of force. Edward rather arrogantly considered that he could sort out his Irish subjects as he had done his French enemies. The only result, however, was to increase the long-standing animosity towards the king's representatives in the lordship. From the end of the decade, when Lionel's place was taken by William of Windsor, the crown's controversial Irish policy threatened to become a major issue in English politics. Such developments indicate that, despite the Anglo-French truce, Edward III's government was still inevitably preoccupied with the possibility, and sometimes the reality, of war.

A NEW GENERATION

Against this uneasy background, it is not surprising that the king achieved comparatively little at home. Edward celebrated his fiftieth birthday in 1362, and was already, by contemporary standards, an old man. By the end of the decade, not one of the six earls created in 1337 was still alive. And as the older generation died off, Edward failed to fill up the comital ranks with new supporters. The only new creations of the 1360s were in favour of his children and their spouses. By 1370 the court was dominated by the Earl of Pembroke, a former royal ward who had been married briefly to the king's daughter, Margaret, and by Edward's third son John of Gaunt, whose marriage to the joint-heiress of Henry of Grosmont had brought him the title of Duke of Lancaster in 1362. While England was at peace, it mattered little that the king's following was so small. But in the early 1370s, when Gaunt and Pembroke spent much time away on campaigns, the removal of the new generation of magnates from the immediate royal circle was to prove a serious political weakness for the crown.

The 1360s also saw significant changes in the government offices. Thoresby had resigned the chancellorship in 1357, and Edington retired from royal service in 1363. Thereafter, administrative power passed increasingly into the hands of the king's new favourite, William Wykeham. Wykeham's first important job had been as clerk of the works at Windsor in 1356. This appointment coincided with a major new building programme designed to make Windsor the greatest castle in the realm. Inevitably, the clerk attracted royal attention, and Wykeham was soon being styled 'chief keeper and surveyor' of the king's works, with control over all the major royal residences. By 1361 he was the king's secretary, or keeper of the secret seal. In 1363 he became keeper of the privy seal, and in 1367 he was made chancellor. Ecclesiastical preferment followed fast. By 1366 he was the wealthiest pluralist in England, and in 1367 he was appointed to succeed Edington as Bishop of Winchester.

Wykeham's influence was enormous: as the chronicler Jean Froissart later commented, 'everything was done by him, and nothing was done without him'.[1] His political ambition, however, put a strain on the government offices. Wykeham had little time for bureaucratic minutiae, and administrative practice inevitably became somewhat lax. Accusations of bribery broke out in the exchequer of receipt in 1365, and the chief baron of the exchequer and the chief justice of king's bench were both dismissed from office on unspecified charges. In 1368 the steward of the royal household, Sir John Lee, was imprisoned after protests over the abuse of his special legal powers.[2] Corruption, inefficiency and maladministration were nothing new; but the frequency and seriousness of such scandals in the 1360s can have done little to improve the reputation of the government.

One of the major problems that Wykeham and his colleagues had to face was the recurrence of the plague. Both the exchequer and the central courts were forced to close down in May 1361 when a second epidemic broke out, and by July Archbishop Thoresby of York was ordering prayers for safe delivery from this pestilence.[3] It has generally been assumed that the second plague was much less serious than the first: one of the few sets of comparative figures, for the clergy of the diocese of York, indicates a mortality rate of only 14 per cent in 1361–2, as against 39 per cent in 1348–9.[4] Nevertheless, this attack, and further outbreaks in 1369, 1371 and 1374–5, ruined any remaining chances of a return to the economic conditions prevailing before 1348. Agricultural wages continued to rise. On the estates of the Bishop of Winchester, for instance, there was a particularly sudden increase in the going rate for casual labour at harvest time after 1362.[5] It is interesting to notice that the fees paid to the senior exchequer officials were increased in the mid-1360s, presumably to keep up with this inflationary spiral.[6] During the 1360s prices remained high; but in 1375 they fell, and began the downward trend which was to last for the rest of the fourteenth century and beyond.

Landholders were forced to take stock of this threat to their profits. Some decided to commute the old labour services demanded of their tenants, to give up the direct farming of their demesnes, and to lease out their lands for fixed rents. In 1369 all labour services on the royal manor of Windsor were abandoned;[7] and by the 1370s a substantial number of great estate holders had begun to change over to leases in an attempt to forestall any further drop in revenue. Not surprisingly, the employers also brought increasing pressure on the government to reinforce the labour legislation. The Ordinance and Statute of Labourers were reintroduced in 1361–2, and after 1368 the justices of the peace were given permanent responsibility for their enforcement.[8] The landed classes were indeed becoming obsessed with maintaining social distinctions. An extraordinary act of 1363, 'for the outrageous and excessive apparel of divers people, contrary to their estate and degree', even tried to regulate the clothing and food allowed to different ranks of society.[9] By the 1370s such fanciful measures were giving way to real and ominous tensions. There were frequent complaints in parliament about the presumptuous attitude of the lower classes; and those landholders who were still farming some of their demesnes chose to revive or increase the services and dues owed by their unfree tenants. This 'feudal reaction' of the 1370s explains many of the grievances and fears aired during the Peasants' Revolt of 1381. It also created dissatisfaction and disillusionment among the political community, and contributed to the general malaise of Edward III's last years.

In the light of this evidence, it is possible to argue that many of the political problems of the 1370s arose out of the diplomatic setbacks, administrative blunders and economic misfortunes suffered in the previous decade. During the 1360s it became apparent that the crown could only maintain its popularity at home by making larger and increasingly ominous compromises with the political community. The change in the commissions of the peace is a case in point.[10] Between 1361 and 1364 the government dropped its earlier policy of including professional assize judges on the commissions, and handed over total responsibility for local law enforcement to the county gentry. The crown actually judged this a mistake and in 1368 returned to its old policy, insisting that the assize judges should be present when cases of felony were brought to trial. By this stage, however, the justices of the peace had won so much control over petty crime that the qualification was of comparatively little significance. So far as the landholding classes were concerned, the privilege of maintaining the peace in the shires was now very largely their own.

It would clearly be a mistake to exaggerate the degree of political pressure applied on the crown during the 1360s. There were only six parliaments held in the period of peace, and the amount of business done in them was fairly limited. In many ways, the king's relations with his subjects were better than ever before. Direct taxation had ceased: indeed, the years from 1360 to 1371 marked the longest respite from such charges since the time of Henry III. The wool subsidy continued to be collected, but at a reduced rate. The king himself was little worried by the resulting loss of revenue, for he was already amassing a considerable personal fortune from the ransom of John II. Consequently, both sides were well satisfied with the politics of peace. In 1363, the commons thanked God for giving them 'a lord and governor who has delivered them from servitude to other lands and from the charges sustained by them in times past'.[11] But this statement also summed up the potential problem. If war began again, proved expensive and failed to get results, the king might well find that the power enjoyed by the political community could be turned against him. That possibility became a painful reality in Edward's last years.

MILITARY REVERSALS AND FINANCIAL CRISES

In the late 1360s certain of the Black Prince's subjects in Aquitaine decided to challenge his right to levy taxes, and presented their case to the French king in the *parlement* of Paris. Charles V quickly seized this opportunity to challenge English power in the south of France. Ignoring the terms of the Brétigny agreement, he claimed feudal suzerainty over Aquitaine and summoned the prince to answer for his actions in 1369. The latter refused, was pronounced a contumacious vassal, and had all his lands in France declared forfeit. When these events were reported to the English parliament in June 1369, the lords and commons agreed to support Edward III's resumption of the French royal title and granted a generous wool subsidy to pay for the now inevitable war. But Edward and his subjects were quite mistaken if they expected another round of easy victories. The English commanders dispatched to the continent after 1369 continued to use the old strategy of the 1340s and 1350s, intervening in Brittany and Normandy and launching raids into the heartlands of the French kingdom. This was intended to divert Charles V's attention away

5 Tomb of William of Wykeham at Winchester Cathedral

from the south. But in practice it simply divided and weakened Edward's military resources. England was also diplomatically isolated. Flanders and Castile counted for nothing, and the Valois king had won over Scotland and Navarre. In 1371 John of Gaunt married the daughter of Edward III's old ally Peter I, and through her was to claim the Castilian throne. But this revival of English interests south of the Pyrenees simply provided a further military distraction and left Aquitaine open to attack.

Even without these difficulties, the English would have faced a considerable challenge from the armies of Charles V. Under the direction of the ubiquitous du Guesclin, the French had learned the tactical mistakes of Crécy and Poitiers, and refused to be drawn into pitched battles where they might be defeated by the English mixed formation. England also lost the initiative at sea after Pembroke's humiliating naval defeat off La Rochelle in 1372. To some extent Edward's lieutenants were the victims of circumstance, ill equipped for a defensive war and caught unawares by the revival of Valois power. But this was not how the king's subjects interpreted the dismal reversals of the 1370s. Ineffective leadership, bad advice, the absence of a co-ordinated strategy, and wanton dissipation of resources: these were the causes of English defeat according to the parliaments of the period. It became increasingly obvious that continued failure abroad would result in a major political upheaval at home.

The greatest of all the military problems of the 1370s was provided by Aquitaine. Not only did the English have to defend the principality from outside attack, but they also had to cope with the increasing animosity of its inhabitants. The only answer they could find to the latter problem was repression. In 1370 the Black Prince led a force against Limoges, which had formed part of the English territories in 1360 but had now fallen under the control of Charles V. He proceeded to destroy any last vestige of English sympathy by plundering the city. His reputation tarnished and his health severely impaired, the prince then returned to England, never to fight again. Those left to carry on the struggle found that they could not even depend on Gascony, the very heart of the English possessions in the south of France. Arnaud Amanieu, Sire d'Albret, one of the most powerful Gascon lords, renounced his allegiance to Edward III in 1369 and threw in his lot with Charles V. Such desertions left Edward's commanders in an untenable position. In 1372, French forces took over much of the northern part of Aquitaine, and within a short while English control was confined to a narrow strip of coastline between Bordeaux and Bayonne. The only substantial counter-measure attempted by the English was the large expedition led by John of Gaunt through France in 1373, which achieved no military advantage and simply ran up enormous debts for the already embarrassed exchequer. In the same year Edward's principal ally, the Duke of Brittany, found his duchy overrun by Charles V's troops. There was nothing for it but to buy time, and an Anglo-French truce was concluded at Bruges in 1375. This amounted to a public declaration of defeat for the English. Everything that Edward III had won by conquest and negotiation up to 1360 had vanished in the space of six short years.

One of the reasons for this dramatic reversal of fortunes was the absence of effective leadership by the king. Queen Philippa's death apparently prevented Edward III from taking charge of operations in 1369,[12] and a further royal expedition planned in 1372 was called off before it ever set sail. [13] In the early 1370s the king withdrew increasingly from public life, and became dangerously dependent on a small group of unscrupulous sycophants at court.[14] Both the chamberlain, William Latimer, and the steward, Lord Neville, seem to have taken advantage of the elderly and feeble-minded king to advance their personal interests. Latimer also negotiated a series of dubious financial deals with the London financier Richard Lyons. The most influential and remarkable member of this inner circle, however, was the king's mistress, Alice Perrers. Queen Philippa had been content with childbearing and collecting fine clothes, but her successor in Edward III's bed was a woman of altogether greater political ambitions.[15] By the early 1370s, in fact, Latimer, Neville and Perrers virtually controlled all access to the king. The court had ceased to epitomize the political unity of the realm, and had instead become dominated by a narrow, exclusive and unpopular clique. It was not long before the country began to blame the courtiers for the evils which had now befallen the realm.

Opposition was once again sparked off by the government's financial demands. Between 1369 and 1375 the crown spent something in excess of £670,000 on the war.[16] Neither the wool subsidy of 1369 nor the triennial tenth secured from the church in 1370 proved sufficient, and in 1371 the laity and clergy were each asked to grant £50,000 towards the war effort. In 1372–3 parliament authorized three fifteenths and tenths; and in 1373 the clergy conceded yet another tenth. It seemed almost incredible that such high taxation could produce so little return, and from 1371 the commons began to voice their suspicions about the misappropriation of subsidies granted for the war effort. More seriously, the parliament of 1371 demanded the dismissals of Chancellor Wykeham and Treasurer Brantingham and their replacement by laymen. Edward was forced to sacrifice his closest advisers in a desperate effort to retain the goodwill of the community. Such actions would have been unthinkable in the 1340s and 1350s, and did not bode well for the future. Even the truce of 1375 was unpopular, for it was seen as an opportunity for Charles V to regroup his forces and prepare for the final onslaught on Gascony. The English government was sufficiently worried about the attitude in the country that it refused to call parliament in 1374 and 1375. When an assembly was eventually summoned in April 1376 it was inevitable that the anger and frustration which had built up over the preceding years would produce an acrimonious debate. But few men on either side can have been ready for the extraordinary course which this political crisis was to take.

THE GOOD PARLIAMENT

The parliament of 1376 was remarkable in many ways. Contemporaries recognized this by identifying it with a special name, the 'Good Parliament'. It was a record-breaking session, lasting longer than any previous assembly (ten weeks) and producing the largest recorded list of common petitions to date (146 items). It witnessed the first appointment of a speaker to act as the commons' chairman and representative, and the first use in parliament of the judicial procedure known as impeachment. We know more about this assembly than any other parliament in the fourteenth century, thanks to several valuable chronicle accounts which supplement the official record of proceedings. There is therefore an understandable tendency to exaggerate the significance of the Good Parliament, and it is important to remember that all its achievements had been undone by the time Edward III died in 1377. Nevertheless, the events of 1376 are a natural focus for our study, since they provide a rare and valuable insight into the attitudes of the new political society that had grown up in the course of Edward III's reign.

The parliament opened with an appeal for taxation. The commons met in the chapter house of Westminster Abbey to debate this request, and after much deliberation came to the conclusion that if the king had been better advised, no taxes would now be necessary. They decided to deliver this message to the government, and chose as their spokesman Sir Peter de la Mare, knight of the shire for Herefordshire and steward of the Earl of March. De la Mare treated with John of Gaunt, the king's representative, and after some delay secured the appointment of a small committee of lords and bishops to join in discussion with the knights and burgesses. The commons subsequently persuaded Gaunt to accept their proposal for a new royal council, which included several members of the earlier consultative committee (Bishop Courtenay of London, the Earls of March and Stafford, Lord Percy, Sir Guy Brian and Sir Roger Beauchamp) together with Archbishop Sudbury, Bishop Wykeham and the new Earl of Arundel. A number of these men had personal grievances against the court, and both March and Wykeham were to make public attacks on the king's advisers in the course of this parliament. The knowledge that there was a group of peers sympathetic to their cause undoubtedly gave the commons a greater sense of security in their ensuing battle against the courtiers.

On 12 May, Peter de la Mare appeared before John of Gaunt and set forth the principal grievance of the opposition: that the king 'has with him certain councillors and servants who are not loyal or profitable to him or the kingdom'.[17] The attack centred on Latimer, Neville, Alice Perrers and Richard Lyons, though a number of other financiers were also implicated in the ensuing scandal. In presenting his case, de la Mare insisted that he was acting for the commons as a whole, and thus stumbled upon the process of impeachment. This was already a well-established procedure in the common law courts, involving a joint charge by a group of accusers acting in the name of the king. In 1376 it was used for the first time in parliament, where the charges were heard and tried by the lords, presided over by John of Gaunt. The most serious accusations were those against Latimer and Lyons, who were said to have sold licences exempting merchants from the Calais staple and to have organized loans for the crown at extortionate rates of interest. Latimer was also blamed for the loss of the fortresses of St Sauveur and Bécherel during his period as the king's lieutenant in Brittany. Some of the charges were without foundation, and many others misrepresented or exaggerated the true facts. But when the former treasurer Sir Richard Scrope declared that the loans negotiated by Latimer and Lyons had been made without his knowledge, Gaunt had to accept that the court was defeated. Latimer and Neville were dismissed from office, Richard Lyons was imprisoned, and Alice Perrers was banished from the household. Behind all the complicated details, the basic issue in 1376 was the same as in 1258, 1311 or 1341: namely, the desire of a section of the political community to removal evil counsellors from the king's side. But there was one great difference which marked the Good Parliament out from earlier disputes, for it was the commons, not the barons, who had now taken the initiative in ousting court favourites and dictating a wiser form of counsel.

It is a measure of the gravity of this crisis that the parliament did not end with these impeachments but continued in session for another month. The commons compiled a long list of grievances, and made it clear that they would not be satisfied until the king had carried out a comprehensive reform of government. They also turned their suspicion on John of Gaunt. After the Black Prince's death on 8 June there were rumours that the Duke of Lancaster intended to take the throne, and the commons hastily requested that the young Prince Richard be installed as Prince of Wales in order to guarantee the rightful succession. The king's representatives were prepared to prolong the troublesome session in the hope of gaining taxes, and were eventually rewarded with a grant of the wool subsidy for three years. But the Good Parliament did what no assembly since 1325 had apparently dared to do: it rejected the crown's requests for direct taxation and refused to the last to authorize a lay subsidy.[18] The session therefore ended on 10 July with a massive vote of no confidence in the government. The court, not surprisingly, was in disarray. The king's two younger sons, Edmund and Thomas, who had dissociated themselves from Gaunt, joined in the celebrations hosted by de la Mare. Edward himself had already retired to Eltham before the end of the parliament, and was soon totally incapacitated by a serious illness from which he never fully recovered.

6 *The body — or funeral effigy — of the king lying in state*

The Good Parliament witnessed one of the most serious attacks on the English crown in the whole of the later Middle Ages. Had it not been for the residual respect accorded to a once great and now aged ruler, the parliament might indeed have made an all-out attack on Edward III himself. In the event, the king's power remained intact, and was used by John of Gaunt to avenge the humiliations suffered at the hands of a presumptuous opposition. By October 1376 the displaced courtiers had been pardoned and restored to their titles, lands and influence. De la Mare was arrested and put in Nottingham Castle; the Earl of March was deprived of his title of marshal; and Wykeham, who had dared to speak out against Lord Latimer, was stripped of his estates and brought before the council. Such arbitrary measures inevitably provoked more hostile reaction. In February 1377 Lancaster's protégé John Wyclif was summoned before Bishop Courtenay to answer charges of seditious preaching. If John of Gaunt intended to abuse the immunities of the church, then the church would be forced to take vengeance on one of Gaunt's own clerical associates. At the same time Gaunt fell foul of the governing elite in London. Rumours spread about his plans to infringe the administrative and judicial privileges of the city. Serious disturbances broke out in the capital and a mob attacked Lancaster's palace of the Savoy. It must have seemed to many in the autumn of 1376 that the whole fabric of political life was about to be torn apart.

Ironically, however, the new parliament which assembled at Westminster in January 1377 proved astonishingly amenable to Lancaster's will. It accepted the reversal of the earlier impeachments and granted a direct subsidy in the novel form of a poll tax. Historians used to think that this parliament was packed with John of Gaunt's supporters and placemen.[19] But it seems more likely that the absence or defection of some of the principal actors in the earlier drama severely weakened the remaining opposition, and left the assembly with no alternative but to accept a *fait accompli*. As in 1341, parliament was forced to acknowledge that the king had the right to renege on political concessions made against his will. In the following months the government also made some concessions to public opinion, giving up its unpopular attack on Wykeham, and stage-managing a reconciliation between Lancaster and the Londoners. By the late spring John of Gaunt's policy seemed to have paid off, and some degree of normality was restored to political life. It remained to be seen how long this uneasy equilibrium could last.

The principal reason for the hasty compromise patched together in the early months of 1377 was the growing concern about the king's health, the succession to the throne, and the security of the realm. Edward III was seriously ill by September 1376, and remained inactive for the next five months.[20] In the following February, parliament was given encouraging news of his health and notified of a general amnesty to celebrate his jubilee.[21] But within a short while the sickness had returned, and the king died of a stroke at Sheen on 21 June 1377.

> The gallant and noble King Edward III departed this life to the deep distress of the whole realm of England, for he had been a good king for them. His like had not been seen since the days of King Arthur … So King Edward was embalmed and placed with great pomp and reverence on a bier borne by twenty-four knights dressed in black, his three sons and the duke of Brittany and the earl of March walking behind him, and carried thus at a slow march through the city of London, the face uncovered. To witness and hear the grief of the people, their sobs and screams and lamentations on that day, would have rended anyone's heart.[22]

Froissart, like many other chroniclers, took Edward's death and burial as an opportunity to indulge fond memories of a great and glorious king. In 1377 some may have been less kind in their comments about a rather pathetic old man whose indolence and incapacity had jeopardized the welfare of the realm. But for all his failings, Edward III had provided a sense of stability in English politics, a stability now threatened by rumours of French invasions and the prospect of a minority government. Some years later an English versifier made the obvious but apposite analogy with the ship of state, deprived of its rudder since the death of this 'noble knight' and set adrift on a troubled sea.[23] It is not surprising that an old man's weaknesses were soon forgiven, and the cult of Edward III was quickly under way.

★ ★ ★

It is not easy to sum up the achievements of Edward III. His reign was too long and his fortunes too changeable to allow for any bold generalizations. Had he died in 1340, he would undoubtedly have been judged a failure; had he died in 1360, he would probably have been seen as one of the most successful men ever to sit on the English throne. Edward II's regime had demonstrated the perils as well as the futility of political conflict, and it must be admitted that the youthful Edward III was somewhat slow to realize the advantages to be derived from conciliation. After 1341, however, the king deliberately made himself more accessible and amenable to a broad cross-section of political society, and enjoyed a degree of popularity virtually unparalleled in the history of the Plantagenet dynasty. This inevitably created a challenge for the monarchy, and both Edward III and his successors often found it difficult to live up to the new expectations placed upon them. But Edward's ability to accommodate the interests of so many of his subjects for so long a period of time sets him apart from most other medieval kings. To understand the full significance of that achievement we need to look beyond the battles and treaties and examine in detail the structure and the motives of political society in fourteenth-century England.

4 The king

Medieval politics was dictated very largely by the character and the ambitions of the king. By the later Middle Ages the crown was tending to become more anonymous: personal monarchy had begun to give way to impersonal bureaucracy. But the king remained the fount of justice and patronage, the protector of his subjects, and the defender of the realm. If he was too young, too old or too inept, the whole political and administrative machine could easily break down. In 1327 it was convenient to maintain the fiction that Edward III was of an age to rule. But there was also a keen awareness that certain great matters, such as a proposed revision to the Charter of the Forests, could not be dealt with until he reached maturity.[1] Similarly Edward's final illness meant that the government was unable for some months to respond to the request of the Good Parliament that Prince Richard be created Prince of Wales.[2] These are just two examples of the problems that arose whenever the country found itself without an effective ruler. Conversely, too much intervention could also pose a threat to political stability. The wilful abuse of power by kings and their aristocratic cronies provoked widespread opposition and led ultimately to the overthrow of both Edward II and Richard II. In the later Middle Ages, then, it was important not only that the king should rule effectively, but that he should be seen to rule well and wisely. This demanded a perception, a sensitivity and a flexibility all too often lacking in the Plantagenet dynasty. It is our present task to describe how Edward III developed such skills, and to assess the wider implications for the state of politics in his reign.

THE CHARACTER OF EDWARD III

Edward III had little formal instruction in the art of kingship. He was given a collection of handbooks or 'mirrors for princes' on his betrothal to Philippa of Hainault in 1326, but it is extremely doubtful that he read or comprehended these works.[3] When he received from Walter de Milemete his very own tract on kingship, Edward was probably much more impressed with the sumptuous illustrations than with the implications of the text.[4] His conception of the royal office was formed not by theory but by practice, and in particular by the models provided among his historical and mythical ancestors. The anonymous author of the *Life of Edward II* had wished on the future Edward III all the virtues of his predecessors: the industry of Henry II, the bravery of Richard I, the longevity of Henry III, the wisdom of Edward I, and — the best he could do — the good looks of Edward II.[5] This habit of referring to the past obviously appealed to Edward III. He collected chronicles of English history, and in 1352 he consulted the writer Ranulph

Higden on some unspecified point in the latter's *Polychronicon*.[6] He was especially taken by the achievements of Henry II and Edward I, and tried to emulate their imperialist policies.[7] By appealing to the glories of the past, Edward III indicated his hopes for the future and advertised to contemporaries his plan for the revival of the monarchy.

Edward III was a man of conventional tastes and habits. He was bluff, brave, generous, slightly boorish, heartily heterosexual, fair-minded and, on the whole, even-tempered. Above all, he fitted the contemporary image of kingship. In his religious observances, for instance, Edward was careful to follow fashion, patronizing the friars, founding colleges of secular clerks, visiting shrines, and showing due devotion to the Virgin.[8] He was a natural showman, and proved remarkably successful at manipulating public opinion through displays of majesty. A notable example is provided by the royal touch, the practice whereby anointed kings blessed (and reputedly healed) those suffering from scrofula.[9] Between November 1340 and November 1341, for instance, when his popularity was otherwise extremely low, Edward carried out no fewer than 355 ritual healings, at least 257 of them at Westminster.[10] We can perhaps better understand the collapse of Stratford's opposition during the summer of 1341 when we realize the symbolic significance of these and other ceremonies going on in the capital. The king's cultural interests also had a political dimension. Edward's principal love was architecture, and the major building programme initiated at Windsor Castle in the 1350s was particularly close to his heart. His total expenditure on palaces, castles, chapels and hunting lodges was at least £130,000.[11] But this extravagance never incited criticism, partly because a good deal of it was funded out of Edward's private income, and partly because it was deemed an appropriate princely pastime. The pageantry and spectacle of the Tudor regime was still some way off; but the trend was set by the mid-fourteenth century, and Edward III's contemporaries liked it.

Much of Edward's popularity rested on his success as a soldier. Several of his escapades — like the rescue of the Countess of Atholl from the siege of Lochindorb in 1336 — had a strongly romantic flavour.[12] Others were distinctly dangerous. At Christmas 1349, for example, Edward was informed that the town of Calais, only recently won after a long siege, was about to be betrayed to the French. With scant regard for his own safety, he immediately crossed the Channel in the company of a small band of soldiers and helped to save the town.[13] Such impetuosity did not always serve the king so well. Edward's tactics at Crécy in 1346 indicate a high degree of planning and organization; but as the campaign of 1360 showed, he was too often distracted from his principal purpose — in this case the siege of Rheims — by the prospect of easy pickings in the shape of plunder and ransoms.[14] For contemporaries, however, there was no such questioning of the king's accomplishments. Indeed, his prowess in war did much to redeem his mistakes at home. Like his grandfather, Edward deliberately encouraged the equation between his own victories and the feats of King Arthur. In 1331 he visited the centre of the Arthurian cult at Glastonbury, and in 1345 he ordered a search to be made for the body of Arthur's supposed ancestor, Joseph of Arimathea.[15] Similarly, in 1343, Edward invoked more recent memories of the battle of Sluys by presenting five model ships crafted in gold to the principal pilgrimage centres of the English church.[16] Shortly afterwards he issued a new gold coin, the noble, with a striking representation of himself aboard a ship of war. This imagery sank deep into the public consciousness, and earned the king a special reputation as lord of the seas both in his own and in later generations.[17] Edward III, in fact, emerges from the records as one of the most image-conscious kings of the later Middle Ages.

THE DEPOSITION OF EDWARD II

It is a commonplace of historical writing that Edward III's vision of kingship was conditioned by the fate of Edward II. There is much truth to this. The monarchy had suffered a considerable blow as a result of the revolution of 1326–7, and many of the policies of Edward III were inevitably designed to wipe clean the soiled reputation of his dynasty. It would be quite wrong, however, to suggest that Edward was much troubled by the ghost of his father. The so-called articles of deposition, which detailed the reasons why Edward II had forfeited his right to rule, may have been read before the parliament of January 1327; but no attempt was made to publicize them throughout the country and they were never cited against Edward III in political debate.[18] Initially, there was a tendency for those aggrieved by the crown to refer in a general way to the punishment meted out to the previous king. William of Pagula, the articulate vicar of Winkfield (Berkshire), held forth on the evils of royal purveyance in the early 1330s, and made some pointed remarks to Edward III about the fate of tyrants.[19] John Stratford, whose name has often been linked with the earlier articles of deposition, also made various references to the downfall of Edward II during his quarrel with Edward III in the winter of 1340–1.[20] But it is interesting to note that these allusions were never taken up by parliament, even at the height of the ensuing crisis. And with the improvement in the political climate after the 1340s, such references ceased altogether. There was no suggestion at the end of Edward III's reign that the king stood in any danger of deposition. It was only Richard II's obstinacy that forced the magnates once again to cite, and finally to use, the precedent of 1326–7.[21]

One of the principal reasons for Edward III's comparative security was his position as the legitimate heir to the throne. Unlike the later usurper Henry IV, Edward never had to resort to deceit in order to justify his title.[22] As a mere youth, he could also claim that he was innocent of the violent deeds of 1326–7. It is almost certain that Edward II was murdered at Berkeley Castle in September 1327;[23] but Edward III was not implicated in the event, and after his own coup in 1330 he was quick to lay the blame for the old king's death on the discredited Earl of March.[24] Edward was indeed sufficiently confident of his own position to pay public respect to his predecessor. He was generous to the monks of Gloucester who had charge of Edward II's remains, and he diligently fulfilled his father's various bequests and religious foundations.[25] He had little to fear from the occasional rumours that the former king was still alive, and responded discreetly and calmly to such reports. Edward III clearly appreciated that his own position rested heavily on the principle of dynastic continuity.

This sense of continuity also explains why the revolution of 1326–7 was not accompanied by any formal statement restricting the power of the crown. Edward III's accession marked a new dispensation only in the sense that it provided his subjects with the opportunity to rebuild the old political structures undermined by Edward II. Although

7 & 8   *Corbel heads of Edward III and Queen Phillipa at Ely Cathedral*

Mortimer and Isabella betrayed that hope, the elite simply trusted that things would improve when the young king came of age. On Edward's assumption of power in 1330, the mood was therefore conciliatory, conservative, and optimistic. The community anticipated the restoration of normality, and eagerly awaited proof of a similar commitment on the part of the king.

THE ROYAL POLICY OF EDWARD III

The idea that Edward III had a consistent 'policy' has not found favour with constitutional historians. Stubbs believed that Edward's opportunism marked a weakness of character and a deficiency of statesmanship, and most historians still attribute the king's success merely to his conciliatory attitude.[26] The common picture is that of a ruler prepared to compromise his power in order to maintain personal popularity and political peace. But it would be quite unrealistic to suppose that Edward III consciously and recklessly destroyed the authority of the throne. A reconsideration of the fortunes of the royal prerogative during the mid-fourteenth century will reveal that Edward's political objectives were considerably more consistent and ambitious than has usually been suggested.

The royal prerogative consisted of those powers which were exercised by the king alone, and which could not be taken away from him without his express permission. They fell into two broad categories.[27] On the one hand there were the feudal perquisites. These included rights of wardship over the persons and estates of tenants-in-chief; the power to collect feudal aids from the tenants-in-chief for the knighting of the king's eldest son and the marriage of his eldest daughter; the authority to impose scutage, a payment made in lieu of knight service; the right to impose arbitrary taxes called tallages on the royal demesne; and the ability to levy prises from the whole country for the upkeep of the household and army. On the other hand, there were what we might call the king's political rights: namely, the authority to appoint and dismiss ministers, to issue laws for the better governance of the kingdom, to summon and prorogue parliaments at will, and to repeal all measures passed in parliament which had been made without his free consent or were injurious to his own position. Edward III's policy seems to have been to compromise on his feudal privileges and safeguard the political ones: in other words, to give up archaic or outmoded rights in order that he might more easily preserve the power that really mattered in fourteenth-century politics.

The results can best be judged by examining a few specific cases. It was in the course of Edward III's reign that parliament successfully abolished or restricted a number of the crown's more contentious feudal prerogatives. In 1340, for instance, it was agreed to release the country from the threat of tallage and scutage, and for the rest of his reign Edward III made no further attempt to levy these arbitrary taxes.[28] Moreover, in 1352 the crown conceded that in future feudal aids should be collected only with the consent of parliament.[29] It is important to recognize, however, that such promises were usually only given when the levies had proved unproductive (as in the case of tallage and scutage),[30] or when Edward had already exercised such rights (as in the case of the feudal aid).[31] The timing of these concessions is therefore of crucial importance.

Much the same holds true for the contemporary legislation on purveyance. Most of the statutes passed between 1330 and 1360 were intended to reduce corruption among the king's purveyors rather than restrict the levies themselves. It was only in 1362, when the war was apparently over, that the king was prepared to abolish country-wide prises for the upkeep of his armies and garrisons, and to restrict compulsory purveyance to the maintenance of the royal household.[32] Indeed, there are reasons to question the effectiveness of this statute once the French war broke out again in 1369.[33] Nevertheless, the importance of such legislation should not be minimized. By the end of Edward III's reign, parliament had made a permanent and considerable impact on the king's feudal rights.

The crown's constitutional powers fared very differently. Edward III was far too much of a traditionalist to ignore the ancient privileges of the crown, and he could cling as jealously as any of his predecessors to those rights deemed to be inherent to his title. It was only in 1340–1 that the desperate financial situation forced Edward to make major concessions. In April 1340 he had to accept a series of special parliamentary tribunals to investigate the activities of royal tax collectors and financiers, and agreed in principle to the idea of a permanent baronial committee nominated in parliament and enjoying comprehensive power over the crown's income and expenditure.[34] The regency council subsequently appointed to run the country in Edward's absence was actually permitted to exercise the king's feudal rights, to appoint and dismiss ministers, and to do all that was necessary for the administration of the realm.[35] In effect, then, royal government was put into commission. Edward's return from the continent in December 1340 marked the end of this extraordinary council, but not of the political arguments behind it. Indeed, in April

1341 the king was forced to accept the appointment of another audit committee, to allow the peers a say in the selection of royal ministers, and to give parliament the right to attaint such officers of state.[36] These new concessions represented a substantial infringement of the royal prerogative. But the renunciation of this legislation later in 1341 made it clear that the king was determined to protect his political rights.[37] Edward may have sworn at his coronation to uphold the just laws and customs which the community of the realm might choose; but as events in 1341 showed, it was the king alone who remained the arbiter of what was good and just.

In theory, this action restored Edward to the plenitude of power. He now enjoyed the same authority claimed by his father in the years following the Statute of York of 1322 or by Richard II after the collapse of the Appellant regime in 1388–9.[38] The vital difference, of course, was that Edward III refused to use the royal prerogative as an instrument of tyranny. In particular, he avoided those arbitrary trials and executions which had claimed so many aristocratic victims between 1322 and 1330. Indeed, in 1352 he made what was arguably one of the most significant political concessions of his reign by defining the various crimes which could be treated as high or petty treason. This made it impossible for the king to proceed against his political opponents on the trumped-up charge of 'accroaching the royal power'.[39] Richard II later had good reason to regret the restrictions contained in this statute. But it is most unlikely that Edward III saw the legislation as damaging to the prerogative. Treason was a political irrelevance in the 1350s; and the king never actually had occasion to test his remaining powers by citing the legislation against an opponent. The Statute of Treasons may have represented a safeguard against tyranny, but it did little to alter the practical power of the crown in the mid-fourteenth century.

The real test of the king's authority, as Edward III well appreciated, was in the financial sphere. It was during this reign, as we shall see, that parliament came to enjoy exclusive control over the granting of direct and indirect taxes. This undoubtedly gave the commons greater influence and encouraged them to intervene in many areas of high politics.[40] But this is not to say that parliament had any real control over the king's financial administration. From 1340 the commons tried to establish the principle that taxes granted for the defence of the realm should be spent solely on war; but the king clearly made free with such supplies, and by the 1350s was reserving at least some of the profits of direct and indirect taxation for the expenses of his increasingly extravagant court.[41] Again, parliament argued that all extraordinary levies should cease in the event of a truce being drawn up. Edward III, however, carried on collecting taxes for their full duration, regardless of the state of war or diplomacy.[42] There was apparently no question, for instance, that the six-year wool subsidy begun in 1356 should not run its course, despite the fact that peace was concluded in 1360.[43] Finally, after 1371, the commons began to agitate for the appointment of groups of barons to administer extraordinary taxes.[44] The apparent intention (not made specific until after Edward's death) was to provide parliament with detailed statements on the expenditure of wartime subsidies. But this clearly aroused memories of the audit committees of 1340–1, and the requests were summarily dismissed. It might be argued that Edward III's ministers were only delaying the inevitable, for the parliaments of Richard II and Henry IV were to take important stands on the appropriation of supplies and the accountability of war treasurers.[45]

Nevertheless, Edward's refusal to compromise on this matter is a notable example of his determination to maintain the initiative and to avoid the damaging political compromises into which he had been forced in 1340–1.

The last and most obvious demonstration of Edward's constitutional rights came during the political squabbles of the 1370s. In 1371 the government was forced to dismiss the chancellor, treasurer and keeper of the privy seal, and to replace them by laymen.[46] But this was no mere repeat of the ministerial crisis of 1340–1. The new officials were appointed by and answerable to the king, not parliament; and although the three principal offices of state remained in the hands of laymen for the next six years, parliament was certainly not consulted on the government's decision to revert to clerical chancellors and treasurers in January 1377. Indeed, the whole royalist *revanche* in the months following the Good Parliament drew directly on the precedent of 1341 and demonstrated very clearly that the prerogative was still a powerful instrument with which to outmanoeuvre the king's enemies. The authority of the crown therefore remained very much a political reality in the mid-fourteenth century. The rarity with which Edward III actually asserted the prerogative was a sign not of some constitutional weakness but of the extraordinary consensus which prevailed for so much of his reign.

THE KING AND GOVERNMENT

Much as they may have disliked it, medieval kings had to apply themselves to the task of government. In the twelfth century, this had meant being constantly on the move: both Henry I and Henry II had travelled around their dominions with a rapidity that remains impressive even today. By the fourteenth century, however, the king's itinerary tended to be more restricted. Indeed, Edward III's personal knowledge of his kingdom was remarkably limited. The Scottish campaigns of the 1330s often led the king through the midlands and the north.[47] But a detailed analysis of his itinerary in the decade 1345–55 reveals that, in normal circumstances, Edward rarely went further west than Wiltshire and Dorset or north of Northamptonshire.[48] By the 1360s his geographical range had become still more restricted, and during the last years of the reign the court was usually lodged either at the queen's manor of Havering (Essex) or at the royal palaces of Woodstock (Oxfordshire), Windsor (Berkshire), Sheen (Middlesex), Eltham and Queenborough (Kent).[49]

There was, of course, a very practical reason why Edward chose to spend the majority of his time in one particular corner of the realm. All his principal residences were within a day's journey of the capital. Ministers were summoned to attend the king at his country seats,[50] and a squadron of royal messengers maintained constant communication between the court and its professional advisers at Westminster.[51] Edward retained his private quarters in Westminster Palace, and made frequent if brief visits there to meet foreign envoys,[52] to consult with his councillors, and to hold parliaments. The itinerary of Edward III indicates a deliberate attempt to balance the king's personal preference for country life with the constant pressures of government; and the evidence suggests that, for most of the reign at least, this compromise proved remarkably successful.

Edward III was not a bureaucrat by inclination: pen-pushing had no place in his vision in kingship. But impatience with administration did not mean a total disregard for business. The king well appreciated the essential distinction between mundane matters 'of course' (*de cursu*) which could safely be left to the professional administrators, and important matters 'of grace' (*de gratia*) which should be dealt with by him alone.[53] There were three principal means by which Edward III communicated his will to the central government: by word of mouth; by writs under the privy seal; and by letters under the secret seal or signet. The frequency with which the first method was used can be attested by the large number of instruments issued from the chancery and warranted *per ipsum regem* (by the king himself). As Edward III's reign wound on, however, both the chancery and the exchequer showed a marked preference for written warrants.[54] The matters which feature in the resulting correspondence are predictable enough: the administration of war; the regulation of government officials; the operation of justice; and the distribution of patronage. But the following analysis of these subjects provides a more general insight into the nature and success of Edward III's regime. The king was attentive to administrative detail not because he liked it, but because it was the very stuff of politics.

The Administration of War

It was undoubtedly in times of war that Edward III was most actively involved in government. During the Scottish campaigns of the 1330s the king actually transferred the chancery, exchequer and court of common pleas to a northern base at York, the better to control his administration.[55] When he went to the continent, these departments were left at Westminster under the token charge of one of the infant princes. On these occasions, Edward took both his great and privy seals with him, and created a great seal of absence for the use of the domestic government. Convention, or specific written instructions, then divided responsibility between the king and the regency council.[56]

Inevitably, this situation sometimes caused problems. In 1336, while at Perth, the king discovered that the chancery had failed to carry out his wishes with regard to a grant made to Lady Mortimer.[57] Similarly, in the winter of 1355–6 when Edward was called north to deal with the Scots, his ministers at Westminster chose to ignore a controversial royal order for the seizure of the Bishop of Ely's estates.[58] By far the most serious conflict arose in 1338–9, when the regency council refused to be bound by the restrictions of the Walton Ordinances and found itself unable to raise sufficient money to meet the considerable costs of Edward's campaign in the Low Countries. After 1341, however, there is little to suggest any real administrative conflict during the king's military expeditions. Edward was every bit as determined to maintain his own scale of priorities in 1346–7 and 1359–60 as he had been in 1338–40.[59] The difference was not that he had given up his special wartime powers, but that his administrators were content to abide by his decisions and in particular were able to meet his financial demands.

Edward III was much involved in the elaborate preparations that went on before each of his military campaigns. He frequently issued instructions for the array of soldiers and for the levy of horses, arms and victuals for his armies.[60] He seems to have shown particular concern for the defence of the seas. In 1337 the council drew up a memorandum on shipping for his attention; and in 1372 when awaiting embarkation on his last abortive campaign, Edward personally ordered the arrest of all those who had deserted, or might desert, from the royal fleet.[61] In 1351 he issued instructions to the sheriff of Somerset and Dorset for the preparation of 6,000lb of rope for the rigging of his ships; and he took a keen interest in the convoy system instituted in the early 1350s to protect the wine fleet trading with Gascony.[62]

The king was also personally involved in diplomacy. His secret correspondence with the Pope in 1330 and his meetings with the French kings in 1325, 1329 and 1331 gave him an early grounding in international affairs, and he remained actively interested in the work of his ambassadors and negotiators for most of the reign. On the eve of Edward's departure for the continent in 1338, for instance, the treasury of the exchequer was opened up and certain documents — probably concerning his claims in France — were made available for royal inspection.[63] In 1362, Edward actually wrote *E. Rex* in his own hand at the foot of a diplomatic document sent to the King of Castile.[64] In November 1348, he crossed the Channel in the company of the Prince of Wales, the Earl of Warwick, Treasurer Edington and others, in order to put the finishing touches to a projected treaty with the Count of Flanders.[65] And in 1360 he intervened directly and decisively in the negotiations at Calais in order to ensure that the renunciation clauses were removed from the main text of the Brétigny settlement.[66] Edward was clearly much more than a figurehead for his armies and his diplomatic service; he emerges from the records as an active and, by his own standards, a conscientious war leader.

Domestic Government

When Edward was not fighting or planning a campaign, he was inevitably rather less involved in administration. In the early years of the reign, indeed, it was only the shortage of funds that usually led the king to interfere in the business of government.[67] But the crisis of 1340–1 did much to stir him from his early complacency. When he returned secretly from the continent in December 1340 to take his vengeance on the domestic administration, Edward had his great and privy seals with him, and swiftly took charge of the whole governmental machine. The invitation to his subject to submit complaints against royal ministers and agents,[68] the subsequent order for the appointment of special commissions of oyer and terminer,[69] and the ensuing announcement of the king's sincere desire to wipe out corruption and oppression:[70] all these actions betray Edward's highly personal interpretation of the problem facing the country early in 1341. His administrative output during these weeks and months was indeed considerable, and it heralded a period of much more active and consistent participation in government.

Although it is impossible to make statistical comparisons, it seems that an appreciable proportion of government business during the central period of the reign arose directly from Edward's personal wishes. He intervened in a whole range of subjects: from special arrangements for the governance of Calais to an inquiry into the forgery of wardrobe bills;[71] from instructions on the disposition of the temporalities of the bishopric of Norwich to a ban on the construction of a new cemetery near the Tower of London during the plague of 1349.[72] Very occasionally, as in 1350, he would write his own response on a document in order to authorize further government action.[73] More frequently, he ordered the chancery to send the great seal to him so that charters, letters patent and writs drawn up at his instruction might be validated.[74] Some of these solemn documents were checked by the king personally, and if he objected to a particular wording, as in a grant made to the Earl of Arundel in 1361, the whole thing had to be written out again.[75] Even during the summer months, when the pace of government slackened and the royal family went off hunting, such duties did not cease. In August-September 1361, for example, while taking his leisure at Beaulieu Abbey in the New Forest (Hampshire), Edward was called upon to authorize numerous grants of ecclesiastical benefices, to ratify the appointment of a new household official, to make a gift of a royal wardship, and to order a special judicial inquiry into hostilities between various towns on the south coast.[76] The king was the ultimate source of all authority: wherever he went, the channels of communication had to be kept open and the ceaseless round of business carried on.

Given the scale and the complexity of royal administration, however, it was inevitable that most of the work had to be undertaken by professional bureaucrats in the capital and trustworthy local amateurs in the shires. Once again, the challenge posed to his authority in 1340–1 seems to have persuaded Edward that he must make more active use of his right to appoint, regulate and dismiss these ministers. The selection of laymen to fill the offices of chancellor and treasurer in December 1340 was deliberately intended to make the civil service more accountable to the crown; and the dismissal of William Thorp, chief justice of king's bench, on charges of corruption in 1350, illustrates the ultimate dependence of even the most trusted ministers on the whim of the king.[77] On occasions, Edward could also be found intervening at lower levels in the bureaucracy. In 1343 he personally selected chancery clerks to take custody of the great seal on the death of the chancellor, and in 1349 he informed another group of custodians that no important documents should be issued during the current vacancy without his knowledge.[78] In 1365 he presided in person over a special inquiry in the exchequer which resulted in the removal of the two chamberlains, Ralph Brantingham and Richard Piriton, and a number of lesser clerks.[79] Edward's newly developed interest in government even extended into the shires. In 1345 he gave personal instructions for the appointment of a commission to deliver the gaol at Baldock (Hertfordshire), and sent a list of recommended judges to the chancellor.[80] In 1360 he decided that Nicholas Seymour was unfit to hold office as sheriff of Somerset; and in 1356 he wrote angrily to the chancellor that the ex-sheriff of Herefordshire should be reinstated immediately and not dismissed without a specific royal command.[81] These snippets of information suggest that Edward III maintained a considerable hold over the personnel of central and local administration during the middle years of his reign. It was precisely by such means that he could best regulate the government carried out in his name and ensure the active co-operation of his ministers in the task of rebuilding royal authority.

The King and the Law

One of the principal responsibilities of a medieval king was to uphold the law. All justice flowed in theory from the throne: indeed, the court of king's bench, as well as the council and the chancery, maintained the fiction that their sessions were held *coram rege* (before the king). In reality, of course, the king left the bulk of civil and criminal proceedings to the professional judges, and tended to involve himself only in cases concerning men of high rank. In a more general sense, however, he was expected to uphold the rights of his subjects and to protect them from the corruption and iniquities of the legal system.[82] The king's record on law-keeping therefore did much to determine public opinion of his regime.

There is little to indicate that Edward III took much interest in judicial administration during his early years. In 1332 he was present at Stamford (Lincolnshire) when a member of the notorious Folville gang, which had been terrorizing the east midlands, was committed to Lincoln gaol by the justices of trailbaston.[83] But the king was inevitably preoccupied with war, first in Scotland and then in France, and gave no real thought to the operation of criminal law in his absence. Indeed, his principal intervention in judicial administration during this period turned out to be highly controversial, for the king began to offer pardons to those criminals who agreed to serve in his armies.[84] There was nothing new about this form of inducement, but the dramatic escalation in the number of pardons issued by the crown — at least 850 in 1339–40 alone — inevitably created disquiet. There was a widespread belief that soldiers returning from the wars were responsible for the increasing level of crime and violence, and there were frequent requests in parliament that charters of pardon should be restricted. The king, however, refused to compromise. The statutes of 1328–36 limiting the crimes for which pardons might be granted were simply ignored; and the system undoubtedly continued to be abused throughout the 1340s and 1350s.[85] This evidence, and more occasional references to arbitrary royal intervention in the courts,[86] suggest that the young Edward III had a distinctly opportunistic attitude to the law.

Nevertheless, royal involvement in justice was not wholly negative. Edward's interest was evidently aroused by the events of 1340–1, when he set up special inquiries into maladministration in the shires.[87] The king played no direct part in these proceedings, and was content merely to reserve for himself the punishment of certain malefactors such as Sir John Coggeshall, a former sheriff of Essex.[88] Undoubtedly, however, he was impressed by the political implications and the potential financial profits of such extraordinary judicial sessions, and the experience made him more inclined to involve himself at all levels in legal administration. Late in 1341, for instance, when he visited Newcastle upon Tyne, Edward ordered a special investigation into civil government to be presided over by the controversial keeper of the privy seal, William Kilsby.[89] In March 1344, when he made a brief visit to East Anglia, he established contact with the justices of oyer and terminer then working in Suffolk, ordered the immediate payment of their expenses, and subsequently sent to the chancellor a list of thirty men indicted in the sessions with orders that they should be punished.[90] In 1349 he issued personal instructions to the justices in eyre in Kent to negotiate a fine with the shire community for the cessation of judicial proceedings.[91] Finally, in January 1356 when Edward again passed through Newcastle on his way to the border, he appointed a group of household officers and royal judges to look into the work of the customs collectors in the port.[92] The king's active participation in justice during the 1340s and 1350s provides one of the most graphic examples of his determination to recover the ground earlier lost by the crown through ineptitude and negligence.

Much the same pattern emerges from a study of Edward's role as arbitrator in disputes involving the great lay and ecclesiastical lords. Such cases can be found all through the reign, from his intervention in the quarrel between the Abbot and townsmen of Bury St Edmunds in 1331 to his mediation in a conflict between Oseney Abbey and the men of Oxford in 1374.[93] Nevertheless, it is noticeable that the majority of royal judgments fell within the period of political harmony from the 1340s to the 1360s, when Edward's reputation was at its height and his decisions universally respected. The king was particularly concerned to establish his authority over the Marcher lords, and intervened regularly in their private disputes. In 1345, for example, he insisted that he should have the final say in a quarrel involving the Welsh lands of Gilbert Talbot; and in 1353–4 he intervened decisively to support the Earls of Warwick and March in separate disputes over the lordships of Gower and Denbigh.[94] Many such decisions were purely arbitrary, and were motivated by political considerations. Between 1346 and 1348, for instance, the council found itself unable to resolve a jurisdictional dispute between the Bishop of Norwich and the town authorities of Lynn; but the king was clear as to who should win, and in 1350 settled the contested judicial powers on his trusted councillor, Bishop Bateman.[95] Where two powerful parties were involved, the loser could obviously create trouble. The Earl of Salisbury felt much aggrieved at the loss of Denbigh and other Welsh lands to the new Earl of March in 1354, although he seems to have done no more than to petition for compensation from the crown.[96] On the whole, in fact, a clever political balancing act seems to have kept most of the magnates satisfied. In 1347, for instance, Edward took the side of his aunt, the Countess of Norfolk, against his cousin, the Earl of Northampton, in a private land dispute; but in the same year he showed favour to Northampton by personally supporting the latter's claim to a portion of the manor of Thaxted (Essex).[97] When the king's grasp of politics declined in the 1370s, his reputation as adjudicator inevitably deteriorated.[98] But for most of his reign Edward III appreciated that the manipulation of justice was an essential part of political management; and by working within the bounds of propriety he was able to maintain widespread respect for his role as supreme judge.

The King and Patronage

Judicial discretion was simply one element in the elaborate machinery of royal patronage. The range of titles and privileges in the king's gift was prodigious: dukedoms, earldoms and knighthoods; bishoprics and benefices; public offices and sinecures; franchises, pardons, protections, exemptions, licences, wardships, annuities — the list is apparently endless. Almost all patronage was a matter of grace, to be exercised by the king alone.

When he went abroad in 1338, indeed, Edward III specifically ordered that no business touching the royal grace should be dealt with by the home government unless a special authorization was received from the king under the privy seal.[99] Admittedly, some lesser forms of royal patronage were exercised by the king's ministers. The chancellor, for instance, had the right to present to all ecclesiastical benefices in the king's gift valued at less than 20 marks (£13 6s. 8d.) a year,[100] and was occasionally tempted to interfere with other more valuable offices. In December 1344, Edward III discovered that Robert Sadington had dared to counteract his orders about a presentation to Fugglestone church (Wiltshire), and as punishment ordered the immediate suspension of all the chancellor's rights of patronage.[101] But until the mid-1370s at least, there is little reason to doubt that the vast majority of grants emanating from the chancery did indeed represent the personal preferences of Edward III.[102]

Much of this business arose from requests made by the king's subjects. Indeed, the audience of petitions formed the bulk of Edward III's daily work.[103] There was an inevitable tendency for the king to favour his servants, his relatives and his great men. His attention was naturally drawn to the wage demands of a royal chaplain, to Prince Edmund's appeal for help in a land dispute, to the Earl of Stafford's concern over the infringement of his liberties, and to the Archbishop of Canterbury's application for permission to extend one of his parks.[104] But petitions normally concerned matters of grace, and the majority therefore needed to go before the king. In 1349, when parliament was adjourned at the last moment because of the plague, Edward conceded that private petitions might be taken to the chancellor and the keeper of the privy seal; but he specifically reserved to himself all requests touching the royal grace.[105] Consequently, there were many matters brought before the king by individuals with little or no political influence. Edward involved himself personally in an attempt by Peter Corbet to escape appointment as sheriff of Gloucestershire, in the protest of the rector of Horncastle (Lincolnshire) against persons challenging his right to the benefice, in the plight of the friars minor of Bristol who had inadvertently taken control of certain property in the town without permission, and in the plea of a Plymouth innkeeper, John Baygge, who had lost several good drinking cups and all his wine as a result of a break-in at his premises.[106] Even routine requests could end up coming before the king. The one surviving petition endorsed with a note in Edward's own hand is an application from two royal clerks for a licence to travel to Rome in 1350, a matter that was normally dealt with quite satisfactorily by the bureaucrats.[107]

The widespread belief that requests could only be satisfied if they reached the king's person meant that Edward was constantly and relentlessly pursued. He received petitions while fighting on the Scottish border and preparing expeditions on the Kentish coast.[108] Some persistent suitors even got their requests sent across the Channel when the king was at Calais in 1346–7.[109] At other times, petitioners or their messengers had to roam around the royal forests in the hope of finding the king out hunting. In August 1362, for instance, while he was at Shipton under Wychwood (Oxfordshire), Edward received several petitions, including one from the Black Prince's councillor Sir James Audley requesting rights of patronage over a parish church.[110] In formal terms at least, the king's responsibility for such business continued right to the end of his life. As late as May–June

1377 petitions were still being taken down to the court at Sheen and approved by the application of the royal signet.[111] Edward III clearly regarded the audience of petitions as a vital and regular part of his system of patronage, and a formative influence on the individuals who made up the political society of his day.

Undoubtedly the most important aspect of royal patronage was the distribution of titles and property to support the peerage.[112] From the Norman Conquest onwards the kings of England had looked upon their landed resources and their feudal rights primarily as a means of rewarding good service. It was not their custom to maintain a large demesne or to reserve escheats for the upkeep of the crown. It is true that Edward II used the lands forfeited from his baronial opponents to build up a new royal estate in the 1320s, but even he made free use of confiscations to create gifts for his favourites. Consequently, when Edward III began to redistribute that estate in the 1330s, he was not resorting to reckless alienation but simply reverting to earlier practice. At first, he concentrated on members of the royal family. But in 1337 he began to use the royal estates as a means of endowing his new batch of earls. Huntingdon, Suffolk and Salisbury were each promised incomes of 1,000 marks (£666 13s. 4d.) a year, and Northampton £1,000. These sums were made up from grants of lands (many of them escheats from the king's deceased brother, John of Eltham), expectations (promises of lands in the future, chiefly from the estates of Queen Isabella and the childless Earl of Surrey), and cash (paid out of the county farms and the customs).

Such generous patronage did not go uncriticized. According to parliament in 1340 and 1343, Edward's alienations prevented him from supporting himself out of crown revenues, and made the country liable to heavy taxation. It is noticeable that the king made fewer expectancies after the 1340s, and tended to rely on wealthy heiresses or on cash payments as a means of endowing new earls. Ralph Stafford derived his income chiefly from his wife Margaret Audley's inheritance, and from an annuity of 1,000 marks (£666 13s. 4d.) at the ports of London and Boston. Elizabeth Burgh and Blanche of Lancaster were quickly snapped up as brides for the king's second and third sons, and the Warenne lands were used to create an endowments for the fourth, Edmund of Langley. In fact, the decline in new creations, together with the re-leasing of large estates on the deaths of the two queens and the gradual maturing of older expectancies, meant that the pressures of patronage were somewhat reduced in the second half of Edward's reign. Nevertheless, it is probably true that the king's unrestrained largesse in the 1330s restricted his patronage in later years. At the time of the Good Parliament it was apparently felt that neither Edmund of Langley nor Thomas of Woodstock had sufficient lands and titles to support their princely status.[113] If the king lacked the resources with which to endow his own children, then he clearly had little chance of satisfying the demands of all the magnates.

It was largely for this reason that Edward III began in the 1370s to make more use of his feudal resources as a means of rewarding servants and courtiers. The sale of wardships and marriages and the leasing of escheated lands was nothing new: after the Black Death of 1348–9, for instance, there had been particularly lively competition for the lands and heirs of tenants-in-chief. But on that occasion leases and wardships had been spread fairly evenly between close relatives of the deceased tenants, neighbouring magnates, and professional servants of the crown.[114] In the 1370s, by contrast, the balance swung decisively in favour of the king's friends. It was Lord Latimer who secured the wardship of two of the most valuable estates falling to the crown in these years, those of Edward Courtenay and Henry Beaumont.[115] There is little to suggest that the terms of such leases were any more favourable than those offered earlier in the reign. But the preferential treatment accorded to unpopular figures led parliament to conclude that the king was dissipating his feudal resources. In 1376 the commons demanded that the income from 'archbishoprics, bishoprics, abbacies, baronies, escheats, fines, ransoms, wardships, marriages, and all profits belonging and escheating into the king's hand', should be reserved for the upkeep of the war, and not granted away by the king without the 'good and wise deliberation of his great council'.[116] This was a direct challenge to the royal prerogative, and the government's response was understandably evasive. But in Richard II's first parliament the commons again asked that the council consider those grants which had impoverished the crown during the previous reign; and finally, in 1404, parliament demanded the resumption of all lands and rights 'of the ancient inheritance of the crown' granted away since the fortieth year of Edward III's reign (that is, 1366).[117] Whether or not the disposition of feudal perquisites in the 1370s had actually weakened the crown's finances, the blatant favouritism shown by Edward during his last years had obviously created an enduring political tradition.

What is most remarkable, however, is that between 1343 and 1376 parliament never once criticized the wisdom of the king's policy or challenged his right to control patronage. For over thirty years, Edward's treatment of the nobility went largely unquestioned. The principal reason was that the king's favours were spread widely, evenly and temperately. Changes in the nature of landholding and inheritance undoubtedly restricted the supply of wardships in the second half of Edward's reign; but it was primarily the misuse of patronage, not the shortage of it, that led to problems in the 1370s.[118] Throughout his reign Edward III tended to use the vast majority of the lands and rights falling into his hands as a means of promoting the aristocracy, and he never seems to have thought of employing such resources to create a new financial base for the monarchy. In this respect, however, he was simply following the traditions of his predecessors. Indeed, he would have come in for a good deal more criticism had he failed to be so open-handed. It was a considerable achievement, in a century punctuated by several major political crises over patronage, that Edward III kept both the magnates and the wider political community satisfied for so long.

EDWARD III AND PARLIAMENT

The time at which the king's political skills came most obviously into play was during a session of parliament. The *Modus Tenendi Parliamentum* ('Method of Holding Parliament'), a private tract composed in 1321–2, placed particular importance on the fact that the king should be present in parliament and take an active part in its proceedings.[119] Edward III certainly agreed with this. Admittedly, a number of assemblies were held in 1339–40 and 1346 while he was on the continent; and in 1351 and 1372 the king was again planning to be away from the country when parliament met.[120] But such absences inevitably tended to hinder proceedings. Common petitions put forward in 1340 could not be answered without being referred directly to the king;[121] and even in 1376–7 as Edward lay paralysed by illness, it was deemed necessary to take the lists of petitions to him in order that the replies, supplied in this case by the council, could be confirmed.[122] Parliament was the acknowledged forum in which to debate the affairs of state, to discuss the making of war and peace, to settle the grievances of the community, and to dispense patronage. At each level of business, the king's involvement was obviously crucial. A session of parliament therefore provided the most important test of the crown's political authority in the later Middle Ages.

Because the mid-fourteenth century witnessed such a substantial growth in the power and influence of parliament, it has usually been concluded that the monarchy lost ground, and ended up compromising its authority for the sake of political harmony. But this is not necessarily how Edward III, or his subjects, viewed the situation. The idea of a constant struggle for power, an attempt to 'win the initiative', is a fallacy bred by Whig historians.[123] Before the seventeenth century, parliament had no real intention of controlling the monarchy or the executive, and any influence that it enjoyed was largely dependent on the goodwill of the crown. The remainder of this chapter will offer a new perspective on Edward III's reign by looking at parliament not from the viewpoint of the community, but from that of the king.

The Functions of Parliament: Petitioning and Taxation

During the reign of Edward I parliament had taken on two new and important functions. First, it had come to be seen as a court in which private individuals could seek judicial remedies by appealing directly to the king's grace. Although petitions could be presented at any time and in any place, it was only during a session of parliament that the suitor was actually guaranteed access to the king and promised some form of response before the end of the session. This was a very important principle, and some historians believe that it set parliament apart from all other assemblies and institutions.[124] It certainly made parliament extremely popular. From an early stage there had been real concern that meetings were becoming inundated with private business. By the early fourteenth century it had become official policy only to encourage complaints against the king's ministers and local agents, matters which had little chance of being judged fairly in the common law courts.[125] Indeed, it was only when Edward III wished to investigate the ranks of central and local government, as in 1330 and 1340–1, that he specifically invited his subjects to enter private petitions in parliament.[126] At other times, war and diplomacy provided the focus of debate, and lesser matters were all too frequently neglected. In three successive assemblies in 1332 other pressing business or poor attendance prevented the audience of private petitions; and thirty years later concern was being expressed about the fate of such requests sent before the king.[127] The public response was swift, and by the middle of Edward III's reign the number of private petitions received in parliament had already fallen dramatically.[128]

This did not mean that parliament ceased to fulfil its special function as a forum for the

9   *The king, seated in state, receives tribute from his subjects*

redress of grievances. Indeed, by the 1320s a new and more important form of document — the *commune* or common petition — had come to take precedence over private bills in the business agenda of parliament.[129] The earliest common petitions, dating from Edward I's time, were so called not because they were drawn up by the commons, but because the matters contained in them were deemed to be of common interest to the realm. Then, in the 1320s and 1330s, an important change occurred. The knights and burgesses in parliament began to articulate the grievances of the community and to draw up lists of demands to be presented to the crown. Although the lords sometimes participated in this process,[130] the *commune* petitions had now effectively become the petitions of the commons. In 1327 the new regime of Isabella and Mortimer set an important precedent by responding to the list of grievances aired in parliament and offering remedial legislation which was written up on the statute roll and proclaimed in the shires.[131] Neither at this point nor at any other stage in Edward III's reign did the knights and burgesses win the *right* to have their petitions answered in this way.[132] But the clear expectation after 1327 was that the crown would offer solutions, and if necessary create statutes, in response to the lists of common petitions presented in parliament.

The political importance of this development can best be appreciated when we turn to the second of the special functions taken on by parliament since Edward I's time: namely, the granting of taxation. By the 1290s it had been accepted that direct taxes charged on the whole realm ought to be sanctioned by assemblies containing representatives of the community.[133] Between 1290 and 1322 successive governments had been able to raise over £635,000 from such subsidies, making these by far the most profitable taxes then available to the English crown.[134] The names applied to the authorizing bodies varied widely until the 1310s, and the terms *colloquium* or *tractatum* were actually used more often than *parliamentum*.[135] In Edward I's day the distinction was probably of little importance. But by 1327 the terminology was becoming more precise, and an increasing number of representative assemblies granting taxes were being labelled parliaments.[136] If parliament were to gain exclusive control over taxation, then presumably it would only be a matter of time before the commons brought their petitions into play and made the redress of grievances a condition of the grant of supply.

Edward III, not surprisingly, did not relish such a prospect. Indeed, the early years of his reign witnessed several attempts to avoid the specific association between taxation and petitioning. It is interesting to note that four of the seven direct subsidies raised between 1327 and 1338 were authorized not in parliaments but in assemblies officially designated as great councils.[137] These were held at Lincoln in September 1327, at Nottingham in September 1336, at Westminster in September 1337, and at Northampton in July 1338 (see Table 5). In terms of personnel, such councils were more or less identical to parliaments; and most historians have called them such.[138] But there may well have been an important distinction. If it was only in parliament that the commons had the right to present petitions, then the knights and burgesses sitting in these great councils would have no formal opportunity to demand concessions. When the political situation was uneasy, as in 1327, or when the king was in need of very heavy taxation, as in 1336–8, we can well understand why the government would prefer to avoid negotiating with parliament. Inevitably, the councils were not completely silent. At Lincoln in 1327 the commons entered a petition concerning a legal technicality; and in 1336 the Nottingham council requested the enforcement of legislation made in the previous parliament.[139] But it may be significant that the two administrative concessions won by the Northampton assembly of 1338 (on the appointment of sheriffs and the granting of respites from debts) were secured specifically by the magnates.[140] There is certainly nothing to compare with the lengthy lists of common petitions surviving from the parliaments of 1324, 1325, 1327, 1333, 1334 and 1339.[141] Until the outbreak of the Hundred Years War, then, it is quite possible that Edward III was deliberately trying to prevent parliament from claiming exclusive authority over wartime subsidies.

This plan failed. Events in the late 1330s showed that the complaints of the community were simply compounded by efforts to silence them. Intense suspicion also arose as a result of the crown's parallel attempts to use merchant councils to grant indirect taxation in the form of wool subsidies.[142] In January 1340 the commons in parliament took a new and daring step when they authorized a forced loan of 30,000 sacks of wool. The grant was made 'under certain conditions, comprised in indentures and sealed with the seals of the prelates and other lords'. If these conditions were not fulfilled then the community 'would not be bound to grant the aid'.[143] The conditions have not survived, but they probably bore a close affinity with the extant list of common petitions put forward in the subsequent parliament of March 1340.[144] For the first time, the commons had made a specific link between grants of supply and the redress of grievances. After 1340, Edward III was forced to accept that direct subsidies should always be negotiated in parliament, and that the commons should always be allowed an opportunity to express their opinions on government policy. By the 1350s he was also prepared to concede that parliament should have sole control of the wool subsidy. In turn, it became regular practice for the crown to use its replies to the common petitions as a basis for formal legislation. The statute roll was therefore transformed from a series of government-inspired legal codes into a collection of short-term measures designed to placate the king's subjects.[145] This is one of the most pronounced and remarkable political developments of Edward III's reign. And yet it would be quite wrong to suppose that it deprived the king of authority. To understand the new working relationship built up after 1340 we need to recognize the way in which the crown could manipulate parliament for its own benefit, and to appreciate the considerable political acumen displayed by Edward III in his dealings with the lords and commons.

The Management of Parliament

By the 1330s it was widely recognized that parliament should always be consulted before the king made war on a foreign power.[146] Edward III certainly never flouted this convention. But this is not to say that king and parliament were always of one mind. The discussions held in the winter of 1332–3, for instance, indicated widespread indifference or even hostility to the king's planned attack on Scotland.[147] Unfortunately, we have no record of the great council of 1337 when Edward's plan for the impending French war was discussed and approved. Again, the assembly was probably required to give token assent to a strategy already worked out in detail by the king and his close advisers. Nevertheless, in the following years Edward was to make much political capital out of this, constantly reminding the lords and commons that they had consented to the war, and were therefore under a direct obligation to finance it.[148] In order to reinforce these arguments, parliament was sent reports on the king's movements in 1338–9 and news of the victory at Sluys in 1340.[149] Such efforts did comparatively little to alter the perception of a wasteful and reckless campaign. But after the Stratford crisis and the improvement in Edward's military fortunes, parliament was gradually forced to acknowledge both the legitimacy and the practicability of the war. Edward's propaganda campaign reached a climax in 1346, when letters recounting the king's progress were sent out with the summonses to parliament, and a document found at Caen purporting to be a plan for an invasion of England was read out to the assembly in order to drum up xenophobic hatred of the French.[150] Meanwhile, the speeches made by the chancellor or the chief justice of king's bench at the start of each session regularly referred to the latest military advances, and the lords and commons were encouraged to believe that their advice would be sought on all proposed truces and treaties.[151] Even the terms of the Brétigny settlement were apparently presented to parliament for confirmation in January 1361.[152]

After the reopening of the war in 1369 it became an increasing embarrassment to the government to have to report on the fortunes of English armies. But parliament still provided an opportunity to rally support. In the assembly of 1369, for example, the king urged men to take up arms against France, promising — rather unrealistically — that those who followed his standard would be assured of rewards in the shape of conquered lands.[153] It is hardly likely that the commons were taken in by mere words: they needed evidence of success before they happily handed the realm over to the king's tax collectors. From Edward's point of view, however, reference to parliament had its desired effect, for it allowed him to present his wars as the supreme expression of the public will.

Once parliament had accepted the need for war, there was actually very little it could do to resist the king's demands for taxes. According to the principles of roman and canon law, 'urgent necessity' bound the people to assist the public authorities in the event of a national emergency.[154] Not surprisingly, the English crown had eagerly seized upon this idea in the thirteenth century, and by the 1310s the full details of the doctrine of necessity were being cited in government documents.[155] It remains doubtful, however, whether such scholastic notions had much impact on the majority of the taxpaying public. Indeed, as recently as 1324–5 parliament had twice refused to subsidize Edward II's war with France.[156] The fact that this was not repeated until 1376 probably says more about the different personalities of Edward II and Edward III than about any sudden change in the political theory of the state.[157] On the other hand, parliament must have recognized that it had some formal obligation to support the king. The ninth of 1340 and the wool tax of 1341 — two of the heaviest direct subsidies granted in the whole of Edward III's reign — were authorized in parliaments which otherwise proved fundamentally hostile to the crown's military schemes. For the most part, Edward's success in reconciling the community to the obligations of long-term warfare after 1341 may be attributed to two great practical advantages: namely, the right to decide when parliament should meet, and the ability to hold out on political concessions until a tax had been granted.

The reign of Edward III witnessed a major decline in the frequency of parliaments. From the late thirteenth century until 1341, sessions had normally been summoned at least once, and often two or three times, a year.[158] But after 1341 the number dwindled, and the timing of assemblies became, in effect, a form of political management. It was now most unusual for two parliaments to be held in the same year; and it was not unknown for two or even three years to elapse between meetings (see Table 5). Since parliament no longer met at any particular season, the king was free to summon it whenever suited him best. In the 1340s it became normal practice to issue writs just as truces were about to terminate or fresh campaigns were about to begin. The clear intention was to reaffirm the country's commitment to the war and to extract further grants of taxation. In February 1351, the fact that Edward was busy planning a new continental campaign undoubtedly encouraged the commons to authorize an extension of the wool subsidy; and in January 1352 the king deliberately emphasized the uneasy state of Anglo-French talks in order to justify his request for another three years of direct taxation.[159]

The commons clearly resented the decline in the number of parliaments, and in 1362 and 1376 they demanded that there should be at least one assembly a year.[160] Yet, by their own actions, they tended to play into the king's hands. One of the most effective ways to secure regular meetings would have been to grant taxes for one year only, as had been normal practice until the 1330s. But the three fifteenths and tenths awarded to the king on the eve of the French war in 1337 set an important precedent; and during the 1340s and 1350s it became common for parliament to grant direct taxation for two or three years in succession. The tendency was even more marked with indirect taxation. Between 1343 and the end of the reign, the wool subsidy was never authorized for less than two years, and on one occasion, in November 1355, it was conceded for a remarkable six years (see Table 3). This obviously reduced the number of occasions on which the king needed to appeal for money, and left the commons with fewer opportunities to present their grievances. Whether it was the plea of necessity or the king's war record that persuaded the commons to give such generous support, parliament's new fiscal authority ironically made Edward III one of the richest rulers of medieval England.

Perhaps the most important of all the discretionary powers enjoyed by the king in the management of parliament was his right to answer common petitions *after* the required subsidy had been won.[161] In 1340 and 1341, during a time of acute political and financial crisis, the commons were able to delay the formal grants of taxation until the king had issued the statutes. But after 1341 this was no longer possible. Usually the schedule of taxation and the list of common petitions were submitted together. The commons clearly hoped that their generosity would encourage the government to give positive replies to their political demands. But the king remained free to answer petitions as he saw fit; and having secured his taxes, he could obviously afford to be more selective in the choice of matters to be made up into legislation. Thus, in 1372, one of the common petitions referred optimistically to 'the statute that will be made in this present parliament'.[162] But in fact there is not a single entry on the statute roll relating to this assembly. This example demonstrates vividly the very different attitudes of king and commons towards the process of political debate in parliament.

On other occasions, of course, the crown could act considerably more generously. Nevertheless, it was still perfectly normal for requests to be refused, delayed or ignored. In March 1371, for instance, when the commons granted a subsidy of £50,000, several of their petitions were left unanswered at the end of the assembly. A special council containing selected members of the parliament was summoned to Winchester in June to receive replies to the relevant items; but by this stage a number of the petitions — including a complaint against the equitable jurisdiction of the chancery and a request for the reservation of taxes to pay the expenses of troops arrayed in the shires — had already been dismissed and crossed off the parliament roll.[163] If petitions threatened to infringe the crown's freedom of action — as, for example, on the appointment of ministers (1343), the movements of the king's bench (1352), or the rights of tenants-in-chief (1372) — then Edward was particularly quick to refute them.[164] One of the most frequent replies given to common petitions, in fact, was *le roi s'avisera* (the king will reflect), a delaying tactic which usually ensured that nothing at all got done. The net result of all this was that the concessions allowed by the crown and made up into formal legislation on the statute roll represented only a proportion — and sometimes a small proportion — of the total business brought before the king in the common petitions.

Finally, it is important to realize that even the statute roll possessed a good deal less sanctity in the fourteenth century than in later times. Magna Carta, the Charter of the Forests, and the great codes of Edward I were certainly revered. It was an established principle that they could not be altered outside parliament, and that any legislation which conflicted with them was invalid.[165] The attitude to more recent legislation, however, was a good deal more flexible. In 1348 it was stated categorically that the king made the statutes only with the *assent* of the lords and commons, and not *through* them.[166] And what the king did, he could also undo. In extreme circumstances, as in 1341, Edward III simply revoked laws which were held to be contrary to his prerogative. And on many other less controversial issues he maintained his right to review, amend and repeal the statutes without the necessary consent of the commons.[167] One notable instance concerned the king's right to present vacant benefices in the gift of bishops on the grounds that he or his predecessors had filled such offices during earlier episcopal vacancies. A statute of 1340 stated that this right could only be claimed within three years of the relevant vacancy; but the legislation was interpreted very loosely by the courts, and in 1352 it was actually revoked, without reference to parliament, on the grounds that it infringed the king's regalian rights.[168]

In 1377, it is true, Edward III's advisers agreed to a petition that statutes should not be repealed without the assent of parliament. But this petition seems to have arisen less from a point of principle and more from the commons' concern over the neglect of the statutes on purveyance.[169] Consequently, no formal statement was made on the statute roll, and the council's reply was of little use as a political precedent. In fact, what the petition of 1377 really demonstrates is the crown's remarkably selective and opportunistic approach to the actual *enforcement* of legislation. Undoubtedly the most striking case of all in this respect is provided by the legislation of 1330 and 1362 requiring annual parliaments.[170] The fact that only twenty-four such assemblies met in the last thirty-six years of Edward III's reign says more for his government's policy than any bland statement of good intent. The theory that no statute could limit the power of the throne seems to have meant in practice that only those pieces of legislation positively advantageous to the king were ever really observed by him and actively enforced by his government.

Edward III's deliberate attempt to place the war at the forefront of parliamentary business therefore had extremely important consequences in the period between 1341 and 1371. It allowed the king to recover the procedural advantages temporarily lost in 1340–1, and gave him the opportunity to rebuild the political and financial authority undermined during the Stratford crisis. It would, of course, be wrong to ignore the considerable advances also made by the lords and commons during these years. Although parliaments became less frequent after 1341, the individual sessions were generally longer and probably harder fought (see Table 5). Nevertheless, it is important to realize that parliament became the very epitome of the new political consensus built up in the 1350s and 1360s. Alongside the hard bargaining, there was also a great deal of back-slapping. In the assembly of 1368, for instance, Edward repeatedly expressed his thanks to the community, in the most florid language, for its past and continuing support; and in reply the assembly prefaced its petitions with a high-flown address to 'our highest, most excellent and most redoubted lord', the king. Such pandering had the required effect:

Edward got his wool subsidy, the parliament got its statutes, and the meeting was rounded off agreeably with a state banquet to which the king invited all of the lords and many of the commons.[171]

This episode says much for Edward III's extraordinary achievement. The king used a highly sophisticated system of political management to create one of the longest periods of domestic peace in the whole of the later Middle Ages. That system collapsed not because it was inherently unworkable but because Edward's sons and grandsons lacked the military success and political perception on which it had been based. It was not until the time of Henry V that England once more found a king able to identify both the risks, and the rewards, offered by Edward III's style of monarchy.[172]

★   ★   ★

Edward III, like every other medieval king, remains an enigma. We know far too little of his private life, his personal prejudices and his political ambitions to be able to construct an authoritative picture of his character. What we can say, on the basis of the evidence reviewed so far, is that his policies were a good deal more coherent and consistent than has usually been suggested. Edward was far too much of an opportunist to resist short-term compromises or vote-winning concessions. But after 1341 at least, he never lost sight of his ultimate goal: the restoration of royal power. At no point between 1341 and 1376 did Edward ever allow parliament to appoint, dismiss or judge his ministers, to set up and nominate permanent councils, to challenge his exclusive rights over patronage, to dictate military or diplomatic policy, or to restrict the expenditure of taxes. These matters, which had been central to the opposition's programme in 1340–1, all came up again in 1376–7, and were to provide some of the main points of friction between crown and parliament under Richard II and Henry IV. The fact that they did not emerge for over thirty years in the mid-fourteenth century is striking testimony both to Edward III's popularity and to his success in rebuilding and maintaining the authority of the crown.

5 The ministers

The Plantagenet kings possessed one of the most sophisticated systems of government in later medieval Europe. Royal administration had developed early in England, and by the time Edward III succeeded to the throne the principal departments of state already had a continuous history stretching back over a hundred years and more. The honourable traditions of their offices gave the ministers great personal esteem and political influence. These were the men most regularly in touch with the king, most frequently summoned to his council, and most immediately involved in the implementation of his policies. Their actions therefore did much to mould the attitudes of political society. Our main concern here is with the most senior officials, the chancellor and treasurer, the keeper of the privy seal, and the judges. We may begin, however, with a more general analysis of the structure of the administration and the influence of the civil service in fourteenth-century England.

Edward III's government may be subdivided according to function into three groups: the secretarial, financial and judicial offices. The most important of the secretarial departments was the chancery, presided over by the king's senior minister, the chancellor. This office was responsible for writing the charters, letters patent and writs issued in the king's name and validated with his great seal. It was the largest of all the administrative departments, employing about a hundred full-time staff. Except on rare occasions, the chancery was housed in the Great Hall of Westminster Palace. Next came the privy seal. Prior to Edward III's reign, this office had formed part of the royal household, but in the mid-fourteenth century it emerged as a separate department of government. It was much smaller than the chancery, employing only about a dozen clerks, but it managed to cope with an astonishing amount of business. It was used especially to draw up writs expressing the wishes of the king and his advisers, which were then sent to the chancery and exchequer as warrants for further administrative action. The last of the secretarial offices was an *ad hoc* affair staffed by clerks of the royal household, who drew up the letters issued under the king's secret seal or signet. This correspondence was quite small in volume, but had a special importance because it communicated Edward's most personal opinions and decisions. By the end of the reign the king's 'secretary', who had custody of the secret seal, was becoming an influential figure at court and in government.

The financial departments were also three in number. Chief in importance was the exchequer, which had become a self-contained department of state as early as the twelfth century. It was headed by the treasurer, and had approximately sixty permanent members of staff. The department was subdivided into the exchequer of receipt (or lower exchequer), which organized the collection and expenditure of royal revenue, and the exchequer of account (or upper exchequer), which audited the returns made by the

10   *Medieval lawyers in disputation*

government's financial agents. These offices were housed in two purpose-built chambers situated off the Great Hall at Westminster. The other financial departments were contained within the royal household. The wardrobe was responsible for the domestic expenses of the court, and for military expenditure during royal campaigns. Finally the chamber, the office of the privy purse, looked after the store of cash reserved for the king's personal use.

The judicial administration was headed by the courts of king's bench and common pleas. Both these tribunals heard large numbers of civil suits; the king's bench also acted as a criminal court. Each employed a total of about forty officials, and was presided over by a chief justice and a bench of 'puisne' or junior judges. These men were professional lawyers, thoroughly immersed in common law procedures and well versed in the statutes. They and various other legal experts from the central courts also staffed the judicial commissions which went out into the provinces to hear assizes and try the prisoners held in royal gaols. While common pleas normally carried on its business in the Great Hall of Westminster Palace, the king's bench often moved around the provinces, assuming jurisdiction over all cases pending in the shires. In the fourteenth century the judiciary was neither separate from nor independent of the administration, and there was a considerable overlap between the courts and the other offices of government: the lawyers, for instance, were often co-opted to serve as barons of the exchequer. Medieval administrators did not recognize fine bureaucratic distinctions or jurisdictional boundaries because, no matter what their departments, they were all occupied in the service of the crown.

The amount of work done by the civil service in the mid-fourteenth century was prodigious. The business of government had increased enormously since the time of Edward I, and there was a marked tendency to commit more and more of it to writing.[1] Despite the fact that all documents had to be written up by hand, certain departments, particularly the exchequer and the courts, thought nothing of making duplicate or even triplicate copies of their main records. The sheer bulk of administrative documentation surviving from Edward III's reign is impressive. The patent and close rolls, just two of the many series of records kept in the chancery, fill thirty large volumes in their printed and highly abbreviated form.[2] The plea rolls of the king's bench for the same period run to some 28,500 pieces of parchment, each about nine inches wide and between two and three feet long, and written up closely on both sides.[3] These random statistics are all the more remarkable when we remember that the surviving records represent only a small part of all the work done. Many thousands of writs issued by the crown to regulate local administration and justice have disappeared, leaving little trace in the central records.[4] Chance references indicate that the burden of such business was considerable. On 13 May 1342, for example, the sheriff of Shropshire and Staffordshire received at Wolverhampton a batch of thirty-one exchequer writs, each one requiring him to locate men within the counties and have them, or information supplied by them, returned to Westminster within the following four weeks.[5] Between June 1333 and November 1334, the sheriff of Bedfordshire and Buckinghamshire had to deal with a total of some 2,400 writs sent out by the chancery, exchequer, king's bench and common pleas.[6] Under special circumstances, this substantial workload could increase still further. When the king's bench visited York in the Michaelmas term of 1348, for instance, a very large number of local litigants used the opportunity to instigate private proceedings in the court; and long after the judges had left, the sheriff was kept busy clearing the enormous backlog of writs arising from this session.[7] These examples provide a graphic illustration of the very real impact that the central government had on its agents in the provinces.

To understand the political influence of the civil service, we must appreciate the elaborate network of personal and professional ties that linked Westminster with the provinces. The regional identification of royal bureaucrats was of great importance in this respect. Many of the clerks in the chancery and exchequer during this period hailed from Lincolnshire, Nottinghamshire and Yorkshire, and kept up close contact with their native areas.[8] An outstanding example is Thomas Sibthorpe, who came from a village outside Newark (Nottinghamshire). Despite his more or less continuous employment in the chancery from 1317 to his death in 1351, Sibthorpe maintained regular links with his home territory, securing benefices in the dioceses of Lincoln and York and getting himself appointed to all sorts of judicial commissions in the east midlands.[9] It is interesting that much of the money he made as a royal clerk was channelled back into the collegiate foundation he established at his birthplace of Sibthorpe.[10] Many others followed a similar course. John Winwick, keeper of the privy seal (1355–60) established a chantry at Huyton church in his native Lancashire; and in the 1350s William Edington was busily involved with the creation and endowment of the ambitious priory church of Sts Mary and Katherine in his home village of Edington (Wiltshire).[11] Service to the crown clearly did not disconnect civil servants from their roots; and it was inevitable that the relatives and friends of these men would seek to take advantage of their contacts at the seat of power.

The royal officials most susceptible to outside influence were undoubtedly the professional lawyers. When it came time to appoint judicial commissions in the shires, the judges were almost invariably given responsibility in the areas where they had personal interests. In the midst of his busy career in the central courts, for instance, Sir William Shareshull usually found time to serve on the assize, gaol delivery and peace commissions in his native Staffordshire and his adopted county of Oxfordshire.[12] He and most of his colleagues in the king's bench and common pleas came under constant pressure from individuals and communities anxious to improve their prospects in the courts. When the royal judges arrived in provincial towns such as Norwich or Leicester, the civic authorities often set aside funds in order to fill the bellies and the pockets of their honoured visitors.[13] Indeed, the Abbot of Peterborough was said to have spent more than £1,000 to ensure favourable judgments during the Northamptonshire eyre of 1329–30.[14] Some magnates and religious houses even paid regular fees to the judges in recognition of past and future favours.[15] This practice of retaining royal justices was very common in the early fourteenth century; and although judges were occasionally dismissed for corruption, it was rare for the crown to challenge the network of influences which underlay the royal courts. The lawyers therefore provide a particularly illuminating example of the double allegiances which were such a feature of late medieval government and society.

It is easy to assume that such external contacts worked to the detriment of the crown. Medieval administrators inevitably tended to put private concerns first, and the resulting conflict of interests could reflect badly on the king. Under proper control, however, there was no reason why the links between royal administrators and other members of political society should cause embarrassment. Edward III appreciated that his ministers could help guide public opinion in both their professional and personal capacities. He also endeavoured to maintain a sense of loyalty and corporate identity within the civil service. The middle and lower levels of the bureaucracy were still dominated by clerks who expected ecclesiastical benefices in lieu of salaries, and were constantly competing for the richest pickings in the king's store of patronage. Edward's two collegiate foundations, at St George's Windsor and St Stephen's Westminster, were both conveniently close to the centres of power and provided additional titles and incomes for these acquisitive officials.[16] The deanery and canonries of St Stephen's became especially popular among the clerks of the exchequer and the king's works, and carried the added bonus of free accommodation within the palace of Westminster.[17] The prospect of such preferment obviously provided a powerful incentive to work loyally and efficiently. Finally, the king had the power to investigate and sack all those who proved less than committed to his cause. Robert Wodehouse was peremptorily dismissed from the treasurership in 1338 because of his failure to collect sufficient funds for Edward's continental campaign.[18] In 1353 the chamberlains of the lower exchequer were hauled up before Treasurer Edington on a charge that they had lost counter-tallies (notched sticks recording real or anticipated revenue) to the value of £2,500;[19] and in 1365 their successors were subjected to a long corruption trial before the king's council.[20] If there was a clash of principles, even the most exalted of ministers had to go. In 1356 John Thoresby was forced to resign the chancellorship because, in his capacity as Archbishop of York, he had opposed the flagrant violation of ecclesiastical privilege resulting from the king's arbitrary seizure of the Bishop of Ely's estates.[21] Edward III's administrators were acutely aware that it was only the goodwill of the king which allowed them continued membership of this exclusive and privileged society.

THE COUNCIL

The centre of political life for the king's chief ministers was the council. A certain degree of initiative was allowed in each department, but it was only by corporate decisions that the administrators could effect major governmental changes. Unfortunately, it was not until the reign of Richard II that the council began to take steps to record its proceedings and preserve its own archives.[22] Many details about the membership and work of Edward III's council therefore remain obscure. Enough evidence survives, however, for us to be able to discern four fairly distinct uses of the term 'council' in this period.[23] First, there were great councils, to which the king summoned large numbers of magnates and prelates, and which on some occasions also included representatives of the shires and boroughs. These were extraordinary assemblies summoned only intermittently to discuss important matters of state, such as the making of war (1337) or the setting up of domestic staples (1353).[24] Secondly, there were the councils attended by nobles and bishops closely connected with the king and actively involved in his military and diplomatic service. These met rather more frequently. We may reasonably assume, for instance, that it was assemblies of this sort which drew up the numerous schemes for the defence of the realm and the dispatch of troops to Scotland and France in 1337–8, and which in 1341 compiled an elaborate list of soldiers and provisions needed for the king's forthcoming campaign in Brittany.[25] Thirdly, there were the extraordinary councils appointed during the king's youth in 1327, and his final incapacitating illness in 1376. These assemblies, staffed by magnates and prelates, also provided the model for the regency administration created by Edward III on his departure for the continent in 1338, and the council forced on him by parliament before his return to the Low Countries in 1340. Finally, there was the administrative council, which sat more or less permanently during the legal and financial terms, was staffed by the ministers of state, and regulated much of the day-to-day government of the realm. It is with this last form of council that we are particularly concerned here.

It is important to remember that there was a considerable overlap between these four tiers of councils. The magnates believed that they were the king's natural advisers, and some of them actually applied themselves remarkably diligently to the work of government. The Earls of Arundel and Warwick, for instance, appear so frequently in the records of the 1340s and 1350s that they probably deserve to be counted among the members of the administrative council.[26] But the king and the majority of the nobility were eager to relieve themselves of governmental responsibilities and get on with their main task, fighting the enemy. Accordingly, for most of Edward III's reign the core of the permanent council was made up of the chancellor, the treasurer, the judges and the barons of the exchequer. They met wherever was most convenient for them and for the king: in Westminster Palace, at the Tower, at the church of St Mary le Strand,[27] at the London houses of various mendicant orders,[28] or, during the plague of 1349, at Edward's country retreat of Woodstock.[29] But in the early 1340s a 'new chamber' at Westminster was put at their disposal; and it was in this building, later known as the Star Chamber, that the council came to do more and more of its work.[30]

This move heralded some important procedural changes. The council had no seal of its own, and most of its decisions were implemented through the chancery and exchequer. But in the 1350s, the privy seal office also established headquarters at Westminster, and began to put its secretarial resources at the service of the council.[31] By the 1370s the keeper of the privy seal was clearly recognized as the third great officer of state alongside the chancellor and treasurer, and had already become a regular member of the administrative council.[32] From the later 1350s it was also agreed that the expenses of the council, previously met only at the whim of the king, should be considered official expenditure and properly subsidized by the exchequer.[33] By the second half of Edward III's reign, the administrative council probably enjoyed a more established place in the structure of government and a greater capacity for business than ever before.

The council was the supreme expression of corporate government, and it is difficult to find any aspect of administration in which it was not involved. Occasional royal letters addressed jointly to the chancellor and treasurer indicate that the majority of important concerns, such as the regulation of the coinage in 1353, were discussed and authorized by the king's ministers.[34] They, like the king, were much occupied with the selection and supervision of lesser officials. It was the council which decided that John Dabernoun should be dismissed from his post as sheriff of Surrey and Sussex in the early 1330s, and which recommended the appointment of Richard Talbot, Richard Willoughby and Robert Thorp to a special commission of oyer and terminer in the 1340s.[35] The ministers were often involved in discussions with the merchants and representatives of port towns, and this provided them with valuable information on candidates for the customs administration. The mayors and constables of the new English staples set up in the summer of 1353, for example, were chosen from among the merchants who attended a special meeting with the government in July that year.[36] In 1370 the council drew up a complete new list of customs officials; and the extant memorandum, with its various deletions and additions, suggests that there was a lively debate as to the best men for these posts.[37] The council also sometimes made recommendations about the personnel of central administration and the regulation of government in the king's dependent territories of Wales, Ireland and Gascony.[38]

Undoubtedly the most interesting work done by the council during Edward III's reign was in the judicial sphere. The ministers obviously had some general influence over the administration of the law. It was they, for instance, who decided that the king's bench should move into East Anglia to hold special trailbaston sessions in 1344–5, and who devised the special machinery to enforce the Ordinance of Labourers in 1349.[39] But the council also enjoyed considerable judicial authority of its own; and circumstantial evidence suggests that this power was expanding rapidly during Edward III's reign.[40] The council traditionally acted as a tribunal to try cases that could not be resolved at common law, issues involving persons of high rank, and matters too controversial to be heard in the regular courts. Thus, it was the council which in 1354 took proceedings against Sir Walter Mauny's new wife, Margaret Marshal, on the charge that she had ignored an earlier ban on foreign travel.[41] Lady Mauny, who was Edward III's cousin and a major landholder in her own right, was actually imprisoned as a result. Inevitably, king and ministers did not always see eye to eye on cases such as this. While the council clung to the letter of the law, the king was often swayed by political considerations. There was a substantial difference of opinion, for example, over Henry of Grosmont's attempt to secure exemption from the farm charged on his bailiwick of Scalby (Yorkshire). Between 1351 and 1353 the chancellor, treasurer, judges, serjeants at law and barons of the exchequer several times gave their unanimous opinion that Duke Henry should be forced to pay his dues to the crown; but in 1354 the king simply overturned their judgment in one stroke and put an end to any ambiguity on the matter by granting his cousin full rights to the farm of Scalby.[42] Disagreements of this kind are interesting; but they were relatively unusual. Edward III, as we have seen, was generally prudent and calculating in his judicial favours to the members of the nobility, and did not normally offend the sensibilities of his councillors.

Edward also appreciated the speed and efficiency of conciliar justice, and encouraged his ministers to increase the range and volume of their work. An important step forward came in 1340 when he returned from the continent and replaced the chancellor and treasurer with laymen. Between 1340 and 1345 the chancery was in the hands of three professional common lawyers: Sir Robert Bourchier, Sir Robert Parving, and Sir Robert Sadington.[43] These men frequently intervened in the proceedings of the king's bench, common pleas, and the exchequer, in order to safeguard the interests of the crown and to uphold the jurisdiction claimed by the chancery and the council.[44] Such practices continued after the return to clerical chancellors. It was John Thoresby (1349–56), for instance, who was probably responsible for devising the famous *sub pena* writ, which summoned defendants to appear before the council on unspecified charges and threatened them with a fine for default.[45] This writ became the very basis of royal prerogative justice in the late Middle Ages, and marked an important breakthrough in judicial administration. All of these developments enhanced the reputation of the council as a particularly efficient, if somewhat brutal, tribunal dedicated to upholding the authority of the throne. By their actions Edward III's ministers therefore proved themselves not only to be capable and inventive lawyers, but also loyal political supporters of the regime.

THE MINISTERS AND PARLIAMENT

The expertise and influence of the administrators was particularly valuable to the king during a session of parliament.[46] When Edward III called a parliament, he sent personal summonses to various bureaucrats and lawyers who took their place alongside the bishops, abbots and magnates in the lords. This 'official' group could vary in size. It usually comprised between ten and fifteen men, although in the consecutive parliaments of September 1334 and May 1335 the number rose to as many as twenty-three.[47] Those regularly included in the lists were the judges and serjeants of king's bench and common pleas, the barons and chancellor of the exchequer, and the high-ranking clerks of the royal diplomatic service. The chancellor and treasurer and various household officials such as the chamberlain and steward would also be present in the lords in their capacity as prelates and barons. Furthermore, many other royal officials were involved to some degree in the work of parliament. Chancery clerks acted as receivers of petitions and compiled the parliament rolls.[48] The committees of triers appointed to deal with private petitions normally included the chancellor, treasurer and judges, and were encouraged to take advice from the officers of the king's chamber and the chief ministers of Ireland and Gascony. Finally, the common petitions were generally heard by the king and his council, who drew up the formal replies and framed the resulting statutes. The influence of the king's agents was therefore considerably greater than mere numbers might suggest. Parliament had begun life in the thirteenth century as a solemn meeting of the council; and although it had developed into a major political forum by the time of Edward III, it had not altogether lost its earlier character.

It was in the audience of common petitions and the making of legislation that Edward's administrators really came into their own. The range of issues covered in these petitions, and the technical know-how needed to translate the crown's replies into statutes, made it imperative that the king should call on expert advice. For example, Sir Geoffrey Scrope, chief justice of king's bench, has been identified as the likely author of the important peace-keeping regulations contained in the Statute of Northampton of 1328.[49] The unique legislative committee appointed in the parliament of March 1340 included four royal lawyers (Scrope, Sadington and Parving, along with Sir John Stonor),[50] and their influence may well have been decisive in ensuring that certain important legal reforms were incorporated in the resulting statute.[51] Another chief justice of king's bench, Sir William Shareshull (1350–61), has been associated with the programme of judicial, economic and ecclesiastical legislation carried through in response to a series of common petitions in 1351–2.[52] Clearly, then, judicial expertise counted for much in the making of parliamentary statutes.

Not all the legislators, however, were common lawyers. The committee of 1340 to which we have just referred also included Archbishop Stratford and the treasurer, William Zouche. It was Stratford's involvement that probably ensured the passing of an important statute confirming the privileges and immunities of the church.[53] And in the years that followed, clerical chancellors and treasurers apparently became increasingly influential in the making of legislation. John Thoresby was probably responsible for effecting a major change in the procedure for the recovery of mercantile debts in 1353.[54] It was the treasurer William Edington whom chroniclers identified as the author of the important coinage reform of 1351.[55] Edington also deserves credit for helping to devise the novel scheme adopted in the parliament of 1352, whereby money raised under the Ordinance and Statute of Labourers was used to subsidize direct taxes.[56] The considerable legislative output during the middle years of Edward's reign is testimony to the industry and expertise of these and other like-minded ministers.

Beyond these specific examples, a more general point emerges. We have already noted that, despite the growing influence of the common petitions, Edward III still managed to retain a degree of initiative in the legislative process. The assistance of his ministers was crucial in this respect. It was they who tested the opinions of the lords and commons and advised when it was necessary or advantageous for the crown to make concessions. An interesting example is provided by the debate over weights and measures. The government's failure to enforce clause 35 of Magna Carta, guaranteeing standard weights and measures, was a constant theme in the common petitions of the 1320s and 1330s, but the crown made only the most cursory of efforts to respond to such criticisms.[57] In 1340, the desperate financial situation forced the king to confirm earlier regulations on this subject, and to set up special commissions to regulate weights and measures in the shires.[58] But the government saw no particular advantage to be had from the legislation, and the commissions were abandoned in 1344.[59] It was only in the early 1350s that the official attitude changed. Shareshull's work in the provincial sessions of the king's bench and Edington's experiences in the reform of the customs service impressed on the government the positive advantages to be had from a rigorous weights and measures policy. Consequently in 1352, when the commons repeated their demand for the confirmation of clause 35 of Magna Carta, the ministers eagerly responded with fresh legislation and an enthusiastic programme of enforcement in the shires and the ports.[60] This example, like the statutes on feudal levies and purveyance already discussed,[61] shows that the government retained a vital hold over the timing, and therefore the political implications, of its legislation.

It should by now be obvious that the superficial connections often made between the common petitions and the statutes tend to underrate the discretionary power enjoyed by Edward III and his council. To state that the seven articles of the 1344 statute and the twenty-three clauses of the statute of 1352 all arose from common petitions is, in a limited sense, correct.[62] But we cannot assume from this that the commons were actively involved in formulating the statutes. The legislative committee set up in the parliament of March 1340 actually included twelve knights and six burgesses, as well as a number of prelates, magnates and ministers.[63] This, however, was quite extraordinary. Under normal conditions, parliament was quite content to make general requests and leave the details to the experts. Some of the most important legislation of the mid-fourteenth century, such as the Statute of Provisors (1351), the Statute of Treasons (1352) and the Statute of the Staple (1354), may have resulted from petitions made by the commons in parliament; but their actual formulation was almost wholly the work of the council.[64] Even in the 1360s when the king was more inclined to make sweeping concessions, the initiative was still not completely surrendered. The parliament of 1365, for instance, produced some eighteen common petitions.[65] Of these, only six were taken up as a basis for formal legislation; and on a number of issues the government substantially qualified parliament's original suggestions. Thus, while the commons demanded complete freedom of trade, the crown insisted that certain restrictions on wool exports be maintained, and gave the chancellor important powers to decide ambiguous cases.[66] It is also worth noting that both sides used the parliament of 1365 to carry through changes in existing legislation. While the commons successfully petitioned for the repeal of the recent sumptuary laws and the alteration of the

Statute of the Staple,[67] the council seized the opportunity to re-enact the Statute of Provisors, to confirm its legislation on the Gascon wine trade, and to change an earlier law on the penalty for bringing unsubstantiated charges before the king's courts.[68] The making of legislation was still very much a two-way process in Edward III's later years.

Finally, it is important to remember that the king's ministers largely dictated how legislation was enforced. In this respect, a clear distinction needs to be drawn between those legal reforms which could be used to the king's benefit and the more broad-ranging statements about the administrative, judicial or fiscal practices of the government. The labour legislation of 1349–51, for instance, was deliberately designed not only to placate the political community but also to increase the crown's judicial profits; and it was therefore enforced with a consistency and ruthlessness hitherto unknown in medieval England.[69] This contrasts sharply with the government's casual approach to other more restrictive legislation. The long series of early fourteenth-century statutes requiring the annual replacement of sheriffs was almost completely ignored by Edward's ministers until after 1371; and the king's judges seem to have paid remarkably little attention to the frequent legislative changes in common law procedure.[70] In 1365 the commons were still demanding that all justices be required to abide by the statutes, and that judgments given by them in contravention of the statutes should be nullified.[71] The enforcement of solemn legislation was indeed a matter of constant concern to parliament throughout the fourteenth century. The fact that the commons were so frequently frustrated on this matter says much about the political influence and administrative discretion enjoyed by the king's professional advisers.

EDWARD III'S CHIEF MINISTERS

So far, we have confined ourselves to assessing the importance of the civil service in politics, and identifying the particular areas of administration in which the king's ministers were involved. It is now time to focus more closely on the different phases of Edward III's reign and to try to identify what changes took place within the government in the course of these fifty years. We have already noted that each period of the reign tended to be dominated by a single powerful administrator Stratford in the early stages, Edington in the 1340s and 1350s, and Wykeham in the later years. Enough has also been said about the king's attitudes to government and about the evolving role of the council to indicate that the most successful period of the reign in administrative terms was the 1350s. But we must now place those developments in a firmer context, by analysing the state of government under each of the king's principal ministers.

John Stratford

Considering the political turmoil of the period 1326–30, there was a remarkable degree of continuity between the successive regimes of the Despensers, Queen Isabella, and Edward III. This was partly because middle-ranking officials tended to keep out of politics, and

John Stratford: Abp. of Canterbury   John Stratford: Abp. Caur.

11 & 12   The seal of John Stratford, Archbishop of Canterbury, with its image of the murder of Thomas Becket

partly because the men who filled the great offices of state simply found party labels too confusing and hazardous. During the insurrection in London in the winter of 1326–7, Edward II's former treasurer, Walter Stapeldon, was murdered by the mob; and his last chancellor, Robert Baldock, died at Newgate prison.[72] These violent events impressed upon the official class the dangers of becoming too closely associated with a divisive political regime, and made them eager to seek an accommodation with the new government of Edward III.

It is therefore misleading to group Edward's early ministers into two parties, the so-called 'curialists' (former supporters of Edward II and the Despensers, or members of Edward III's own household) and the 'Lancastrians' (those who had sympathized with the aims of the baronial opposition in the 1320s, and eventually came out in sympathy with Stratford in the crisis of 1340–1).[73] Between 1327 and 1341 there were so many shifts in the political balance that such labels are largely meaningless. In fact, this was the age of the trimmer. Sir Geoffrey Scrope, who remained chief justice of king's bench more or less permanently from 1324 to 1338, is the classic example of a civil servant who preferred to reach an accommodation with each successive regime rather than lose the income, perquisites and social standing associated with high office.[74] However, it is important to recognize that Scrope's long tenure of office was exceptional. The political sympathies of individual ministers may have shifted in the course of the 1320s and 1330s, but many personal animosities remained. And the resulting tensions manifested themselves in a high turnover of personnel. Since the death of Edward I, there had been chronic instability in the chancellorship and treasurership, and this continued to some extent during Edward III's early years. Between 1307 and 1340, no one had uninterrupted tenure of these offices for more than three and a half years, and many were in power for much shorter periods.[75] The real problem in the 1330s was not some innate ideological conflict, but the failure of Edward III to break down old feuds and establish a proper following for himself within the administrative departments.

This does much to explain the problems encountered by John Stratford during these years. Stratford, who was Bishop of Winchester from 1323 to 1333 and Archbishop of Canterbury from 1333 to his death in 1348, had been one of the principal opponents of the Despenser regime and a staunch supporter of Queen Isabella. Indeed, he had been given custody of the exchequer while the revolution was in hand during the winter of 1326–7. But he had rapidly fallen out with the Earl of March and dissociated himself from Mortimer's rule.[76] When Edward III seized power in 1330, Stratford was therefore a natural candidate for the chancellorship. He resigned this post on his enthronement as Archbishop of Canterbury in September 1334, but very rapidly found that secular government was more to his taste and went back to the chancery in 1335–7. He was also an experienced diplomat, and accompanied the king to the continent in July 1338. He returned to England late in the following year to act as head of the regency council, and had a further short spell as chancellor in April–June 1340. Stratford's influence in the chancery was indeed sufficient for a number of his relatives and associates to find employment there; and his own brother Robert, Bishop of Chichester, twice succeeded him as chancellor (March 1337–July 1338 and June–December 1340).

Whether the king felt completely satisfied with Stratford's ascendancy is another matter. John was at least fifty when the seventeen-year-old Edward III seized power, and the two men seem to have had little in common. It was rumoured that when he had travelled to Kenilworth to receive the abdication of Edward II, Stratford had threatened that the king's rightful heir might also be disinherited.[77] If this is true, it is hardly likely to have endeared him to Edward III. Stratford's sensitivity to possible rivals also suggested that he often felt politically insecure. In the early 1330s the exchequer gave him much cause for concern. Although his brother served as chancellor of the exchequer in 1331–4, the treasurers of this period — William Melton (November 1330–April 1331), William Airmyn (April 1331–March 1332) and Robert Ayleston (March 1332–February 1334) — had all been prominently associated with the Despenser regime, and at least one (Airmyn) had personal grievances against Stratford.[78] They are unlikely to have been much in sympathy with their former opponent turned first minister. It is interesting that Stratford was not even certain of his former allies. In 1333 he became involved in an unseemly dispute with Adam Orleton over the latter's promotion to the bishopric of Winchester. In the course of the debate, damaging accusations were made about the archbishop's role in the supposed abdication of Edward II.[79] Finally, in 1341, Stratford was to make bitter personal attacks on certain royal servants — Bishop Burghersh of Lincoln, Sir Geoffrey Scrope, and, above all, William Kilsby — claiming that they had poisoned the king's mind against him during the campaigns of 1339–40.[80] Whether Edward deliberately tried to antagonize the Stratfords by his choice of advisers is uncertain. But the intense jealousies which broke out in official circles in 1340–1 can clearly be seen as the natural culmination of a decade of resentment and rivalry in government circles.

Against this background, it is not surprising to find that there were few significant administrative advances during the 1330s. In contrast to the major reorganization of the royal archives carried out by Stapeldon in the last years of Edward II,[81] and the various administrative novelties introduced by Thoresby and Edington in the middle years of Edward III, the 1330s seem notably unproductive. This in part was the result of the king's concentration on the Scottish and French wars. All the principal ministers were actively involved in the great spurt of diplomatic activity which preceded the outbreak of the Hundred Years War, and they had little time to devote to mere domestic matters. On several occasions Stratford's departure from the realm or his preoccupation with other business caused delays in the chancery.[82] The removal of the exchequer, chancery and common pleas to York in the mid-1330s, and the king's absence on the continent in 1338–40, also impeded any efforts to pursue far-reaching reforms. And with the treasurership so frequently changing hands, it was very difficult to maintain the momentum of reform. In 1331 William Airmyn tried to improve the administration of the customs service by appointing resident controllers to supervise the collectors in the ports.[83] But within months Airmyn had been removed from the treasurership, and the reform was abandoned. The government's faltering policy towards the wool staple and the keeping of the peace also suggests that it was incapable of consistent policy in these years.[84] But undoubtedly the most outstanding example is provided by its attitude towards the escheators. These officials were responsible for administering the lands and other feudal perquisites which fell to the king on the death of any of his tenants-in-chief. Ever since 1311 there had been a difference of opinion as to whether such duties should be undertaken by two high-ranking officials or be divided between eight regional escheators; and between 1327 and 1341 there were no fewer than five changes in government policy on this matter.[85] This example strongly suggests that the political and diplomatic pressures on the civil service in the 1330s severely hampered any effective bureaucratic advances, and may indeed have reduced the strength of government at just the time when Edward III needed his administrative resources most.

Had it not been for the king's financial recklessness in the late 1330s, John Stratford might well have remained a loyal servant of the crown and taken his place among the numerous unremarkable bureaucrat bishops of the Middle Ages. As it was, the quarrel which broke out between king and archbishop in the winter of 1340–1 has given Stratford an enduring fame surpassed only by his predecessor and hero Thomas Becket. The origins and events of this crisis have already been outlined; the intention here is to assess the implications of the dispute for the royal administration. On his return to England late in 1340, Edward dismissed a number of high-ranking officials, and forced several others to resign. Among these were the judges John Stonor, John Shardlow, John Inge and William Shareshull; the chancellor Robert Stratford and the treasurer Roger Northborough; and a number of lesser officials including John St Pol (keeper of the chancery rolls), Henry Stratford, Robert Chigwell and John Wath (senior chancery clerks), John Hildesley (chancellor of the exchequer), and John Thorp (treasurer's clerk in the exchequer of receipt).[86] This represented the most radical and violent reform of government personnel carried out in the whole reign. Unfortunately for the king, the inquiries he launched into official malpractice generally failed to uncover charges on which these dismissed ministers might be indicted. The lawyers were certainly accused, and in some cases convicted, of corrupt practices. Indeed, Richard Willoughby, the former chief justice of king's bench, was upbraided as an unscrupulous judge who had sold the laws 'as if they had been oxen or cows'.[87] But none of the royal judges was closely involved in the central issue, namely the king's quarrel with the regency council; and within a short while both Willoughby and a number of his associates were reappointed to senior posts in the courts.[88] The real focus of Edward's blatantly political attack would inevitably be the Stratfords.

Robert Stratford, the dismissed chancellor, was the first to feel the king's wrath. On 1 December 1340 he was accused of failing to supply the money Edward so desperately needed to fight the war; and he was given until after Epiphany (6 January) to prepare his case.[89] Robert obdurately refused to answer these and other accusations, not only because he regarded them as unfounded, but also because, as a prelate, he had immunity from the royal courts.[90] Edward seems to have dropped the attack at this point, but only in order to bring increased pressure to bear on the archbishop.

John Stratford had no post in the government in December 1340, and it was therefore doubly difficult to argue that he should answer for his crimes before a secular court. But Edward pressed ahead, and issued a formal statement which accused the archbishop of refusing to provide adequate financial resources, of encouraging opposition to royal taxes, of advocating a policy of largesse which impoverished the crown, and of abusing his authority in order to promote his own and his followers' interests. This catalogue of half-truths, distortions, and moral imputations — promptly dubbed a *libellus famosus* (infamous libel) by the outraged archbishop — indicates that the crisis was as much a clash of personalities as a conflict of principles.[91] Stratford was certainly not blameless, on either a professional or a personal level. It has been pointed out, for instance, that although the tax of the ninth granted in 1340 was very difficult to collect, it might have raised a good deal more had it been subject to better management by the regency council.[92] Edward may also have been justified in complaining that Stratford had incited treason and sedition, for the threats of excommunication issued by the archbishop in 1340 against persons infringing the privileges of the church implied public criticism of the king's iniquitous financial policies.[93] And although accusations of corruption were probably unfounded, it is undeniable that Stratford had done very well out of his connection with the court, securing the greatest ecclesiastical office in the land and regularly being pardoned his debts in the exchequer.[94]

For all this, however, Edward III had the utmost difficulty in finding a specific offence on which to indict the archbishop. Stratford answered the *libellus famosus* point by point, disclaiming the charges and stressing his loyalty to the crown. When he arrived at Westminster Palace in April 1341, the government was forced to use a dubious charge of non-payment of wool in order to prevent the archbishop from gaining access to parliament.[95] For it was there that he had his supporters, and had decided to take his stand on the issue of privilege. The two main points of the opposition programme — namely, that the ministers of state should be appointed, judged and dismissed in parliament, and that the nobles and prelates should answer for their offences only before their peers — both arose directly from Edward III's attempts to take arbitrary proceedings against the Stratford brothers. When the king was induced to grant a statute conceding those points in modified form, the Stratfords could claim a major personal victory.

Edward III badly misjudged the situation in 1341. His attempt to punish the members of the regency council for his own ineptitude had rebounded on him, and he had no choice but to patch up his differences with the noblemen and prelates he had alienated since 1338. Edward tactfully dropped the accusations against Stratford, and was formally reconciled with the archbishop later in 1341.[96] The exchequer was also instructed to ignore certain small fines (presumably for wool) charged on Stratford, and to abandon their attempts to levy the sum of £220 in amercements imposed on him by the justices of oyer and terminer in Kent and Sussex.[97] But despite these marks of favour, the king clearly had no intention of bringing the Stratfords or their followers back into government. The archbishop and his brother never again held official posts; and although John St Pol later went on to a distinguished career in Ireland, neither he nor the other clerks dismissed in 1340 succeeded in gaining readmission to the English chancery and exchequer.[98] Both John and Robert Stratford, as well as their nephew Ralph, Bishop of London, served on the regency councils of 1345 and 1346–7,[99] but this reflected their importance as churchmen and did not necessarily imply political rehabilitation.[100] The Sratford family's influence was therefore permanently eclipsed after 1340. Edward III learned many a bitter lesson from the events of 1341; and not the least was the need to create a reliable and efficient civil service which would implement his policies and uphold his interests. The ascendancy of Stratford was over, and a very different form of government was to take its place.

William Edington

If the ministerial history of the 1330s was dominated by Stratford, the 1340s and 1350s belonged to William Edington, Bishop of Winchester.[101] Edington was one of a group of administrators closely identified with the king's party during the opening stages of the Hundred Years War; and it was these men who replaced the older generation in the chancery and exchequer during the early 1340s. This brought about some fundamental changes in the bureaucracy. The most obvious was the notable increase in the length of tenure of high office. John Thoresby held the chancellorship for a continuous period of seven years (1349–56), while Edington was treasurer for a remarkable twelve years (1344–56) before going on to an additional six at the chancery (1356–63). The security of tenure so lacking since Edward I's time was restored: indeed, Edington's record at the exchequer was not to be equalled again until Tudor times.[102] After the disruptions of 1340–2, the courts also settled down: Sir John Stonor was chief justice of common pleas from 1342 to 1354, and Sir William Shareshull remained chief justice of king's bench from 1350 to 1361.[103] The lower echelons of the bureaucracy always tended to be more stable; but the continuity in the middle ranks during this period is particularly noteworthy. The post of chancellor of the exchequer, for instance, which had changed hands fifteen times

13   *Tomb of William Edington at Winchester Cathedral*

between 1305 and 1345, was held continuously by William Stow between 1346 and 1359; while at the chancery, David Wollor acted as keeper of the rolls for some twenty-five years (1345–70).[104] Nor did the Black Death seriously disrupt this new-found stability. The plague carried off Chancellor Offord, three of the twelve senior chancery clerks, and a number of key exchequer officials; but their colleagues and successors quickly reverted to normality.[105] It is particularly striking how many exchequer officials remained in the same posts throughout the 1350s: in addition to William Stow, these included Ralph Brantingham, the king's chamberlain (1349–65), Hugh Appleby, the king's remembrancer (1350–62), William Peek, the treasurer's remembrancer (1344–61) and Hugh Colwick, the clerk of the pipe rolls (1347–61).[106] All this was bound to have some effect on administrative practice, as the inconsistencies of the 1330s gave way to long-term planning and effective implementation of policy. The most important feature of this period, however, and the real key to the administrative strength of the regime, was the co-operation established between all departments of government. Both Stratford in the 1330s and Wykeham in the 1360s tended to stand alone. Edington, by contrast, was simply one of the many capable men who served the crown and influenced its policies in the middle years of Edward III's reign.

One of the special features of the 1340s and 1350s was the considerable overlap which developed between the major government departments and the lesser offices of the royal household. Historians used to think that there was an innate antagonism between the chancery and exchequer on the one hand and the privy seal and wardrobe on the other.[107] This idea has been greatly exaggerated, and is now largely discredited.[108] Nevertheless, it is clear that the physical separation of the departments of state and the household, as in

1338–40, could create considerable conflict within the administration. It is no surprise that William Kilsby, keeper of the privy seal, was one of the royal advisers most intensely criticized by Stratford and his allies in 1341.[109] So long as the whole administration was prepared to accept the king's scale of priorities, however, there was no reason why good relations between departments should not be re-established. This is precisely what happened after 1341. During the continental campaign of 1346–7, for instance, close links were built up between Chancellor Offord, who had control of the great seal of absence in England, and John Thoresby, who acted as joint keeper of the privy seal and custodian of the great seal at Calais.[110] Both men were of like mind and background, trained at Oxford and experienced in royal diplomacy.[111] It was therefore a relatively easy matter to maintain contact between the domestic and continental administrations, and there were only a few minor disagreements between king and chancellor (mostly over ecclesiastical patronage) in the course of this lengthy campaign.[112] Such links were kept up after Offord's death and Thoresby's promotion to the chancellorship, when two other university men, Simon Islip (1347–50) and Michael Northborough (1350–4), were brought in as keepers of the privy seal.[113] Indeed, so similar did the practices of the two departments become that for a while it seemed the English crown might adopt French custom and have a single writing office incorporating both the great and privy seals.[114] One notable result of this consolidation of resources was that diplomatic correspondence, previously the preserve of the chancery, was largely taken over by the privy seal clerks John Welwick and William Tirrington in the early 1350s.[115] The administrative departments, which had threatened to pull apart under the political conditions of the late 1330s, had now resumed their unity of purpose and action.

This development is most strikingly illustrated by Edington's reforms in the financial offices. Edington's apprenticeship as receiver of the ninth and keeper of the wardrobe in 1340–4 coincided with the period of greatest financial chaos in the whole of Edward III's reign.[116] The crown had exhausted all its traditional and extraordinary forms of revenue, and had resorted to huge loans of money and wool which it could never hope to repay.[117] Edward chose simply to renege on his debts, driving his Italian financiers into bankruptcy and entering into dubious credit deals with English merchants. When Edington took office as treasurer in 1344 he had not only to clear a backlog of royal debts, but also to re-establish public confidence in the crown's financial administration. His task was made all the more difficult by Edward's refusal to limit his military operations. While Edington was reasonably successful in convincing the king that his campaigns must be more economical, he still had to find large amounts of cash for the war during the mid-1340s. The Crécy-Calais campaign, which cost in the region of £225,000,[118] was funded largely by a merchant company set up in 1343–4 and given control over wool exports in return for an annual farm of £50,000. The financial demands on the farmers were so intense that, when the Black Death caused a temporary collapse in overseas trade, they promptly went bankrupt.[119] Edington was acutely aware that if stability was ever to be restored to the exchequer, it was essential that the treasurer should have some overall knowledge of income and expenditure and be capable of some basic budgeting. This was a very ambitious plan, for the exchequer was by origin a counting house, and its records and staff were not naturally geared towards the larger task of financial management. Given these limitations, however, the scale and the achievements of the ensuing reform were indeed remarkable.

Edington began with the exchequer itself.[120] By introducing a series of new book-keeping devices between 1344 and 1353, he was able to improve his own knowledge of the revenue and expenditure recorded in the receipt and issue rolls. He followed this up in 1348–53 with a concerted effort to achieve comprehensive knowledge of the king's household finances. He persuaded Edward III to appoint certain prominent exchequer officials to posts in the household: William Cusance as keeper of the wardrobe, John Buckingham as controller and later keeper of the wardrobe, and William Rothwell as receiver of the chamber. By 1355 Edington had established the principle that all the revenue of the royal household, even the money supplied to the king's privy purse, should be recorded in the exchequer. This was intended not to limit household expenditure (a thing the king would very much have resented), but simply to obtain an overall picture of the state of the royal finances. By the early 1360s, indeed, financial procedures had become so sophisticated that the exchequer was able to draw up detailed statements of royal income and expenditure, something that would have been unimaginable in the 1330s.[121]

Meanwhile, in 1351, the exchequer had resumed direct control of the customs service, and had proceeded to make a thoroughgoing reform of the officials and procedures at the ports.[122] Particular efforts were made to give the exchequer a better knowledge of how the customs revenues were collected and spent. Consequently, by the mid-1350s, when enormous sums were flowing into the royal coffers from both direct and indirect taxation, the exchequer was much better equipped to administer these resources effectively. And since the increase in taxation coincided with a decline in military activity, the king's ministers found themselves in the enviable and unusual position of having greater revenue than expenditure. The various campaigns of 1355–6, for instance, which culminated in the battle of Poitiers, cost the exchequer just £110,000,[123] at a time when the customs system alone was producing an average of about £87,500 a year (see Table 4). Indeed, the financial situation had been transformed to such an extent that when Edward III announced his plans for an invasion of France in 1359, the government was able to lay out approximately £75,000 in current or anticipated revenue from the customs, and did not even find it necessary to approach parliament for a grant of direct taxation. This was the first time in the Hundred Years War that the crown was able to mount a major expedition without imposing such burdens on the lay population, and it undoubtedly reflected well on both Edward III and his chief minister.

It is clearly unwise to become too enamoured of Edington's motives and achievements. Like all other royal ministers, he benefited personally from high office, and was evidently not immune from corrupting influences. During his period as chancellor, for instance, he was given substantial bribes by the monks of Meaux Abbey in order to ensure royal assistance in their dispute with the villein tenants of Wawne in Holderness (Yorkshire).[124] Nevertheless, the contemporary image of Edington was that of a scrupulous and public-spirited minister. The chronicler John of Reading described him as a friend of the community who, during the whole period of his office, saved the people from royal extortions and by his hard work and prudence was able to do much for the profit of the king and the realm.[125] Clearly, then, Edington's reforms did much more than transform government finances. They also helped create a sense of trust and common purpose between crown and community, and enormously increased the political prestige of Edward III's regime.

William Wykeham

In the 1360s the situation changed. By the time Edington retired from the chancellorship in 1363, influence was already passing to William Wykeham, who became the dominant figure in government during the decade after the treaty of Brétigny. Wykeham's rapid rise to power has already been charted, from his appointment as keeper of the king's works at Windsor to his elevation to the chancellorship in 1367.[126] The Windsor posting seems to have earned him early notoriety, for it was apparently at his instigation that the crown began to offer excess wages and to impress building workers in order to create a ready supply of labour at the castle.[127] Wykeham's real influence, however, depended not so much on official titles as on his intimacy with the king. As a member of the royal household between 1360 and 1367, he had many valuable opportunities to meddle in almost every aspect of government. In 1360, for instance, he was closely involved in the negotiations leading up to the treaty of Calais.[128] As the clerk of the signet, Wykeham was constantly by the king's side; and he continued to act as Edward's conscience and mouthpiece throughout the mid-1360s.[129] It was he who provided the essential link between the king and the chancery during the summer of 1361 when Edward was out hunting; and it was he who wrote somewhat imperiously to the chancellor and treasurer in 1366, instructing them not to make arrangements for the recently vacated archbishopric of Canterbury until he brought them the king's personal instructions on the matter.[130] Wykeham clearly inspired enormous confidence in Edward III, and reaped the rewards. The king was prepared to put considerable pressure on the Pope in order to secure his favourite's appointment as Bishop of Winchester in 1366–7.[131] Not surprisingly, this close relationship aroused some resentment. The uneducated Wykeham was disliked by certain members of the ecclesiastical hierarchy; and the chroniclers were to reserve some of their most damning comments for this self-seeking upstart.[132] By the end of the reign, however, Wykeham's greatest enemies were to be found in the very circles he had once dominated, the royal household and the court.

As an administrator, Wykeham had a much easier task than either Stratford or Edington. In the 1360s England was at peace, and the crown enjoyed a popularity and a financial security unparalleled since the late thirteenth century. Yet there were certain serious weaknesses in the administration, several of which arose directly out of Wykeham's ambitious drive for power. It became increasingly apparent that a single powerful minister could not hope to run the government with the same grasp of detail that had characterized the 1340s and 1350s. It is uncertain whether Wykeham deliberately encouraged the king to select obscure men for the principal offices of state, but it is striking that none of Edington's immediate successors at the exchequer — John Sheppey (1356–60), Simon Langham (1360–3) and John Barnet (1363–9) — had any experience in financial administration.[133] Early in the 1360s the lords complained that Treasurer Sheppey had abandoned the time-honoured practice of allowing men to have written records of the debts they owed to the exchequer.[134] This was probably done in the interests of economy, but it can hardly be said to have addressed the main problems of financial administration. Langham in particular, who went on to replace Edington as chancellor (1363–7), seems to have held on to office largely because he was prepared to accept the other influences at work in central government. Indeed, it was later said that it had been Wykeham, not Chancellor Langham, who had acted as 'chief of the privy council, and governor of the great council' in the middle years of the decade.[135]

For a short while in the early 1360s the influence of Thoresby and Edington endured. Household finances were subject to further reform; there was a brief attempt to restore the close working relations between the chancery and the privy seal; and steps were taken to revive the budgeting responsibilities of the exchequer.[136] But by 1365 all such efforts had been abandoned; and it was only a matter of time before administrative inertia collapsed into inefficiency and corruption. For instance, there was a marked deterioration in the standard of record-keeping, first detectable in the court of common pleas in 1363–5 and increasingly evident in the exchequer by the end of the decade.[137] The high degree of accountability established in both the financial and secretarial offices during the 1340s and 1350s also began to break down. In 1365 it was claimed that the treasurer's clerk in the lower exchequer, Richard Chesterfield, had taken advantage of the administrative disruption caused by the plague of 1361 in order to embezzle funds.[138] In 1364 a writ was issued from the chancery ordering the observance of a clause in the statute of 1341 relating to usury; but it had to be cancelled 'for having surreptitiously emanated from the chancery without the knowledge of the chancellor and others of the council'.[139] Later, Wykeham was to be accused of manipulating the chancery to obtain an illicit pardon of debts for one John Kirkton, who claimed the manors of Tumby and Tattershall (Lincolnshire).[140] These examples suggest that government was becoming increasingly prone to outside influence and to certain sharp practices during the 1360s. If this ever became public knowledge, it would inevitably reflect badly on the crown.

The state of the administration was in fact destined to become one of the most serious political issues after the reopening of hostilities with France. On the declaration of war in June 1369, Treasurer Barnet was replaced at the exchequer by Thomas Brantingham, a former official of the wardrobe and treasurer of Calais.[141] But the restoration of a financial expert proved of little use. The government apparently tried to repeat the experiment of 1359, appealing to the parliament of 1369 for a renewal of the wool subsidy but deliberately avoiding any demand for direct taxes on the laity. However, overseas trade was temporarily disrupted by the war, and in the exchequer year 1369–70 the customs collectors raised only about £49,000. This was clearly insufficient to fund a major new offensive, and the crown therefore appealed for substantial loans from its lay and clerical subjects.[142] In turn, these credit deals pushed up the level of assignment and put additional pressure on the king's remaining resources. By 1371 there was no option but to appeal to the kingdom for an emergency tax of £100,000, divided equally between the laity and the clergy.

When this subsidy was discussed in parliament, it was made a virtual condition of the grant that Chancellor Wykeham and Treasurer Brantingham, together with the keeper of the privy seal, Peter Lacy, should be dismissed from office.[143] Some historians have argued that Wykeham and his colleagues were opposed to the war, and were ousted in 1371 by a group of bellicose magnates led by the young Earl of Pembroke.[144] Others have suggested, more plausibly, that they were the victims of a violent anti-clerical reaction in the commons.[145] Like Edward III in 1340, the commons were apparently concerned about the immunity that clerical ministers enjoyed from prosecution in the royal courts. Each of the three ministers was therefore replaced by a layman — Robert Thorp as chancellor, Richard Scrope as treasurer, and Nicholas Carew as keeper of the privy seal. However, the opposition is unlikely to have been moved by a mere point of principle. It seems most likely that the lords and commons wished to use Wykeham and Brantingham as scapegoats and to blame them for the military failures and the heavy financial exactions which had accompanied the new phase of the war. It is particularly interesting that Wykeham's name was closely associated with the campaign to collect loans in 1369–70.[146] Whether or not these ministers really deserved such harsh treatment is an open question. What is clear is that the reputation for integrity and sound policy earlier associated with Edington's regime had now broken down.

The new regime of Treasurer Scrope appears to have responded to some of the complaints and misgivings voiced in the parliament of 1371. A period of financial stringency set in;[147] a statement of the king's outstanding commitments was attempted;[148] every effort was made to collect revenues in cash, rather than assigning them in advance;[149] and a special treasurer of war was appointed in the person of Adam Hartington, a chamberlain of the exchequer.[150] For a while, Scrope was successful, and some sense of order returned to the royal finances.[151] But when Lord Latimer began to strike his private deals with the London financiers, administrative co-ordination rapidly broke down. During the Good Parliament both Brantingham and Scrope were called upon to give evidence against the king's own creditors. Such events openly advertised the many tensions existing within the administration, and between the administration and the court, in these last years of Edward III's reign.

Another of those who publicly attacked the courtiers in the Good Parliament was William Wykeham, present in his capacity as Bishop of Winchester. Wykeham was also appointed to the abortive continual council set up at the end of the session.[152] When the court recovered the initiative later in 1376, John of Gaunt was determined to avenge what he saw as a betrayal of trust, and summoned Wykeham before the council on a series of charges relating to his time in government. The only specific point that could actually be proved was that Wykeham, as chancellor, had remitted certain fines which ought to have been paid by Sir John Grey of Rotherfield and others for the issue of solemn documents under the great seal.[153] In fact, there may have been some truth behind the other accusations. The charge of peculation was no doubt exaggerated, but it is true that Wykeham had helped the king to divert the revenue from John II's ransom into the chamber, and to deprive the exchequer of any knowledge or control of the sums involved.[154] The same idea may lie behind the statement that Wykeham had taken money from Matthew Gourney, Thomas Fog and John St Loo, for all three of these men are known to have paid fines and ransoms into the chamber in 1361.[155] Finally, the charge that Wykeham employed certain of the French hostages, notably the Duke of Bourbon, to go to Avignon and argue his case for the bishopric of Winchester fits perfectly well with the known facts of the case.[156] But it is also clear that Wykeham's enemies were motivated by politics, not the desire for justice. John of Gaunt was attempting to revive official and public suspicion against Wykeham, and to use this as a means of deflecting popular sympathy back towards the crown.

Under these circumstances, the judgment on Wykeham was a foregone conclusion. On 17 November 1376 his estates were confiscated. Unfortunately for the government, however, the church now took up Wykeham's cause.[157] The other bishops could hardly countenance such arbitrary actions and blatant infringements of ecclesiastical liberty, and early in 1377 the clergy formally protested about the seizure of the Winchester estates.[158] The whole affair ironically served to restore Wykeham's political credibility, and to ensure a place for him, and for his former colleague Thomas Brantingham, in the minority councils of Richard II.[159] The trial of Wykeham is an interesting example of the rapid and sometimes bewildering shifts of political opinion during Edward III's last years. But more than anything else, it reveals the lack of purpose and leadership within the government. The Good Parliament and the death of Edward III ushered in a new period of uncertainty and instability which was to culminate in Richard II's first major crisis of 1386.

★ ★ ★

The link between the administrative and political history of Edward III's reign has now been clearly established. The uneasy equilibrium of the Stratford regime, the confident reforms of Edington and his colleagues, and the slow slide into corruption during and after Wykeham's supremacy: all these reflect, and to some extent explain, the political mood prevailing in different phases of the reign. The king's reputation with his people depended a good deal on his choice of ministers and his ability to supervise and constrain them. In his early years, Edward III either neglected or failed to find men of his own age and outlook, and created a dangerous rift between the household and the central administration that ultimately precipitated the crisis of 1340–1. In the following twenty years the mature king was lucky enough to find and promote a series of quite exceptional administrators who played a major role in restoring public confidence in the crown. But after Edington's retirement, Edward became increasingly complacent, and allowed power to pass into the hands of unpopular and ultimately unscrupulous men. It was common throughout the Middle Ages for kings and their subjects to blame the ministers when things went wrong. This was not altogether fair: both Stratford and Wykeham were ultimately the victims of circumstance. But the crucial point about the ministerial history of the reign of Edward III lies not in the dismissals of 1341 and 1371, but in the intervening three decades. What happened in the civil service during this period is far too important to be relegated to the annals of mere administrative history, for it provided the very institutional base on which Edward rebuilt the reputation of the English monarchy.

6 The magnates

Medieval English society was headed by an oligarchy of great men who saw themselves as the natural companions and counsellors of the king. Despite the growing importance of lesser landholders and merchants, the magnates remained socially pre-eminent throughout the later Middle Ages, and to a large extent dictated the political fortunes of the crown. It is therefore of fundamental importance to establish how Edward III treated these men, and how they in turn responded to their king.

Historians use various terms to describe the highest levels of lay society in the Middle Ages. 'Nobles', 'aristocrats', 'lords', 'barons' and 'peers' all have slightly different connotations, but all tend to be used synonymously to describe the 'magnates' — literally the great men. Inevitably, there is some ambiguity about the membership of this group. The top ranks of the aristocracy were made up of those holding formal hereditary titles: the earls and (after 1337) the dukes. In the reign of Edward III, however, there were never more than about a dozen such men at any one time, and the greater proportion of the nobility was made up of the barons, who used the title 'lord' followed by a family name. In the thirteenth century, a baron had been defined as a tenant-in-chief of the crown who held sufficient land to warrant the payment of a relief (entry fine) of £100, later reduced to 100 marks (£66 13s. 4d.). By the fourteenth century, however, the magnates came to be identified not by tenure but by membership of the house of lords. From the time of Edward II there was a marked tendency for the same families to receive personal summonses to successive parliaments.[1] As a result, the lords developed a keen sense of their own identity, claiming the right to consent to impositions charged on their number and to judge accusations made against their equals or 'peers'. For this reason, most historians have taken membership of the lords as the criterion for defining the nobility of late medieval England; and such a definition will broadly be followed here.

Having established a means by which to test membership of the magnate class, it is relatively easy to assess its numerical strength. The average number of temporal peers receiving personal summonses to parliament between 1327 and 1377 was fifty-eight.[2] Inevitably, there was some fluctuation across this period. In 1346, for instance, when the king and the majority of the nobility were detained abroad at the siege of Calais, only twenty-seven lords were called to parliament; and as a result of a spate of deaths during the second outbreak of the Black Death, there were only thirty-eight magnates summoned to the assembly of 1362. Conversely, the number could rise quite dramatically as a result of a conscious decision to fill up depleted ranks. As many as seventy-eight lords received personal summonses to the parliament of March 1332; and sixty-six were called to an abortive session in 1349. Our average of fifty-eight does, however, provide a reasonably accurate impression of the size of the English nobility in this reign. Taking into account the immediate families of these men, the entire magnate class cannot have numbered much in excess of 500 people. Even in the period after the Black Death, this represented a mere fraction of one per cent of the entire population. Yet it was these families which comprised the most powerful group in the polity of late medieval England.

The wealth of the magnates varied greatly. The top end of the scale comprised members of the royal family. The Black Prince's lands in England and Wales were said to yield about £10,000 per annum at the time of his death; and the Lancastrian inheritance, valued at some £8,400 a year under Henry of Grosmont, increased under John of Gaunt until it was worth approximately £12,500 in 1399.[3] Few other members of the nobility had even a quarter of these resources. The landed estates of the younger Despenser, valued at over £7,000 in Edward II's last years, were altogether exceptional, and were never fully reassembled after the revolution of 1326–7.[4] In fact, £4,000 a year was probably enough to put a nobleman in the top income bracket. The lands and annuities bestowed by Edward III on his new earls in 1337 indicate that the minimum income commensurate with comital status was about £1,000.[5] Still more modestly endowed were the bannerets. A banneret was a cavalry officer who was permitted to have a rectangular banner carried before him on the field of battle, as distinct from the triangular pennon of the knight. Certain of the bannerets associated with the royal household received personal summonses to parliament, and are therefore normally included in the ranks of the peerage. In economic terms, however, they were often indistinguishable from the wealthier knightly families, and could consider themselves fortunate if their annual income from land and fees reached about £500. The majority of the barons stood somewhere between this and the wealthier earls.

All the magnates shared a natural desire to increase their family holdings and thus improve their political standing. Some did so by purchase. Sir Thomas Berkeley of Berkeley (Gloucestershire) raised his annual income from £659 in 1335 to £1,150 in 1346 as a result of some judicious property speculation.[6] Others benefited from marriage. In the course of the fourteenth century, four successive generations of the Zouche family of Harringworth (Northamptonshire) took wealthy heiresses as brides, and built up a formidable array of estates in the midlands and the north.[7] The best way to enhance one's prospects, however, was to win favour at court. The history of the lordship of Denbigh well illustrates the king's power to raise or depress aristocratic fortunes.[8] These valuable marcher lands, worth over £1,000 a year, were seized from Thomas of Lancaster in 1322 and granted to the younger Despenser, only to be lost to Roger Mortimer after the coup of 1327. On March's fall in 1330, the estate reverted to the crown, and was granted to Edward III's friend, William Montagu. But with Montagu's death, and the rise to favour of March's grandson, another Roger, the king decided to transfer Denbigh back into the hands of the Mortimers in 1354. Royal favour therefore did more than anything else to determine the relative standing of aristocratic families in fourteenth-century England.

The history of the later Middle Ages has often been portrayed as a continuous struggle for power between the king and the magnates. But the reign of Edward III witnessed a long period of political calm, and provides an obvious opportunity to pause and discuss how a king could reach a successful working compromise with his great men. The following analysis will indicate that Edward III took a lot longer than has sometimes been suggested to reach an accommodation with the nobility. But it will also show that he hit on a highly successful formula during his middle years, one which was equally advantageous to king and magnates, and which continued to function with some degree of success right through to the end of the reign.

THE LEGACY OF THE 1320s

The last years of Edward II and the minority of Edward III formed a particularly difficult period for the nobility. Between 1322 and 1330 a total of seven earls lost their lives and lands, and numerous barons were executed, imprisoned or hounded by the Despenser and Mortimer regimes. Edward II's own brother-in-law, the Earl of Hereford, was slain at Boroughbridge in 1322, and his first cousin, Thomas of Lancaster, was summarily executed shortly after the battle.[9] The coup of 1326–7 produced fewer sacrifices, mainly because most of the barons had already defected to Queen Isabella. Apart from the two Despensers, the only other leading nobleman to be executed was Edmund Fitzalan, Earl of Arundel. Isabella was also quick to restore the families of prominent barons who had fallen at Boroughbridge, such as the Badlesmeres, Cliffords and Mowbrays.[10] But the rise of Roger Mortimer prevented any real sense of reconciliation, and the rebellion of Henry of Lancaster in 1328 and the execution of the Earl of Kent in 1330 revealed deep divisions within the top ranks of political society.

It would be natural to assume that the blatant mistreatment of the magnates during the 1320s produced a public reaction in their favour. But this was not so. Many of the lords were believed to have taken advantage of the disturbed state of politics to pursue their own selfish interests. Three matters in particular caused great concern around 1330. First, there was the general interference in the course of government by those holding power at court. The Despensers and Roger Mortimer had undoubtedly used their influence to cover up the widespread corruption and intimidation associated with their regimes in the provinces.[11] Secondly, the civil wars of 1321–2 and 1326–7 had resulted in widespread and indiscriminate plundering, during which the peasantry inevitably suffered much.[12] The third and by far the most serious problem was 'maintenance' — the protection of criminals from prosecution in the king's courts, and the bribery or harassment of judges and juries.[13] None of these offences was peculiar to the magnates. But on a number of occasions in the 1320s and early 1330s when the commons in parliament complained about such matters, it is significant that they singled out the great men of the realm for particular criticism.[14]

Edward III was acute enough to realize that such behaviour reflected badly on the crown, and quickly tried to improve the reputation of his nobles. In the parliament of October 1331 he appealed directly to their better natures, and drew up a formal compact which was then proclaimed throughout the realm.[15] The lords promised that they would not protect criminals from legal proceedings; that they would assist royal agents in the task of government; that they would no longer disturb the law, but keep it; and that they would refrain from seizing provisions from the king's poor subjects. Edward also took this

14 *Edward III grants a charter to the Earl of Arundel*

opportunity to settle some outstanding baronial disputes. Lord Zouche of Ashby and Sir John Grey of Rotherfield, for instance, who had been quarrelling over the right to marry the younger Despenser's widow Eleanor (a major landholder in her own right), were both committed to prison pending a proper investigation of the case.[16] In the same parliament, the lords requested that Roger Mortimer's son Edmund be restored to his family's ancient inheritance in the marches; and although the king refused to compromise his prerogative, he acted on the suggestion shortly after parliament had disbanded.[17] Edward III was evidently trying to persuade political society of his firm resolve to control the magnates, while at the same time offering the sons of former rebels the chance to prove their commitment and loyalty to the new regime.

All this, however, had little effect. In 1334 the commons complained once more about the magnates' abuse of prises and maintenance, and special commissions had to be set up to investigate such matters.[18] Even then, problems continued unabated. Sir Robert Clifford, who had failed to recover a piece of property by legal means, organized a band of thugs to beat up his rival and occupy the land in 1335.[19] It was reported in 1337 that the Earl of Arundel's steward Sir Roger Lestrange had caused such distress by his raids across the Welsh border that the people were about to rise against him.[20] And in 1338, when investigating a case concerning the Earls of Norfolk and Northampton, Lord Scales and Sir Gilbert Pecche, the sheriff of Norfolk reported that he could not find a single knight in his county who was not a relative, tenant or retainer of one or more of these men, and who would be capable of giving dispassionate evidence.[21]

In some respects, the government's policies simply compounded these problems. Under Edward II the nobility had been allowed considerable influence over local justice through their appointment as supervisors of the keepers of the peace.[22] This practice continued in various different guises during most of the first decade of Edward III's personal rule, with the lords serving either as presidents of the county commissions of the peace (in 1332) or as overseers of the justices of the peace (in 1338).[23] Either way, the magnates rapidly won a reputation for inefficiency and corruption.[24] Meanwhile, the king also made free with the franchise of return of writs, a special privilege which allowed a private lord to take on a function normally fulfilled by the sheriff and to receive and answer all royal writs relating to his lands and tenants. Among those receiving this franchise were the Earl of Arundel and two of the king's closest friends, William Montagu and John Molyns.[25] The result, once again, was to interrupt or distort the course of justice. It seems no coincidence that another of Edward's confidants, Thomas Breadstone, was accused of holding the whole of Gloucestershire to ransom as a result of his influence over local juries.[26] In 1341, moreover, Molyns was to be exposed as a notorious bully and brigand, who for several years had terrorized the area around his native Stoke Poges (Buckinghamshire) with complete impunity.[27] Edward's frequent absence on campaigns made matters still worse, allowing corruption to spread through all levels of government and society. The men of Dunwich complained that while the king was out of the country, Sir John Clavering had manipulated juries in order to deprive them of control over some 200 acres of Suffolk marshland.[28] By 1340 it was possible to assert that confederacies, conspiracies and lawlessness in the midland shires were worse than ever before.[29] Clearly, it was not only the crown's reputation that had suffered as a result of the break-down of law and order. The selfishness of the lords had also come to be seen as a major impediment to the restoration of social and political harmony.

THE MAGNATES AND THE KING'S WARS, 1330–41

In the end, it was not domestic politics but foreign policy which transformed the reputation of the nobility. Medieval chroniclers and modern historians are all agreed that the magnates played a key role in the military adventures launched by Edward III against Scotland and France. Sir Thomas Gray of Heton, a northern knight writing in the mid-1350s at the very high point of Edward's military fortunes, assumed that the brotherhood of arms then so apparent among the aristocracy had been carefully nurtured by the king from the very start of his personal rule.[30] But this view accords ill with the official records of the 1330s. The military fiascos of Edward II and Roger Mortimer had created considerable resentment; and when the lords were consulted on how to proceed against France in 1331, they insisted on a diplomatic solution rather than risking the outbreak of war.[31] Again, when Edward III decided to intervene in Scotland late in 1332, the magnates were at best indifferent and at worst positively hostile to the plan.[32] Even the initial euphoria surrounding Edward's claims in France in 1337 rapidly gave way to apathy and opposition, culminating in the political crisis of 1341. There is little to suggest that the majority of the English nobility relished the prospect of war in the 1330s.

Part of the problem was the magnates' uncertainty over their role in the army.[33] The decline of the feudal levy in the early fourteenth century and the development of volunteer forces paid directly by the crown had left the nobility in a rather anomalous position. Sometimes, particularly when Edward I and Edward II had been absent from expeditions, the great tenants-in-chief had accepted the new cash nexus and taken the top levels of pay offered by the crown. But when they were asked to fight alongside the king, they resented the subordinate status implied by wages, and made clear their preference for more traditional forms of service. This was an unrealistic position to adopt, for on the rare occasions that the crown chose to revert to feudal armies, as in 1327, the tenants-in-chief proved unable or unwilling to provide the necessary quotas of knights.[34] Faced with such problems, it is not altogether surprising that the young Edward III attempted to do without the massed ranks of the English barons in the 1330s, and depended heavily on a group of self-interested northerners and personal friends to organize his campaigns in Scotland and the Low Countries.

Strategic reasons also necessitated a strong aristocratic presence at home. England was under constant threat of attack in the later 1330s, and an adequate system of defence was imperative. The lords were the natural choice for such a task. The great northern families — Wake, Neville, Percy, Umfraville, Clifford and Lucy — were always primarily concerned with guarding the Scottish march, and did not normally go on continental campaigns. Indeed, in 1339 the border communities requested that nothing, not even a summons to parliament, should distract Sir Thomas Lucy from his primary duty of defence.[35] The French raids on the Channel ports, culminating in the sack of Southampton in 1338, encouraged a similar attitude in the southern shires.[36] In 1336 the king instructed the Earls of Arundel, Surrey and Devon to equip and man their castles in readiness for attack.[37] In the following year many of the magnates were appointed to special commissions set up to defend the counties south of the Trent.[38] Finally, in August 1338, ten regional committees were appointed, under the leadership of nine earls and a large number of eminent barons, to organize the array of troops and to over-see the keeping of the peace.[39] There were indeed sound arguments why prominent figures such as the Earls of Arundel, Huntingdon and Warwick, and Lords Berkeley, Wake, Mowbray and Basset, were on this occasion omitted from the king's foreign enterprise and associated in the defence and governance of the realm.

Where Edward went wrong was in failing to convince these and other members of the regency administration that his military schemes had any real chance of success. In this sense, the crisis of 1340–1 must be seen as the inevitable outcome of ten years of political mismanagement, during which an important section of the English nobility had been deprived of any real influence over military and diplomatic affairs. The opposition of 1341 represented a complete cross-section of the nobility, from political veterans such as John Warenne, Earl of Surrey, to some of the principal beneficiaries of Edward III's regime, Arundel and Huntingdon.[40] It was a major indictment of the king's system of patronage, as well as his military policy, that he was unable to retain the support of such men at this vital moment.

Nevertheless, there are reasons to question the strength and success of the baronial alliance. Once the crisis parliament was over, Edward was able to fall back on a number of leading nobles who had remained loyal or had been absent from England during the quarrel with Stratford. These included the Earls of Derby, Devon, Gloucester, Northampton, Oxford, Pembroke, Salisbury, Suffolk and Warwick.[41] It was with their consent that Edward annulled the legislation of 1341 and mounted expeditions to Scotland and Brittany in 1341–3. Such men can hardly have been indifferent to the constitutional principles embodied in the discarded statute. But they probably interpreted the clause guaranteeing trial by peers as a specific reference to Stratford's case. Once the king had dropped his charges against the archbishop and arranged a personal reconciliation, the majority of the magnates were loath to risk royal displeasure on an abstract principle. Far from being a resounding victory for baronial constitutionalism, then, the crisis of 1341 rapidly dissolved into a political compromise.

The eagerness of most magnates to patch up their differences with the crown can best be explained by what was happening in the shires. The nobles had good reason to worry about the special courts set up by Edward in the winter of 1340–1 to inquire into corruption and lawlessness. When first issued, these commissions included a number of earls and barons, representing all shades of political opinion: close friends of the king, such as Sir Nicholas Cantilupe of Ilkeston (Derbyshire); political neutrals like John de Vere, Earl of Oxford; and some who would shortly defect from the king's party, including the Earl of Arundel.[42] But a number of the magnates were subsequently relieved of their responsibilities, leaving the commissions under the control of royal judges and local gentry.[43] The serious accusations of corruption, maintenance, robbery and murder brought against prominent knights and royal favourites, such as Sir Thomas Gurney (Somerset), Sir Edward Creting (Suffolk) and Sir John Molyns (Buckinghamshire), must have left many of the magnates wondering how long they could conceal their own criminal activities.[44] The inquiries also begged comparison with the eyres of Edward I's time, and seemed to herald a return to that king's policy of curbing the privileges of the nobility. More ominous still was the removal of the magnates from participation in local peace-keeping. The supervisory committees were not renewed after 1340, and by 1344 only the Earls of Angus and Arundel and a handful of barons such as Sir Thomas Berkeley remained to represent their class on the commissions of the peace.[45] In the mid-1340s many members of the nobility saw their private interests and political influence under attack, and must have been increasingly disillusioned by the consequences of their opposition during the Stratford crisis. With the commons still profoundly suspicious of baronial behaviour, there was little chance of political support from below. The net result of the 1341 crisis was to leave the magnates relatively weak and isolated, unnerved by Edward's swift recovery and uncertain of their next move. The only real solution, in fact, was to seek an accommodation with the crown.

THE PROCESS OF RECONCILIATION: WAR AND CHIVALRY

This interpretation of the Stratford crisis does much to explain the speed and success of Edward III's subsequent reconciliation with the nobility. Many historians have assumed that Edward bowed to pressure after 1341 and deliberately pandered to aristocratic interests. But this is to forget the magnates' side of the bargain. Their abuse of power during the 1320s and 1330s had severely damaged their reputation as political and military leaders. The eagerness of the nobles to co-operate with the crown after 1341 stemmed not merely from the king's change of heart, but from their own anxiety to regain credibility. The political system of the 1340s and 1350s, then, was a distinctly reciprocal affair.

The most obvious manifestation of this was to be found in the war. The great series of campaigns launched in Aquitaine, Brittany and Normandy after 1341 became a 'joint-stock enterprise',[46] drawing together king and nobility in the common pursuit of glory. The English occupation of western France would indeed have been unthinkable without the active involvement of a whole series of aristocratic lieutenants: figures such as Henry of Grosmont, William Clinton, Ralph Stafford, William Bohun, William Montagu II, John de Vere, Roger Mortimer II, and Thomas Beauchamp among the earls and Thomas Holand, John Lisle of Rougemont, Guy Brian, Michael Poynings, Walter Mauny, Robert Morley, Thomas Breadstone and Thomas Dagworth among the barons and bannerets. Apart from the fame to be won on the battlefield, there were two very practical reasons why so many such men entered into military service in the 1340s. These were the indenture system and the profits of war.

After 1341 it became common for military commanders to draw up contracts or 'indentures' with the crown, promising to provide a specified number of soldiers for an agreed period of time, and receiving guarantees that all their resulting expenses would be met by the royal exchequer.[47] Such contracts gave the nobles several distinct advantages. The employment of their own armies in the king's service inevitably gave them a greater influence over strategy.[48] The development of the indenture also put an end to the question of whether or not noblemen ought to receive payment for military service. Wages were now the norm for all ranks, and ranged from 13s. 4d. a day for a duke to 2d. a day for an ordinary infantry soldier.[49] Even more important were the arrangements laid down in indentures for the disposition of prisoners and plunder.[50] Edward III managed to establish by the 1350s that important prisoners ought to be reserved to him, and that a third of all the profits of war should pass to the crown. In turn, however, military leaders expected rich rewards for surrendering their captives, and claimed a proportion of the booty and ransoms taken by their own soldiers. Consequently, many of Edward's lieutenants made considerable fortunes out of the war. Sir Thomas Holand, who captured the count of Eu at Caen in 1346, sold his prisoner to the king for the enormous sum of 20,000 marks (£13,333 6s. 8d.).[51] After the battle of Poitiers, the Earl of Warwick ransomed the Archbishop of Sens for £8,000, and Sir Bartholomew Burghersh the younger secured 10,000 marks (£6,666 13s. 4d.) from Edward III for his captive, the Count of Ventadour.[52] Extravagant building projects such as Henry of Grosmont's palace of the Savoy, Lord Berkeley's castle at Beverstone (Gloucestershire), Thomas Beauchamp's extensions at Warwick Castle, Gilbert Umfraville's tower house at South Kyme (Lincolnshire), and the

Scropes' great fortress at Bolton in Wensleydale (Yorkshire), all suggest a considerable accumulation of capital out of the French and Scottish wars.[53] Nor did the victors of Neville's Cross, Crécy and Poitiers forget their duty to the anglophile Almighty. Sir Walter Mauny founded a Carthusian monastery in London, and Sir Thomas Breadstone glazed the huge east window of Gloucester Abbey in memory of the local landholders who had fought alongside him on the battlefields of France.[54] In the absence of noble archives, these and other monuments provide the most tangible evidence of the extraordinary financial benefits accruing to the English nobility from participation in Edward III's wars.

Such were the advantages of service. But there was also a debit side. It was usual for the crown to pay advances to contractors on the sealing of indentures, but these only accounted for a proportion of the costs of a campaign. In 1345, Henry of Grosmont received an unusually generous £20,800 for his projected war in Aquitaine. But he still overspent to the tune of £17,700, for which he was not fully reimbursed until 1350.[55] Personal resources, then, just as much as martial skills, counted for much in the choice of royal lieutenants. Indeed, financial contributions in themselves came to be seen as a form of service. The Earl of Lancaster advanced over £4,500 to the exchequer in the course of 1348;[56] and between 1370 and 1374 the Earl of Arundel loaned the king at least £38,500 — an astonishing sum equivalent to one fifteenth and tenth levied on the whole kingdom.[57] Most of Arundel's loans were quickly repaid, and at good rates of interest.[58] But other loans and war debts had to take their turn among the exchequer's other commitments; and an immediate return was most unlikely. It has been suggested that Edward III's indebtedness to so many of the magnates created a serious political weakness in his regime.[59] But until the 1370s there is no real evidence to suggest that the lords were angered by the crown's inability or refusal to pay up. In 1344 the Earl of Salisbury left instructions in his will that all debts still unpaid by the crown at the time of his death (calculated at £6,734) should be cancelled — a welcome precedent much commended by the king.[60] It is quite possible, therefore, that the wages and loans paid by the magnates out of their own pockets were not considered debts at all, but necessary investment in a profit-making war. Edward III himself made large advances out of his private treasure to subsidize military enterprises, and although some of these were listed as loans in the exchequer records, only a small proportion were ever paid back.[61] In a joint-stock enterprise, it was only reasonable that the nobility should act similarly, sharing the burdens, as well as the profits, of war.

Royal patronage also worked by the same principles. In 1341 Edward III accused Stratford of advocating a policy of largesse that had seriously impoverished the crown.[62] By throwing responsibility for his early generosity on to the shoulders of a disgraced minister, Edward was clearly advertising a change of policy. Thereafter, only conspicuous and continuous service could expect to be rewarded. Roger Mortimer II is a case in point.[63] After distinguishing himself at Crécy, Mortimer was made a founder member of the Garter and was raised to the ranks of the parliamentary peerage. But it was not until 1354, when he was a seasoned campaigner, that he received back the earldom of March lost by his grandfather in 1330. Appropriately enough, the new earl died while on active service in France in 1360. The strong sense of commitment bred into the magnates during this period is also demonstrated by the annuities of 1,000 marks (£666 13s. 4d.) promised by Edward to the Earls of Warwick and Stafford in 1348 and 1353.[64] In both cases, payment was conditional upon the earls holding themselves in constant readiness to serve the king, each with a minimum of a hundred men-at-arms. In effect, Warwick and Stafford had become permanent retainers of the crown, just like the household bannerets and knights. The political distinctions between the high nobility and the courtiers had therefore broken down into a common bond of service.

This new sense of unity and camaraderie was most perfectly manifested, of course, in the Order of the Garter. Those admitted to the fraternity in the 1350s and 1360s included household servants like Richard la Vache, prominent soldiers of fortune such as Reginald Cobham and Walter Mauny, loyal barons like Edward Despenser, Thomas Ughtred and Ralph Basset of Drayton, and great aristocrats such as Humphrey Bohun and the Princes Lionel, John and Edmund.[65] The omissions, too, were of some significance. It is particularly noticeable that the two surviving opposition leaders of 1341, Arundel and Huntingdon, never became knights of the Garter.[66] Commercial considerations apart, it is just possible that Arundel's large loans to the crown in the 1350s and 1370s were an attempt to wipe clean the stain of revolt and win this final and elusive honour. That he failed says something about the animosities aroused during the Stratford crisis. But the fact that he remained one of Edward's most active generals, diplomats and councillors throughout the middle years of the reign seems more significant still. Service was no longer an imposition for the nobility; it had become a matter of political necessity and personal honour.

THE MAGNATES IN PARLIAMENTS AND COUNCILS

One of the principal reasons for Edward III's rapid political recovery after 1341 was his greater willingness to act on the recommendations of the barons. The two principal channels through which such advice was conveyed were parliament and the council. The records of these assemblies are sparse and formal, and give a strong impression that matters proceeded in much the same way throughout the fourteenth century and long beyond. But this is to forget important changes of attitude. The political transformation of the 1340s and 1350s arose not from some fundamental reform of institutions, but from the magnates' belief that Edward was now observing their own preferred policies.

This can best be demonstrated by the record of baronial attendance at parliament. Given the political importance of this institution, it is somewhat disarming to discover that so few members of the aristocracy actually responded to parliamentary summonses and turned up in person.[67] In one assembly after another the story is the same: proceedings delayed and business abandoned as a result of the non-arrival of the peers. So far as we can tell, there was no major departure from this norm at any point in Edward III's reign. But it is possible to argue that the motives for absenteeism varied across the period. Throughout the 1320s, there had been real risks involved in attending parliament. Henry of Lancaster, for instance, had refused to attend an assembly at Salisbury in 1328 because he feared arrest and trial by Roger Mortimer. Edward III's aggressive policy towards Scotland, coupled with the inconvenience of winter journeys to York, had been the chief reason for abstentions during the 1330s. In the 1340s and 1350s, however, we may detect a change of heart. It was the very involvement of the nobility in the king's wars, rather than any negative political feeling, that now prevented men from attending. Even during the years of peace in the 1360s, the barons' failure to get to parliament on time was probably a result of their general satisfaction with the diplomatic and domestic settlement rather than any sense of political disillusionment. In statistical terms, then, there was no demonstrable increase in the level of baronial participation in parliament during Edward III's middle years. What really changed was the degree of confidence in the king. and the assumption that his policies now stemmed from the wiser counsels of the nobility.

The barons' influence over the workings of parliament in the middle decades of the fourteenth century was therefore considerably greater than mere numbers might suggest. The peers always tended to look upon parliament as a court where they could advance their private interests, and the new political conditions prevailing after 1341 gave them a much greater chance of success. In 1348 and 1351, for instance, the Earl of Arundel petitioned for full enjoyment of his father's former lands and titles, and he achieved his aim in 1354 when the sentence passed against Edmund Fitzalan in 1327 was finally and formally annulled.[68] The peers could also act in concert. In 1343 a debate had arisen in parliament over the inheritance rights of children born to English parents serving on the continent.[69] This matter was of considerable importance to the nobility, and in 1351 the claims of Henry Beaumont, Giles Daubeney and Elizabeth Brian were submitted to the council for special consideration. As a result, a statute was issued confirming the rights of those born overseas.[70] Undoubtedly the most important of the barons' responsibilities, however, was to act as advisers on war and diplomacy. Edward III may have called upon the commons to give formal approval for his campaigns and treaties; but when more detailed matters were under discussion, like the proposals for an Anglo-Scottish peace in 1362 and 1368, it was to the lords that he naturally turned for advice.[71] In many and diverse respects, then, parliament provided a natural forum of debate between crown and nobility in the mid-fourteenth century.

When we turn to the work of the council, we need to distinguish three broad groupings among the magnates. First, there were the knights and bannerets of the royal household who were in regular attendance on the monarch and formed an inner phalanx of councillors. Secondly, there were the earls and barons who did not spend all of their time at court, but were in frequent attendance on the king and took an active part in central politics. Finally, there was the larger body of magnates who had little personal contact with Edward but were summoned on selected occasions to treat with him in afforced or great councils. The crown's reputation with the aristocracy largely depended on the power accorded to these various groups; and by comparing their influence at different points in the reign we can do much to explain the radical shifts in the king's political reputation.

Enough has already been said to indicate that it was household men who really dominated Edward III's council during his early years. The fact that several members of this inner clique were raised to earldoms in 1337 did little to disguise the considerable social and political gulf between favourites like William Montagu, Robert Ufford and William Clinton, and the established aristocracy led by the royal Earls of Norfolk and Lancaster. Montagu in particular exercised an influence quite out of proportion to his

15   The choir of Gloucester Abbey, built in the 1330s

station.[72] He accompanied the king on all military and diplomatic expeditions, and was always in attendance at court when the great seal changed hands or new ministers were admitted to office.[73] His own seal was occasionally used to validate royal letters;[74] and he sometimes claimed to act as a spokesman for the council in communicating its decisions to the chancery.[75] He even took it upon himself to authorize official business, ordering the appointment of a commission to deliver Colchester gaol, and postponing the settlement of the sheriff of Hampshire's account at the exchequer.[76] Not surprisingly, other members of the Montagu family benefited directly from the court connection. One of William's brothers, Simon, ended up as bishop of Ely; another, Edward, became a knight in the royal household, married the king's cousin Alice of Brotherton, and was eventually raised to the peerage.[77] The unenviable reputation earned by Salisbury and others during the campaigns of 1338–40 is better understood when we appreciate the extraordinary influence which these men had exerted over the king throughout the first decade of his effective rule.

It would be a mistake, of course, to push the distinction between courtiers and magnates too far. Some of the bannerets and knights who served in the king's household during the 1330s were themselves the scions of baronial houses: John Beaumont, Thomas Lucy, John Faucomberg, Maurice Berkeley, the two Beauchamp brothers, John and Giles, and their distant and more famous cousin Roger.[78] Nevertheless, the king's failure to secure the confidence of the earls and barons became ominously apparent within weeks of his departure for the continent in 1338. In a great council held at Northampton in August, the magnates objected to proposals set out in the Walton Ordinances for the ending of estallments and respites.[79] These were licences allowing debts owed to the crown to be paid off by instalment or to be excused for a specified period. The ruling on estallments seems to have remained in effect;[80] but by September 1339 the king had been forced to raise the ban on respites.[81] This example is of relatively little significance on its own. But when set against the growing opposition of parliaments and councils in the period 1338–40, it suggests an ambivalent attitude on the part of many noblemen from the very start of the French war. Edward's failure to convince the magnates left in England that he would act on their recommendations simply reinforced the prejudice against his inner circle of advisers. The crisis of 1341 was the direct result of a serious rift within the ranks of the king's council.

By the end of the 1340s, however, that conflict was over. Any political distinction between the courtiers and the aristocracy was now largely irrelevant. Edward's choice of household officials undoubtedly helped in this respect. The much-despised John Darcy, who had served first as steward (1337–40) and then as chamberlain (1342–6),[82] was now replaced by less controversial figures like Sir Bartholomew Burghersh the elder (chamberlain, 1347–55), Richard Talbot (steward, 1345–9) and John Grey of Rotherfield (steward, 1350–9). Significantly, these men were drawn from prominent baronial families, and were well qualified to represent the interests of their class even in the most secret and select meetings of the council. This attempt to draw the nobility back into regular contact with the court reached its climax in 1362, when Thomas de Vere, Earl of Oxford, successfully asserted an ancient family claim to act as hereditary chamberlain.[83] De Vere did not actually fulfil his office in person.[84] But at least one other earl, Richard Fitzalan, seems to have taken up more or less permanent residence at court during the years of peace in the 1360s.[85] This was a powerful symbol of baronial influence at the very centre of politics, the king's household.

Such developments had a profound effect on the wider group of magnates who normally only attended great councils. In 1342 Edward III called an extraordinary assembly of prelates and peers to discuss the defence of the realm, the state of the war in Scotland and the proposed campaign in Brittany.[86] A total of ten earls and ninety-six lay magnates were invited: more than twice the number that had been summoned to attend the parliament held in the previous year. There is no way of telling how many of these actually attended; and we may well suppose that the real influence rested, as always, with the king's closest friends. But by deliberately broadening the base of aristocratic council, Edward III was clearly attempting to make good the mistakes of the 1330s. This policy paid rich dividends. In March 1347, when the great majority of the magnates were occupied in the north or detained at the siege of Calais, a great council was summoned to meet at Westminster under the formal presidency of the king's infant son, Prince Lionel.[87] The secular peers summoned were the Earls of Lancaster, Surrey, Hereford, Pembroke, Devon, Oxford, Arundel and Huntingdon, and Lords Wake, Segrave, Despenser, Berkeley, and Grey of Ruthin. It is a vivid indication of the new political climate that this council was prepared to grant the king a forced loan of wool, a new duty on the export of cloth, and a temporary subsidy for the protection of shipping.[88] By authorizing levies which should arguably have been sanctioned by representatives of the community, the lords were laying themselves open to considerable political criticism. That they were prepared to accept this situation surely says much for their new-found confidence in the king and his cause.

Unfortunately, it becomes more difficult after 1347 to ascertain the frequency and composition of such extraordinary councils. From about 1350, summonses tended to be issued under the privy and secret seals and no record of such writs was kept in the central administration.[89] What evidence we have suggests that great councils were still only called on rare occasions, to discuss the problems of defence in 1359–60 and 1369–70, or the king's proposals for the government of Ireland in 1361–2.[90] On the other hand, not a year went by without some members of the nobility being called to attend on Edward and his innermost circle of advisers. In April 1353, for instance, a legal agreement made at Westminster between Sir James Audley and the king was witnessed by the Duke of Lancaster and the Earls of Northampton, Arundel, Warwick and Stafford, together with Roger Mortimer, Henry Percy, Bartholomew Burghersh, John Beauchamp and John Grey.[91] Later, in 1356, Richard Fitzalan, Guy Brian and Walter Mauny were among the lords assembled in council when news of the capture of John II reached England. And in May 1358 the exchequer met the expenses of the Earls of Warwick, Arundel, Suffolk and Stafford, dwelling at Westminster for two days on business probably associated with the negotiation of the French king's ransom.[92] These high-ranking noblemen provided just the sort of political influence which had been so lacking in the 1330s, and their active involvement in the business of state probably convinced most of the barons that the king was now receptive to their ideas. That this was done without any formal statutory guarantee, and with no real change in the actual process of consultation, says much about the pragmatic nature of Edward's regime.

THE MAGNATES AND THE LOCALITIES

The primary concern of any medieval nobleman lay with his family, his estates, and his 'country' — the region where he enjoyed political and social pre-eminence. Affairs of state might occupy a proportion of his time; but it was on his record as a husband, father, landholder and lord that he was most likely to be judged. Any medieval king wishing to create a successful and workable polity was therefore forced to acknowledge the lords' power in the provinces. Without a professional civil service in the shires, the crown inevitably depended on the magnates and their followers to ensure that administration and justice operated effectively. What distinguished the strong rulers of the later Middle Ages was their ability to restrain the more corrupt elements in the aristocracy and to ensure that the crown, rather than the magnates, derived the principal benefit from this system. Edward III's early record on such matters, as we have already seen, was hardly impressive. But the political conditions prevailing during the central period of the reign were much more encouraging, and allowed the king to establish a system of local government advantageous both to him and to his aristocratic supporters.

The authority wielded by the magnates after 1341 was indeed considerable. Throughout the later Middle Ages, the crown inevitably referred to the magnates when filling administrative posts in the shires. It was only natural, for instance, that the government should have followed up the Earl of Lancaster's suggestions for the replacement of a tax collector in Staffordshire in 1337, John Talbot's request for the removal of a commissioner of array in Gloucestershire in 1352, and John Beauchamp's recommendations for the replacement of searchers at the port of Southampton in 1355.[93] During his middle years, however, Edward III went notably further than this. Between 1344 and 1351 he granted several sheriffdoms as life interests to members of the nobility, temporarily increasing the total number of counties under such aristocratic control from five to eleven (Cambridgeshire and Huntingdonshire, Cornwall, Lancashire, Rutland, Shropshire, Staffordshire, Warwickshire and Leicestershire, Westmorland, and Worcestershire).[94] After 1350, Edward also allowed the peers to regain their place on the commissions of the peace.[95] By 1368, indeed, John of Gaunt was president of no fewer than nine such commissions (Leicestershire, Derbyshire, Hertfordshire, the three Parts of Lincolnshire, and the three Ridings of Yorkshire), and the Earl of Hereford of three (Essex, Huntingdonshire and Rutland).[96] In 1353 it was also agreed that a local lord be appointed to help keep the peace within each of the new provincial staples.[97] The regional authority temporarily jeopardized during the early 1340s was now being restored to the nobility, and with handsome interest.

It must be admitted that powers of this sort created many valuable opportunities for the more ambitious and unscrupulous members of the aristocracy. By appointing members of their own affinities as undersheriffs and deputy justices, they could exert a powerful, and not altogether beneficial, influence over administration and justice in the shires.[98] Edward III, moreover, was apparently happy to accept these implications. The ordinance of 1346 against the giving of fees to royal judges remained virtually a dead letter; and there is no indication that the government took steps to enforce the statutes of 1361 against the bribing of jurors and the nomination of judicial commissioners by interested parties.[99]

Queen Isabella nicely articulated the prevailing attitude in 1348, when she stated that her stewards should be put on judicial commissions 'to save and maintain our right and that which pertains to us'.[100] A whole series of formal and informal privileges, deliberately designed to build up the magnates' influence in the localities, had apparently become the necessary price paid by the crown for political peace.

This interpretation, however, is singularly one-sided. Given the nature of politics after the crisis of 1341, it seems highly unlikely that the king would have been prepared to increase the authority enjoyed by his great men without imposing some conditions on them. In particular, Edward expected his beneficiaries to observe standards of behaviour more acceptable to him and to the political community. If they failed in this duty, then they were publicly discredited. Thus in 1351 John, Lord Fitzwalter, was condemned to gaol by the court of king's bench for an alarming series of crimes committed in Essex during the previous decade. Although he subsequently secured a pardon, Fitzwalter had to pay the king nearly £850 to recover his lost estates.[101] Even John Molyns, whose restoration to favour after the inquiries of 1341 is so often taken as an example of Edward III's poor record on law and order, was eventually disgraced in 1357 and spent the last three years of his life in prison.[102] Such cases, like the trials of Chief Justice Thorp and Sir William de la Pole,[103] obviously harked back to the events of 1340–1 and left the magnates with a timely reminder of their responsibilities to the king and his subjects.

From the commons' point of view at least, this policy evidently proved successful. The period after 1341 witnessed a marked decline in the number of common petitions directed specifically against the nobles. Despite continued complaints about royal purveyance, for instance, there was no further mention of the magnates' abuse of prise between 1341 and the great Statute of Purveyance in 1362.[104] The lords also ceased to be singled out for criticism in the petitions on maintenance. The Ordinance of Justices of 1346 asserted that the magnates were still maintaining quarrels, and in 1348 the commons requested that the nobility be charged not to conceal and protect criminal gangs.[105] But for the next two decades such complaints were conspicuously lacking.[106] Nor was there any real disquiet about the influence of the magnates on the bench. Indeed, in 1352 the commons actively encouraged the king to involve the nobility in local justice by requesting that 'the great men of the realm, earls and barons, each in his own region' be associated with other loyal subjects in the commissions of the peace.[107] It is true that there were continued misgivings over the large number of franchises created in the 1330s, particularly since the king allowed the lords and tenants of liberties exemption from local levies to pay the wages of members of parliament.[108] But after the long and acrimonious debates over the abuse of privilege by the aristocracy during the 1320s and 1330s, the virtual silence of the commons during the mid-fourteenth century is indeed striking.

That silence is inevitably somewhat ambiguous. After the Black Death, the common petitions were dominated by the class interests of the gentry and the merchants, and had very little to say about the grievances of the lower classes.[109] The ending of complaints about the lords' abuse of prise and maintenance may simply suggest that the petty landholders in the commons were concealing practices in which they also indulged. This, however, is to ignore the revival of public hostility towards the magnates during the 1370s. In the Good Parliament, the knights and burgesses claimed that the great men of the realm were seizing crops and foodstuffs; that maintenance was rife among the king's courtiers and the justices of the peace; and that the lords were failing in their duty to defend the kingdom.[110] On the death of Richard Fitzalan in 1376, the people of Shropshire appealed to the king not to renew the life shrievalty of the county, complaining that they had suffered many injustices during the earl's regime.[111] The Good Parliament extended this into a general request for the cessation of all life sheriffdom.[112] There was also growing unease over the actions and influence of those who served in contract armies. In 1371 it was decided in parliament that no retainer of a great lord should be appointed as a tax collector, and in 1376 the military contingents of several leading noblemen were accused of oppressing the people of southern England.[113] By 1377 the granting of liveries (gifts of robes, caps or badges by great lords to their followers) was being perceived as a form of maintenance, and throughout the 1380s and 1390s attacks were to be made on the government of Richard II for its failure to constrain aristocratic influence in the courts.[114] It would obviously be naive to suggest that the magnates had been totally blameless during the middle decades of Edward III's reign. But this evidence does imply that they had exercised their powers altogether more discreetly. In the generation after 1341, the barons once more became responsible and respected members of the political community.

THE JOINTURE, THE USE AND THE ENTAIL

To suggest that the magnates ousted the king from control in the provinces, then, is to misinterpret the consequences of the Stratford crisis and to ignore the traditions of honour and service successfully revived by Edward III during his middle years. This bond of trust must also be kept in mind when examining the management of noble estates.[115] From the late thirteenth century the tenurial relationship between the crown and its tenants-in-chief had been undergoing major changes, and already by 1327 the nobility enjoyed much greater control over the disposition of their lands. It was becoming increasingly common, for instance, for tenants-in-chief to make 'jointures', settling their lands on themselves and their wives in joint tenure and thus preventing the king's agents from seizing the lands on the death of one or other partner. During Edward's middle years, the barons went one step further and began to adopt the device known as 'enfeoffment to use'. Under this arrangement, trustees were appointed to take charge of the family estate (or part of it), managing the lands on the lord's behalf and paying the profits to his receivers. The great advantage of the use was that when a tenant-in-chief died, his feoffees remained in control, and the king had no right to claim wardship of the estates during the period of vacancy before the heir rendered homage. Not surprisingly, therefore, the use has often been seen as a wily attempt to deprive a complacent king of his rights as feudal overlord. But to impute such sinister motives to the baronage is seriously to distort the context and the purpose of this development.

The earliest enfeoffments — such as those made by the Earls of Suffolk (1342), Warwick (1345), Lancaster (1349) and March (1359) — were *ad hoc* affairs designed to protect estates while the lords were away from England fighting for the king. If they returned safely, the uses were terminated. Indeed, it was not in the magnates' interests to allow trustees to take permanent control of their estates, for the use was a legal fiction and there was no proper judicial process for removing unscrupulous feoffees.[116] Such were the complications arising from the illegal seizure of the manor of Speen (Berkshire) by two former feoffees of William Hastings in 1349, for instance, that the case ended up coming before the council in parliament.[117] Such considerations presumably explain why the use took off only very slowly among the peerage, and why a good proportion of baronial estates were never subject to enfeoffment during Edward III's reign.

In fact, the earliest enfeoffments by tenants-in-chief seem to have been intended not so much to deprive the king of his rights of escheat as to prevent the government from granting custody of lands to other members of the nobility. We must remember that it was common practice for the crown to sell wardships to the highest bidders. The Earl of Warwick, for instance, offered £800 for Lord Clifford's lands in 1346; and in 1349 Sir Bartholomew Burghersh the elder secured temporary control of the valuable Despenser lands at a farm of £1,000 a year.[118] Bereaved families were naturally concerned about the exactions which such men might make on their estates and tenants, and on at least two occasions (in 1339 and 1376) the lords asked the king for a guarantee that wardships should always be granted to the next of kin.[119] It is possible, then, that the wider adoption of the use after the 1340s may have been precipitated by Edward's refusal to co-operate on this matter.[120] However, the crucial point about the whole system was that enfeoffments of lands held in chief required formal royal consent. And although there is little to suggest that Edward III adopted a very selective approach to requests for such licences, the fact remains that the majority of uses licensed by the crown before 1377 continued to be made by members of the nobility setting off for the king's wars. Quite simply, the use became another of those incentives — like respites of debts and immunity from assizes — offered to the aristocracy in return for military service.[121]

In the long term, of course, the use was bound to reduce the king's store of patronage and to restrict his control over the great estates. Indeed, Edward's apparent willingness to accommodate this new procedure is often seen as one of the most ominous political concessions of his reign.[122] It must be admitted that the king took the development somewhat lightly: no doubt his popular policy of compromising on feudal rights, already discussed, made him too eager to give up potentially important rights of wardship and escheat.[123] On the other hand, it would be a mistake to assume that the king was blind to the wider implications of his actions. The use certainly seems to have protected estates from being forfeited for acts of treason; but in 1361 Edward made it quite clear that no such immunity would exist in the (highly unlikely) event of full-scale rebellion against the crown.[124] Nor should we conclude that all the legal developments of this period automatically worked against the king's interests. The increasing tendency of the magnates in the fourteenth century to 'entail' their estates — that is, to specify the exact line of succession to the family holdings (normally through the male line only) — once again meant that the crown was deprived of its rights of wardship. But on some occasions it actually allowed the king to take over noble estates when the direct line failed.[125] Thus, when John Hastings enfeoffed and entailed a portion of the earldom of Pembroke in 1369, he granted the reversion of the property to the king; so that when the Hastings line eventually died out in 1389, the valuable lordship of Pembroke fell directly into the hands of Richard II.[126] This example may be atypical, but it does demonstrate that the legal developments of the fourteenth century still allowed the crown some room for manoeuvre. The most important point of all, however, is the apparent absence of any deliberate malice towards Edward III on the part of the nobility. It was only when Richard II began to abuse his seigneurial rights that the use became an important instrument of political opposition. If the barons felt greater security of tenure in the middle decades of the fourteenth century, it was not because they had radically altered the law of property, but simply because they had a king who could be trusted. Edward III was well aware that the easiest route to a nobleman's heart was via his land. It was the crown's great misfortune that Richard II failed to appreciate that maxim.

COURTIERS AND MAGNATES IN THE 1370s

A whole range of political factors therefore came together in the mid-fourteenth century to create one of the most productive alliances between crown and nobility known in the later Middle Ages. Inevitably, these happy conditions could not last for ever. The stability of this period depended on the personal relationships built up between the king and a small group of like-minded contemporaries. When Edward's friends died off in the 1360s and 1370s, the weaknesses in the system were bound to become evident. The campaigns of 1359–60 and the plague of 1361–2 took a heavy toll on the aristocracy, and several of Edward's leading supporters, including Robert Morley, John Beauchamp, Thomas Breadstone, Reginald Cobham, the Earls of March and Northampton and the Duke of Lancaster, died during this period. Subsequently, a number of leading magnates became disaffected with the regime and threw in their lot with the opposition during the Good Parliament. It is not surprising, therefore, that some historians have traced Richard II's political problems with the nobility back to the last years of Edward III.[127] But while there were undeniable deficiencies in the old king's policies, it seems highly unlikely that Richard was merely the innocent victim of his grandfather's mismanagement. This chapter will end with a fresh assessment of Edward's last years, and an attempt to re-evaluate the state of baronial politics at the time of his death in 1377.

One of the most striking features of the 1360s and 1370s was Edward III's reluctance to create new earldoms and baronies outside the royal family. Instead, he concentrated on integrating as many noble titles as possible into the Plantagenet line. There was a great spate of weddings between 1358 and 1362 which brought the young Earls of March and Pembroke and the heiresses to the duchy of Lancaster and the earldom of Kent into the royal family.[128] Lionel of Antwerp and John of Gaunt were raised to the rank of duke in 1362, and Edmund of Langley became Earl of Cambridge in the same year. Princess Isabella's husband Enguerrand de Coucy was made Earl of Bedford in 1366; and in 1374 the king's youngest son Thomas of Woodstock married the co-heiress to the Bohun estates, with the apparent expectation that he would become Earl of Hereford, Essex and Northampton.[129] These moves obviously beg comparison with Edward I's attempts to graft some of the greatest baronial dynasties on to his own family tree. Like his grandfather, Edward III was simply responding to a very obvious need to provide titles and

16   *The king presides in*
       parliament

inheritances for his younger children, and there was no real suggestion of a deliberate anti-baronial policy. But the tendency to view domestic and foreign policy primarily as a means of dynastic advancement meant that Edward neglected the younger generation of non-royal noblemen who came into their father's titles during the 1360s and 1370s. Until 1375, for instance, vacancies in the Order of the Garter were filled either by the king's sons and sons-in-law or by prominent members of the household, such as Richard Pembridge, Guy Brian and Alan Buxhull.[130] Edward maintained reasonably close contact with the Earl of Salisbury, and also with the new Earl of Warwick, Thomas Beauchamp II, who had earlier been a knight of the chamber.[131] But the new Earls of Devon, Stafford, Oxford and Suffolk seem to have had few links with the court. The only non-royal earl who kept up regular contact with the king in these years was Richard Fitzalan, whose death on the eve of the Good Parliament deprived Edward III of the last of his close contemporaries and advisers.

The king's dynastic plans were finally ruined by the series of mortalities and misfortunes that befell his children.[132] Lionel of Clarence died in 1368; the Earl of Pembroke spent the last three years of his life a prisoner of war, dying in 1375; and the Black Prince's illness removed him from effective military and political command after 1371. Edmund of Langley was in regular attendance at court in the 1370s, but his more able brother John of Gaunt spent most of his time on campaign in Scotland and on the continent. Thomas of Woodstock and the Earl of March were only in their teens and early twenties, and hardly provided an adequate royal following. The royal family also fell prey to faction. Historians have often seen the politics of the 1370s in terms of two rival aristocratic groupings: a 'court party', led by Pembroke and John of Gaunt, and a 'popular party' represented by the Black Prince and supported by his brothers Edmund and Thomas, together with their niece's husband the Earl of March.[133] It would be a mistake to see the divisions within the royal family in such stark terms, or to assume that all the aristocracy lined up conveniently under one or other party label. But the friction within the court was undeniable. There were indications, for instance, of a clash between March and John of Gaunt after the latter's inconclusive and expensive foray through France in 1373.[134] When the commons also became disillusioned by the war and the corruption of the court, it was inevitable that they would try to make political capital out of these tensions at the very highest levels of society.

This is not to say that Edward III totally neglected the magnates during his last years. Until about 1373, the war still united king and nobility in a common purpose. Although it became increasingly unlikely that they would be able to emulate the achievements of their fathers, the lords continued to give active support to Edward's military enterprise. They were encouraged to do so by the advantageous terms offered in their indentures: the right to castles, towns and lands captured in the king's name, and anything up to double the wage paid during the years of victory.[135] These incentives helped to offset the mounting war debts owed by the crown to leading members of the nobility.[136] The king's projected campaign of 1372, although called off, also served as an opportunity to reaffirm older solidarities. When aboard the Grace Dieu preparing this expedition, Edward personally received the homage of the new Earl of Stafford,[137] and no doubt expressed his hope that this newest recruit to the peerage would serve as loyally as his esteemed father. After the cessation of hostilities in 1375, moreover, the Earls of Warwick, Stafford and Suffolk reappeared at court.[138] Finally, the Garter also opened its ranks to the high nobility again: the new knights elected in 1375–6 included Suffolk and Stafford, as well as Sir Thomas Holand and Sir Thomas Percy.[139] Gestures of this sort compensated to some extent for the unpopularity of the courtiers, and probably made many of the nobility somewhat ambivalent about the prospect of an all-out attack on the crown.

What finally alienated the magnates, of course, was the ascendancy of Latimer, Neville and Perrers, and the control which they and other members of the household came to enjoy over royal patronage. Indeed, the real problem of Edward III's last years was not the supposed division of the aristocracy into two rival camps, but the frustration aroused in the vast majority of the baronage by a small group of royal favourites. The political conditions of the 1370s were in many ways similar to those of the 1330s, except that Edward's declining health allowed his courtiers even greater influence. Lord Latimer now virtually dictated who might have access to the monarch. In 1371, for instance, when the Earl of Pembroke tried to see the king at Marlborough on business arising from his dispute with Lord Grey of Ruthin, he was told that he would have to present his case through Latimer.[140] And when the monks of the alien priory at Takeley (Essex) wished to complain about Latimer's actions as custodian of their lands, they found it inadvisable to appeal to the king alone, and begged the assistance of Latimer's father-in-law, the elderly

Earl of Arundel.[141] By 1375, in fact, certain petitions received at court were even being endorsed with notes in Latimer's own hand purporting to represent the king's wishes. Significantly enough, the two earliest such petitions were made by the keeper of the privy seal, Nicholas Carew.[142] Certain officials were evidently taking advantage of Edward's infirmity to manipulate the machinery of patronage for their own advantage. This was certainly the view taken by the commons in 1376. We have already noted the attack which the Good Parliament made on the disposition of royal escheats and other feudal prerogatives.[143] The parallel debate over the leasing of hundreds provides further evidence of the intense suspicion aroused by the courtiers during these last years of the reign.

Throughout the fourteenth century it was common for certain hundreds and wapentakes (subdivisions of shires) to be leased out to the king's family or friends.[144] Those lucky enough to receive such grants paid an agreed rent to the exchequer, and took all the extra profits of the hundreds for themselves. At the start of Edward III's reign there had been complaints about this practice, and in the Statute of Northampton (1328) it had been stated that all hundreds should be rejoined to their counties.[145] But little had been done, and after the 1330s the issue had largely been forgotten. It was only after 1371 that fresh demands were made for the enforcement of the Statute of Northampton, culminating in an all-out attack on the leasing of hundreds in 1376.[146] Since the number of leases had not notably increased,[147] public concern must have been sparked off by other considerations. The chancery records provide the clue. The death of Queen Philippa in 1369 had brought a large number of manors and hundreds back into the king's hands. Rather than using these to strengthen the royal demesne or to endow high-ranking noblemen, the king simply assigned them to favoured soldiers and courtiers, who often paid very little for the privilege. Thus, the household knight Sir John Ipre received the manor and hundred of Isleworth (Middlesex) in 1374, at a farm of £123; but he was allowed to take £100 of this sum as his fee.[148] In 1370 an esquire of the royal household, George Felbridge, obtained the farm of North and South Erpingham (Norfolk); and in July 1376 he was granted the hundred of Rochford (Essex) for an indefinite period, and free of all payments to the exchequer.[149] Felbridge was one of many who narrowly escaped the wrath of the commons in 1376, for he was also involved in the controversial farm of the customs at Great Yarmouth and had close links with Hugh Fastolf and William Ellis, two Yarmouth merchants impeached in the course of the Good Parliament.[150] The commons' criticisms of hundred farmers in 1376 are better understood when they are seen as part of a general unease about the distribution of royal patronage and a particular suspicion of certain members of the royal household. Patronage, which had been exercised so effectively and successfully in the middle years of the reign, had once more become a pressing issue not only with the nobility but among the whole political community.

The deficiencies in Edward III's later policy towards the nobility are therefore undeniable. The political alienation of a large proportion of the peerage ensured a sympathetic hearing for the commons' programme in 1376 and sealed the fate of the courtiers. But whether the crisis of 1376 left a deep and permanent division in the ranks of the English nobility is another matter. The counter-attack launched by John of Gaunt in the winter of 1376–7 certainly antagonized some. In particular, the Earl of March resented losing the title of marshal to one of Gaunt's closest allies, Henry Percy.[151] But it is noticeable that most of the other leading opponents of the court had already been won over by the time Lord Latimer and Alice Perrers received their royal pardons in October 1376. Edmund of Langley and Thomas of Woodstock were both partly compensated for their rather meagre endowments by receiving offices, profits and property formerly held by Latimer and Richard Lyons.[152] Thomas, the more active and influential of the two, also seems to have made peace with his brother Gaunt.[153] By the time parliament and convocation met again in January 1377, even March was prepared to co-operate with the government in putting forward its urgent request for taxation.[154] The Good Parliament may well have produced a larger number of defections among the peerage than the crisis of 1341. But the outcome was much the same. A widespread reluctance to perpetuate the conflict and a general desire to re-establish friendly relations ensured that the intricate and rather tenuous alignments of 1376 rapidly broke down.

The general move towards reconciliation was undoubtedly spurred on by a growing concern over the king's health and the question of the succession. Edward III left no formal instructions for a regency in 1377. This apparent dereliction of duty has been variously explained as a result of his incapacitating illness, the bureaucratic inconvenience of ruling by committee, or the vaunting ambition of John of Gaunt.[155] However, it is quite possible that an informal consensus had actually been reached on this matter before the king's death. Edward rallied a little during the early months of 1377, and on 17 April he summoned a great council, including Salisbury, Warwick, Stafford, March, Suffolk and the new Earl of Arundel, Lords Percy, Basset and Fitzwalter, Sir Roger Beauchamp, and several other prominent laymen and clerics.[156] The king then moved on to the St George's Day celebrations at Windsor, where a large number of young noblemen and royals were knighted. Prince Richard and his cousin, Henry of Bolingbroke, were also admitted to the Order of the Garter.[157] The discussions which took place in these assemblies are unknown to us; but it is at least possible that the king and the barons used the occasions to make arrangements for the impending succession. Certainly, we know that some sort of regency administration was functioning in the weeks between Edward's death and the formal appointment of a continual council after Richard's coronation.[158] The old king had evidently appealed to that residue of respect which he could still command from his barons, asking them to unite in loyal support of his young grandson. This may have been naive, but it worked. The exile of Alice Perrers and a rush of new creations after Richard's succession appeased the majority of the nobility, and even allowed former rivals such as William Latimer and the Earl of March to work together on the various regency councils appointed between 1377 and 1381. Consequently, there is very little to suggest that the political issues of 1376–7 divided the baronage into opposing camps and created long-term factions that survived the minority of Richard II. Richard's problems with the nobility in the 1380s and 1390s were an indictment of his own style of monarchy, not that of his grandfather.

★   ★   ★

Edward III came as near as any medieval king to reconciling the interests of crown and nobility. At the start of his reign the magnates were an unruly and uncooperative group, suspicious of the government and resentful at their loss of public esteem. The crisis of 1341 taught them not only about political opposition, but also about the absolute necessity of reaching an understanding with the king. The reconciliation of the 1340s and 1350s was successful precisely because it was bilateral. Generosity may have been the hallmark of Edward's regime, but it was generosity with a purpose. Even in his last years, the king never resorted to the indiscriminate patronage lavished by Edward II on the Despensers or by Richard II on Robert de Vere. Edward III's aim — and one of his greatest achievements — was to revive the tradition of aristocratic service destroyed in the civil wars and political conflicts of the 1320s. That a vestige of unity and loyalty still remained in 1377 says much about the enduring qualities of the new alliance. Edward III may have avoided the strong-armed tactics of his grandfather. He may even have lacked something of Henry V's charismatic appeal. But his reign proved that there was nothing inherently incompatible between a powerful monarchy and a satisfied nobility. His *rapprochement* with the magnates made him one of the foremost exponents of the art of political management in the whole of the later Middle Ages.

7 The clergy

Next to the crown, the most powerful institution in medieval England was the church. The clergy belonged to a great international order which was highly conscious of its status and rights. Consequently, they formed an articulate and often highly critical force in politics. In a sense, of course, the 'church' included all those who, through personal conviction or sheer inertia, conformed to the beliefs and practices of catholic Christianity. But contemporaries tended to define the church as a select body of professional clergy whose vocation and status set them apart from the rest of society. It is with the latter group that we are presently concerned.

The numerical strength of the clergy under Edward III is difficult to judge. On the basis of the poll tax returns of 1377–81, it has been calculated that there were some 35,500 people in clerical and monastic orders, out of a total population of some two and a half to three million.[1] Unfortunately, it is virtually impossible to tell what the numbers were like before the Black Death. The monasteries, which were already in a state of decline before 1350, probably never recovered from the shock.[2] The plague of 1348–9 also carried off large numbers of beneficed secular clergy: an average of 40 per cent in the dioceses of York, Lincoln and Coventry and Lichfield.[3] On the other hand, there was a rush of vocations in the 1350s; and although the wage demands of chaplains suggest a slight decline in the number of unbeneficed seculars by the 1360s,[4] the grand total probably did not alter very much between 1348 and 1377. On a very rough estimate, we may conclude that 1–1.5 per cent of the population — and perhaps as many as 3 per cent of all adult males — would have been classified as clergy in mid–fourteenth–century England.

The clergy were a diverse and disparate group, and a huge gulf separated the elite corps of seventeen English and four Welsh bishops from the great mass of unbeneficed clerks. Many ecclesiastics identified more easily with their counterparts in secular society: prelates with peers, and parish priests with peasants. On the other hand, the church transcended social class and secular loyalties, and offered its professional servants many opportunities for collective action. Most important in this respect were the periodic meetings of the clergy in diocesan and provincial councils (which dealt with matters of discipline and doctrine) and convocations (which discussed more practical issues, such as taxation). As we shall see, these assemblies could make a considerable impression on the political life of the nation, debating royal policy, helping to fund the king's wars, and securing statements on the legal and constitutional rights of the church. The *communitas cleri* (community of the clergy) was indeed an active force in the medieval polity.[5]

THE KING AND THE CLERGY

For much of his reign, Edward III enjoyed an enviable reputation with the church. Despite his occasional clashes with the English hierarchy and the papal court at Avignon, Edward was generally regarded as a pious man, and his wars as a kind of divine mission fought for the defence of true religion. Around 1350, clerical writers were drawing enthusiastic parallels with Judas Maccabeus and Solomon, with Arthur and Charlemagne.[6] By the end of the century, indeed, Thomas Walsingham was describing Edward III as a great Christian king, 'outstanding in his devotion to God, often making pilgrimages, and venerating and honouring priests of the church'.[7] Much of this later tradition arose from mere nostalgia, and did not necessarily reflect the reality of church-state relations in the 1340s and 1350s. Nevertheless, Edward's prodigious successes in France and Scotland impressed the clergy just as much, if not more, than they did the laity; and for most of the second half of his reign at least, the king had little difficulty in reconciling the English church with his own political and military ambitions.

It had not always been thus. The clergy, like the rest of society, were deeply divided and disrupted by the events of the 1320s, and it took some years before the young Edward III won the confidence of the hierarchy.[8] Certain bishops — notably Orleton of Worcester, Stratford of Winchester, Burghersh of Lincoln and Airmyn of Norwich — had backed the palace revolution of 1326–7. But Isabella and Mortimer had been incapable of sustaining this support, and personal quarrels had soon broken out within the episcopate. By 1328 Stratford, together with Bishop Gravesend of London and Archbishop Mepham of Canterbury, had become closely identified with the political opposition of Henry of Lancaster; and in 1330 both Gravesend and Archbishop Melton of York were implicated in the rebellion of the Earl of Kent. Although the bishops naturally rallied around the young king when he seized power late in 1330, Edward III did comparatively little to reduce underlying tensions. Particularly divisive were the king's efforts to deprive William Zouche of the archbishopric of York and to set up his own man, William Kilsby, as northern metropolitan in 1340.[9]

The church also suffered considerable hardships as a result of the collapse of law and order in the provinces. In 1327–8 there was a series of attacks on the great monastic houses of Abingdon, St Albans and Bury St Edmunds.[10] In 1336 the villeins of Darnhall and Over (Cheshire) rose in open rebellion against their lord, the Abbot of Vale Royal.[11] Bishop Grandisson of Exeter complained of the ransacking of ecclesiastical property in his diocese; and in 1333 the new bishop of Carlisle, John Kirkby, was subjected to verbal and physical threats in his own city.[12] Failing to get satisfaction from the king, some members of the higher clergy themselves resorted to dubious or even criminal practices. Several monastic houses set up special funds with which to bribe judges and juries, while the canons of Lichfield Cathedral employed the notorious Coterel gang to carry out a campaign of intimidation against their rivals.[13] Meanwhile, the king and his agents inflicted further material damage by flouting the church's theoretical immunity from purveyance and taking foodstuffs from ecclesiastical estates.[14] In 1328 Edward was said to be riding around the country seizing the goods of churches, in direct contravention of his coronation oath and Magna Carta.[15] The oppressions suffered on the Kent manors of

Christ Church, Canterbury during the 1330s indicate the harsh reality behind such generalizations.[16] Had Edward III been deposed in 1340–1 (as Archbishop Stratford at least thought possible)[17] it is most unlikely that he would ever have been regarded as a friend of the church.

Twenty years later, the king's image was strikingly different. By a mixture of good luck and sound strategy, Edward had restored authority over the church and respect within it. Political thought and public opinion were now virtually unanimous in seeing the monarch as the natural head of the church within his lands. In the past, such an Erastian viewpoint had created considerable conflict: both Henry II and Edward I had provoked major constitutional crises in their attempts to take over the ecclesiastical courts and to exploit the financial resources of the church. The reign of Edward III was certainly not without its conflicts: both John Stratford and John Thoresby made important stands on points of clerical privilege. But so long as Edward III continued to embody the ideals of militant Christianity, most of his clerical subjects were quite happy to accept the reality of royal sovereignty. The church never ceased to be sensitive about the infringement of its liberties, and constantly grumbled about the weight of royal taxation. But the vast majority of the clergy had no hesitation in expressing their personal loyalty to the king and giving public support to his cause.

There were four particular ways in which the church contributed to the regime of Edward III: it provided the king with a source of patronage; it gave administrative support to the state; it helped to promote the war effort; and it supplied revenue for the royal treasury. It may be instructive to examine each of these four areas before proceeding to a more general assessment of ecclesiastical politics in this eventful reign.

The Church and Patronage

The church was the single greatest source of patronage available to the crown in the Middle Ages. The king had a certain number of ecclesiastical offices directly in his gift, and many other appointments were influenced by him. Edward III's predecessors had long appreciated that the best way of maintaining good relations with the church was by controlling its personnel, and since the late thirteenth century the crown had deliberately set out to increase the number of benefices under its control.[18] This campaign took a number of directions. To begin with, more use was now made of advowsons attached to the noble and ecclesiastical estates periodically falling into the king's hands. The seizure of the alien priories during periods of war with France was of particular importance in this respect: indeed, the benefices normally under the control of these religious houses accounted for almost half the titles granted by Edward III between 1337 and 1360. In addition, the early years of the fourteenth century saw the development of a new principle whereby any benefice attached to a cathedral or monastic house and filled by the king during an episcopal or abbatial vacancy was thereafter deemed to be in the permanent gift of the crown. In order to uphold this often controversial claim, the government began to prosecute rival patrons in the common law courts, and not surprisingly secured favourable judgments even in the most dubious of cases.[19] The cumulative effect of this aggressive policy was very striking. On average, Edward I had presented to about twenty-six benefices a year. But in the period 1307–37 the annual figure shot up to seventy, and by 1337–47 it stood still higher at a remarkable 123. It is small wonder that by the 1340s Edward III was being heralded as 'patron paramount' of the English church.[20]

This achievement was all the more impressive given the efforts of contemporary popes to appropriate English benefices for their own use. John XXII granted a total of 630 provisions and expectancies to English benefices during his seven-year pontificate (1328–34).[21] The number of papal provisions dropped under Benedict XII, but rose again sharply after the election of Clement VI, and averaged about 150 a year between 1342 and 1352.[22] By the middle of Edward III's reign, papal provisions had become a permanent reality in the church and an increasingly important issue in ecclesiastical politics.

It would be easy to assume that the simultaneous development of royal and papal claims created competition and hostility. In fact, the consequences varied according to the offices in question. So far as bishoprics were concerned, there was no real clash of interests between Westminster and Avignon. The appointment of Ralph Stratford to the see of London in 1340 was the last occasion on which a bishop was elected and consecrated without formal authority from Avignon.[23] But far from threatening royal interests, papal provisions normally worked in the king's favour, and Edward III usually had little difficulty in persuading the Curia to accept his own nominees for English sees. The real losers were the cathedral chapters, which greatly resented the infringement of their traditional right to elect bishops. The king's attitude to this problem is extremely revealing. There were at least twenty-seven occasions in Edward III's reign when a bishop was elected by the relevant chapter, only to be challenged by an alternative candidate holding a papal provision.[24] In eight of these cases the king formally consented to the election, but withdrew without protest as soon as the papacy intervened.[25] And in five further cases he actively opposed the capitular candidates for the very good reason that the Pope already had royal servants lined up for the relevant bishoprics.[26] There were, admittedly, a number of occasions when the king had a struggle to get his own men in. Diplomatic tensions and genuine disquiet about the educational backgrounds of royal nominees made Urban V extremely reluctant to accept the appointment of John Buckingham to Lincoln in 1362–3 and of William Wykeham to Winchester in 1366–7.[27] In general, however, papal provisions rarely threatened the crown's *de facto* control over the episcopate, and indeed did much to create a loyal and amenable bench of bishops.

Lower down in the church the results of royal and papal patronage were rather more complicated. Both the crown and the papacy tended to concentrate on the prebendal stalls of secular cathedrals and collegiate churches. These were titular benefices which could be held *in absentia* and in plurality, and were therefore ideally suited to the needs of busy royal clerks and curial officials. It would probably have been possible for the two sides to co-operate here had it not been for the competing claims of other interested parties. Both king and Pope tended to ignore the rights of the original patrons of the benefices, who in the case of cathedral prebends were usually the relevant bishops. By the 1340s this situation was creating considerable dissatisfaction. If the king secured a legal judgment confirming his right to appoint to a contested benefice, the dispossessed patron and his protégé were forced to appeal to the Curia and secure a provision challenging the royal presentation. The bishops were well aware that this might simply allow the Pope to appropriate the disputed benefice for his own — or even the king's — use. But they had no other means of redress. Consequently the 1340s witnessed a very notable increase both in the number of appeals registered at Avignon and in the number of English benefices being contested between royal clerks and papal provisors.[28] Edward III was forced to admit that papal provisions might soon begin to threaten his influence over some of the most prized sinecures in the English church.

What eventually drove the king to action were the anti-papal sentiments expressed in a series of parliamentary petitions between 1343 and 1351.[29] The commons believed — mistakenly — that the English church was being filled with foreigners and that good English money was being drained into the pockets of a corrupt cardinalate and a Francophile Pope. In 1343–4 Edward III responded by imposing a ban on the admission of all aliens bearing provisions to English benefices and instigating inquiries into the number of foreign clergy resident in England. Finally, in 1351, he issued the Statute of Provisors, which theoretically prohibited the execution of all papal provisions within the English church.[30]

This legislation has often been dismissed as a publicity stunt intended to placate parliament and to put added pressure on the Pope at a difficult moment in the Anglo-French negotiations. There is certainly no sign that Edward III tried to implement its more far-reaching clauses. Papal provisions to bishoprics and prebends continued as before, and the king never actively used the right (claimed directly from the Pope) to appoint to all benefices left vacant by their patrons for six months. Nevertheless, it would be a mistake to dismiss the statute as a mere irrelevance. The most significant clause was that which gave the crown the right to take action against dispossessed provisors who appealed to Avignon against the decisions of the royal courts. There was nothing particularly new about this procedure, or about the minor amendments made to it in the Statute of Praemunire of 1353.[31] But the inclusion of these details in formal legislation enrolled on the statute roll may be seen as a public declaration of intent by the crown. Even as the Statute of Provisors was being formulated, the king was embroiled in a dispute with Bishop Grandisson over the appointment of a wardrobe official, Richard Eccleshall, to a church in the diocese of Exeter. When all the hyperbole is stripped away, the Statutes of Provisors and Praemunire can be seen as a wily attempt to seize still more benefices for the use of the crown and to eliminate all effective opposition to the king's more controversial claims.

The results, however, were unsatisfactory. Edward had reckoned without the powerful opposition developing within the church. In 1352 the clergy complained bitterly about the king's arbitrary seizure of Bishop Grandisson's temporalities, and his habit of searching ever further back into history for examples of cathedral prebends filled by the crown during episcopal vacancies.[32] Edward was forced to step down, and agreed that he would no longer collate to benefices reserved by the crown prior to his own accession.[33] The crisis therefore ended in a tactful truce. Indeed, Edward became notably more scrupulous in the years after 1352, and even revoked some of the more dubious presentations made earlier in his reign.[34] Consequently, by the time that the ban on proceedings in foreign courts was reiterated in the Statute of Praemunire, the number of appeals registered at Avignon against royal presentees was already declining.[35] The records of the 1350s leave the distinct impression that the crown, private patrons, and the papacy had reached a successful compromise which guaranteed to each party a portion of the available patronage in the English church.

From the king's point of view, there was much to be said for this new agreement. Between 1352 and 1359 the number of royal presentations to English benefices averaged 108 a year, a figure only slightly lower than in the 1340s.[36] Admittedly, the restoration of the alien priories during the truce of 1360–9 substantially reduced the available stock of patronage: during the regnal year 1364–5, for instance, the total number of royal presentations was only forty-nine.[37] But this alone does not explain the crown's decision in 1365 to reissue the Statutes of Provisors and Praemunire. The real aggressor in the 1360s was the Pope. Urban V not only made numerous provisions to English benefices, he also issued a bull in 1364 denouncing and outlawing pluralism in the church.[38] The English bishops were forced to make inquiries into the number of benefices held in plurality in their dioceses, and the returns made it quite obvious that royal civil servants stood to lose most from the ban.[39] The only way Edward could protect his clerks was by preventing papal providees from entering their benefices, and the statutes of 1351–3 were therefore put back into operation.[40] In 1375, however, Gregory XI formally gave up his predecessor's attempts to reserve benefices resigned by or seized from pluralists and agreed to support the claims of certain English clerks currently in dispute with papal provisors. Finally, in February 1377, the crown agreed to a sort of amnesty on ecclesiastical appointments, stating that all benefices vacant before that date and not yet filled should be surrendered to their customary patrons.[41] By the time of Edward III's death, then, the crown and the papacy had realized that both their interests were probably best served by a return to the compromise of the 1350s.

The ecclesiastical patronage of the English crown is a large and complicated subject, and we have focused on only one aspect of it here. Undoubtedly the king's main concern was to provide for the large and acquisitive group of clerks employed in his household and in the government departments. If he was unable to give them church offices he would be forced to pay them large salaries, and this would undoubtedly prove a severe financial strain on the crown. Apart from its more symbolic value, then, ecclesiastical patronage was of great practical importance. It also had a political dimension. Edward III's ability to manipulate the system of papal provisions to English bishoprics and his successful appropriation of so many cathedral prebends ensured that amenable civil servants filled some of the greatest offices in the English church. Contrary to contemporary assumptions, the hierarchy was never entirely staffed by the creatures of Edward III. But the decline of effective political opposition from the church, to which we shall return, undoubtedly owed something to the king's extraordinary influence over the higher clergy. All medieval kings enjoyed power in the church; but few could match the achievement of Edward III.

The Church and Government

The English crown inevitably looked to the clergy for support in the formidable task of running the country. Not only did the church possess a sophisticated system of administration and justice, but many of its more powerful members also exercised secular jurisdiction delegated to them by the crown.[42] The heads of some of the old-established monasteries, notably the East Anglian and fenland houses of Bury St Edmunds, Ely, Peterborough, Croyland and Ramsey, ruled over their own liberties, where they had the right to hold their own courts, to execute royal writs, and to receive some of the judicial penalties normally accruing to the king. The greatest of all the ecclesiastical liberty-holders was the Bishop of Durham, whose county palatine was run as an autonomous unit normally immune from the king's judges, sheriffs and tax collectors. At many different levels, then, the church was expected to represent the authority of the crown and to maintain the interests of the state.

During the early years of Edward III's reign the government tried to win popularity by bestowing further secular power on members of the higher clergy. Mortimer and Isabella granted generous privileges to Bishop Beaumont of Durham and Archbishop Melton of York, and allowed the clergy of Lincoln Minster to run their cathedral close as an independent unit free from intervention by the city authorities.[43] Edward III seems to have agreed with this policy, for in 1335 he granted Archbishop Stratford additional rights of jurisdiction on the Canterbury estates.[44] In the 1340s and 1350s, however, official attitudes changed markedly. Stratford's quarrel with the king and his refusal to accept trial in a royal court made the crown much more suspicious of the power of the prelates. Consequently, Edward's government began to override some of the privileges claimed by ecclesiastical liberty-holders, particularly with regard to judicial penalties imposed by royal judges.[45] There were even efforts to challenge the bishopric of Durham's immunity from national taxation and to force the laity of this region to contribute to direct subsidies in 1338, 1344, 1348 and 1371.[46]

It would be a mistake, however, to suppose that these initiatives represented a co-ordinated attack on ecclesiastical privileges. On the whole, Edward III concentrated less on challenging long-standing rights and more on building up the loyalty and co-operation of his prelates. According to the chroniclers, the king established close friendships with Abbot Thomas de la Mare of St Albans and with William Clowne, head of the great Augustinian house at Leicester.[47] His success in securing the promotion of two royal clerks, Richard Bury and Thomas Hatfield, to the bishopric of Durham was particularly important in guaranteeing sound government in the north. One tangible result was the agreement reached in 1341 whereby felons from the northern counties who attempted to evade justice by escaping into the palatinate of Durham were to be captured and delivered back to the relevant authorities for trial.[48] Edward also made good use of his powers as arbitrator to resolve a number of serious squabbles between high-ranking churchmen. In 1351, for instance, he appealed directly to Bishop Bateman of Norwich to end an acrimonious dispute with the Abbot of Bury St Edmunds which had been raging in the royal and papal courts for over six years.[49] The king's character and reputation therefore did just as much as his government's aggressive attitude to re-establish authority over the church in the years following the Stratford crisis.

17   Edington Priory, Wiltshire

The bishops and abbots were most obviously involved in matters of government and high politics during their visits to the capital. Despite owning town houses, most of the members of the episcopate seem to have disliked spending long periods in London: apart from the chancellor and treasurer, indeed, the only prelates who usually attended meetings of the administrative council were the Archbishop of Canterbury (normally resident at Lambeth Palace) and the Bishop of London.[50] On the other hand, the episcopal bench always included a number of distinguished diplomats and former civil servants who were naturally called upon to give advice in plenary sessions or great councils. In the first half of Edward III's reign this group was dominated by veterans of the previous regime: William Airmyn of Norwich (d. 1336), Henry Burghersh of Lincoln (d. 1340), Adam Orleton of Worcester, and subsequently of Winchester (d. 1345), and Roger Northborough of Coventry and Lichfield (d. 1358). The only councillor-bishop of this period who had close personal links with the young king himself was Richard Bury of Durham (1333–45). Later, however, the old guard gave way to a collection of curialist bishops, all of whom owed their promotion directly to Edward III. These included Thomas Hatfield of Durham (1345–81), Adam Houghton of St David's (1362–89), John Buckingham of Lincoln (1363–98) and Thomas Brantingham of Exeter (1370–94).[51] In addition, there was usually a small number of bishops who did not travel regularly to the capital, but who were occasionally employed as royal envoys and whose particular connections or skills allowed them to be considered as royal councillors. The most important members of this category were Henry Gower of St David's (1328–47), Simon Montagu of Worcester (1334–7) and Ely (1337–45), Ralph Shrewbury of Bath and Wells (1329–63), William Bateman of Norwich (1344–55) and Robert Wyville, the former secretary of Queen Isabella and long-lived bishop of Salisbury (1330–75).[52] Although the total number of the higher clergy actively involved in politics at any one time was therefore comparatively small, it is probably fair to say that the hierarchy provided a regular source of expertise and advice for Edward III's regime.

In theory at least, the higher clergy were also expected to fulfil their role as royal councillors during meetings of parliament. All the English and Welsh bishops, and certain abbots and priors, received personal summonses to the king's parliaments. The writ sent to each bishop also included the so-called *praemunientes* clause, which required the attendance at parliament of representatives of his cathedral and diocesan clergy. This clause had been a source of much controversy when it was first introduced in 1295, for the clergy denied the king's right to summon them before a secular court. Although the phrase was permanently incorporated into writs of summons after 1334, the crown made no attempt to enforce it after 1340, and while some clerical proctors continued to attend parliament in the later fourteenth century, their number and influence was negligible.[53] Consequently, any remaining ecclesiastical influence in these assemblies was maintained largely by the prelates.

Even the higher clergy, however, seem to have been very reluctant to accept their obligation to attend parliaments. In part, this was a point of principle. In 1341 a number of abbots secured exemptions from summons on the grounds that they did not hold their estates by barony, and several other religious were relieved of such responsibilities in Edward III's later years.[54] Consequently, the number of heads of monastic houses summoned to parliament dropped from between thirty and thirty-three in the 1330s to an average of twenty-six in the years 1343–77. In any case, that figure considerably exceeded the number that actually turned up, for neither the abbots nor the bishops proved at all enthusiastic about the supposed honour of receiving a personal summons to parliament. Absenteeism was the norm. In the winter of 1332–3 only the Archbishop of York, the Bishops of Carlisle and Lincoln, and the Abbots of York and Selby bothered to attend an assembly at York; and the opening speech in the parliament of 1344 was heard by just four bishops and four abbots and priors.[55] The prelates covered themselves by appointing proxies: the scholar Thomas Bradwardine acted as representative for Bishop Bury of Durham in the parliament of 1344,[56] and in 1352 the Abbot of St Augustine's, Canterbury employed the services of Michael Northborough, keeper of the privy seal and a close kinsman of the Bishop of Coventry and Lichfield.[57] The government clearly disliked this practice, and sometimes issued supplementary letters requesting the personal attendance of the prelates.[58] In 1354 Edward III even provided ships to transport the victuals needed by Hatfield of Durham and his retinue during their stay at parliament.[59] But none of this had much effect. We are left with the distinct impression that participation in parliament was confined to a hard core of 'political' bishops, abbots and proctors.

The clergy themselves probably regarded this development as a modest constitutional achievement, since it showed that the crown was incapable of forcing clerics to attend secular courts. Ironically, however, it was to be highly damaging to the other ambitions of the church, for it isolated the clergy from the rest of political society and hindered their efforts to obtain concessions from the crown. This situation, as we shall see, was already becoming evident after the 1350s, and was considerably to strengthen the crown's position in relation to its clerical subjects during Edward III's later years.

The Clergy and the King's Wars

Despite their membership of an international order based on the precepts of Christian charity, the clergy came to be some of the most enthusiastic supporters of Edward III's military adventures. For some at least, the war provided professional advancement. The acquisition of territory in France was particularly important in this respect, since the king needed able clerks to take on the administration of his new dominions. The treasurership of Calais, for instance, was filled by a succession of former wardrobe officials, William Shrewsbury (1348–50), Richard Eccleshall (1351–61), Thomas Brantingham (1361–8) and William Gunthorpe (1368–73); while John Buckingham, a former keeper of the privy seal, became co-lieutenant of Brittany in 1358–9.[60] One of the Black Prince's associates, John Harwell, did especially well in Gascony, moving from the office of constable of Bordeaux to become the first English chancellor of Aquitaine (1364–*c*.1370).[61]

Churchmen were also much in demand for the king's diplomatic service. The closest thing to an international lawyer in the fourteenth century was a graduate in civil or canon law, and Edward III showed a distinct preference for such men when selecting his advisers.[62] Among the bishops who acted as royal ambassadors during this reign were Adam Orleton, William Airmyn, Henry Burghersh, Richard Bury, Richard Bentworth, John Stratford, John Thoresby and John Offord in the first half of the reign, and William Bateman, Simon Islip, Gilbert Welton, Adam Houghton, John Barnet and Simon Sudbury in the later years.[63] At a lower level, there was a veritable army of university graduates and notaries who helped to organize negotiations and to compile the copious correspondence associated with international diplomacy. During the 1340s and 1350s, this group included John Carlton, William Loughborough, Henry Chaddesden, John Lecche, and Chancellor Offord's brother Andrew, together with John Branketre, John Welwick and William Tirrington.[64] The Hundred Years War clearly provided an important outlet for the academic and administrative qualifications of a considerable number of English clerics.

The lure of war was such that some ecclesiastics even took up arms. The soldier clerk was still very much a reality in the fourteenth century. William Beauchamp, son of the Earl of Warwick, renounced his clergy and gave up a promising career in the church in order to take part in the military exploits which delighted so many other members of his family.[65] The clerical contribution to the Scottish war was particularly important. The northern prelates had always been involved in the defence of the Scottish border, and the bishops of Carlisle were regularly appointed as wardens of the march during Edward III's reign.[66] Archbishop Zouche of York, accompanied by John Kirkby of Carlisle, actually led the

English forces at the battle of Neville's Cross. The greatest of the warrior bishops, however, was Thomas Hatfield, who fought in the Crécy-Calais campaign and served in the king's Scottish expedition during the winter of 1355–6. Away from the northern march, other high-ranking clergy were also expected to take on responsibility for military matters. Eleven bishops and five abbots were among those appointed to supervise the defence of the southern shires when war broke out in 1337.[67] In the late 1330s the doughty Abbot of Battle put together his own fighting force to protect the abbey and help guard the south coast from invasion.[68] The church was officially exempt from arrays for local defence, but in 1369 the prelates of the southern province agreed in parliament that ecclesiastics should henceforth contribute to such levies. Consequently, in the 1370s the parish clergy became fully and actively involved in the medieval equivalent of a home guard.[69]

For the great majority of churchmen, however, the war effort was concentrated not on the battlefield but in the pulpit. The church provided one of the most effective means of broadcasting news and propaganda, and Edward III regularly called upon the clergy to advertise his military needs and the justice of his cause. After each of the great victories — Halidon Hill, Sluys, Crécy, Les Espagnols sur Mer, Poitiers, Nájera — the king wrote to the bishops requesting that thanks be offered to the Almighty for the deliverance of the realm.[70] They were apparently happy to respond. Successive bishops of Lincoln, for instance, offered forty days' indulgence to all those attending masses and processions for war and peace, and regularly enjoined their clergy to supplement the liturgy with special wartime prayers in the vernacular.[71] Some of the greatest preachers of the day also lent their support to Edward's cause. After the battle of Crécy, Thomas Bradwardine preached before the king on the text 'God who always leads us in triumph grants victory to those whom he wills, and he wills to grant victory to the virtuous' (2 Corinthians ii: 14).[72] When news of the same event reached London, the scholarly Richard FitzRalph found an even more promising hook on which to hang a tub-thumping sermon: 'May they offer sacrifices of sweet savours unto the God of heaven, and pray for the life of the king and of his sons' (Ezra vi: 10).[73] With such attitudes prevailing among the clergy, it is no surprise to find that a strong sense of political nationalism and moral superiority developed in mid-fourteenth-century England.

This is not to say that the church was a helpless instrument of royal propaganda. At some points in the reign, indeed, churchmen showed themselves fundamentally critical of the war and its effects. Much of the protest literature of the 1330s probably flowed from the quills of parish priests and friars well aware of the intense hardships suffered by the king's ordinary subjects through oppressive taxation.[74] After Edward made his claim to the throne of France, and began by his victories to prove that he had God on his side, many a clerical conscience was eased. FitzRalph, for instance, though still troubled by the social consequences of fighting, did not hesitate to declare Edward's French enterprise a just war.[75] Moreover, the clergy themselves were drawn more and more into the process of diplomacy. Royal envoys were sent to convocation to keep the church well informed of the progress of negotiations; and in 1354 the bishops actually appointed proctors to attend the current round of talks with the French.[76] In this way the church, like other sections of political society, became inextricably bound up in the king's military and diplomatic ambitions, and had little choice but to give public support to his cause.

Later in the reign, when English fortunes declined, it was inevitable that some members of the clergy should again question both the practicality and the morality of war. Thomas Brinton, Bishop of Rochester (1373–89), the most famous preacher of his day, believed in the essential rightness of Edward's cause, but was highly critical of the new round of campaigns in France, seeing the English defeats as the punishment of God on an irreligious people.[77] By the late 1370s, John Wyclif and John Gower were beginning to question the whole idea of the just war, and by extension to condemn some forty years of military activity.[78] Nor were these sentiments confined to a few intellectuals and extremists. The activities of the clerical proletariat during the Peasants' Revolt suggest considerable political disillusionment among the parish clergy in Edward's declining years.[79] It would therefore be a great mistake to suppose that churchmen stood by meekly as the government requisitioned their pulpits for political service. But so long as Edward III lived, these rumbles of discontent did little to threaten the mutual support system built up between crown and church. The majority of the clergy volunteered their services freely and gladly to promote the virtues of the war and the valour of their king. The political consequences were incalculable.

The Clergy and Royal Finance

For all the administrative and moral support which it provided, the church was most useful to Edward III as a source of supplies. The king spent much of his reign begging money from his subjects, and since the clergy controlled a significant proportion of landed property and movable wealth it was deemed only reasonable that they should contribute their share of the cost of war.[80] There were three ways by which the crown might tap such resources: by exploiting its feudal rights over the church; by demanding loans; and by levying direct taxes. As money-making enterprises, the first two methods were much less successful than the last, but they deserve some brief mention before we proceed to a more detailed analysis of clerical taxation in the mid–fourteenth century.

The lands of the bishops and some of the great monastic houses were held in chief from the crown, and were therefore liable to be taken into the king's hands on the death of an incumbent or as punishment for some serious offence.[81] Earlier rulers had often left bishoprics empty for long periods in order to reap substantial profits from their estates. By the fourteenth century, however, vacancies were much shorter. Under Edward III, indeed, the gap between the death of one bishop and the delivery of lands to his successor was rarely more than twelve months.[82] A statute of 1340 also allowed the relevant cathedral or monastic chapter the option of farming the vacant temporalities;[83] and although there were later to be some complaints about the unscrupulous actions of royal agents on church lands,[84] this legislation seems to have proved effective in protecting the interests of the great ecclesiastical landholders.

The seizure of temporalities from contumacious bishops was a slightly different matter. This had a political as well as a financial dimension, and was therefore a more jealously guarded privilege. Early in his reign, Edward III had to tread warily, for some of his principal supporters (Bishops Burghersh, Orleton and Airmyn) had suffered arbitrary confiscations at the hands of the Despensers, and were likely to oppose any similar attacks on their colleagues.[85] In 1340, the king actually declared that ecclesiastical estates could not be seized without due cause.[86] The confiscation of Bishop Grandisson's temporalities in 1350–1 also provoked controversy, and in 1352 the clergy demanded that a mere judgment for contempt should not be sufficient grounds for seizure.[87] The results can be seen in 1355, when the king took the side of his cousin, Lady Wake, in a dispute with the Bishop of Ely, and ordered the seizure of the temporalities pending a trial.[88] The royal councillors advised that this action would be contrary to the statute of 1340, and refused to carry out Edward's instructions.[89] It was only when a judgment of felony was passed against Bishop Lisle in October 1356 that the ministers were prepared to co-operate and to take the episcopal estates into the king's hands.[90] Edward successfully confiscated the Chichester temporalities in 1365, when Bishop Lynn contravened the recently reissued Statute of Praemunire.[91] But in 1376–7 the crown once again excited controversy by its apparently arbitrary seizure of Bishop Wykeham's estates.[92] The king was certainly not indifferent to the financial advantages which such confiscations brought: the Ely estates alone provided him with an extra income of £2,000 a year between 1356 and 1362.[93] But the political repercussions, coupled with the problems of direct estate management after the Black Death,[94] persuaded him to use his regalian rights sparingly. Edward appreciated the symbolic importance of his feudal prerogatives, but he had other, more lucrative, ways of making money.

The king also seems to have made surprisingly little use of the clergy as a source of credit. Indeed, it has been calculated that of the £54,000 raised in royal loans between 1328 and 1331, only a few hundred pounds came from the church.[95] In the mid- to late 1330s, some of the wealthier bishops and cathedral and monastic clergy were persuaded to invest more substantial sums in the Scottish and French wars. We know that Archbishop Melton of York loaned over £3,300 to Edward III, most of it between 1332 and 1340;[96] and in the summer of 1338 a number of religious houses made loans in cash or kind.[97] Archbishop Stratford also agreed to lend the king £1,000 for his first French campaign, although the sum was never actually handed over.[98] However, Edward's first concerted attempt to get the church to contribute loans ended in failure. The clergy, like all the king's subjects, were made liable for the forced loans of wool raised in 1337–8. But in 1338, when these levies were commuted to a tax in wool, the clergy demanded exemption on the grounds that they were not liable to direct subsidies granted by the laity.[99] This principle was later applied to all forced loans, as well as taxes, authorized by secular assemblies. Thus, in March 1347, when a great council granted the king a loan of 20,000 sacks of wool, it was necessary for the government to write to all the monastic and cathedral churches asking for specific contributions before the levy could be extended beyond those bishops and abbots actually present in the relevant assembly.[100] The grumbles and refusals that came back hardly suggested a major financial breakthrough for the government.[101]

On the other hand, the later 1340s did see the first successful efforts to get the higher clergy to contribute cash loans for the upkeep of Edward III's wars. Early in 1346 the king wrote to about 200 high-ranking ecclesiastics asking for loans amounting to nearly £14,000.[102] The contributions were fixed unrealistically high, and most of the clergy consequently declined to provide assistance. But in the spring of 1347 another request

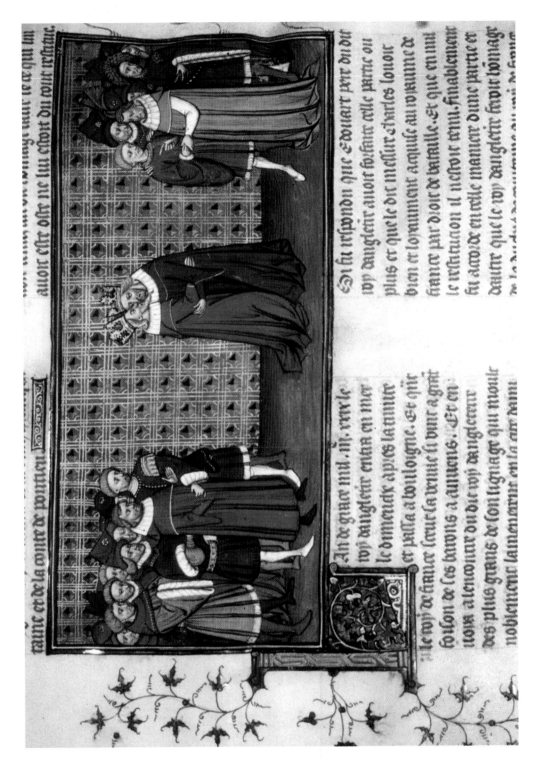

1 *Edward III performs homage to Philip VI of France*

2   *David II of Scotland with Edward III*

3   *Tomb of Queen Philippa at Westminster Abbey*

4 (left)
Edward III
and the
Black Prince
as benefactors
of St Albans
Abbey

5 (right)
Edward III
grants the
title of Prince
of Aquitaine
to the Black
Prince

6   *Tomb of Edward III at Westminster Abbey: detailed view of the effigy*

7   *Tomb of Edward III at Westminster Abbey: general view*

8   *Fifteenth-century depiction of Edward III as patron of the Order of the Garter*

went out, and loans amounting to just over £2,000 were collected.[103] Given Edward III's popularity in the period immediately after Crécy and Calais, the government might well have followed up this modest success with further attempts to mobilize the cash reserves of the church. In fact, however, the only other occasion in the reign when the king made a general appeal to the higher clergy came after the resumption of the French war in 1369.[104] As a result of this, loans amounting to nearly £10,000 were received from ecclesiastics between the spring of 1370 and the summer of 1371.[105] This figure is slightly less impressive, however, when we note that some of the largest advances came from civil servants, including a remarkable £3,000 from William Wykeham.[106] Some bishops certainly became regular lenders in the 1370s: Thomas Hatfield, for instance, later claimed that he had advanced £2,666 13s. 4d. to the government between 1369 and 1375.[107] For the rest of the reign, however, the crown appears to have made no general appeals for clerical loans. We are left with the distinct impression that the church played only a modest role in Edward III's credit operations.

The crown's major source of revenue from the church was therefore direct taxation. Contemporary political theorists were all agreed that the clergy should contribute towards the defence of the realm; and by the end of Edward's reign indeed, certain extremists were beginning to argue that the church's wealth should actually be turned over to the service of the state.[108] The general custom after 1327 was for the king to appeal to the convocations of Canterbury and York and to be granted a tenth of the value of ecclesiastical property. These successive subsidies were levied on the basis of a valuation originally carried out in 1291, and revised in 1318 in order to take account of the damage incurred by many northern churches during the Scottish raids. After 1327, the amount charged on the clergy for a tenth was somewhere between £18,700 and £19,000 (see Table 2). Both provinces granted Edward III twenty-three tenths, making a total value of approximately £421,000. In addition, the king was granted half the profits of the four papal tenths collected from the English clergy in 1330–4, which ought to have brought him about £35,500. In 1371 the church also conceded a special subsidy of £50,000; and in 1377 it sanctioned the first clerical poll tax, though this proved only a very modest levy. On a rough estimate, we can calculate that the total value of the clerical subsidies granted in the course of this reign was some £507,000.

It is important to recognize that not all of this sum was actually raised. The first four tenths collected under Edward III (in 1327, 1334 and 1336–7) yielded an average of £16,800, or about 88 per cent of the total charged. After 1337, however, the percentage dropped. One of the main reasons for this was the seizure of the alien priories on the outbreak of war with France, and the king's decision to exempt them from taxation in return for the payment of regular fee farms.[109] The poverty of clerical taxpayers was also probably a factor.[110] Thus the biennial tenth of 1351–3 — the first clerical tax to be collected after the Black Death — yielded only about £15,000 a year. When the clergy offered another tenth in 1356, they actually made it a condition that those in need should be treated with compassion, and numerous requests for tax relief were received by the government.[111] The result seems to have been a slow but definite erosion in the profits from clerical tenths over the fifty years of Edward's reign. Nevertheless, the sheer frequency of such taxes meant that an impressive amount of ecclesiastical wealth

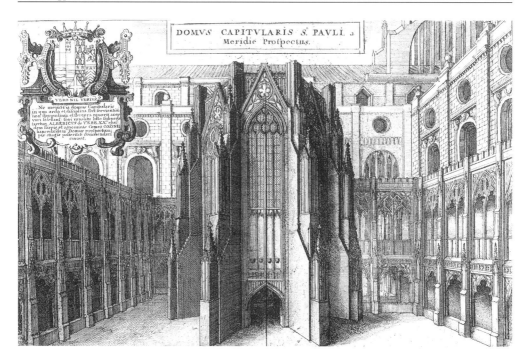

18   The chapter house of Old St Paul's Cathedral, London

continued to pour into the royal coffers. Even on a conservative estimate, the clerical tenths, the allocations from the papal subsidy of 1330–4, and the profits from the special levies of 1371 and 1377 probably yielded over £435,000. Furthermore, the income from the farms of the alien priories, which stood at anything between £3,500 and £5,000 a year,[112] clearly compensated more than adequately for the shortfall in revenues from direct taxation.

The full significance of our figures becomes apparent when we compare them with the records of earlier kings and contemporary popes. In the course of his thirty-five-year reign, for instance, Edward I had imposed some of the most oppressive taxes ever experienced by the clergy, including one demand for half the entire value of the English church.[113] But the total assessment for all these subsidies and for the portions of papal taxes appropriated by the crown between 1272 and 1307 was some £342,000, of which about £285,000 was actually collected.[114] A still more striking contrast is provided by the papacy's efforts to tax the English clergy during Edward III's time. Between 1327 and 1377 successive popes collected only about £58,000 in direct taxes from England, and some £15,000 of this sum actually found its way into the king's pocket by way of a papal contribution to the ransom of John II.[115] In financial terms at least, it is clear that Edward III enjoyed both unparalleled and unrivalled authority over the English church.

THE CHURCH AND POLITICS

It would be quite wrong to suppose that the clergy stood by silently while the crown helped itself to their financial resources. Under Edward III, direct taxation was more frequent than ever before; and, like the commons, the clergy were anxious to find ways of opposing or limiting the more onerous fiscal demands. Although the parliamentary subsidies of this period have been closely analysed, very little attention has been given to the constitutional implications of clerical taxation.[116] We may therefore conclude this survey of the church's place in the fourteenth-century polity by examining its response to the numerous tax demands made in the course of Edward III's reign.

When the clergy were asked for a subsidy, they could respond in one of three ways: by making a free and unrestricted grant; by offering a tax under certain conditions; or by rejecting the demand altogether.[117] The first course was rarely followed during this period, except in 1337, when the initial excitement over an impending war with France persuaded the convocations of Canterbury and York to make an unusually generous offer of three successive tenths.[118] To refuse a request was also rare, and became progressively more difficult as Edward III began to exploit the plea of necessity and effectively obliged his subjects to contribute to the cost of war. Although there were important precedents for opposing the crown's fiscal demands, particularly from the time of Archbishop Winchelsey (1293–1313),[119] the only really acceptable reason for rejecting Edward III's demands was if a papal subsidy was currently being collected from the English church. There were two occasions during the reign — in 1330 and 1376 — when the clergy were able to use this situation to immunize themselves from royal taxation.[120] Otherwise, the only known refusal came in 1338, when the northern convocation declined to follow the lead set by the clergy of Canterbury and resisted the request for a further tenth on top of the triennial subsidy of 1337 on the grounds that they were seriously impoverished by the Scottish war.[121]

The great majority of requests for aid were therefore met positively, but on the proviso that the king would make certain concessions to clerical taxpayers. At the beginning of the reign, the conditions all concerned the way in which the tax was to be assessed and collected.[122] The clergy of the northern province were particularly preoccupied with these matters, for they had long complained about the effects of Scottish depredations in the hope of securing reductions in their quotas. In 1327 they actually made it a condition of their grant that a new valuation be made of impoverished churches,[123] and in 1330 when the profits of the papal tenth were appropriated by the crown it was agreed that these lower assessments should still apply.[124] It was also standard practice for both convocations to request that tenths should cease to be collected in the event of the Pope imposing a subsidy or of the king making any other extraordinary charges on the clergy. Throughout the first half of Edward III's reign, for instance, the northern dioceses tried to use this principle as a means of immunizing themselves from royal prises.[125] In 1347 the convocation of York also demanded that its taxes should be spent solely on the defence of the northern march, and that in the event of a truce with Scotland the subsidy should immediately cease.[126] Very similar restrictions were being placed on the expenditure and duration of lay fifteenths and tenths granted for the Scottish and French wars in the

1340s.[127] Unfortunately, the fragmentary nature of the evidence makes it difficult to decide whether parliament or convocation set such precedents. What is apparent is that these assemblies maintained close links during Edward III's early years, and drew considerable strength from each other's achievements.

This situation is most strikingly demonstrated by the presentation in parliament of a number of sets of clerical *gravamina* (grievances).[128] It must be remembered that meetings of the convocation of Canterbury were frequently timed to coincide with sessions of parliament, and it was comparatively easy for the bishops of the southern province to communicate between the assemblies meeting at St Paul's Cathedral and Westminster Palace. The church had presented its political demands in parliament before, and in 1327 the Canterbury clergy revived the custom by submitting a list of ten items, mostly concerning technical points of jurisdiction. These were used by the crown as a basis for formal legislation recorded on the statute roll. The *gravamina* were usually quite narrow in scope, but represented an important summary of the church's political concerns. Before 1327, however, they seem to have been quite distinct from the more specific demands about the application of royal taxes put in with grants of clerical tenths. In particular, there is no indication that the clergy had previously attempted to link grants of supply with redress of grievance and to make the payment of taxes conditional upon the issue of remedial legislation.[129] Nor was this vital link ever made during the first decade of Edward III's personal rule.

By 1340, however, the situation had changed. In January of that year, as we have seen, the commons granted the king 30,000 sacks of wool on the understanding that he would receive and act upon their demands incorporated in a schedule of petitions.[130] This was the first time in the history of parliament that precise political conditions were set on the grant of a tax, and it created a very important precedent. The clergy were not slow to realize its significance. In February 1340 convocations of both provinces granted the king a new tax: a single tenth from the clergy of Canterbury and a double tenth from those of York. We know that the northern convocation set certain conditions on their grant (probably concerning the form of collection), for they subsequently requested a formal statement of the king's willingness to abide by their requests.[131] More important, however, is the possibility that the southern province presented a general list of grievances linked directly to the grant of supply. This would certainly explain the origins of the important new statute on ecclesiastical privilege drawn up by the legislative committee appointed in the Lent parliament of 1340.[132] It would also explain why the northern clergy, when asked to grant an additional tenth in 1342, drew up a list of *gravamina* and stated that unless formal replies were embodied in royal letters patent before Lent 1343, the tax would simply not be paid.[133]

These developments suggest that there was an unusually high level of communication between parliament and the two convocations during the troubled years around 1340. If that situation can be attributed to any one man, it was very probably Archbishop Stratford. Despite his association with the government, Stratford was highly critical of the general infringement of clerical liberties and the oppressive taxes being charged on the clergy in the late 1330s, and was consistently to champion the cause of the church in parliaments, convocations and ecclesiastical councils during the early 1340s. It was he, as head of the legislative committee of 1340, who undoubtedly insisted on the inclusion of clerical demands in the new statutes.[134] This indeed says much for Stratford's ability — demonstrated again in the crisis of 1341 — to unite disaffected political groups and exact major constitutional concessions from the crown.

For the next decade, the clergy successfully consolidated their gains. In 1341, 1344 and 1352 the *gravamina* of the southern convocation were not only delivered to the king in parliament but were transcribed on to the parliament rolls and used by the council to frame further remedial legislation.[135] Although the important concessions made to the clergy in 1341 were lost when the king revoked the legislation of that year, several of the points were revived in 1344 as the price of a triennial tenth. These included two important clauses confirming the exemption of bishops and ecclesiastical judges from liability to criminal proceedings before the king's courts. When a biennial tenth was granted in 1346–7, the northern clergy actually declared, in direct imitation of parliament, that payment of the second year of the subsidy would depend on the observation of the attached conditions.[136] This threat was somewhat difficult to sustain. But it provided a useful bartering position, and was sufficient on a number of subsequent occasions to force the government into substantial concessions. In May 1351 both provinces made the payment of the second year of a new biennial tenth conditional upon the redress of grievances,[137] and they successfully held up the formal confirmation of the second year of the tax until the further demands registered by the southern province in the parliament of January 1352 were finally accepted and enacted by the crown in July of that year.[138]

The hard bargaining between king and clergy reached its peak in 1356. When the representatives of the southern province assembled at St Paul's in May, they were visited by a number of courtiers and civil servants who expounded to them the king's case for demanding no fewer than six tenths. Long discussion followed, during which convocation expressed much disquiet about the crown's failure to reform abuses and about the already considerable financial pressure imposed on a much impoverished church. Eventually the clergy relented, but they offered only one tenth, and made the payment of the second half of this tax conditional upon the redress of grievances.[139] The convocation of York made similar stipulations when it authorized a tenth in June.[140] The Canterbury clergy had adopted notably dramatic language in order to press home their demands, declaring that 'the keys of the church are despised in such a way that the catholic faith is imperilled and the greatest danger to souls is incurred'.[141] But Edward III was not to be outdone at his own game. He countered with a well-timed appeal to the loyalty of the clergy and ordered special convocations in 1357 to discuss the defence of the church and the realm. In response to the plea of necessity, both provinces were forced to concede the second half of the tenth and agreed to drop their earlier conditions, except those concerning the exemption of impoverished churches.[142] The negotiations therefore ended in compromise. The king had been forced considerably to reduce the scale of his demands, and the clergy had acknowledged their obligation to pay free and unconditional taxes for the war effort.

At the time, it may well have seemed that Edward had made the greater concession. But as the reign wound on it became increasingly evident that the real loss had actually been sustained by the church. Like the commons, the clergy discovered that it was extremely difficult to force the king to observe limitations on taxation or to be bound by statutes based on their political grievances. There is no evidence, for instance, that the northern clergy got the charters demanded in 1342; but Edward went ahead in any case and collected a subsidy from them. The constant repetition of the same issues in the clerical *gravamina* — the defence of ecclesiastical liberties, the freedom of the church courts, the rights of episcopal and monastic churches during vacancies, clerical immunity from purveyance, and so on — indicates that the clergy found it almost impossible to secure the enforcement of legislation in which the crown had no active interest.

The real political weakness of the clergy, however, lay not in the fragile nature of the concessions won during the 1340s and early 1350s but in their failure to follow up on those achievements during the last years of Edward III's reign. In particular, the church appears to have stopped using parliament as a means of advancing its demands. No lists of clerical *gravamina* were recorded on the parliament rolls between 1352 and 1376, and the crown made no further statutory concessions to the church until the very last parliament of the reign.[143] During the 1360s, when the king's lay and clerical subjects were free from direct taxation, this political isolation mattered comparatively little. But with the renewal of the French war in 1369 and the imposition of extremely heavy fiscal charges on the church, the clergy found themselves bereft of lay support and at the mercy of an increasingly oppressive regime. There were many reasons for this shift in political alignments. The breakdown of consensus during Edward III's last years meant that very few groups were able to make much impression on government policy: witness the commons' failure to secure any more than a handful of entries on the statute roll between 1369 and 1377.[144] After 1370, moreover, parliament became violently anti-clerical, and it was extremely unlikely that the clergy would make any headway in this hostile environment.[145] But anti-clericalism had been known before, particularly in the 1340s, when it certainly had not prevented the clergy from securing constitutional recognition. It is therefore difficult to escape the conclusion that the church itself was in large measure responsible for its political demise during the later years of Edward III.

One symptom of this internal weakness was the growing tension between the northern and southern provinces. In 1371 the convocation of Canterbury gave its consent to a royal levy of £50,000. The northern clergy were more or less forced to accept the tax voted on them by their colleagues in the south, and an acrimonious debate ensued over the exact proportions of the sum to be paid by the dioceses of York, Durham and Carlisle.[146] But the greatest impediment to concerted political activity among the clergy was undoubtedly the attitude of the bishops. Historians have been at pains to point out that the later fourteenth-century episcopate was not simply packed with curialists and time-servers.[147] But it is clear that the prelates of the 1370s were much more inclined than their predecessors to co-operate with the government. And this attitude increasingly isolated them from their own lesser clergy. There was a good deal of bad feeling, for instance, about the bishops' decision in the parliament of 1369 to authorize arrays of the clergy, and in 1370 the convocation of York actually tried to secure immunity from this charge as a condition of the new triennial subsidy.[148] In the southern province, a difference of opinion was also developing over the level of financial support which the clergy ought to provide for the king's wars. In 1370 Archbishop Whittlesey overrode the attempts of convocation to limit the duration of a new tax and ordered the collection of three successive tenths.[149] The conflict came to a head in 1373. Simon Sudbury, Bishop of London, was commissioned to put the king's case to convocation; but on this occasion the lower orders stood firm, and were successful in limiting the grant to a single tenth. It is very striking that only one member of the episcopate, William Courtenay of Hereford, was apparently prepared to identify himself with the opposition movement, declaring that his diocese would not pay a single penny unless the king heard and redressed the grievances of the clergy.[150]

It was only the exceptional political circumstances of 1376 which re-established some semblance of unity between the higher and lower clergy. The southern convocation met while the Good Parliament was in session, and contrary to recent practice delivered a unanimous rejection of the government's demand for further supplies.[151] It also drew up a list of grievances, mostly concerning the jurisdiction of the ecclesiastical courts, and these were transcribed on to the parliament roll.[152] Far from representing a return to the political co-operation of the 1340s, however, the Good Parliament merely disguised the considerable suspicion which now existed between secular and spiritual assemblies. It is particularly noticeable that the clerical *gravamina* put on to the parliament roll were carefully loaded with complaints against the papacy. Realizing their political isolation, the clergy had been forced to match the mood of the laity. Moreover, the knights and burgesses in this parliament were sufficiently suspicious of clerical motives to demand that 'no statute or ordinance be made or granted on the petition of the clergy without the assent of the commons'.[153] Eventually, in February 1377, some of the clerical grievances presented in the Good Parliament were accepted by the crown and answered on the statute roll.[154] But by this point the conflicts within the church had once again become evident, with Sudbury (now Archbishop of Canterbury) acting as the spokesman of the court and defending the king's request for a poll tax, and Courtenay (recently translated to London) standing as the champion of clerical liberties.[155] The only issue that had really united the clergy was the seizure of Bishop Wykeham's temporalities; and once the Winchester estates were restored in July 1377, clerical solidarity once more crumbled.

The collapse of unity within the hierarchy and the isolation of the clergy from other sections of the community was seriously to compromise the church's political standing in the late fourteenth and fifteenth centuries. From the crown's point of view, however, the implications were altogether more positive. In the 1340s, the clergy had been able to use the political legacy of Archbishop Stratford and to play on the king's continued financial embarrassment in order to press their demands. By the 1370s this was no longer possible, and although the crown avoided a major offensive on ecclesiastical privilege, it undoubtedly used the church's political weakness as an excuse to extract very large sums of money in loans and taxes. What is most remarkable is that all of this aroused barely a murmur from the bishops. Such a situation would have been unthinkable in the time of Islip and Thoresby, let alone Winchelsey or Stratford.

★ ★ ★

The relations between church and state under Edward III provide some interesting insights into royal policy, and obviously invite comparison with what was going on in secular politics at the same time. Edward III encountered little effective pressure from his clerical subjects until after the opening of the Hundred Years War, and it was only the precedents set by parliament and taken up by Archbishop Stratford which probably persuaded the clergy to seek legislative concessions in return for grants of taxation. Between 1340 and 1352 they won some notable victories which theoretically guaranteed their immunity from the royal courts, their exemption from purveyance and other prerogative levies, the limitation of regalian rights over the church, and the restriction of the crown's ecclesiastical patronage. On some matters — notably the question of appointments — the king was prepared to honour the new settlement and stood by his promises for most of the rest of the reign. But in 1356–7 he reasserted his authority over the church by seizing the Bishop of Ely's temporalities and by refusing the clergy the right to make conditions on the payment of taxation. This royal *revanche* caused considerable unease in clerical circles, and may even have precipitated Archbishop Thoresby's resignation from the chancellorship. But in the end no political crisis occurred. And by the 1370s, when some of the lower clergy and at least one of the bishops began once more to question the king's policies, the opportunity to advance their political programme had passed. The emptiness of so much of the ecclesiastical legislation passed during the middle years of the fourteenth century serves to remind us of the crown's tendency to forget its former promises once the moment of conflict had passed. The inability of the lower clergy to forward their demands in the 1370s also provides an obvious parallel with the growing political frustration felt by the commons after the reopening of the French war. And the fact that these disaffected groups were increasingly antagonistic to each other possibly explains why the crisis of 1376 did not take place earlier. In its later stages, Edward III's regime was maintained not so much by the strength of the monarchy as by the inability of its opponents to mount an effective opposition.

To conclude this chapter on such a negative point would be a great mistake. It should be remembered that for much of his long reign Edward III was able to mobilize the resources of the church in the service of the state and to persuade the English clergy to give active and enthusiastic support to his foreign ambitions. The undercurrent of discontent, unmistakable though it was in the 1330s and the 1370s, never really threatened the king's *de facto* sovereignty over the clergy. In the end, the quarrel with Archbishop Stratford did little to alter the balance of power between church and state, and the very absence of similar controversies later in the reign served to emphasize the king's growing authority over the ecclesiastical hierarchy. Edward III was able to manage the church with an ease and an impunity that would indeed have been the envy of many a medieval king.

8 Provincial society and the gentry

For most of the fourteenth century the realm of England was subdivided into thirty-eight shires or counties. The city of London had shire status, and the same privilege was extended to Bristol in 1373. But the other thirty-seven units, although including cities and towns, were basically rural; and for the present we shall look at the landed classes and village communities of these regions, leaving urban society for separate treatment in the next chapter. There has been considerable debate about the influence of the 'county communities' in later medieval England, and some historians are now prepared to argue that it was the shire, rather than the kingdom, which provided the essential focus for the political aspirations of provincial society. It has already been remarked in several places that Edward III's reign witnessed the devolution of administrative and political influence to the provinces; and the king's relations with the shires are therefore of crucial importance in helping to characterize his regime.

We have already met several individuals and groups who might be regarded as part of 'county society' in the later Middle Ages. The magnates, with their vast landed estates, and the parish clergy, with their responsibility for the spiritual welfare of the rural community, obviously had important roles to play in provincial life. Most of this chapter will be devoted to the middling landholders or 'gentry'. To begin with, however, it may be instructive to ask whether the lesser members of rural society contributed anything to the development of the fourteenth-century polity.

THE PEASANTRY

The role of the peasantry in politics was inevitably extremely limited. The peasant's world was a narrow one, and he often had little knowledge of conditions in other parts of his own shire, let alone at opposite ends of the country. For this and many other reasons, concerted political action by the peasantry was most unlikely. On the other hand, the rural population certainly had no shortage of grievances.[1] The real problem was to find channels for legitimate and effective protest.

The ability to seek redress largely depended on the legal status of the complainant. Free tenants were at liberty to petition their lords, and often used this right to make accusations against unscrupulous estate managers.[2] Tenants on the royal demesne had a special advantage in this respect, for their appeals went straight to the king. Thus in 1328, and again in the 1340s, Edward III's tenants at Boothby Graffoe (Lincolnshire) protested in parliament about the unjust seizure of their common pastures by the constable of

Somerton Castle.[3] When free peasant communities had grievances which fell outside the scope of the manorial court, they were also at liberty to register petitions in parliament. The great majority of such petitions surviving from Edward III's reign deal, predictably enough, with taxation: abuses by the collectors, the unfairness of the quotas, and the failure of absentee lords and tenants to pay their due share. In the parliaments of January and March 1348, for instance, we find complaints on these and other related matters from the nine poor tenants of Hardwick (Oxfordshire), the men of Broadway (Somerset), the tenants of Hungerford (Berkshire), the community of Skeldale in the West Riding of Yorkshire, and many others.[4] But the mere presentation of a petition was no guarantee of redress. The evasive responses made by the crown and the perennial problem of regulating local administrators made it highly unlikely that many communities got real satisfaction. The crown's response to petitions was all too often conditioned by the social status of the petitioner, and peasants simply did not have the clout to guarantee preferential treatment.

For the unfree, there was not even the hope of satisfaction through such channels. Villeins were subject only to their lords: they were not recognized by the royal courts, and could not appeal to the king. Their only chance was to claim the privilege of ancient demesne: that is, to assert that their manors had once been part of the crown estate and that they, like the king's villeins, should have access to royal justice.[5] In 1335 the men of Macclesfield Forest claimed this privilege in order to appeal against the bailiffs of the Earl of Chester.[6] During the 1330s the tenants of Darnhall and Over took a similar course, protesting to the king and to parliament against the villein services being imposed on them by their lord, the Abbot of Vale Royal. They got no satisfaction, and were ultimately subjected to a humiliating penance by the victorious abbot.[7] Not all appeals ended thus, for some villeins found friends in surprisingly high places. In 1334 the Archbishop of Canterbury accused Richard Ward, sheriff of Buckinghamshire, of assisting the villein tenants of Prince's Risborough in their claim to the privilege of ancient demesne.[8] And in 1364 the king himself upheld the rights of the tenants of Crondall (Hampshire) in a similar dispute with the Prior of Winchester.[9] On the whole, however, the balance of justice weighed heavily against the unfree peasantry. They had identified a means of gaining access to the crown, only to find the way repeatedly barred.

Claims to the privilege of ancient demesne are interesting in a more general sense, for they provide a useful index of peasant grievances. The escalation in the number of such appeals during the later fourteenth century has often been taken as a sign of the increasingly harsh and intrusive lordship which characterized the period after the Black Death.[10] There are occasional signs of tension even before 1350. In 1344, for instance, the men of Tuxford (Nottinghamshire) protested to the king about certain customary dues newly imposed by the lord of the manor, Sir Thomas Beckering.[11] Nevertheless, the plague undoubtedly heralded a new era. Parliament and government now gave official backing to the efforts being made by landholders to revive villein tenancies and services, and deliberately restricted the means by which unfree peasants might gain access to royal justice. In 1348 the crown reformed the procedure on the writ *exceptio villenagi* ('exception of villeinage') in order to make it easier for lords to challenge presumptuous serfs impleading them in the courts.[12] And in 1352, at the instigation of the commons, the king severely restricted the use of the writ de *libertate probanda* ('proof of liberty'), thus eliminating the means by which a former villein might prove his freedom and escape repossession.[13] The resulting frustration felt by unfree peasant communities can be measured by the remarkable number of appeals of ancient demesne registered in the later 1370s. Between the autumn of 1376 and the spring of 1378, no fewer than forty villages, most of them in Surrey, Hampshire and Wiltshire, made petitions of this kind to the crown.[14] The failure of so many of these appeals may well have persuaded peasants in other parts of the country that the crown had effectively turned its back on the majority of its subjects, and that the only effective means of protest now left was insurrection. The peasantry, who formed anything up to 90 per cent of the total population, had been effectively barred from legitimate political action.

THE GENTRY

It is no surprise to find that local politics in the fourteenth century was dominated by the landholders. Problems only arise when we try to define the different ranks of landholding society. Historians have identified a group below the nobility to whom they have applied the anachronistic label 'gentry'. The members of this class demonstrated their gentility by bearing coats of arms, by exercising some form of lordship over dependent tenants, and by participating in the administration of the shires. Within this group, however, there was considerable diversity. The upper levels were dominated by the knights. According to the crown, everyone with a landed income of over £40 a year ought to be a knight, and although there were some evasions and exceptions, the great majority of the more substantial landholders in Edward III's reign continued to conform to this rule.[15] Below the knights was a larger group of middling and minor gentry generally described in the mid-fourteenth century as *armigeri* or *valletti*. By 1400 more precision had crept in, and two discernible classes had emerged: the 'esquires', holding estates valued between £20 and £40 a year; and the 'gentlemen' with annual incomes of £10–£20.[16] Looking at the situation in the mid-fourteenth century, when the terminology was still vague, it is difficult to establish a minimum qualification for membership of the gentry. When royal officials were called upon to draw up lists of important county landholders, they not infrequently included those with incomes as small as £5 a year.[17] But the influence of these lesser men was obviously extremely limited, and they have left very little trace in royal records. The following discussion will therefore concentrate on the more substantial members of the class, often referred to as the 'county gentry'.

How many gentry families were there in mid-fourteenth-century England? There are a number of ways of calculating this, though any such exercise is bound to contain a degree of guesswork. The ratio of knights to non-knights altered considerably in the later Middle Ages, as it became acceptable for men of quite substantial means to remain mere esquires. This to some extent accounts for the drop in the total number of knights, from as many as 2,000 in the thirteenth century to well under 1,000 in the early fifteenth century.[18] But the esquires did not increase sufficiently to compensate for this: the total number of knights and non-knights valued between £20 and £100 in the taxation returns of 1436 was still under 2,000.[19] In Gloucestershire at least, this reduction in numbers was already evident by the last quarter of the fourteenth century.[20] Working from the available evidence, it would seem that there were about 1,500 knights or potential knights valued in excess of £40, and about the same number of lesser men valued at £20–£40, in the first half of Edward III's reign. But the Black Death and the subsequent redistribution of incomes seem to have had a significant effect, and by the end of our period it is possible that the number of county gentry had fallen by as much as a third to a total of only about 2,000 men.[21] The main point to emerge from these very rough statistics is that the gentry never formed more than a tiny proportion of the entire population of medieval England. In extending our analysis of political society into the shires, and referring somewhat glibly to the wider political community represented in the parliamentary commons, we should clearly not be deluded into the idea that Edwardian England was some form of democracy.

THE GENTRY IN ARMS

The primary function of the landed classes was the profession of arms. The gentry were the direct successors of the knights, the elite mounted force in the feudal armies of the Norman kings. By the mid-fourteenth century the feudal host had given way to contract armies, and new methods of fighting had tended to reduce the importance of heavily armed cavalry officers. But it is quite wrong to suppose that the knights simply renounced their traditional function and allowed royal armies to pass under the control of professional mercenaries. Edward III's adventures in Scotland and France offered considerable potential for fame and fortune, and a high proportion of the gentry eagerly took up their place on the battlefields of Europe.

The cavalry forces in Edward's armies were usually divided into four ranks: earls, bannerets, knights and men-at-arms (not to be confused with the 'armed men' who made up the infantry). Not all the knights were English, and not all the men-at-arms were established members of landed society. Indeed, Edward III's reign witnessed the emergence of a new class of professional captains, men such as Hugh Calveley, Robert Knollys, Walter Huet, John Norbury, David Hulgreve and Gregory Sais, who came of relatively humble stock and who used the war as a means of social advancement.[22] Nevertheless, the records we have suggest that a considerable proportion of the gentry must have been involved in the armies of the mid-fourteenth century.[23] In 1335 the royal forces in Scotland included 450 knights and some 2,250 men-at-arms. In 1341 when Edward III planned a major expedition to Brittany he budgeted for 489 knights and over 2,000 men-at-arms.[24] The army actually collected in 1342 was somewhat smaller, but still had 330 knights and 1,470 men-at-arms. Over 900 knights apparently served at Crécy and Calais, though this figure was unusually large as a result of the virtual conscription of English knights and the mass dubbings carried out by the king in the course of the campaign.[25] Even so, the royal expedition to France in 1359–60 still included 870 knights, of whom no fewer than 680 were English. These examples represent some of the largest armies mobilized in the whole of the Hundred Years War. Inevitably, many of the contract armies led by members of the nobility were somewhat smaller: Henry of

Grosmont's force of 2,000 men for the campaign in Aquitaine in 1345, for instance, included just ninety-two knights and 150 esquires. John of Gaunt's French expeditionary force of 1373, on the other hand, contained no fewer than 248 knights and 1,766 men-at-arms. When we remember that England was fighting on several different fronts for much of this period, and that crown and nobility had only a restricted number of cavalrymen on whom to draw, then the extent of gentry involvement in the wars is indeed remarkable.

There were many practical reasons why so many members of provincial landholding families took up arms in defence of Edward III's claims in Scotland and France. While they were on active service, bannerets normally received wages of 4s. a day, knights 2s., and ordinary men-at-arms 1s. On their own, however, these wages were probably insufficient to draw many voluntary recruits: indeed, during Edward's uneventful and increasingly unpopular campaign in the Low Countries in 1338–40, the cavalry forces had to be paid precisely twice the normal rates.[26] It was considerably more lucrative to act as a recruiting agent for the king or the nobility and negotiate a premium for each soldier thus found: Sir John Strother of Kirknewton (Northumberland), for instance, made at least £255 out of such a deal with the Earl of March in 1374.[27] As with the nobility, however, it was probably the prospect of ransoms and plunder that really proved attractive. An excellent example of a fortune made on the basis of a single lucky break in war is provided by John Coupland. This obscure northerner was fortunate enough to capture David II at the battle of Neville's Cross, and was awarded the rank of knight banneret and an annuity of £500 by a grateful Edward III. His career was thus transformed, and he rapidly emerged as a leading member of the northern gentry, building up a large landed estate in Northumberland and Westmorland, and getting himself appointed sheriff and justice of the peace, warden of the march and keeper of Berwick upon Tweed.[28] His sudden rise may have offended some members of the Northumberland gentry, for in 1363 Coupland was murdered at Bolton Moor by a gang led by Sir John Clifford.[29] But in spite of such hazards, there were many others who followed Coupland's example. Even in the less favourable conditions of the 1370s and 1380s, a good number of lesser landholders seem to have continued to prosper in the wars: the castles erected by Sir John de la Mare at Nunney (Somerset) and by Sir Edward Dallingridge at Bodiam (Sussex) during this period are striking testimony to the very tangible benefits of the military life.[30]

There were other incentives, too, and not all of them wholly honourable. Some members of the gentry took advantage of the general pardons granted in return for military service to immunize themselves from prosecution in the courts. Sir Thomas Beckering, whom we have already met, got off a major inquiry into his conduct as sheriff and purveyor of Nottinghamshire and Derbyshire in 1347 as a result of a pardon obtained at Calais.[31] Others used their time in the army to secure writs halting judicial proceedings in which they were involved at home. It was common form for the crown to adjourn assizes until defendants returned from the war;[32] and in 1375 it was discovered that Sir John Roucliff, currently serving at Berwick, had maliciously used such a device to block an action being taken against him by the cathedral chapter of York.[33] Those on military service were also exempt from the king's attempts in 1344–6 to raise soldiers on the basis of landed wealth, and from the periodic fines levied to support troops arrayed in the shires.[34] In the late 1350s the commissioners in Leicestershire reported that no fewer than sixty-seven of the magnates and gentry holding land in that county were claiming immunity from array because they were currently serving in the wars.[35] Finally, those with little inclination to serve in local government sometimes found the war a useful excuse. In 1374, John Berkeley was discharged from the office of sheriff of Warwickshire and Leicestershire because he had already contracted to serve in the war with Lord Berkeley.[36] Sometimes it was less of a liability to take up arms than to stay at home.

There is little evidence, however, to suggest that the war created a shortage of manpower in the administration of the shires. It was perfectly possible to combine a military and a civilian career: Thomas Wake of Blisworth, for example, who went abroad with the king in 1340, managed to keep his post as sheriff of Northamptonshire while serving on the continent.[37] Moreover, many of the cavalry officers in Edward III's armies were probably the sons of county landholders, doing their time in the military before succeeding to the family estates and the family responsibilities in local government. In this respect it may be significant that Sir John Hardreshull, who rose to prominence during the Breton civil war of the 1340s, retired from active service at precisely the time when his son William first appeared on the battlefields of France.[38] Finally, a good number of the men-at-arms seem in any case to have been younger sons of minor landed families. A good example is Sir Ralph Ferrers, the second son of William Ferrers of Groby (Leicestershire), who rose through military service in France, Scotland and Ireland to become keeper of the Channel Islands (1373) and a royal councillor (1377).[39] In fine, the wars of Edward III provided an outlet and an opportunity for a large section of gentry society. In discussing the political attitudes of the knights and esquires, we will do well to remember that they, like the nobility, were the king's companions in arms and partners in glory.

BASTARD FEUDALISM

The contracts of military service made between commanders and cavalry officers are of particular interest to our study since they sometimes represented more permanent associations. The network of contacts built up between magnates and gentry in the later Middle Ages created that phenomenon which historians have chosen to call 'bastard feudalism'. This form of lordship manifested itself in three ways: the indenture of retinue, a formal contract specifying the nature of the service demanded and the rewards offered; the payment of annuities; and the granting of liveries.[40] The essential difference between bastard feudalism and the 'legitimate' feudalism that it replaced was therefore the cash nexus: the bond between patron and client was symbolized not by the grant of a piece of land (a fief) but by a regular payment in money (a fee) or in kind (robes and badges). Such arrangements had been known in the thirteenth century, but the reign of Edward III is often seen as the period when their more sinister implications first became evident. The development of contract armies during the 1340s supposedly encouraged magnates to take on larger numbers of permanent retainers, and the king's apparent deference to the

19   *An indenture between the king and John Coupland for the custody of the town of Berwick*

nobility allowed lords to use their client networks as a means of infiltrating local government, of intimidating rivals, and of securing favourable judgments in the courts. It has already been pointed out, however, that the parliament rolls of the mid-fourteenth century are remarkably silent on the abuse of aristocratic power; and specific complaints about the evil consequences of lordship were not made until after Edward III's death.[41] We need to take a fresh look at the available evidence before assuming that the fourteenth-century gentry were mere pawns in the baronial power game.

The absence of noble archives makes it very difficult to assess what proportion of the gentry were active members of magnate affinities in this period. The evidence we have, derived mainly from the indentures of war, inevitably tends to exaggerate the numbers. It would be quite unrealistic to suggest that the twenty-five bannerets, 119 knights and 1,117 men-at-arms who accompanied the Earl of Stafford to Aquitaine in 1352 were all life annuitants of this new and modestly endowed nobleman.[42] It has been calculated that Thomas of Lancaster's retinue in 1314 numbered as many as 150 knights and esquires, while John of Gaunt's permanent following in 1386 probably included some 169 knights and esquires.[43] Both these cases, however, are quite exceptional, not only because they refer to the wealthiest noble house in England, but also because they concern periods when the Lancastrian affinity itself was unusually large. In fact, in the settled political circumstances of Edward III's reign, few noblemen seem to have had more than about twenty knights and perhaps twice as many esquires on their books at any one time.[44] The image of a society dominated by indentures of retainer is therefore palpably false.

Inevitably, there were geographical variations to this general pattern. In those shires where power were concentrated in the hands of a single powerful lord, the majority of the local gentry would naturally seek his fees and favours. The Black Prince, for instance, enjoyed a virtual monopoly of patronage in Cornwall and Cheshire. Even in the palatinates, however, bastard feudalism did not rule supreme. A detailed study of Lancashire society in the late fourteenth century has shown that only just over half the major office-holders in the county were members of John of Gaunt's affinity, and only a handful of the minor gentry had any Lancastrian connection at all.[45] In certain other counties, the absence of resident lords or the division of authority between several magnates clearly fostered a strong tradition of independence among the lesser landholders. In Bedfordshire, for instance, there was no substantial aristocratic influence for the greater part of the fourteenth century, and politics was dominated by the major gentry families such as the Braybrooks and the Birminghams. The same was true in many parts of the midlands, including Lincolnshire, Leicestershire and Derbyshire.[46] In the present state of our knowledge, it is difficult to tell whether any one of these cases can really be regarded as 'typical'. What is clear is that a proportion — perhaps a significant proportion — of the gentry remained outside the formal ties of bastard feudalism in the mid-fourteenth century.

It is interesting to speculate about this situation. The unscrupulous actions of the nobility during the 1320s and 1330s may well have dissuaded some men from seeking noble patronage: lordship, after all, was only attractive if it was 'good' lordship. To associate oneself with a magnate had been particularly hazardous during the unstable 1320s: witness the desertions from Thomas of Lancaster's retinue in the months preceding the battle of Boroughbridge.[47] Those who survived the successive revolutions of this decade must have been highly cautious about aligning themselves with particular factions. After the 1340s the aristocracy's political reputation improved. But just at this point the Black Death intervened; and the economic conditions following the plague may well have put constraints on noble budgets and prevented the rapid growth of peacetime affinities during the second half of Edward III's reign.

The most important reason why bastard feudalism failed to establish itself as the prime force in English politics during this period, however, was probably the crown's willingness to accept that the gentry ought to be actively and directly involved both in local government and in central politics. With the knightly classes securing so much through their own representatives in the commons, they simply did not need to seek the support of noble patrons. Indeed, the actions of the gentry sometimes showed them to be sharply at variance with the magnates. In 1339–40, for instance, a striking difference of opinion arose in parliament over the king's demands for more taxes, with the lords offering to pay a tenth of their agricultural produce and the commons holding out against any further fiscal exactions.[48] Similar conflicts sometimes arose at the local level. For example, when John of Gaunt tried to impose new and controversial services on his estates in Sussex during the 1370s, he encountered considerable opposition from local landholders led by Sir Edward Dallingridge.[49] The 'horizontal' links within gentry society were evidently just as important as the 'vertical' links created by bastard feudalism.

Having registered these qualifications, we must also point out that membership of a baronial retinue undoubtedly offered the best hope of advancement for many members of the gentry. Examples of relatively obscure men rising to distinction through aristocratic service abound in the mid-fourteenth century. John Cokayn of Ashbourne in Derbyshire, for instance, came to prominence as Henry of Grosmont's under-sheriff of Lancashire, had a busy career in Lancastrian and royal service until his death in the 1360s, and founded a long-lasting dynasty of gentlemen-lawyers.[50] In 1339 the Earl of Warwick appointed one of his retainers, Walter Shakenhurst, as under-sheriff of Worcestershire, and continued to sponsor the latter's career as a local justice and member of parliament during the 1340s and 1350s.[51] Even well-established members of the gentry appreciated the benefits of aristocratic service. For example, Sir Ralph Bocking, a distinguished Suffolk landholder, acted as steward to Edward III's uncle, the Earl of Norfolk, in the 1330s.[52] Bastard feudalism was popular precisely because it created a reciprocal relationship: it was the client, just as much as the patron, who benefited from the arrangement.

Nor was the king averse to using the same techniques as his great men. It was not until the 1390s that the English crown apparently made any conscious attempt to build up an independent following among the gentry by granting fees to provincial landholders.[53] But it is worth noting that a number of the minor peerage and greater gentry were at some time or other employed in Edward III's household. Apart from the elite corps of bannerets and knights, there was also a large group of esquires retained by the royal household and listed in the accounts of the king's wardrobe. During the early years of the reign there were about a hundred such esquires at any one time, though after the 1340s the number dropped to around seventy.[54] Many of these men were obscure figures; others had distinguished military and political careers and worked their way up into the minor aristocracy. Nigel Loring, for instance, who was one of the founder members of the Order of the Garter, had served as an esquire of the household in the 1330s.[55] Similarly, the list of esquires in the household accounts for 1353–4 includes a number of men who would later rise to prominence as knights of the king's chamber — Guy Warr, Oliver Brocas, Richard Stury, Roger Elmrugge, John Foxley and John Beauchamp of Holt.[56] Most interesting from our present point of view, however, is the appearance in these same lists of men drawn from several of the leading baronial and gentry families: the Uffords, Beauchamps, Zouches, Umfravilles, Fitzwalters, Chandoses, Swynnertons, and so on. These were apparently young apprentice knights attached to the royal household to learn the arts of war and pick up some of the culture of the court. They presumably acted as important channels of communication between king and country; and the sense of loyalty bred into them and their like may well have helped to sustain Edward's regime in the provinces during his last declining years. Nevertheless, it is significant that Edward III never attempted to turn this amorphous group of king's friends into a recognizable political party. Astute and popular rulers preferred to draw on the baronial retinues and the more general tradition of service in order to build up a broad base of support among the gentry in the shires. Edward III's ability to work with, rather than against, the forces of bastard feudalism demonstrates not only his political realism but also his sheer popularity in both noble and gentry society.

THE GENTRY AND LOCAL GOVERNMENT

The goodwill of the gentry was particularly important since it was they who provided the manpower and skills needed to run local government. Administrative and judicial posts in the shires fell into two broad categories. The greater gentry dominated the offices of sheriff, escheator, justice of the peace, and chief collector of taxes, while the minor gentry filled the less important or less popular offices of under-sheriff, hundred bailiff, coroner, verderer, commissioner of array, sub-collector of taxes and purveyor. Some officials were elected locally (coroners and verderers, for instance, were chosen by the county courts); but in most cases the king retained the right to appoint his own representatives in the shires. It was only in 1338, when Edward III was absent from the country, that the 'good people' of the shires were empowered to choose their own sheriffs and other officials. In fact, this experiment proved unpopular, since the county communities feared that they would incur liability for the actions and debts of their nominees, and the government rapidly returned to the system of central appointments.[57] Thereafter, local officials were selected on the advice of the chancellor, treasurer, and other senior ministers, or on the basis of personal recommendations received from magnates and prelates. It was only in exceptional circumstances that members of the gentry were consulted, as in 1369 when three Essex men were summoned before the council to decide which of them should be appointed sheriff.[58] This is not to say, however, that the lesser landholders were indifferent to the question of local appointments. Indeed, their demands for better-qualified officials, and their particular concern to win greater participation in the work of the peace commissions, created a considerable political challenge for the government of Edward III.

In the first half of the fourteenth century a candidate for local office was simply expected to be of good reputation and to hold 'sufficient' property in the relevant shire.[59] How much was deemed sufficient was actually far from clear. When Treasurer Zouche advised the removal of collectors of scutage in Nottinghamshire and Derbyshire in 1338–40, he merely stated that they should be replaced by two 'more sufficient' men.[60] In 1337 the Earl of Lancaster did the same thing in suggesting a new collector of lay subsidies in Staffordshire, though in this case we know that the new commissioner, Maketon Wasteneys, held land to the value of £20 in that county.[61] In 1349 John Chastillon was considered suitable for the sheriffdom of Bedfordshire and Buckinghamshire because he was worth £100 a year;[62] but this was well in excess of the average income even of the more prosperous sections of gentry society. The situation was so vague that even the county communities sometimes made mistakes. In 1346 a report came in that Robert Savage, recently elected as coroner in Derbyshire, had been discovered to hold no land in that county.[63] It was to resolve these problems and ambiguities that the commons in parliament began to campaign for a formal system of qualifications, and the government eventually fixed a minimum property requirement of £20 for escheators in 1368, and possibly also for sheriffs in 1371.[64] After 1371 the crown also agreed to observe another of the commons' long-standing demands, namely that sheriffs should not be allowed to serve for long periods but should be replaced annually.[65] The most sustained campaign, however, revolved around the personnel of the peace commissions. In their concern to ensure that local men were appointed to keep the peace in the shires, the commons frequently asked that the names of the justices be submitted to parliament for approval, and it is possible that this was done in 1351, 1361, 1362 and 1363.[66] Such concessions, limited though they were, signified that the workings of local government were the rightful concern of the parliamentary commons, and provided an important guarantee that the landed interest would prevail in the administration of the shires.

The response of those individuals actually selected for royal service varied considerably. A post in the shire administration was an honour. But it was also an obligation, and occasionally a hazard. Those working as justices of labourers in the period after the Black Death not infrequently faced intimidation and violence, and arrayers in particular often tried to wriggle out of their responsibilities when they realized the level of hostility towards them.[67] Tax collectors were another obvious target for abuse. In 1354 Richard Marclesham, a collector of the lay subsidy in Essex, reported that no less a figure than the Abbot of Colchester had mounted an armed attack on him.[68] Nor did the problems cease when men left office. Those charged to account at the exchequer were held personally responsible for all their outstanding debts. Sir Peter Mallory of Litchborough, for instance, who enjoyed brief favour with the government after his distinguished performance at Crécy in 1346, had good reason to regret his brief period as sheriff and escheator of Northamptonshire in 1351. Unable to meet the county farm in full, he was detained several times in the Fleet prison and never really recovered his former prominence in local society.[69] Given such liabilities, it is not surprising that some members of the gentry preferred to seek royal letters patent exempting them from public office.[70]

For the most part, however, the advantages of service outweighed the penalties. Apart from the obvious prestige, for instance, there was often the potential for considerable financial gain. In a formal sense the local officials of the crown did not get paid. The only major exceptions to this rule were special judicial commissioners, such as the justices of weights and measures acting between 1340 and 1344 and the justices of labourers working in the decade after the Black Death, who were permitted to take a quarter of the profits from their sessions as wages.[71] Knights of the shire also qualified for expenses of 4s. a day while they were away from home on the king's business — twice what they could expect to earn for military service. This financial incentive must surely explain in part why Nicholas Stivichall, sheriff of Cambridgeshire and Huntingdonshire in 1356–60 and 1361–71, secured his own return to no fewer than eight parliaments.[72] Sheriffs themselves received no formal emoluments, but made their own rewards by a mixture of fair and foul practice.[73] Since they farmed their shires for fixed sums payable at the exchequer, they were free to take any excess profits for themselves. Some sheriffs also made considerable gains from fees and bribes paid by towns, religious houses and magnates. The authorities in Oxford, for instance, made regular gifts of money, food and wine to the sheriffs, escheators and royal judges visiting the town; and in 1346–7 the burgesses of Cambridge gave the considerable sum of £3 to the sheriff as thanks for exempting them from the recent round of purveyance.[74] William Trussell, escheator of the counties south of the Trent (1327, 1331–2, 1335–40), received a regular annuity of ten marks (£6 13s. 4d.) from the Knights Hospitallers.[75] Finally, in 1366 it was revealed that the sheriff of Yorkshire, Thomas Musgrave, had received £5 from Sir Thomas Ughtred in order to guarantee a favourable judgment in the local assize sessions.[76] These opportunities for personal gain clearly explain why, despite the financial problems experienced by an increasing number of sheriffs after the Black Death, the office continued to be much sought after for the rest of the fourteenth century. In the late 1370s Sir John Basings argued that he ought to have the farm of the county of Rutland because it had been granted to his great-great-great-grandfather Ralph Normanville in 1202.[77] Anyone who could take the trouble of carrying out the genealogical research necessary to back up such a claim obviously regarded the office of sheriff as well worth having.

CORRUPTION AND LAW-KEEPING

The mixture of motives which drove men to seek public office obviously raises worrying questions as to whether the gentry could be trusted to regulate their own affairs. Medieval England was no paradise, and its system of local government inevitably contained a corrupt element. Examples of sharp practice abound in all the shire posts during Edward III's reign. In 1330 Agnes Yetlington accused Sir John Lilburn of unjustly arresting her, and protested to the king that so long as Lilburn remained sheriff of Northumberland she would stand no chance of obtaining justice.[78] Philip Deneys, the member of a special judicial commission in Suffolk, was discovered in 1368 to have colluded with a certain William Dirland to pervert the course of justice by empanelling men of low birth and intimidating juries.[79] Tax collectors understandably had a particularly bad reputation. In 1348 it was reported that Sir John Inge, chief collector in Somerset, had arbitrarily increased the levy charged on the people of Widcombe from 14s. 10d. to an outrageous £3 17s. 8d.; and in 1362 it was alleged that excess money raised towards the special lay subsidy of 1360, which ought to have been paid back to the taxpayers, had in fact been appropriated by John Lanum, one of the collectors in Nottinghamshire.[80] The officials with the worst record, however, were undoubtedly the purveyors. Early in the reign, the keepers of the royal stud in Bedfordshire were accused of extorting supplies from the locals and squandering their money in brothels, to the scandal of all concerned.[81] Among the many charges levelled against Sir Peter Mallory in 1352 were several accusations that in his role as purveyor he had used false weights and made excessive levies, to the great detriment of the people of Northamptonshire.[82] At the same time it was said that the purveyors in neighbouring Leicestershire had taken ransoms from towns and individuals, had sold many of the goods, and had carried off all the profits for themselves.[83] In 1376 the commons of Norfolk complained that no one had yet been paid for the large amounts of food taken in the shire over the previous two years;[84] and in the same year there were grumbles from a number of counties on the south coast about soldiers who seized crops and other goods, leaving letters of obligation which the king's purveyors then refused to honour.[85]

The scandalous record of the shire officials was a reflection of the general level of crime and corruption among the gentry. Again, the records of Edward III's reign furnish many examples of landholders involved in extortion, violence, intimidation and murder. Comparatively few members of this class were professional criminals. For example, there is nothing to suggest that the band of Warwickshire knights, including Fulk Birmingham and John Ryvel, who were accused of attacking and robbing Sir Ralph Basset of Drayton in 1355 were regular partners in crime.[86] On the other hand at least two gentry families, the Folvilles and the Coterels, organized reigns of terror in the midlands during the 1330s, and were often employed by other landholders to harass or even murder their rivals.[87] Other members of the same class lived virtually double lives, fluctuating between thuggery and respectability. The criminal career of Richard Alberd of Yaxley, for instance, spanned thirty years, and included a robbery perpetrated against Queen Isabella. Yet Alberd also enjoyed a prominent place in Huntingdonshire society, acting as knight of the shire, commissioner of array, and justice of the peace throughout the 1350s and 1360s.[88] A disruptive and undesirable element was of course to be found at every level in society. What made the criminal proclivities of the gentry so alarming was that they were also the class that demanded, and ultimately achieved, substantial control over local peace-keeping.

Already in the early years of Edward III's reign it was obvious to many politically active men that the only hope of improving law and order lay in a general overhaul of the legal administration. A limited amount was achieved by the brief revival of the eyre in 1329–30 and by the appointment of comprehensive commissions of oyer and terminer in 1340.[89] One result of these inquiries, indeed, was to expose a considerable number of gentlemen-criminals.[90] John Lestrange of Myddle (Shropshire), for instance, who had been the king's bailiff errant in Norfolk and Suffolk for a number of years, was hauled up before the commissioners in East Anglia in 1341 and fined £3 for numerous extortions and oppressions.[91] This and similar cases may well have persuaded the government that it was inadvisable to grant comprehensive judicial authority to local landholders. But the inquiries also tended to offend the more law-abiding members of provincial society. The appointment of judges drawn from outside the locality was regarded as a major infringement of the county's right of self-government; and in 1341 a number of the shires actually offered hefty fines, amounting in most cases to twice their current assessments for a fifteenth and tenth, in order to immunize themselves from judicial proceedings.[92] The shires certainly wanted justice: there is no shortage of petitions from the county communities requesting more frequent assize and gaol delivery sessions[93] or demanding the building and repair of local prisons for the secure custody of offenders.[94] But they wanted justice on their own terms: and by the 1350s it was clear that this meant nothing less than local control of the commissions of the peace.

Consequently, it was only in the second half of Edward III's reign, when the justices of the peace assumed responsibility for the operation of criminal law, that the landed classes became more satisfied with the king's record on law-keeping. Whether this was accompanied by any real improvement in standards may be doubted. Banditry does seem to have declined after the 1340s,[95] but the presence of friends and neighbours on the bench may simply have made it easier for members of the landed classes to cover up their own criminal activities. Nor should we exaggerate the effectiveness of the peace sessions.[96] Despite the stipulation that the justices should sit four times a year,[97] there are indications of considerable laxity and delay. A petition dating from the later fourteenth century claimed that there had been no peace sessions in Kent for at least eleven years, and in Gloucestershire it seems that the justices of the peace met only once, or at most twice, a year.[98] One reason for this apparent slackness was the fact that, unlike the justices of

20   *Tomb of Sir John Hardreshull at Ashton church, Northamptonshire*

labourers working in the 1350s and the royal judges serving in the central courts and the assizes, the new commissioners of the peace received no salaries. In 1376, indeed, the commons specifically asked that justices of the peace be paid, 'since without wages they do not bother to hold their sessions'.[99] The fact that the government ignored such pleas until 1388 may indeed suggest that the commissions of the peace were still at an experimental stage when Edward III died, and had yet to prove themselves as an essential element of the judicial administration.[100]

This last point may also help to set in context the supposed political implications of the local peace commissions. For to argue that Edward III effectively renounced his control over law-keeping in the shires is fundamentally to misinterpret the issue.[101] Since 1250 there had been an enormous increase in the number of petty crimes ('trespasses') recognized as breaches of the king's peace, and this had put an unprecedented strain on the existing judicial machinery. The justices of the peace were simply the most practical answer to the considerable problem of accommodating all this new business. In a sense, then, the delegation of authority represented a return to that tradition of 'self-government at the king's command' temporarily upset by the intrusive Plantagenet regime of the later thirteenth century.[102] Even so, this was no return to zero. Except for one short period in 1361–4, as we have seen, the commissions of the peace were placed under the general supervision of the professional assize judges, who were required to be in attendance when serious crimes ('felonies') were brought to trial.[103] Consequently, the justices of the peace were not some local mafia operating their own private system of law, but were an integrated part of a much greater whole: they were the king's judges, upholding the king's law in the king's courts. It may be too much to suggest that the development of the peace commissions bred a greater degree of integrity into those who administered the shires.[104] But it did undoubtedly create a new sense of respect, trust and mutual support between king and gentry. Above all, it gave county society a greater sense of its status within the wider community of the realm. To appreciate the significance of this development, we need to examine the political pressure which the gentry were able to exert both at the local level in the county court and at national level in parliament.

THE COUNTY COURTS

The county courts were of ancient origin, and were originally the principal judicial tribunals in the shires.[105] By the fourteenth century their legal powers were negligible, but they continued to have important political functions. They met every four or six weeks, usually in the royal castles of the county towns. The local tenants-in-chief of the crown and their own immediate tenants were theoretically obliged to attend, along with the sheriff, under-sheriff, coroners and bailiffs. A majority of the substantial free landholders in the shire could also be expected to turn up. In practice, the attendance figures probably fluctuated widely, depending on the size and social structure of the shire and the nature of the business being transacted. In the mid-fourteenth century the 'commons' of Northumberland put in a complaint about the successive adjourning of assize sessions in the county, to which nineteen named individuals and 'many others' appended their seals.[106] Yet some years later, in 1388, no fewer than 330 of the 'better born and more worthy' men of Lincolnshire attended the shire court to take oaths of allegiance to the Lords Appellant.[107] On average, it has been suggested that there might have been about 150 notables, officials, litigants and onlookers present at a typical meeting of the county court in the fourteenth century.[108] It was therefore an occasion of major social consequence, and an obvious forum for political debate among the gentry.

The administrative duties imposed on the county court were considerable. It was here, for instance, that the government launched its periodic attempts to force all those with land valued over a certain figure (normally £40) to take up knighthood.[109] The county courts were also occasionally used to negotiate taxes. In 1337 a series of meetings was held with knights and landholders in the shires in order to extract promises of aid for the impending war. Some 104 men attended the Staffordshire assembly.[110] The experiment was a failure, and was superseded by a tax granted in great council. Later, however, in 1360, representatives of the county courts were again summoned to regional meetings which voted subsidies for the defence of their communities.[111] These assemblies were anomalous, half-way between the county court and the national parliament, and the tax they granted was unique in being administered locally and kept outside the control of the exchequer. But it says much for the importance and vitality of provincial politics that during a state of national emergency Edward III's government found it necessary to treat with the shires for their own defence.

The negotiations of 1360 can indeed be seen as the natural culmination of a policy pursued by the crown throughout the first phase of the Hundred Years War. The county courts, like parliament, needed to be persuaded of the justice and feasibility of the king's schemes, and coaxed into giving more active support for his military enterprises. The first and rather hesitant stages of this public information programme were not particularly successful. In 1339–40, when the war was going badly and taxation was particularly oppressive, the regency administration sent commissioners into Norfolk to raise loans from the clergy and other notables. The envoys were instructed to report the recent destruction of naval forces and the need for money to raise a new fleet, but they seem to have returned to Westminster with nothing but refusals and excuses.[112] In 1344, the sheriff of Cumberland was so worried about local hostility to the collection of arrears on the wool tax of 1341–2 that he called a special meeting of the county court to be addressed by the king's envoy, Lambert Hautpierre.[113] Gradually, however, the shires became rather more impressed with the king's record. The achievements of parliament had a particularly important influence in this respect. It was a long-standing tradition that statutes, ordinances, and other major administrative measures should be proclaimed by the sheriffs in the county courts. Copies of the statutes and of taxation schedules were also given to the knights of the shire on a regular basis after 1340, and were delivered back to the constituencies for discussion.[114] The government's considerable legislative output in the 1350s probably did much to mollify the leaders of provincial society, and made the continuing burden of direct and indirect taxation rather more acceptable at least to the landholding classes.

Propaganda was also inclined to create higher expectations. Any failure by the crown to live up to its promises of good governance was liable to be seen as a betrayal of trust. By the mid-fourteenth century there was an increasing tendency for private petitioners to cite the statutes back at the government and to criticize it for failing to enforce its own legislation.[115] The county courts rapidly followed suit. A considerable number of petitions entered during Edward III's reign were made in the name of the 'commons', the 'liege men' or the 'poor men' of the shires, and there is little doubt that the majority of these were drawn up as a result of discussion in the county courts.[116] They fell into four main categories. First, there were the inevitable complaints about the corrupt practices of the crown's local agents: tax collectors, purveyors, peace commissioners, forest officials, and so on.[117] Secondly, there were expressions of concern about the impact of war and the special requirements of local defence.[118] Third, and most frequent, were the demands for relief from fiscal exactions. Particularly prominent in this group were complaints about the burden of the shrieval farms.[119] The twin counties of Nottinghamshire and Derbyshire and of Surrey and Sussex argued consistently that the granting away of hundreds and other franchises ought to be accompanied by a reassessment of the county farm,[120] and late in the reign of Edward III the people of Essex and Hertfordshire began to demand a formal reduction of £100 on their farm as a result of economic problems encountered since the plague.[121]

Finally, the most interesting group of petitions from the shire communities were those accusing the nobility or the crown of attempts to override local privileges. In 1337 the people of Cornwall complained to the king about a new court that had been set up by the officials of the late earl, John of Eltham, at Launceston; and in 1376 the men of Sussex expressed their anger at the excessive profits being taken in a prerogative court held by the Earl of Arundel.[122] Royal intrusions sometimes met with the same response. In the late 1330s the commissioners of array in Warwickshire found that the community would not consent to paying the costs of archers; and in 1341 the county court of Shropshire put up concerted opposition to the new tax in wool.[123] The government's attempt to use the king's bench as a roving commission of trailbaston in the late 1340s and early 1350s met with widespread opposition because it threatened the gentry's preference for self-regulation within the shires.[124] About the same time the men of Norfolk and Suffolk expressed their anger at being summoned outside their county boundaries to attend special inquiries into the evasion of customs duties.[125] The high-handed actions of the nobility and the crown were clearly perceived as a direct threat to local liberties, and helped to create greater solidarity within the shires. The sheer number of communal petitions surviving from Edward III's reign indicates that the county court had now become not simply an agency of royal government but also an important channel through which the localities could articulate their political grievances.

THE GENTRY IN PARLIAMENT

The real focus for the political aspirations of the gentry, however, was not the county court but parliament. At the start of Edward III's reign the commons were still a relatively new phenomenon: even in the mid-1320s it had still been possible for meetings without representatives of the shires and towns to be labelled parliaments.[126] But under Edward III the knights and burgesses emerged as a major political force. From 1327 every parliament included two representatives from each English county, with the exception of Cheshire and Durham.[127] According to the extant returns, these 'knights of the shire' were usually elected 'in full county court' with the assent of 'the whole community of faithful men'.[128] In fact, it was not uncommon for the sheriffs, who acted as returning officers, to rig proceedings. In 1338 it was reported that for the previous seven years the sheriffs of Cambridgeshire had returned their friends without any reference to the wishes of the county court; and in 1372, as a result of long-standing complaints by the commons, the government specifically excluded sheriffs and lawyers from election to parliament.[129] If noblemen held the sheriffdoms, then it was also relatively easy to ensure the appointment of men amenable to their will. In Lancashire, indeed, there are reasons to believe that elections did not always take place in the county court, and that the knights of the shire were simply nominated by the Earl — later the Duke — of Lancaster.[130] In special circumstances, the crown might also intervene in the selection of representatives. In 1354, when parliament was called to confirm legislation put forward in the great council of 1353, the sheriffs were specifically instructed to return those who had sat in the earlier assembly.[131] In 1358, the sheriff of Gloucestershire was told by the government that those chosen to represent the shire were unsuitable, and that he should find two 'wiser and more sufficient' knights to attend parliament.[132] Finally, in 1364, the king actually wrote to the sheriff of London to nominate two men whom he wished to see returned to the forthcoming parliament.[133] In general, however, the government seems to have made remarkably few attempts to manipulate elections. The nature of the commons' activity in parliament during Edward III's reign certainly does not suggest that the county representatives were the puppets either of the lords or of the king. Indeed, their political aims were often pursued in the face of considerable apathy or hostility on the part of the crown, and found support not among the magnates and ministers, but in the provincial communities from which the commons sprang.

The influence of the knights and burgesses on the work of parliament depended on their special power to vote subsidies which would be binding on all the king's subjects.[134] In formal terms, taxes were granted by the lords as well as the commons.[135] But in 1340 it was established that the peers could only impose subsidies on their own number,[136] and thereafter the knights and burgesses became the real arbiters of national taxation. The direct subsidies they granted were assessed not on land or income but on 'movables': chiefly animals and crops in the countryside, and merchandise and domestic goods in the towns.[137] The crown normally claimed a cash payment representing a certain fraction of such wealth. Edward III's first subsidy, raised in 1327, was levied at the rate of a twentieth. In 1332, however, parliament authorized a tax of a fifteenth on the countryside and a tenth on the towns and the ancient demesne, and these became the standard rates for the rest of the reign. In 1334 it was agreed to abandon the time-consuming practice of reassessing individuals for each successive tax, and instead the collectors negotiated a block payment with each community within their shires. So successful was this experiment that the quotas of 1334 became the basis for all subsequent fifteenths and tenths. No fewer than twenty-one such subsidies were granted by parliamentary assemblies between 1332 and 1373, not to mention the special subsidy authorized by the regional gatherings in 1360. There were also a number of experimental taxes collected in the course of Edward's reign. On two occasions — in 1338 and in 1341 — the commons agreed to direct taxes paid not in money but in wool, and in 1340 the king secured a special levy of every ninth lamb, fleece and sheaf of corn produced in the realm. In 1371, a subsidy of £5 16s. was levied on each parish in England. Finally, in 1377, Edward III's last parliament granted a poll tax at the standard rate of 4d. a head on every man and woman over the age of fourteen.

The potential yield from these taxes was very large (see Table 1). The first two lay subsidies of the reign were designed to raise £25,400 and £34,000 respectively. The quotas established for the fifteenth and tenth in 1334 totalled some £37,300; but Cumberland, Westmorland and Northumberland were not assessed for this tax, and when these counties were incorporated into the national system in 1336 the combined assessments rose to £38,500. Thereafter there were minor adjustments, but the gross value of a fifteenth and tenth at the end of Edward III's reign was still £37,800. The extraordinary levies were particularly profitable: the quotas of wool charged on the shires in 1338 and 1341–2, when translated into cash terms, amounted to £79,400 and £151,000 respectively. By adding up all the available figures, we can calculate that the total value of the direct taxes levied between 1327 and 1377 was well in excess of £1,260,000.

The net proceeds were inevitably somewhat smaller. The experimental taxes in kind were particularly unpopular, and yielded well below their estimated value. The exemptions, evasions and collection costs of a subsidy on movables, however, accounted for a remarkably small proportion of the total estimated yield, and these taxes normally netted over 90 per cent of their gross value. This is all the more remarkable given the substantial reduction in the potential taxpaying population after 1348. Moreover, the parish subsidy of 1371 brought in over £49,900, making it one of the most successful taxes ever raised in the later Middle Ages. Even on a conservative estimate, then, the profits of lay taxation between 1327 and 1377 amounted to approximately £1,120,000. Clearly, without these subsidies granted in parliament with the consent of the knights and burgesses, Edward III could never have implemented his audacious plans for full-scale war in Scotland and France.

It was the special authority enjoyed by the commons in connection with taxation that gave them such influence in parliament. In theory, as we have seen, the knights and burgesses had no right to decline the king's request for subsidies during a period of war.[138] Their decision to attach specific conditions to the loan of wool offered in January 1340 was apparently possible only because the king was away at the time and the triennial fifteenth and tenth granted in 1337 was still being collected.[139] It was not until 1376 that parliament flatly rejected a demand for direct taxation, and even then it would seem that the commons were only able to reject the plea of necessity because the truce of Bruges had just been extended for another year.[140] Nor had the knights and burgesses the power to force concessions from the crown as a condition for the grant of a tax. What they could do was to threaten the king and his agents with passive resistance in the provinces if the crown refused to acknowledge and redress at least some of their grievances.[141] In order to press home this point the commons began, under Edward III, to link their complaints directly to grants of supply. By 1352, indeed, they were including detailed lists of common petitions within the actual schedules of taxation. While theoretically free to do as he pleased, the king was obviously coming under increasing pressure to accept and act upon the demands of his subjects. The inclusion of the common petitions in the official records of parliament on a regular basis after 1343 was indeed a tacit acknowledgment of the commons' new-found political influence.

The development of the common petition also gave the commons a greater sense of solidarity. At the start of the fourteenth century it is hardly possible to talk of a house of commons at all, since the knights and burgesses often met and acted separately. In some ways, of course, the shire representatives always had more in common with their fellow-landholders in the lords. Sir Otto Grandisson, for example, who sat for Kent on no fewer than eight occasions between 1332 and 1357, had two brothers among the peers — one a baron, the other a bishop.[142] However, the political conflicts of the 1320s seem to have driven a wedge between the lords and the majority of the gentry in parliament, and created a new sense of unity between the knights and burgesses. By the 1330s, indeed, the parliament rolls normally referred to the knights and burgesses as *la commune* or *les gentz du commun*.[143] One important manifestation of this new political alignment was the development of common petitions directed specifically against the aristocracy.[144] After the Black Death there was admittedly a change of tone, as the petty landholders allied with the crown and the lords in defence of proprietary interests.[145] But even on the central issue of the labour laws it is possible to detect a distinction between the attitudes of the major and minor landholders in parliament. The government's reluctance to allow the justices of the peace permanent authority over labour cases in the 1360s apparently proved particularly harmful to the 'middling men' of the realm. In 1368 the commons claimed that whereas great lords had servile tenants and seigneurial rights to fall back on, lesser landholders were dangerously dependent on paid labour and were therefore suffering much from rising wage demands.[146] It may well be, indeed, that the gentry now identified more easily with the problems of urban employers than with the comparative economic security of the aristocracy. Whatever the case, the parliament rolls make it clear that the two representative groups had now definitely emerged as a single political entity: the commons.

The greater unity and authority enjoyed by the commons in the mid-fourteenth century can best be measured by the considerable impact they made on the statute roll. The success of the knights and burgesses in extracting major legislative concessions from Edward III is well known, and a number of their important victories have already been discussed: the restrictions on purveyance and other prerogative levies, the enforcement of standard weights and measures, the change in the composition and powers of the peace commissions, and so on. It has also been pointed out, however, that the government tended to act on the commons' demands only when the political situation dictated some concession to public opinion or when the resulting legislation could be used to the advantage of the crown. Even if we assume that most of the statutes of this period arose from discussions in parliament, it is worth noting that the take-up rate was extremely uneven (see Table 5).[147] The pattern is clearly to be explained in political terms. The considerable legislative output of 1327–31 was the work of two successive regimes — Queen Isabella's and Edward III's — each anxious to buy popularity after an uncertain start to the new reign. The statutory concessions of 1335–7 were granted as measures of good faith to a realm which had already committed itself to war in Scotland and was now threatened by major hostilities with France. The great code of 1351–3 was a deliberate attempt to win back public confidence after the economic crisis of the plague and the controversies surrounding the regulation of overseas trade. Finally, the statutes of 1361–5 can be explained partly as an expression of thanks to the country for the sustained military activity of the previous twenty years, and partly as a means of extracting further indirect taxes to pay off the king's debts. With the exception of the major statutes of 1340–1, then, most of the parliamentary legislation of Edward III's reign occurred during periods of relative political calm. In the 1340s, when the knights and burgesses were hostile to the government's methods of funding the war, and in the 1370s when the majority of the political community turned against the crown, legislation declined to a mere trickle. Any influence the commons enjoyed over the making of the statutes tended to be a measure of the king's goodwill, and could easily be forgotten if politics turned sour.

Finally, it is important to recognize that matters raised in parliament and taken up by the government were not always resolved according to the precise wishes of the commons. The debate over the money supply is particularly interesting in this respect. Throughout Edward III's early years there were grumbles in parliament about the state of the coinage, which was much devalued by wear and clipping and by a debasement carried out in 1335.[148] The opening of the French war in 1337 meant that the bullion supply dried up, and there was an acute shortage of money in England.[149] Finally, in 1343, the government consulted with the prelates, peers and commons, and announced its intention of creating a new gold currency complementing the existing silver one.[150] The commons clearly believed that this, together with heavy penalties against counterfeiters and smugglers, would be sufficient to resolve the bullion shortage and allow a return to the former weight and fineness of sterling. This was the burden of numerous petitions presented in the parliaments of 1344–54.[151] But the government's policy was very different. Between 1343 and 1351 the weight of sterling was substantially reduced in order to increase the amount of coin in circulation.[152] The commons disliked this measure, claiming that it pushed up prices, and in 1352 they extracted a promise from the king that the ancient standard would be restored 'as soon as a good way is found'.[153] Nothing was done, however; and by the mid-1350s the knights and burgesses were forced to acknowledge that the government's policy had been a success.[154] The currency question provides an interesting example of an issue on which parliament expressed consistent opinions, and could force a somewhat sluggish government into action. But it also demonstrates how the commons and the king's ministers could come up with sharply different solutions to the same problem. The knights and burgesses were encouraged to believe that they could influence government policy, but the direction of that policy remained firmly in the hands of the experts.

It is therefore possible to argue that a great deal of the political initiative enjoyed by the commons during Edward III's reign was an illusion. The involvement of the knights and burgesses in diplomacy is particularly relevant here. In July 1338, the king claimed that his unpopular policy of buying alliances in the Low Countries had been sanctioned by the 'prelates, earls, barons, citizens, burgesses and all the knights of the shires and commons' — an apparent reference to the earlier debate on the French war held in 1337.[155] Again, in 1343, 1348 and 1354, the commons were specifically asked their opinion on possible truces with France. But we must be cautious about assuming that they had any real say in diplomatic policy. In 1348 they actually protested their innocence of such matters and refused to give advice. And when they did offer an opinion on proposals for peace it was almost always, as in 1354, a unanimous 'Yes, yes!'[156] This eagerness was not necessarily shared by the king and the lords. In 1369 Edward III was quick to point out that parliament, which had ratified the treaty of Brétigny, should now acknowledge the breakdown of the Anglo-French peace and accept its obligation to fund a new war.[157] It is difficult to escape the conclusion that the commons were only allowed a say in high politics so long as their opinions did not threaten the king's existing policies. It would be interesting to know how many other debates were terminated when the knights and burgesses showed signs of defecting from the official line.

In the 1370s, of course, this informal system of censorship broke down, and the political influence won by the commons during the middle years of the reign began to rebound on the crown. Indeed, the impeachment of the courtiers and the comprehensive indictment of government policy passed in the Good Parliament is often seen as the natural culmination of Edward III's plan to make the commons participate more fully in political affairs. But the highly exceptional nature of the 1376 crisis makes it difficult to accept such an interpretation. As late as 1373, when the government appealed for money to support an increasingly disastrous war effort, the knights and burgesses simply followed the usual procedures, authorizing a biennial fifteenth and tenth, putting in a list of petitions, and trusting to the government to provide relief.[158] And even in the Good Parliament they expressed the hope that their successors would be 'ready to aid and comfort [the king] ... like no other commons of the world'.[159] The actions of the commons in 1376 were therefore intended not to overturn the political structures of the realm but to restore the sense of co-operation which had existed during the 1350s and 1360s. The essentially conservative nature of their programme helps to explain why their successors failed to keep up the fight. Once John of Gaunt declared the crown hostile to the deeds of the Good Parliament in 1377, the commons could find no legitimate means of prolonging the dispute.[160] The failure of the Good Parliament to extract any statutory concessions from the crown simply highlights the comparative weakness of the opposition's case. The really lasting gains made by the knights and burgesses in the fourteenth century therefore came not through conflict, but consensus. It was the exclusive control over taxation and the ability to request legislation, not the right to impeach royal favourites, which were to be of lasting importance to the commons in the fifteenth and sixteenth centuries. If the knights and burgesses learned anything from Edward III's long reign, it was the positive benefit to be derived from political co-operation with the crown.

★ ★ ★

Our review of the commons' role in mid-fourteenth-century parliaments has carried us far from the provincial peasants and knights with whom this chapter began. Yet parliament has a rightful and prominent place in the history of the county communities. Unlike the kingdom of France, England was a monolithic polity. Edward III's military demands and political techniques certainly encouraged a sense of cohesion in provincial society: the shires had to defend themselves not only against the enemy, but also against the king's own agents. Consequently, it is possible to suggest that the county communities became much more aware of their rights and importance during this period. On the other hand, England was never in danger of breaking down into a series of semi-autonomous political units. The existence of a powerful monarchy and the development of a unitary system of taxation had ensured that public debate would always be focused on a single central institution, parliament. Few provincial societies were sufficiently united in themselves and isolated from others to develop a separate political consciousness, and it is highly unlikely that the gentry, the real leaders of local society, regarded the county boundaries as meaningful political barriers.[161] When the lesser landholders found that they were capable of making a real impression through their representatives in the commons, their ambitions were inevitably channelled into parliament. That membership of the commons came to be seen as a privilege rather than a duty in the later Middle Ages is striking testimony to the political influence won by the gentry in the course of Edward III's reign.

9 Urban society and the merchants

There is no single criterion for judging what constituted a town in fourteenth-century England.[1] It has traditionally been supposed that a town needed to possess a charter from the king or some other lord granting certain distinct privileges in return for the regular payment of a fixed rent or fee farm. The most common such privileges were the right to self-government by locally elected officials, to hold markets and fairs and have a gild merchant, and to claim free or 'burgage' tenure for all inhabitants. This definition, however, is far too restrictive, for many important urban communities, including Westminster, St Albans, Boston, Leicester and Warwick, lacked such comprehensive charters in our period.[2] The medieval town is best defined in economic terms: that is, as a community where the majority of the population was involved in non-agricultural pursuits such as manufacturing, retailing and servicing. Many towns were extremely small, with populations as low as 500.[3] But the poll tax returns of 1377 list some forty places with more than 1,000 taxpayers, and whose total populations were probably in excess of 1,500 or 2,000. Apart from London, which had at least 40,000 inhabitants in 1377, there were only a dozen or so towns with over 4,000 people: these were York, Bristol, Coventry, Norwich, Lincoln, Salisbury, Lynn, Colchester, Boston, Beverley, Newcastle upon Tyne and Canterbury.[4] It is with the political and economic life of these and the other more substantial provincial towns that we are primarily concerned in this chapter.

The records of the first poll tax indicate that the forty largest cities and towns accounted for just over 8 per cent of the entire population of England. It is difficult to tell whether such a proportion holds true for the whole of Edward III's reign, since there are no comparable figures for the period before the plague. Some towns clearly suffered a major reduction as a result of the pestilence: if the population of London in 1300 was as high as 100,000, as now seems possible,[5] then the capital evidently dwindled to less than half its size in the course of the following seventy years. On the other hand, certain large towns such as York and Colchester may well have remained stable after 1348, or even increased in size as a result of considerable immigration from their rural hinterlands.[6] Indeed, the period 1350–75 was one of considerable buoyancy for most provincial towns: the ambitious public building programmes carried out at such places as Coventry, Norwich, Bristol and Colchester provide an important index of urban prosperity, if not of actual size.[7] In the absence of proper statistics, it would probably be fair to say that the ratio of urban to rural dwellers did not alter drastically in the course of the fourteenth century, although the proportion living in towns may have risen slightly after the plague.

The medieval chartered towns have sometimes been regarded as havens of democracy, because all their inhabitants were free. Indeed, even villeins from rural areas who resided for a year and a day in such towns were assumed to have been released from their servile status. In practice, however, the towns were just as hierarchical as county society, and political influence was confined to an elite group of merchants who controlled the export and wholesale trades, dominated the gilds, and monopolized local office. Having made their names and fortunes in business, some of these men actually joined the ranks of landed society. John Pulteney, a prominent London draper knighted by Edward III in 1337, had extensive holdings in the home counties and the midlands and built himself an impressive mansion at Penshurst in Kent.[8] Many others, however, were content with town life and preferred to invest in commercial enterprises rather than land. It was the extraordinary wealth controlled by this comparatively small group that brought them into contact with the government and allowed them a growing influence in affairs of state. In examining the role of the townsmen in the mid-fourteenth-century polity, we shall therefore be concerned primarily with the members of these merchant oligarchies.

THE CITY OF LONDON

London enjoyed by far the largest concentration of population and wealth in medieval England. Its early development as a self-governing community and its proximity to the royal administrative capital often brought the city into conflict with the crown, and it played a major part in some of the political revolutions of the later Middle Ages.[9] It also controlled the domestic money market, and came to dominate the crown's credit dealings in the fourteenth and fifteenth centuries. London is therefore a special case, and obviously cannot be used to illustrate the crown's general policy towards the towns. But the actions of the Londoners often reflected, and sometimes helped to mould, the political will of the realm. Edward III's relations with the city therefore tell us much about the general character of his regime, and deserve first place in our discussion of urban society.

Edward's policy towards London was conditioned largely by the actions of his father and mother. The city had been locked in conflict with Edward II since the 1310s, and had bitterly resented the loss of its privileges during the London eyre of 1321. Not surprisingly, the city authorities supported Queen Isabella's invasion, and during the winter of 1326–7 they organized a 'commune' specifically dedicated to the task of removing Edward II from the throne. Indeed, it was the political pressure applied by this commune, together with the menacing presence of the London mob, that really persuaded those assembled in parliament at Westminster to acknowledge the overthrow of the old regime and support the succession of Edward III. This done, the Londoners lost no time in presenting parliament with a comprehensive list of their grievances. The government responded by pardoning the city from all former offences and debts, and granted a charter containing the most comprehensive and generous statement of the city's liberties yet known. London was never again to be subject to royal wardens; it was to be exempt from purveyance and from the jurisdiction of the household courts; its fee farm was fixed at the token sum of £300; and it was allowed to regulate its own internal trade.[10]

21   Penshurst Place, Kent, built by John Pulteney

It is a striking demonstration of Queen Isabella's ineptitude that these sweeping concessions failed to secure the loyalty of the city. By the time of the Salisbury parliament of October 1328 the Londoners were already finding fault with Roger Mortimer and offering support to Henry of Lancaster.[11] The events of the 1320s had proved that neither confrontation nor liberality could guarantee effective control over the city. What was really needed was trust, consistency and co-operation. It was the majority rule of Edward III that eventually provided those conditions.

The charter of 1327 had been made in the king's name and in full parliament, and it would have been very difficult for Edward III to challenge its validity. As it was, the charter became the most potent symbol of the new political alliance built up between crown and city after 1330, an alliance which lasted, with only minor disruptions, for over forty years. The only real dispute in the course of this reign arose as a result of the statute passed at York in 1335, which allowed all merchants, native and foreign, to trade freely throughout England.[12] This conflicted directly with the clause of the London charter of 1327 allowing the city to organize its own trade. It is doubtful that Edward intended to snub the Londoners, for in 1337 he specifically exempted the city from the statute.[13] Later, however, when the regime of Edington and Thoresby was attempting to claw back the king's lost powers, the crown took a conscious decision to bring London into line with the rest of the country. The Statute of York was reaffirmed in 1351 and, despite regular petitions from the Londoners, the council now refused to acknowledge their former immunity from the legislation.[14] Although the government made a partial concession in 1367 by prohibiting foreigners from trading in retail, it insisted that the other regulations of 1335 and 1351 should stand, and it was not until 1376 that Edward's ministers were once again induced to allow the Londoners to regulate alien trade.[15] This long-running controversy should make us cautious about assuming that Edward III simply bought the goodwill of the city by an endless stream of constitutional concessions. Nevertheless, the trade dispute is interesting largely because it is unique. The parameters of the relationship between crown and city had been determined before Edward III achieved power; but once in control, the king never really challenged the extraordinary range of privileges now enjoyed by the Londoners.

The primary reason for Edward's deferential attitude was that he needed the financial services offered by the city. In March 1340, at a time of considerable political unrest, the king asked the mayor and aldermen to authorize the levy of a corporate loan of £20,000.[16] The figure was pitched artificially high in order to allow room for negotiation, but the sum of £5,000 eventually agreed upon still represented a considerable charge on the citizens. A number of similar loans were raised in the following years: £1,000 in 1342, 2,000 marks (£1,333 6s. 8d.) in 1346, and £5,000 in 1371.[17] The citizens, either corporately or individually, also claimed to have invested at least £120,000 in the various credit operations launched by Edward III between 1337 and 1349.[18] Despite the theoretical obligation on the king's subjects to assist him with loans during times of war, both the city and the private companies were inclined to drive hard bargains. In 1351, shortly after the Statute of York had been reintroduced, the authorities successfully dodged another request for a corporate loan of 20,000 marks (£13,333 6s. 8d.); and in the 1370s, when the king was no longer regarded as creditworthy, the London bankers were able to charge exorbitant rates of interest on the sums advanced to the exchequer.[19] A stable and amicable political relationship was therefore crucial if the king were to be able to tap the city's wealth for the upkeep of his wars.

Such considerations obviously explain why Edward III, in contrast with every other king from Henry III to Richard II, never suspended the Londoners' rights of self-government. He came close to doing so in 1341, when the city was subjected to the general commissions of oyer and terminer set up to investigate administrative abuse throughout the realm. But as soon as the government was informed that this infringed the 1327 charter, it abandoned proceedings in the capital, and the eyre which was to have been held at the Tower of London was quickly bought off by the citizens for the relatively modest sum of 500 marks (£333 6s. 8d.). Although the fiction was maintained that the eyre had been held, and might be renewed in future, this was to be the last such intrusion into the city's rights under Edward III.[20] After the Good Parliament, when John of Gaunt tried to get the discredited financiers Richard Lyons, Adam Bury and John Pecche readmitted to the freedom of the city, it was rumoured that the crown intended to extend the jurisdiction of the marshalsea court into London, and was even planning to take over the administration of London. This created considerable disquiet, and explains why certain prominent Londoners were to support the great revolt of 1381.[21] But the disturbances of 1376–7 were simply another consequence of Edward III's removal from public affairs and the collapse of political consensus in his last years. In the mid-fourteenth century the Londoners emerged as one of the most privileged groups in political society. The fact that Edward III regarded this as an opportunity rather than a threat does much to explain the extraordinary stability of his regime.

THE PROVINCIAL TOWNS

To test whether or not the London model is typical of Edward III's attitude towards the towns, we may turn to the evidence of the royal charters. There are ninety-five separate grants to cities and towns recorded on the charter rolls between 1327 and 1377.[22] Of these, thirty-eight simply confirmed previous grants, and fifty-seven included new privileges. Their chronological spread is very uneven. No fewer than twenty-six charters were granted during the ascendancy of Mortimer and Isabella, and another thirty-eight were issued in the decade between Edward's assumption of power and his return from the continent at the end of 1340.[23] To some extent, this pattern was typical: any new ruler was expected to ratify or amplify his predecessor's grants. But the sheer number of such grants made while Mortimer and Isabella were in power suggests something out of the ordinary. In the parliament of Northampton of 1328 there were already complaints that the king's rights were being eroded by too many lavish concessions to towns, and it was ordered that all new franchises should be withdrawn pending an investigation.[24] This apparently did little to stem the flow of favours; and it was only after the seizure of power by the young king in 1330 that a rather more cautious attitude was adopted. When the government was presented with a request for a full declaration of the franchises of Bristol in January 1331, for instance, it decided only to issue a simple charter of confirmation, and delayed a fuller statement until a proper investigation had been carried out.[25] Even so, the comparatively large number of charters granted in the period 1330–40 suggests that the king had not departed significantly from the policies of his mother. As in so many other areas of government, it was the crisis of 1340–1 that really brought about a permanent change. The last thirty-six years of the reign produced only thirty-one royal charters to towns, two of which were subsequently withdrawn and one of which related to Edward's own new foundation at Queenborough (Kent).[26] On this basis at least, it is possible to argue that Edward's policy of buying favour from the towns largely came to an end after 1341.

There are certain other indications that the crown adopted a firmer attitude towards urban privileges during the second half of the reign. Prior to 1348, for instance, the town courts usually took responsibility for enforcing the Statutes of Winchester and Northampton, and the government only very rarely appointed special peace commissions to serve in towns.[27] Even when it did so, it normally appointed the mayors and bailiffs of the relevant towns to act as justices. After the Black Death, however, the situation changed. In 1354 a complaint was made in parliament about the lax observance of the new statutes on wages and prices in the city of London, and legislation was passed threatening punitive action against the city authorities.[28] Similar shortcomings elsewhere probably explain the spate of separate peace commissions issued for certain urban areas during the 1350s, 1360s and 1370s.[29] It is extremely interesting to notice that most of these commissions were staffed not by town officials but by a mixture of royal lawyers and private individuals drawn from the urban oligarchies. The town authorities were not unduly concerned about this development: indeed, some of them had a vested interest in encouraging the peace sessions since the profits of these courts could be used to pay off their fee farms.[30] Nevertheless, the experiment did have political implications, for it signified the king's right to assume superior jurisdiction within areas normally immune from immediate royal justice. It was only in 1373, when Edward III raised the town of Bristol to the status of a county and made the mayor and sheriff *ex officio* justices of the peace, that the crown abandoned its policy of sending in outside judges; and it was not until the 1390s that town officials generally won the right to act as justices of the peace in their own areas.[31]

The charters and the peace commissions therefore suggest that the second half of Edward III's reign witnessed a general attempt to restrict the amount of power exercised by the towns. It would be unwise to make too much of this, however, since the king's decisions were normally determined by local circumstances and personal preference, not by a pre-ordained policy. This can be shown by Edward's response to the numerous jurisdictional disputes which arose between secular and spiritual authorities within the towns. Sometimes the king sided with the burgesses. By a series of awards between 1334 and 1348, for instance, Edward transferred a considerable amount of power from the Prior of Coventry to the townsmen;[32] and in 1354 he allowed the citizens of York to regain control of Bootham from St Mary's Abbey.[33] In other cases he prevaricated. Between 1327 and 1358 no fewer than four different royal judgments were given in the long-standing dispute between the Abbot and men of St Albans.[34] And on other occasions the support of a powerful ecclesiastical institution meant more to the king than the goodwill of a town. Edward was quick to support successive bishops of Winchester in upholding their various market rights in and around the city;[35] and after the St Scholastica's Day riot in Oxford in 1355 the king transferred many of the town's hard-fought privileges to the university.[36] The most important point about these disputes, in fact, is not so much the way they were resolved as the fact that they were always submitted to the king for arbitration. Under an inadequate or unpopular government, townsmen were often tempted to resolve their internal problems by violence: witness the outbreaks of disorder in London, Bury St Edmunds, Abingdon, St Albans and Northampton in 1326–7, and the many urban uprisings which took place during the great revolt of 1381.[37] The fact that the Oxford riot of 1355 was more or less the only serious disturbance in the intervening period says much for Edward III's reputation as an impartial judge and honoured lord.

This dependence on the king's grace can be further illustrated through the extant financial records of the towns. In the late fourteenth and fifteenth centuries many urban corporations were to pay out quite substantial sums of money to members of the nobility in order to secure influential political support. But in the mid-fourteenth century such *douceurs* were still comparatively rare.[38] Local lords obviously needed to be placated. Lynn, for instance, made regular gifts to the Earl of Suffolk and the Bishop of Norwich; Exeter curried favour with the Earl of Devon; and Winchester and London courted their respective bishops.[39] But there was no general reliance on the magnates to forward the interests of the towns. Instead, it was the king and his officials who were the real beneficiaries of urban generosity. London led the way in this respect, regularly sending wine and victuals to the court and making free gifts of money to both Edward III and the Black Prince.[40] In 1337 the sum of £369 was raised in the city in order to make presents to the king, queen and lords during a great council at which London was endeavouring to obtain exemption from the 1335 Statute of York.[41] It is noticeable that the most regular entries in the accounts of the provincial towns relate to royal administrators. John Thoresby, keeper of the privy seal, was in receipt of a fee of £1 from Cambridge in 1347, and the chamber clerk Thomas Bramber was given £10 by the city of Norwich in 1351.[42] Those who profited most of all from such generosity were the royal judges.[43] The towns freely accepted that quite major expenditure was sometimes necessary in order to secure royal favour: Hull, for instance, paid a fine of 250 marks (£166 13s. 4d.) in order to have the privilege of appointing its own mayor and paying its own fee farm in 1331.[44] In 1373 the authorities of Lynn paid out £107 in their successful bid to obtain a wool staple in the town, and in 1376–7 they spent over £500 on gifts, bribes and other expenses incurred in the capital during a legal dispute with the Bishop of Norwich.[45] So long as Edward III remained king, then, the towns naturally looked to the crown, its courts, and its professional agents for protection and advancement. Their later reliance on the magnates was merely a reflection of the decline of royal authority that set in after Edward's demise.

THE TOWNS AND WAR

That the king attached some importance to maintaining good relations with the towns is shown by his special efforts to keep them informed on the progress of the war. The fact that the sheriffs were instructed to make their proclamations in the principal towns and market places possibly means that townsmen were rather more aware of political and military developments than were their rural neighbours.[46] In any case, the crown was not content simply to rely on this general network of information. In 1346, separate letters recounting news of the victory at Crécy were dispatched to the Cinque Ports and twenty-nine coastal towns.[47] The London records in particular contain transcripts of important diplomatic and personal correspondence: the king's letter to his eldest son relating the events of the battle of Sluys, official responses to papal proposals for peace, a letter of the Black Prince sending news of the victory at Poitiers, and so on.[48] The London material is not necessarily typical, but there are scraps of evidence to suggest that provincial towns were also in regular communication with the king's military and diplomatic agents. The citizens of Winchester were informed of Edward III's safe return home after concluding the treaty of Brétigny in 1360; and the men of Leicester received letters in the 1340s and 1350s both from the king and from their lord, the Earl of Lancaster, on the state of the war.[49]

Townsmen were also encouraged to participate in the celebrations following major campaigns. In 1344 the wives of certain prominent Londoners were invited to attend the tournament at Windsor, and their husbands seem to have taken an active part in many of the jousts held in the capital.[50] Henry Picard of London is said to have put on a great banquet in the 1360s attended by both Edward III and the captive John II.[51] Naturally, there were no merchants in the Order of the Garter, and it was still extremely rare for members of the urban patriciate to be knighted. But the crown was quite prepared to accept and play on the aspirations of the trading classes. The sumptuary legislation of 1363 put merchants owning goods and chattels valued at £1,000 on a par with those holding £200 worth of land, and allowed them — and their wives — to wear fine cloth and silk, silver jewellery and miniver (though not the prestigious ermine).[52] The ostentation which characterized courtly life was therefore aped by the top ranks of urban society, and despite the gibes of the chroniclers,[53] there is little to indicate that the king himself showed any disdain for such developments.

The crown's principal motive here, of course, was a financial one. By keeping the towns well informed on the progress of the war and by appealing to the well-established tradition of mercantile snobbery, the king naturally hoped that he might persuade the leaders of urban society to support his enterprises with hard cash. The contributions made to state finance by the townsmen fell into three main categories: direct taxes, customs duties on overseas trade, and loans. It will be helpful to discuss each of these before attempting to evaluate the more general political implications of the government's fiscal relations with the commercial community.

Direct Taxes

Taxes on movables were in some respects the least oppressive of the charges on the towns in the mid-fourteenth century. The differential scale adopted in such taxes after 1332 ensured that towns paid a higher proportion of their wealth than did the countryside: a tenth as against the rural fifteenth. But tax commissioners seem to have found it particularly difficult to assess the movable property of townsmen, and the decline in certain urban valuations during the early fourteenth century suggests that some towns, or groups of townsmen, became increasingly adept at the art of underassessment.[54] The anomalies became still greater after 1334, when it was decided that the towns, like all other communities, should be responsible for collecting their own contributions to royal taxation. As a result, the number of taxpayers in Leicester rose from seventy-three in 1332 to some 445 in 1336; and it is difficult to escape the conclusion that lesser men were now having to contribute a larger share of the total assessment.[55] A more serious development from the king's point of view was the decision to allow a number of important cities and towns to compound for their taxes with block payments.[56] In 1335 Edward was already complaining that the 1,100 marks (£733 6s. 8d.) offered by the city of London in lieu of assessment was quite inadequate;[57] but he did nothing directly to increase it, and the figure remained unchanged for the rest of the reign. If we take the forty towns and cities which contributed over £25 to the fifteenth and tenth after 1334, we find that their total assessments came to £3,035, or just 8 per cent of the national assessment.[58] This correlates remarkably well with the demographic evidence already discussed. However it is equally clear that it failed to reflect the considerable financial capital controlled by the urban communities.

Nor did the various experiments in direct taxation carried out after 1334 redress this imbalance. The ninth of 1340 seems to have weighed particularly heavily on the countryside.[59] Admittedly, the parish subsidy of 1371 put pressure on those urban areas with large numbers of churches: Norwich, which paid £94 12s. for a conventional tenth, now had to find £266 16s., and the more prosperous parts of the shire were prevailed upon to assist the city.[60] In many other cases, however, the urban assessments seem to have fallen in 1371: London's contribution, for instance, was just £638.[61] In practice, then, the extra burden of this tax was carried almost wholly by the rural population. All this helps to explain why townsmen made so few complaints about taxation. In 1348, at a time when they were suffering from certain other controversial fiscal exactions, a number of towns put in requests for the reduction of their quotas for the tenth.[62] Otherwise, the silence is almost unbroken. So far as direct taxation was concerned, urban dwellers clearly had a vested interest in maintaining the status quo.

The towns also made a comparatively small contribution to the periodic levies of men, arms and victuals taken to support the war effort. London itself is known to have supplied at least 500 archers and 600 armed men for the French war between 1337 and 1360, as well as 200 infantrymen for Edward's campaigns in Scotland.[63] But few other urban areas gave major assistance. In 1327 the men of Oxford promised to send fifty men to Scotland, but only because this was made a condition of the grant of a new royal charter.[64] Although most provincial towns were theoretically subject to arrays and prises, they very often managed to secure immunity by bribing the king's agents.[65] It was only in 1346–7 that the crown made any real effort to remedy the situation by demanding specific quotas of troops from 131 cities and towns in the south and the midlands.[66] The experiment provoked hostile reaction, and the government was forced to commute the levies to cash payments and to promise that they would not be used as a precedent for future demands.[67]

The one wartime levy which did have a major impact at least on the coastal towns was the requisitioning of ships and mariners for the transport of the king's armies.[68] Ships were simply seized from their masters, who rarely received any compensation for the time that their vessels were out of commission. The towns themselves were also responsible for raising and paying the sailors employed on the king's service. The resulting burdens were considerable. The authorities of Lynn paid out well over £200 between 1336 and 1341 on shipping and mariners; and in 1340 the burgesses of Newcastle claimed that they were owed no less than £723 for ships impressed during the Scottish wars.[69] In 1360 Bristol complained that the town was almost completely denuded of ships and open to attack as a result of the king's demands; and the large convoys conscripted for the transport of the Black Prince and his army to Bordeaux led to protests in the parliament of 1362.[70] Finally, in 1372–3, the crown ordered selected towns and cities to build one or two 'barges' or 'balingers' which were then to be maintained at local expense and used for the king's service whenever required. The resulting costs were considerable: London spent £620 on a single vessel.[71] In Edward III's later parliaments there were many complaints about the inordinate demands being placed on shipmasters and others involved in seagoing trade.[72] At the local level, indeed, the results could be catastrophic: one of the chief reasons for the dramatic decline of the port of Yarmouth in the second half of the fourteenth century was the incessant pressure applied by the government on the town's merchant fleet.[73]

It would obviously be a mistake, then, to suppose that the relatively privileged position enjoyed by the towns with regard to direct taxation signified political timidity on the part of the crown. In fact, the major reason why the towns were not required to contribute more to the fifteenths and tenths and to the arrays was that their richest inhabitants were also paying out very substantial sums in customs duties and loans to the king. These sources of income formed an increasingly important element in the system of public finance, and their development does much to explain the course of politics in Edward III's reign.

The Taxation of Overseas Trade

By 1327 there were two permanent taxes on overseas trade.[74] The ancient custom was paid by all merchants, native as well as alien, and consisted of a standard charge of 6s. 8d. on every sack of wool exported from England. The new custom, on the other hand, was paid only by foreigners, and included small charges for the import of cloth, wine and general merchandise, as well as an additional export levy of 3s. 4d. on each sack of wool. The most valuable taxes on overseas trade, however, were the extraordinary wool subsidies or 'maltolts' (literally, 'bad taxes') imposed on top of the customs duties at times of war. Prior to 1327 there had been only one major levy of this type, collected by Edward I between 1294 and 1297 and set at the rate of £1 13s. 4d. on every sack of wool. The first subsidy collected by Edward III, to support his Scottish campaign in 1333, was charged at the relatively modest rate of 10s. per sack (see Table 3). But at the start of the French war in 1336 the subsidy was fixed at £1, rising by 1338 to £1 13s. 4d. for denizens and £2 13s. 4d. for aliens. In 1340 a uniform rate of £1 13s. 4d. was established. After a short break in 1341–2 it was raised to £2, and continued at this level for the next twenty years. In 1362 parliament took a momentous decision by allowing the king to carry on levying the subsidy during peacetime, albeit at the reduced rate of £1 per sack. In 1365 it went up again to £2, and then fell to £1 16s. 8d. in 1368. Finally, on the resumption of the French war in 1369, it rose to £2 3s. 4d. and stayed at this level for the rest of the reign. Other short-term subsidies and forced loans were also charged on overseas trade from time to time, raising the total level of taxation still higher. At one point in 1340, for instance, it was claimed that native merchants were being charged a total of £4 and aliens an amazing £5 3s. 4d. for every sack of wool they exported.[75]

The adoption of the wool subsidy as a permanent element in the taxation of overseas trade meant that the profits of the customs increased enormously (see Table 4). During the first ten financial years of Edward III's reign (Michaelmas 1326–Michaelmas 1336), the customs and other extraordinary levies on overseas trade yielded an average of just over £14,500 per annum. Unfortunately, it is difficult to judge the immediate effect of the new charges imposed in the late 1330s, for the wool trade was subject to a series of embargoes around 1340 and the customs system itself was farmed by syndicates of merchants between 1345 and 1349.[76] But the fact that this farm was fixed at £50,000 a year says much for the transformation that had occurred in the meantime. In 1351 the crown returned to the direct administration of the ports, and we have reasonably comprehensive customs accounts for the rest of the reign. These provide some remarkable statistics. In the exchequer year 1353–4 the taxation of overseas trade produced a total of £113,400, and in 1361–2 it yielded almost £110,000. The mean annual yield in the period 1353–62 was no less than £87,500, over six times the average for the first decade of the reign. The yield dropped to about £61,000 a year in 1362–9, but then recovered slightly to reach some £65,500 a year in 1369–75. Altogether, the crown's net income from the taxation of overseas trade between 1351 and 1376 stood at approximately £1,750,000. In other words, the profits of the customs in these twenty-five years alone exceeded the total income from direct taxation levied on the clergy and the laity in the course of the entire reign. Not only had Edward III's wars produced a dramatic increase in indirect taxation; they had also made the customs and subsidies the single most important weapon in the financial armoury of the late medieval state.

In immediate terms, it was of course the merchants who had to pay the customs duties. Their ability to do so says much both for their wealth and for the extraordinary profits they made out of selling English wool on the continent. In 1336–7, for instance, the price for wool on the domestic market was only about half its value in the Low Countries.[77] Consequently, it was possible to expend considerable sums in purchasing, customing and transporting wool and still benefit from the deal. On the other hand, the merchants were highly sensitive to any erosion of their profit margins, and they inevitably reacted to high customs duties by trying to push down domestic prices. In 1337 the crown agreed to fix a scale of minimum prices in order to protect the interests of wool growers and up-country merchants, and for the next decade the value of wool remained reasonably stable. After the Black Death, however, wool failed to keep up with inflation, and by the early 1360s the domestic market was severely depressed.[78] It is therefore easy to see why the producers claimed that they were indirectly burdened by the taxes on overseas trade.

The resulting political conflict between the greater merchants and the wool growers will be traced later in this chapter. Here we need only mention the economic and financial implications. It was possible to avoid high rates of export duty if one converted raw wool into cloth and sent it to the continent in its finished state. It was not long before enterprising manufacturers and merchants realized this, and sponsored the development of the native cloth industry.[79] In 1347 the crown attempted to make good the gaps in the customs system by imposing a general duty on cloth exports.[80] But low rates meant that the cloth custom was of only marginal significance: indeed, in the decade 1352–62 it produced only about £500 a year for the crown.[81] As wool exports declined and cloth exports rose, the total value of indirect taxation was bound to fall, and fifteenth-century kings were to find it impossible to alter the customs system in their favour. The trend was already evident in Edward III's last years, though it was still a long way from threatening the financial stability of the crown. In fact, Edward III had transformed the economic base of the English monarchy by tapping that potentially enormous supply of wealth controlled by the merchants. That he was the first king to do this on any regular basis says much for the authority and sheer ingenuity of his regime.

Loans

Edward's ability to manipulate the merchants for his own benefit is also demonstrated by the raising of loans. No previous king had systematically attempted to use the domestic money market, and Edward III himself preferred to deal with the Florentine banking firms of the Bardi and Peruzzi during the first decade of his reign.[82] The only general attempt to raise money from English merchants during this period was a forced loan imposed on all those involved in overseas trade in 1327, which yielded some £7,400.[83] The situation was transformed, however, after the opening of the Hundred Years War. The Italian firms remained important until the early 1340s, when they went bankrupt; and certain other foreigners such as the Hanseatic merchants and Tidemann Limberg of Dortmund continued to support Edward's regime thereafter.[84] But the sheer scale of royal expenditure from 1336 forced the government to find alternative sources of credit, and drove it into negotiations with the English merchant classes.

The man responsible for shaping the crown's credit dealings between 1337 and 1349 was William de la Pole, a prominent merchant of Hull who had strong links with the commercial community in London.[85] By July 1337, Pole and his business associate Reginald Conduit had brought together a group of fifty English merchants who agreed to lend the king a total of £200,000. In order to raise this capital, they were allowed to seize 30,000 sacks of wool and export it for sale on the continent. The suppliers of the wool were to be given credit notes redeemable only when the company had received repayment of their loan from the crown. The scheme was a workable one, and potentially highly profitable. But the king's agents in the Low Countries were desperately short of funds, and simply seized the first shipment of wool for their own use. Pole's associates were forced to take debentures for the wool (the so-called Dordrecht bonds), and when the crown subsequently defaulted on these promises, it left both the wool company and the original suppliers substantially out of pocket. The whole enterprise was a costly failure, and created intense bad feeling among the political community.

Not everyone, however, was ruined by the collapse of the wool company. Pole, for instance, continued to provide the king with large amounts of cash: his loans and other related expenses between June 1338 and October 1339 amounted to at least £112,000.[86] Pole was caught up in the political backlash of 1340, and was arrested and imprisoned on the king's return from the continent in November that year. But by 1343 he had managed to ingratiate himself with the government, and put together a new syndicate of merchants led by Thomas Melchbourn, who agreed to lend the king money on the security of the customs.[87] In 1345 the same men were permitted to farm the customs for £50,000 a year, on condition that they would use any other profits from the ports to make additional loans. Between 1343 and 1351 three successive monopoly companies advanced the remarkable total of £369,000 to the crown. Indeed, this proved the most lasting and successful of all Edward's credit schemes. But it had two serious defects. First, the syndicates were themselves forced to borrow money, and too often failed to pay it back. It was later claimed, for instance, that groups of Londoners had advanced some £40,000 to Walter Chiriton's company during the time of the siege of Calais, and that none of this had been recovered. Secondly, the companies were allowed to buy up Dordrecht bonds at a fraction of their original value. This caused considerable resentment among the lesser merchants, who became extremely reluctant to enter into credit deals with the crown.

In 1346–7 the king was desperately short of money, and for the first time his ministers made a general appeal both to individual merchants and to town governments for loans.[88] In the spring and summer of 1347 the exchequer did manage to collect about £11,000 from merchants not immediately involved in the syndicate, but this sum was dominated by a few large donations such as the £4,000 advanced by sixteen citizens of Norwich.[89] In 1351 Edward made a further appeal for funds, and for the first time a number of provincial towns offered corporate loans. But contributions from individual merchants were extremely small, and the total raised amounted to a mere £6,500.[90] The monopolistic practices of the previous fifteen years had clearly alienated a substantial proportion of the merchant community,[91] and the king had little choice but to wind up the farm of the customs between 1349 and 1351.

It was not until 1357 that the crown again required any substantial cash advances. By this stage the political controversy over the monopoly companies had calmed down, and a ban on wool exports by native merchants imposed in 1353 had given the king a powerful bargaining position.[92] In return for special licences allowing them to participate in overseas trade, a number of powerful merchants — mostly Londoners — were persuaded to advance loans totalling over £19,800. The new creditors included several former colleagues of the monopolists, such as Henry Picard, Thomas Dolesley, John Pyel and Thomas Perle, and a group of younger men who rose to prominence in the city after the Black Death, including John Not, John Aubrey, Adam Bury and John Pecche.[93] Whether these men entertained hopes of forming a new cartel is uncertain, since the king required few further loans over the next twelve years. But after the resumption of war in 1369 Edward was to become increasingly dependent on a small group of London financiers, and a return to the dubious commercial practices of his earlier years inevitably precipitated political controversy.

Between 1369 and 1375 the English crown borrowed at least £150,000, and probably considerably more, in order to cover the escalating costs of warfare in France, Scotland and Ireland.[94] The townsmen, like the nobility and the clergy, were expected to meet their share of this debt. Between March and September 1370, corporate advances alone accounted for about £9,200, of which £5,000 came from London, 1,000 marks (£666 13s. 4d.) from Norwich and £600 from York.[95] On 24 May 1370, ninety-three named Londoners contributed loans totalling £1,500; and in February 1371 another group from the capital advanced £4,600.[96] Even William de la Pole's widow Katherine was persuaded to send in £200.[97] Once again, the loans from the merchant classes were part of a deal with the crown. An embargo had been placed on all foreign trade in the summer of 1369, and it was not until substantial loans had been offered and paid that the government finally lifted the ban in August 1370.[98]

So far, there had been no discernible trend back towards monopolistic practices. But in 1371 Treasurer Scrope began to make his economies in the exchequer, and the crown refused to honour many of the debts incurred in 1369–70.[99] Under these circumstances, it was no longer possible to organize simple credit deals: a general request for corporate loans from the provincial towns in 1375 yielded nothing.[100] Instead, the government was forced to offer increasingly advantageous terms to the small number of Londoners still prepared to provide cash advances.[101] These new creditors — John Pyel, Richard Lyons, John Hedingham and William Walworth — were allowed to buy up ancient debts at discount and to charge exorbitant rates of interest. From Christmas 1372 Richard Lyons was also granted the farm of the petty customs (the duties on cloth and general merchandise) in all the ports. Finally, in November 1373 John Pecche was allowed exclusive control of the sale of sweet wines in the city of London on condition that he would share the profits of that office with the king. This marked a return to the discredited practices of the 1340s and provoked hostile reaction in the Good Parliament, where the commons impeached Lyons and Pecche, together with William Ellis (Lyons's deputy in the port of Yarmouth) and Adam Bury (in his capacity as mayor of Calais). The fact that so many of those who had loaned money in 1369–70 had been unable to get satisfaction while the financiers held sway undoubtedly fired the opposition movement: in 1377, for instance, the town authorities of Lynn were still attempting to recover the loan of 500 marks (£333 6s. 8d.) advanced in 1370.[102] But what gave particular vehemence to the attack in 1376 was the widespread belief that the London merchants, acting through Lord Latimer, had deliberately taken advantage of the king's infirmity to reap material and political advantage for themselves.

The story of Edward III's credit dealings is particularly complicated, and only the barest outline has been given here. The main point to emerge from this brief analysis is the considerable antipathy which often developed between the majority of political society — including a good proportion of the merchant class — and the relatively small group of wealthy capitalists who tended to dominate the king's credit transactions. It is often suggested that after the collapse of the farm of the customs in 1349–51 Edward III was forced permanently to abandon his dealings with such cartels and to provide formal guarantees against any further restrictive practices.[103] But it is clear from the comparatively small sums raised in 1351, 1357 and 1369–70 that the merchant community was not prepared to compensate the king for the resulting loss of credit. With the onset of the war in 1369, the crown became increasingly dependent on loans, and inevitably returned to the same practices that had been so roundly condemned in the 1340s. In the meantime, however, there had been an important realignment in politics. One of the principal reasons for the commons' success in 1376 was that they were now able to act in the name of the merchant community. This represented one of the most important political developments of Edward III's reign, and will provide the theme for the remaining sections of this chapter.

THE ESTATE OF MERCHANTS AND THE BURGESSES

Throughout the first half of the fourteenth century it was regular practice for the English crown to summon merchant assemblies, in which it negotiated wool subsidies and forced loans or discussed more general matters concerning trade. Occasionally the king sent writs to town authorities asking for the return of representatives,[104] but more usually the crown itself chose the membership of such meetings. The lists of those to be summoned were probably drawn up with the assistance of prominent merchants such as William de la Pole,

John Pulteney, Reginald Conduit and Henry Picard, who were better acquainted than were the clerks of chancery with the complicated world of trade and finance. So important was the business undertaken in these assemblies that historians have sometimes referred to a separate 'estate of merchants' which often found itself in competition or conflict with parliament. In fact, there is little to indicate that meetings between the council and the merchants were regarded with any particular suspicion by the rest of political society until the start of the Hundred Years War. It was only with the imposition of exorbitant wool subsidies after 1337 that a conflict began to emerge between the relatively narrow group of exporters actively involved in such assemblies and the larger cross-section of wool growers and lesser merchants.

It must not be forgotten, of course, that many merchant communities were directly represented in parliament.[105] The methods by which the sheriffs decided which towns ought to have their own members of parliament were surprisingly haphazard, and there were some significant omissions: Coventry, for instance, did not have separate representation for almost a century after 1353.[106] Nevertheless, most towns appreciated the privilege and guarded it well. This can be illustrated by the calibre of those chosen as members of parliament. These men were usually drawn from among the urban oligarchies they represented: except in the south-west, very few towns as yet called upon outsiders or members of the landed gentry to serve as their spokesmen in parliament. Many, however, had powerful connections. William Fen, who represented Southwark in 1351, was chamberlain to the Archbishop of Canterbury; and Thomas Leggy, skinner of London, who sat in parliament on two occasions in the middle years of Edward III's reign, married a daughter of the Earl of Warwick.[107] Roger Normanville, a freeman of York and twice representative for that city, was also a long-standing royal servant, keeper of the king's stud north of the Trent from 1343 to 1350 and controller of the king's works at York.[108] The urban authorities were also prepared to reward their representatives handsomely. The crown set a standard rate of 2s. a day for the expenses of citizens and burgesses attending parliament, but many towns were considerably more generous. Norwich and Lynn paid 3s. 4d. a day, and London still more.[109] These examples indicate that the towns were anxious to secure the services of able and powerful men who might promote local interests in parliament. By the end of Edward III's reign the same men had also emerged as the principal spokesmen of the merchant class.

The Wool Subsidy

There were two major issues on which parliament and the estate of merchants joined battle: the wool subsidy and the staple. The maltolt, as we have seen, began life as an extraordinary tax collected during periods of active warfare.[110] Like direct taxation, it therefore required some form of consent and had to be renewed at regular intervals. The king naturally turned to the merchants for the necessary authorization, not only because they were immediately responsible for paying the duties at the ports, but also because the wool subsidy often formed part of a more complicated trade deal with the major exporters. Thus, the maltolt granted by a group of forty-one merchants meeting with the king during

22 & 23   The gold noble of Edward III, with its representation of the king aboard a ship of war

the great council held at Nottingham in September 1336 was the first stage in a series of negotiations leading to William de la Pole's wool scheme of 1337.[111] The commons, on the other hand, claimed that the imposition of high rates of duty affected all those involved in the wool trade, whether producers, middlemen or exporters, and that the king ought therefore to seek authority for such taxes in parliament. The collapse of the wool company in 1338, followed by a further large increase in the level of the wool subsidy, quickly convinced the commons that the only way of guaranteeing the interests of the producers was to control the maltolt themselves.

The following decade therefore witnessed a long-running dispute between the crown, the commons and the merchants (see Table 3). In April 1340, when parliament managed to authorize an extension of the wool subsidy, the commons insisted that the high rate set for foreigners should be reduced, and that once the subsidy granted in this parliament had expired all such levies should cease.[112] But the subsequent political crisis left Edward in no mood for compromise, and the renunciation of the statute of 1341 made it clear that he would accept no parliamentary restriction of his rights. Early in 1341 the king negotiated an additional subsidy with the merchants, to be paid over and above the current parliamentary levy; and in 1342 he simply overrode the agreement of 1340 and negotiated a new subsidy of £2 per sack not with parliament but with a broadly based mercantile assembly.[113] The commons reacted quickly, and in 1343 offered to extend the same rates for a further three years.[114] Both sides were probably eager to co-operate with the crown at this stage, since the new merchant company put together in 1343 was promising to help those holding Dordrecht bonds and other credit notes to redeem their debts on the customs.[115] But such hopes were dashed when this company turned into a private speculative venture in 1345. The result was an important new political alignment between the commons and the lesser merchants.

Until 1343 most merchant assemblies had been sufficiently large to claim to represent a cross-section of the commercial community. But after the setting up of the English company and its gradual evolution into a monopolistic enterprise, both the size and the frequency of such meetings declined. It was not only parliament but also a large proportion of the business community which therefore became alienated from the farmers of the customs after 1345. Such was the bad feeling generated by the Melchbourn and Chiriton companies, indeed, that the crown did not dare to approach any representative body for a renewal of the maltolt. Instead the king persuaded a group of bishops and magnates meeting in February 1346 to prolong the levy for another two years.[116] In March 1347 the regency administration forced a similar council to grant a prospective wool subsidy running for three years from Michaelmas 1348. What was more, the 1347 assembly also authorized the imposition of a permanent custom on cloth and an additional subsidy on wine and general merchandise.[117] The assemblies of 1346–7 marked the first occasion in the fourteenth century when the English crown had dared to impose customs and subsidies on overseas trade without the direct consent either of a body of merchants or of parliament.[118] Such high-handed actions seem to have persuaded the majority of the merchants that their only hope of maintaining some political initiative was to make common cause with parliament. Their opportunity came in March 1348. The commons now agreed to ratify the wool subsidy granted by the council in 1347.[119] They probably had little choice in the matter, since the maltolt had already been assigned to pay off the forced loan of 20,000 sacks of wool currently being collected in the shires.[120] But their action provided an important precedent. For the rest of Edward III's reign, the wool subsidy was always renewed in parliament, or at least by a great council containing representatives of the commons.[121] Finally, in 1362, the king formally conceded that no subsidy should be imposed on overseas trade without the proper consent of the community in parliament.[122]

From Edward's point of view, of course, the new deal had much to recommend it. Parliament was more or less obliged to extend the maltolt for as long as the war lasted, and the successive wool subsidies of the 1350s did more than anything else to restore the financial stability of his regime. But the commons also derived benefit from the situation. We have already noted that Edward III's early attempts to extract grants of direct taxation from great councils failed because of his unwillingness to allow such assemblies to present common petitions.[123] Once parliament had won effective control over lay subsidies, it made the vital link between supply and redress of grievance and persuaded the king to concede to some of its demands. The commons' successful bid to control indirect taxation was bound to give this movement further impetus. In September 1353 the king called a great council, including elected representatives from the shires and a limited number of towns, to advertise the new Ordinance of the Staple. This form of assembly, which had fallen out of use since the late 1330s, was probably chosen because the king did not wish to have the new legislation enrolled among the statutes.[124] But the government made a tactical error in asking the assembly to authorize an extension of the maltolt. Since they had been called upon to fulfil one of the functions now associated with parliament, the representatives of the shires and towns insisted on acting like their parliamentary counterparts and presented the king with a list of common petitions.[125] Edward had little choice but to respond, and new laws including the Statute of Praemunire and regulations on the cloth and wine trades were written up on the statute roll.[126] This effectively eliminated that distinction between parliaments and representative great councils which Edward III had tried to maintain in the 1330s, and finally persuaded him that all future financial and political negotiation would have to be undertaken in parliament.

The constitutional implications of this development need to be kept in focus. The king was still under no obligation to accept and act upon the political demands entered by the commons with their schedules of taxation. Indeed, in the parliament of 1355 the government made not a single statutory concession, despite the fact that the assembly extended the wool subsidy for the exceptionally long period of six years. Nevertheless, the commons' position had clearly been enhanced by the new assumption that they alone represented a cross-section of the commercial classes. In January 1348 a number of the common petitions recorded on the parliament roll were addressed specifically in the name of the merchants.[127] This was virtually the first time in Edward III's reign that a parliamentary assembly meeting without a committee of merchants in attendance had claimed to represent the mercantile community.[128] The evidence should not be exaggerated, but the coincidence is striking. The commons' claim to speak for the merchants not only strengthened their case for taking over the negotiation of the wool subsidy, but also allowed them an increasing say in the economic policies of the crown. The political impact can best be assessed by examining the second point of conflict between parliament and the estate of merchants.

The Staple

The staple was a fixed point through which all wool (and sometimes other goods) intended for the foreign market had to pass. From the king's point of view, the staple was a means of applying diplomatic and commercial pressure on England's main markets in the Low Countries. Whenever possible, then, Edward III favoured the idea of locating the staple on the continent. The greater merchants tended to see the staple as an opportunity to monopolize trade and to use the customs as surety for loans to the crown. Because they controlled exports, it suited their purposes also to have a continental staple. The growers and the middlemen, however, were interested in the staple chiefly because they saw it as a means of restricting the activities of alien merchants within England. The only way in which they could participate fully in such a system and ensure a share of the higher prices that English wool then reached on the continent was to have the staple situated at home. The resulting clash of interests between these groups tells us much about the balance of power in mid-fourteenth-century England.

The first recorded staple had been set up in 1313 at St Omer in France, and had remained there, with brief interruptions, until 1326, when domestic staples were established in London, Newcastle, York, Lincoln, Norwich, Winchester, Exeter, Bristol and Shrewsbury.[129] The major wool ports of Hull, Boston, Lynn and Yarmouth were deliberately excluded from this list in order to prevent the staples from being dominated by wealthy exporters. But this did not work. Both the ports and other inland towns resented the inconvenience and expense of taking wool to two separate places before it was ready for export.[130] Although the staple towns themselves put up a vigorous defence of the system,[131] the new government of Queen Isabella bowed to public opinion and abolished the domestic staples in 1328. They were revived briefly in 1332–4; but with the outbreak of the French war and the establishment of a series of monopoly companies, the staple was transferred to the Low Countries, and remained fixed there until the early 1350s.[132]

Because of its close association with the royal financiers and their restrictive practices, this foreign staple became unpopular not only with the producers and up-country merchants but also with many exporters. Consequently, when the farm of the customs was wound up in 1351, it was more or less inevitable that the staple would be transferred back to England. In June 1353 the government ordered the immediate establishment of a series of domestic staples to come into operation in September.[133] Once again, these were to be fixed not in the major ports but at important inland towns. The king's ministers then set about compiling a more detailed ordinance for the administration of the new system. The most important and novel of its regulations was that denizens would be deprived of the right to export wool. This amounted to a drastic but effective guarantee against the creation of further monopoly companies. To compensate for the loss of denizen exports, the government now offered an attractive package of legal and commercial privileges to alien merchants trading in England. The resulting Ordinance of the Staple was presented for ratification in the great council of September-October 1353.[134]

An integral part of this new deal was the reform of the cloth trade. During its earlier experiments with domestic staples the crown had normally given special incentives to cloth manufacturers;[135] and as early as 1334 the men of Northampton had pointed out the positive impact that home staples could have on cloth sales.[136] In 1337 the government implemented a range of measures designed to encourage foreign cloth workers into England and increase domestic output. These included the relaxation of the assize of cloth, an unpopular system requiring the forfeiture of any cloth that failed to conform to a scale of standard measurements.[137] The worsted manufacturers of East Anglia in particular had complained bitterly about the harmful effects of the assize, and the upturn in exports of this cheap cloth during the 1340s probably owed much to the government's policy of deregulation.[138] For a short while in 1348–53 the crown seems to have contemplated a return to more restrictive practices. A short-lived cloth staple was set up at Calais,[139] and the assize of cloth itself was reintroduced in 1351.[140] But in the great council of 1353 the king was persuaded to abandon forfeitures in exchange for a sliding scale of excise charges on all cloth sold on the domestic market. This system continued in force until 1373, when a modified form of the assize was re-established.[141] In commercial terms the concessions of 1353 undoubtedly worked, and there was a substantial increase in the production of cloth, and especially of the cheaper ranges, for both the domestic and foreign markets.[142]

Like most of the legislation of the early 1350s, the Ordinance of the Staple and the cloth regulations can be regarded as conciliatory measures designed to win back public confidence after the financial and political controversies of the 1340s. The government certainly went out of its way to demonstrate that it had parted company with the farmers of the customs. It reopened proceedings against Pole,[143] and it generally refused to allow former colleagues of the monopolists to take posts of responsibility in the new staples.[144] This is not to say, however, that the ordinance of 1353 was forced on the crown against its will. The new Count of Flanders was increasingly hostile towards England, and there was now little diplomatic justification for maintaining a staple in the Low Countries.[145] Moreover, the crown stood to benefit substantially from the new deal by charging the higher alien rates of duty on all wool exports and collecting a small but useful revenue from the excise duty on cloth. Finally, the king had no intention of being permanently bound by the new regulations. The great council requested that the Ordinance of the Staple be confirmed in parliament, and in 1354 the commons in parliament asked that it should be enrolled as a statute 'to last forever'.[146] Edward conceded in part, and the legislation was exemplified on the statute roll along with a number of minor additions and alterations.[147] Like so many other statutes passed in this reign, however, it was effective only so long as the government wished. The subsequent history of the wool staple helps to put the political concessions of the early 1350s into context, and suggests that, for all their control over financial matters, the commons were still somewhat reluctant to challenge the king's right to regulate overseas trade.

The main problem with the new staple system was that it prevented English merchants from participating fully in the remarkable trade boom of the 1350s. In 1357 the king was asked to relax the ban on denizen wool exports, and native merchants were allowed to buy special licences to export wool at the alien rate of duty.[148] It was now only a matter of time before a new group of exporter-capitalists emerged. In 1359 it was ordered that all wool shipments to the continent should be directed through Bruges,[149] and in 1362 the government presented parliament with a proposal for the complete abandonment of the home staples and the setting up of a compulsory entrepôt at Calais. The commons' response is of some interest: they could not agree among themselves on the matter, and suggested that the king should consult with the merchants.[150] So long as the government summoned a broadly based merchant assembly like those of 1337–8 and 1342–3, the knights and burgesses were apparently quite content to offload responsibility for commercial matters. What they did not envisage, however, and what actually happened, was the transfer of the staple to Calais in 1363 on the sole authority of the king's council, and the creation of a syndicate of twenty-six merchants who agreed to govern the town on the king's behalf. This new company had no formal monopoly of the wool trade, but it was inevitable that its members would come to dominate commercial transactions in the new staple.[151] Strictly speaking, the ordinance of 1353 remained in force: former English staples were still allowed to elect their mayors and constables and to operate the special legal services which had become indispensable to the trading community.[152] But by failing to seize the initiative in 1362, the commons had undoubtedly suffered a severe setback to a policy pursued more or less consistently since the 1320s. It was only the revival of blatant monopolistic practices in the 1370s which forced them into action and finally convinced them of their responsibility to speak for the commercial interest.

In 1369 parliament met to authorize the resumption of war with France. Initial unease about the security of Calais meant that the staple was transferred back to England, although this time it was generally fixed in the port towns.[153] But in August 1370 the government on its own authority re-established the Calais staple, which remained in force for the rest of the reign. The English staples were no longer permitted to collect fees for checking wool prepared for export, and they ceased to have any real economic significance.[154] But the removal of the basic administration to the ports suggested that if ever the wool staple should return to England it would inevitably fall under the control of the major exporters. This resulted in an interesting *volte-face* on the part of the commons. While former staple towns like Lincoln kept up the pressure for a return to the arrangements of 1353,[155] the knights and burgesses in parliament now became enthusiastic supporters of the Calais staple.

Issue was finally joined over the government's habit of selling licences to exporters allowing them to take their wool to other foreign ports. In 1372, 1373 and 1376 the commons claimed — erroneously, as it happened — that the Calais staple had been set up on the authority of parliament, and should not be evaded or repealed without their consent.[156] In the Good Parliament it was revealed that Lord Latimer and Richard Lyons had sold so many export licences that both the prosperity and the defence of Calais were severely jeopardized.[157] This charge proved vitally important, and was one of the main points on which Latimer and his associate were impeached. The future of the staple itself was not resolved in this assembly, and there was to be continuing uncertainty over where it should be held during the 1380s and 1390s. Contrary to their assertions, then, the commons actually had no established right to dictate the position or the business of the staple; and the ambiguity surrounding the legislation of 1353–4 allowed the crown considerable room for manoeuvre throughout the second half of the fourteenth century.[158] On the other hand, the Good Parliament demonstrated very dramatically that it was the commons, not a handful of financiers, who now had the moral right to represent the merchant community before the king.

MERCHANTS AND PARLIAMENTS

The decline of the estate of merchants as a separate political force and the resulting increase in the authority of parliament can therefore be traced to a series of important events in 1348–53. After 1353, in fact, merchant assemblies became the exception rather than the rule.[159] In June 1356, 170 merchants were called before the council, presumably to discuss the opening up of overseas trade to denizens; but significantly enough, this matter was actually decided in the ensuing parliament.[160] Another meeting of representatives from the staple towns and from Calais was summoned in June 1361, apparently to discuss the king's plans for the removal of the staple. Once again, however, there was no immediate outcome.[161] After the resumption of the war in 1369 the government was content merely to invite those skilled in shipping to come before the council and discuss the defence of the seas.[162] In 1373 the merchants made it quite clear that they did not regard these assemblies as representative of their will.[163] Rather, it was parliament itself which now voiced their political concerns and demands. The petitions made in the name of the merchants in January 1348 proved the first in a steady trickle of such documents recorded on the parliament rolls for the rest of Edward III's reign.[164] Sometimes these petitions may have been the work of separate groups meeting during sessions of parliament. In 1354, for example, it is known that certain unnamed merchants were summoned to parliament for the king's 'secret business'; and petitions were entered by both denizen and alien merchants in the course of this assembly.[165] But such summonses do not appear to have been a regular occurrence. When Edward III's last parliament addressed its petitions to the king in the name of the 'prelates, dukes, earls, barons, commons, citizens, burgesses and merchants of his realm of England', it was simply reflecting the assertiveness and exclusiveness of parliament as the only assembly which could speak for the whole community of the realm.[166]

In the light of such evidence, it is surely no coincidence that this period also witnessed a small but definite increase in the number of citizens and burgesses returned to sit in parliament. In 1355 the city of London was allowed the special privilege of sending four representatives to parliament, rather than the usual two.[167] Meanwhile, other provincial towns apparently began to make more active use of their rights. Under Edward I, an average of eighty-six towns had made returns to each parliament, but the number had dropped to around seventy during Edward II's reign, and apparently remained at that level until the 1360s, when it rose again to over eighty. The largest recorded attendance at a single parliament in the course of Edward III's reign came in 1362, when at least 174 men, representing some eighty-six cities and towns, were elected to serve.[168] Since there was no demonstrable change in the form of summons, it must be concluded that the decision to revive or demand rights of representation was a matter for local initiative. Unfortunately, the actual attendance rate of the burgesses at parliament is virtually impossible to calculate. But it is tempting to assume that the decline of separate merchant assemblies encouraged the towns to make more active use of their parliamentary representatives and allowed the provincial merchant communities so often excluded from Edward III's credit transactions to make their presence felt in central politics.

The results can be measured by the number of matters of specific interest to the townsmen dealt with in the common petitions and statutes of the 1350s and 1360s. The new legislation of 1351 on the freedom of river traffic and the prevention of forestalling, the special provisions made in 1357 for the protection of Yarmouth's fishing industry, the statutes of 1361 concerning trade with Ireland,[169] the periodic discussions on how to regulate and protect the Gascon wine fleet,[170] and the general requests that the king uphold the franchises of towns and cities:[171] all these examples suggest that the burgesses, acting singly or collectively, had achieved considerable influence over the business of parliament. Their emergence into the very centre of the political arena was finally and dramatically acknowledged in 1376 when they joined in the Earl of March's victory celebrations following the Good Parliament.[172] In social terms the burgesses may still have been regarded as inferior to the knights of the shire; but the successful political alliance between these two groups had allowed the commons to emerge as a major force in English politics.

★ ★ ★

The relationship between the crown and the townsmen was therefore transformed in the mid-fourteenth century. Edward III came to rely increasingly on English merchants to provide the cash advances needed to fund his foreign wars. Few of these men had sufficient personal resources to lend large sums, and even major financiers such as Pole, Chiriton and Lyons could only realize the necessary financial capital by taking on special commercial privileges, acting as brokers for royal debts, or borrowing from lesser men. Consequently, their private deals with the crown affected a much larger number of merchants and had repercussions for almost all those involved in the production and export of English wool. The imposition of the wool subsidy and the location of the staple became matters of fundamental political importance and dominated relations between crown and parliament throughout the middle decades of the reign. The principal result of this conflict was the demise of the estate of merchants and the emergence of the commons as the mouthpiece of the business classes. Consequently, the crown's earlier tendency to treat lay society as a series of separate committees or estates was abandoned, and parliament emerged as the only central representative institution with comprehensive authority over taxation and legislation. In this sense the middle years of the fourteenth century marked a turning point not only for the urban communities, but for the whole of political society.

Conclusion

Edward III has not always enjoyed a good press. His modern reputation derives in part from the critical judgements made by William Stubbs in the late nineteenth century:

> Edward III was not a statesman, although he possessed some of the qualifications which might have made him a successful one. He was a warrior; ambitious, unscrupulous, selfish, extravagant, and ostentatious. His obligations as a king sat very lightly on him. He felt himself bound by no special duty either to maintain the theory of royal supremacy or to follow a policy which would benefit his people. Like Richard I he valued England primarily as a source of supplies, and he saw no risk in parting with prerogatives which his grandfather would never have resigned.[1]

Stubbs deliberately diverted attention away from the 'long and tedious reign' of this 'ideal king of chivalry' and towards those periods he thought more deserving of 'constitutional' analysis. Early twentieth-century historians therefore found themselves caught between a whiggish admiration for Edward, under whom parliament first became an essential element in the constitution, and an uneasy feeling that the king's compromises set the crown on the road to political disaster in the fifteenth century.[2] Since Stubbs's day, Edward's biographers have generally found it easier to retell the events of the Hundred Years War and to perpetuate the cult of chivalry than to make detailed appraisals of his political achievements. This was George Holmes's judgement in 1962:

> In Edward III the Plantagenet line found its happiest king. Not perhaps the greatest and certainly not the most interesting personality, but the one whose designs coincided best with the temper and opportunities of his time. Edward III did not make great constitutional innovations, like Edward I, and in home affairs he was rather a passive inheritor of the legacy of his grandfather. But, unlike grandfather and father, he was essentially a successful warrior, who loved fighting and was good at it, achieved more than he could reasonably have expected, and surrounded himself with a comradely galaxy of warrior magnates and warrior sons.[3]

By the time Holmes's textbook appeared, revisionism was already in fact taking a hold on Edward III's reign. May McKisack's volume in the Oxford History of England series, published in 1959, and her well-known lecture, 'Edward III and the Historians', presented the reign in a new and altogether more favourable light:

Edward III succeeded, where nearly all his predecessors had failed, in winning and holding the loyalty of his people and the affection of his magnates, even in the years of his decline. He accepted the chivalric and militant ambitions of his age and used them, as he used the devotion of his wife and sons, in the service of his dynasty. He raised that dynasty from unexampled depths of degradation to a place of high renown in western Christendom.... He blundered badly in his early years but, after 1341, he chose his servants well and favoured them discreetly. He avoided clashes with his parliaments, with the pope, and with the clergy; and, while maintaining his royal rights to the best of his ability, he never permitted himself his grandson's folly of openly challenging the laws and customs of the realm. . .[His subjects] saw him as the pattern of chivalry and the maker of England's fame, and when he lay upon his death-bed they mourned the passing of a great English king. It is not altogether easy to share Stubbs's confidence that they were wrong.[4]

McKisack's assessments gave Edward a new stature both as warrior and as politician. The posthumous publication of K. B. McFarlane's Ford Lectures in 1973 provided a new and considerably more sympathetic analysis of Edward's relations with the nobility, and G. L. Harriss's studies of fourteenth-century parliaments have now proved that the king was a particularly perceptive and adroit manager of men.[5] Consequently, the modern perspective is considerably more favourable. Michael Prestwich, while stressing the contrast between the political techniques of Edward I and his grandson, has concluded that 'Edward III was far more than a mere military adventurer; he was a skilful ruler as well as a chivalric hero'.[6]

There remains, however, an uneasy ambivalence in the minds of many historians. Edward's single-minded pursuit of military glory is still often seen as a selfish and irresponsible act which not only bled England of her wealth but also seriously weakened the power of the crown. This theme emerges clearly in two textbooks widely read by students of the period: Bertie Wilkinson's *Later Middle Ages in England* and M. H. Keen's *England in the Later Middle Ages*.[7] Indeed, Keen's summary of Edward, 'pliant at home in order to admit adventure abroad', has been the basis of many an essay and examination question on this period. Most recently, Richard W. Kaeuper has picked up the theme again in his stimulating *War, Justice, and Public Order*. Pointing in particular to the development of parliament, the abandonment of ambitious legislative programmes, the ossification of the tax system, and above all the concession of judicial power to the localities, Kaeuper concludes that compromise was the very keynote of Edward's reign:

> What becomes apparent ... is how much the sights and sounds of war can mask the levelling off or even the reduction in royal activism and initiative in so many other areas of kingship, a reduction which was necessary as a part of the price-tag attached, however indirectly, to the prosecution of war ... Edward III secured support for the war he and his nobles wanted so much at least in part by giving the parliamentary commons so much of what they wanted locally ... The point is not to award praise or blame to Edward III, but to recognize that,

however skilful and perceptive he may have been, English kingship of necessity took on a different role by the mid-fourteenth century. Compromise and a scaling-down of efforts other than the war effort were the concomitants of relatively peaceful politics within the realm.[8]

There is, of course, much to be said for this viewpoint. Indeed, if the word 'change' were to be substituted for 'compromise', a good deal of what has been argued in earlier chapters of this book could easily be reconciled with the revived Stubbsian tradition. On the other hand, it is as well to point out that very few of the developments that went to make up the late medieval polity either began or ended in the course of this one reign. Many of the themes that have been identified — the development of parliamentary taxation and legislation, the problem of law and order, the political tensions between church and state, the controversy surrounding royal credit dealings, and so on — find their true origins not in the 1330s but during Edward I's Scottish and French wars of the 1290s.[9] Furthermore, it is a mistake to think that the political concessions which Edward III did make — such as the increase in local control over peace-keeping — marked the permanent and inevitable demise of royal authority. In the 1380s, for instance, there was still a substantial debate over whether or not the commissions of the peace were the best means of maintaining law and order in the localities;[10] and the more vigorous kings of the fifteenth century, such as Henry V and Edward IV, were to make good use of the king's bench and special oyer and terminer commissions as a means of counteracting provincial autonomy and investigating corruption among the official classes in the shires.[11] Above all, the widespread assumption that Edward III had no grander vision, no higher sense of duty to his successors, needs to be challenged. The painful reconstruction of political society after the civil wars of the 1320s and the faction-fighting of the 1330s; the carefully timed concessions on minor prerogatives and the jealous guarding of the major ones; the adaptation of military and diplomatic strategy to match the growing aspirations of his magnates and sons; and the final appeal for a peaceful transition to the impending minority government in 1377: all these and many other things point to a remarkably consistent and ambitious policy on the part of Edward III.

It is the contention of this book that Edward's popularity with contemporaries rested on his ability to reconcile that royal policy with public opinion and political reality. Inevitably, most of Edward's obituaries written between the late fourteenth and sixteen centuries concentrated on his prowess in arms.[12] Nevertheless, it would be quite wrong to assume that the quartered arms of France and England were perceived as Edward's only lasting contribution to the monarchy. The king was seen as the bringer of peace as well as war. He restored harmony to his realm by directing the aggression of the military classes away from internal squabbles and towards the maintenance of national security. As a result, his reign witnessed the development of a new community of interests between crown and people. This idea can be seen as early as the 1340s in the writings of the Oxford philosopher Walter Burley, who argued that every Englishman, according to his own degree, 'ruled in and with the king'.[13] The same theme found echoes in an anonymous poem commemorating the death of Edward III, where the commons were likened to the mast of the ship of state, and in the prologue to the B-text of *Piers Plowman*, where the

24   *Edward III, from the east window of York Minster*

power of the commonalty was said to have given the king his throne.[14] Behind these philosophical and literary allusions lay the belief that the welfare of the realm was best preserved in a polity where every person knew his own rights and respected those of others. The fact that political society altered so little between the fourteenth and the seventeenth centuries gave added credence to the belief that Edward III had created that system of mixed monarchy extolled by Sir John Fortescue and upheld by the opponents of the early Stuarts. It is perhaps no mere coincidence that Joshua Barnes, Regius Professor of Greek in the University of Cambridge, published his definitive biography of Edward III in 1688, the very year of the Glorious Revolution.[15]

This book has tried to evaluate Edward III's achievement less through the formal statements of the statute roll and the rhetoric of the later chroniclers, and more through the reality of contemporary politics. It is difficult to sum up such a large and intangible subject, for politics is made by people, and human nature does not easily conform to generalizations. But it is perhaps admissible to conclude this study by identifying three particular themes that run through our analysis and give this period a special character and unity.

The first is the development of institutions. Edward III's reign witnessed many changes in the administrative, judicial and political structures of the realm. The most important was undoubtedly the emergence of the commons in parliament. The evolution of a single, central agency capable of representing both the minor landholders and the merchant classes marked a constitutional advance of the greatest importance. From the mid-fourteenth century onwards, the political success of the king depended to a large extent on his relations with parliament. But it is also worth noting that parliament was in active session for a total of only about four years during Edward III's fifty-year reign (see Table 5). Unless we appreciate the extraordinary nature of the institution, we are in severe danger of distorting later medieval politics. Indeed, it is arguable that some of the greatest advances of this period occurred not in the political agencies, but in the permanent administrative offices of the state. The emergence of a unitary financial system co-ordinated by the exchequer, for instance, can be traced to the middle years of Edward III's reign, as can the development of the council as a more professional body with its own special judicial authority. We should also remember that the separation of convocation from parliament considerably strengthened the king's hand by isolating the clergy and reducing their influence over high politics. Ultimately, the power of parliament rested on its control of the purse strings. The task of paying for Edward III's wars undoubtedly gave the commons a new political prominence. However, it also made the king an extremely wealthy man. If it was the abundance or lack of money that raised or depressed kings,[16] then Edward III's position was virtually unrivalled in the whole of the Middle Ages.

The second notable feature of Edward's regime was that most of the important changes in the structure of politics were carried through by co-operation and consensus. If Englishmen learned anything from the crises of 1215, 1258, 1297, 1311 and 1341, it was that kings, when cornered, could not be trusted. Time and again the community had extracted promises from the crown only to see them ignored, flouted, or even annulled. The re-establishment of political harmony was therefore imperative not only for the advancement of the king's military ambitions but also for the welfare of his subjects. In the years after 1340, both the commons and the clergy found various ways of restraining the crown and restricting the use of some of its more controversial prerogatives. But it is equally important to remember that such legislation was a gift of grace, and remained effective only so long as the king wished. Edward III never formally acknowledged the commons' right to judge the plea of necessity or to demand concessions in return for taxes. Nor did he allow parliament the authority to make or unmake legislation. And if the crown was prepared to constrain its prerogative powers, it was only because of the strong financial incentives involved. Almost every statute of the 1340s and 1350s was the result of a tax bargain, permitted by the crown in the sure knowledge that it had once again secured generous funding for the defence of the realm and the upkeep of the court. The political negotiation of Edward's middle years may have been a bilateral affair, but it was not a dialogue between equals.

The final point to emerge from this discussion therefore concerns the power of the crown. For all the new pressures and challenges raised by the Hundred Years War, it is remarkable how little politics really changed under Edward III. Public opinion was still to a large extent dictated by the king's ability to reward and restrain the nobility; and apart from certain anxieties in the 1330s and 1370s, the community remained well content with Edward's policy. There is little to indicate that the new rules concerning aristocratic inheritance weakened the crown, or that the forces of bastard feudalism yet threatened royal influence in the localities. Nor, indeed, was the emergence of the knights and burgesses quite so revolutionary as might at first appear. In the 1330s and 1340s the commons apparently tried to represent the interests and concerns of all the king's subjects, and thus to give some genuine meaning to that still rather ambiguous phrase, the 'community of the realm'. But with the development of regular taxation and the sudden economic crisis provoked by the plague, they turned their backs on the peasantry and the urban artisans and pursued policies specifically designed to maintain their own class interests. Consequently, although the number and range of men involved in politics was now greater than before, perceptions and aspirations had actually changed very little. The commons adopted the same attitude as the magnates: namely, that the king should consult them on matters of state, but not bother them with the day-to-day routine of central government. Even in the development of the commissions of the peace, on which so much of the interpretation of Edward III's reign hangs, it seems that the crown was simply reverting to the long tradition of self-government briefly and not altogether satisfactorily challenged by the monarchy of Edward I. Consequently, it can be argued that while the reign of Edward III witnessed important alterations in the structure of politics and government, it also saw remarkably little change in the real distribution of power.

It is often suggested that Edward III left his successors an impossible task. He depended too much on his military victories as a means of appeasing political opposition and winning financial support, and he was too easily persuaded to compromise powers which might be used to shield the crown in less auspicious times. Unfortunately, Edward's position as the last common ancestor of the Lancastrian, Yorkist and Tudor kings has led historians to blame him for all sorts of things quite beyond his control. It is still not uncommon to state that he produced too many sons, made them into overmighty subjects, and was thus responsible for the Wars of the Roses. But this is completely to ignore the fact that contemporary chroniclers regarded Edward's very fecundity as a sign of divine grace, and saw in him all the attributes of the ideal king.[17] Similarly, to argue whether or not the Hundred Years War was a diplomatic or economic mistake is to forget the intractable diplomatic problems left over from Edward I's reign and the equally formidable domestic tensions created by Edward II. Above all, such an argument ignores the contemporary conception of monarchy and the high premium which all the king's subjects set upon the successful defence of the realm. As Froissart so neatly put it, 'The English... will never love or honour [their king] unless he is victorious and a lover of arms and war against his neighbours.'[18] This study has argued that, beyond the trumpets and the drums, there is another history of this reign. When Edward III's achievements in domestic politics are finally and fully evaluated alongside his accomplishments in war, he may yet be permitted to re-enter the august and select band of great medieval rulers.

Table 1: Lay subsidies, 1327–77

Date of grant	Subsidy	Assessment		Yield
1327	twentieth		£25,400	£23,400
1332	fifteenth and tenth		£34,300	£32,400
1334	fifteenth and tenth		£37,300	£36,600
Mar. 1336	fifteenth and tenth		£38,500	£37,500
Sept. 1336	fifteenth and tenth		£38,500	£36,800
1337	3 fifteenths and tenths	(1)	£38,300	£33,900
		(2)	£38,200	£34,100
		(3)	£38,100	£34,700
1338	tax in wool		£79,400	£73,000
1340	ninth		£100,000	£65,000
1341	tax in wool		£151,100	£131,200
1344	2 fifteenths and tenths	(1)	£38,000	£37,000
		(2)	£38,100	£36,800
1346	2 fifteenths and tenths	(1)	£38,200	£37,300
		(2)	£38,200	£36,300
1348	3 fifteenths and tenths	(1)	£38,400	£34,600
		(2)	£38,400	£31,900
		(3)	£38,400	£35,300
1352	3 fifteenths and tenths	(1)	£38,300	£36,800
		(2)	£38,300	£36,800
		(3)	£38,300	£36,700
1357	fifteenth and tenth		£38,100	£37,300
1360	fifteenth and tenth		£38,000	£6,000
1371	parish subsidy		£50,000	£49,900
1372	fifteenth and tenth		£37,800	£36,000
1373	2 fifteenths and tenths	(1)	£37,800	£36,000
		(2)	£37,800	£36,000
1377	poll tax		£22,600	£21,600

Sources

1327–48: W. M. Ormrod, 'The Crown and the English Economy, 1290–1348', in B. M. S. Campbell, ed., *Before the Black Death: Essays in the Crisis of the Early Fourteenth Century* (Manchester, 1991), Tables 1 and 5.

1348–57: W. M. Ormrod, 'The English Government and the Black Death of 1348–49', in W. M. Ormrod, ed., *England in the Fourteenth Century: Proceedings of the 1985 Harlaxton Symposium* (Woodbridge, Suffolk, 1986), pp. 184–5.

1360: G. L. Harriss, *King, Parliament and Public Finance in Medieval England to 1369* (Oxford, 1975), pp. 396–400; Public Record Office, E401/457, 460. Neither the assessment nor the yield of this tax can be calculated properly, because it was kept out of the control of the exchequer and spent locally. The sum of £6,000 given here represents only that fraction which happened to be handed over to royal agents and was recorded on the receipt rolls.

1371: W. M. Ormrod, 'An Experiment in Taxation: The English Parish Subsidy of 1371', *Speculum*, lxiii (1988), 80. To the figure of £49,600 given there I have added the £353 16s. paid by the men of Co. Durham as a free-will offering in lieu of the tax (Public Record Office, E401/518, 21 Nov. 1374).

1372–77: E. B. Fryde, 'Introduction to the New Edition', in C. Oman, *The Great Revolt of 1381*, 2nd edn (Oxford, 1969), p. xii, n. 6, and p. xvii. The figures for yields for 1372–3 are my own estimates.

Table 2: Clerical subsidies, 1327–77

A. *Clerical subsidies granted to the king*

Canterbury		York		Assessment	Yield
Date of grant	Subsidy	Date of grant	Subsidy		
Nov. 1327	tenth	Oct. 1327	tenth	£18,800	£17,000
Sept. 1334	tenth	Oct. 1334	tenth	£19,000	£16,900
Mar. 1336	tenth	May 1336	tenth	£19,000	£16,600
Sept. 1336	tenth	Oct. 1336	tenth	£19,100	£16,700
Sept. 1337	3 tenths	Nov. 1337	3 tenths	£57,000	£45,000
Oct. 1338	tenth	—	—	£16,000	£14,000
Feb. 1340	tenth	—	—	£16,000	£14,000
—	—	Feb. 1340	2 tenths	£4,000	£3,000
Oct. 1342	tenth	Dec. 1342	tenth	£18,000	£16,000
May 1344	3 tenths	June 1344	3 tenths	£54,000	£48,000
Oct. 1346	2 tenths	Jan. 1347	2 tenths	£36,000	£32,000
May 1351	2 tenths	May 1351	2 tenths	£36,000	£30,000
May 1356	tenth	June 1356	tenth	£18,000	£15,000
Feb. 1360	tenth	Feb. 1360	tenth	£18,000	£15,000
Jan. 1370	3 tenths	Feb. 1370	3 tenths	£54,000	£45,000
May 1371	special subsidy	May 1371	special subsidy	£50,000	£42,100
Dec. 1373	tenth	Feb. 1374	tenth	£18,000	£15,000
Feb. 1377	poll tax	Apr. 1377	poll tax	£1,000	£800

B. *Clerical subsidies imposed by the Pope*

Date	Subsidy	Share for king	Royal share	
			Assessment	Yield
1330	4 tenths	half	£35,600	£35,000

Sources
1327–37: W. M. Ormrod, 'The Crown and the English Economy, 1290–1348', in B. M. S. Campbell, ed., *Before the Black Death: Studies in the Crisis of the Early Fourteenth Century* (Manchester, 1991), Tables 2 and 3.

1338–42: Public Record Office, E359/3 (the assessments and yields are estimates).

1344–73: D. B. Weske, *Convocation of the Clergy* (London, 1937), pp. 252–9, 284–7. The assessments and yields are estimates based on those for 1351, found in Public Record Office, E359/3.

1377: Public Record Office, E359/4B.

Table 3: The wool subsidy, 1327–77

| Date of grant | Duration | Rate per sack | | Authorizing agency |
		Denizens	Aliens	
May 1333	May 1333–May 1334	10s.	10s.	merchants
Sept. 1336	indefinite	20s.	20s.	merchants
May 1338	indefinite	33s.4d.	53s.4d.	? merchants
Apr. 1340	Apr. 1340–May 1341	33s.4d.	33s.4d.	parliament
July 1342	July 1342–June 1343	40s.	40s.	merchants
Apr. 1343	June 1343–Sept. 1346	40s.	40s.	parliament
Feb. 1346	Sept. 1346–Sept. 1348	40s.	40s.	lords in council
Mar. 1347	Sept. 1348–Sept. 1351	40s.	40s.	lords in council (? with merchants)[1]
Apr. 1348	confirmation of above	40s.	40s.	parliament
Feb. 1351	Sept. 1351–Sept. 1353	40s.	40s.	parliament
Oct. 1353	1353–56	40s.	40s.	commons in great council
Nov. 1355	1356–62	40s.	40s.	parliament
Oct. 1362	1362–65	20s.	20s.	parliament
Feb. 1365	1365–68	40s.	40s.	parliament
May 1368	1368–70	36s.8d.	36s.8d.	parliament
June 1369	1369–72	43s.4d.	43s.4d.	parliament
Nov. 1372	1372–74	43s.4d.	43s.4d.	parliament
Nov. 1373	1374–76	43s.4d.	43s.4d.	parliament
June 1376	1376–79	43s.4d.	43s.4d.	parliament

Notes
1. See p. 232, n. 118.
2. This cancelled the preceding grant and came into immediate effect.

Sources
1333: *Calendar of Fine Rolls, 1327–37*, p. 365; Public Record Office, E356/5, m. 2.

1336–42: E. B. Fryde, 'Edward III's War Finance, 1337–41: Transactions in Wool and Credit Operations', University of Oxford D. Phil. thesis (1947), i. 54–5, 78–80, 487–90; *Calendar of Close Rolls, 1341–3*, p. 553; E. B. Fryde, *William de la Pole, Merchant and King's Banker* (London, 1988), pp. 182–3, 201.

1343–76: G. L. Harriss, *King, Parliament and Public Finance in Medieval England to 1369* (Oxford, 1975), pp. 420–49, 468–9; A. Beardwood, *Alien Merchants in England, 1350 to 1377* (Cambridge, Mass., 1931), pp. 44–5; corroborated by the parliament rolls (as cited by J. G. Edwards, *The Second Century of the English Parliament*, Oxford, 1975, p. 21, nn. 5, 6), and Public Record Office, E356/8.

Table 4: The customs revenues, 1326–76

Financial year (Sept. to Sept.)	Total receipt	Financial year (Sept. to Sept.)	Total receipt
1326–27	£19,200	1356–57	£96,100
1327–28	£9,300	1357–58	£87,700
1328–29	£13,300	1358–59	£75,100
1329–30	£12,400	1359–60	£86,500
1330–31	£14,200	1360–61	£66,800
1331–32	£15,100	1361–62	£110,000
1332–33	£12,000	1362–63	£41,700
1333–34	£30,800	1363–64	£40,200
1334–35	£13,600	1364–65	£71,900
1335–36	£7,800	1365–66	£79,200
		1366–67	£73,000
1336–51	Trade subject to	1367–68	£58,600
	embargoes, exemptions,	1368–69	£64,700
	monopolies and farms.	1369–70	£49,100
		1370–71	£74,000
1351–52	£54,600	1371–72	£70,000
1352–53	£42,800	1372–73	£71,000
1353–54	£113,400	1373–74	£64,000
1354–55	£83,900	1374–75	£75,200
1355–56	£70,600	1375–76	£55,000

Sources

1326–36: W. M. Ormrod, 'The Crown and the English Economy, 1290–1348', in B. M. S. Campbell, ed., *Before the Black Death: Essays in the Crisis of the Early Fourteenth Century* (Manchester, 1991), Table 4.

1351–64: W. M. Ormrod, 'The English Crown and the Customs, 1349–63', *Economic History Review*, 2nd ser., xl (1987), 33, 39.

1364–76: Public Record Office, E356/7, 8, 9, 14, *passim*.

Table 5: Parliaments and representative councils, 1327–77

| Year | Place | Designation[1] | Dates of session[2] | Taxes granted | | Statutes |
				Direct	Indirect[3]	enrolled
1327	Westminster	parliament	3 Feb.–9 Mar.	No	No	Yes
1327	Lincoln	council	15 Sept.–23 Sept.	Yes	No	No
1328	York	parliament	7 Feb.–5 Mar.	No	No	No
1328	Northampton	parliament	24 Apr.–14 May	No	No	Yes
1328	York	council	31 July–6 Aug.	No	No	No
1328	Salisbury	parliament	16 Oct.–31 Oct.	No	No	No
1329	Westminster	parliament	9 Feb.–22 Feb.	No	No	No
1330	Winchester	parliament	11 Mar.–21 Mar.	No	No	No
1330	Westminster	parliament	26 Nov.–9 Dec.	No	No	Yes
1331	Westminster	parliament	30 Sept.–9 Oct.	No	No	Yes
1332	Westminster	parliament	16 Mar.–21 Mar.	Yes	No	No
1332	Westminster	parliament	9 Sept.–12 Sept.	No	No	No
1332	York	parliament	2 Dec.–11 Dec.	No	No	No
1333	York	parliament[4]	20 Jan.–27 Jan.	No	No	No
1334	York	parliament	21 Feb.–2 Mar.	Yes	No	No
1334	Westminster	parliament	19 Sept.–23 Sept.	No	No	No
1335	York	parliament	26 May–3 June	No	No	Yes
1336	Westminster	parliament	11 Mar.–20 Mar.	Yes	No	Yes
1336	Nottingham	council	23 Sept.–27 Sept.	Yes	No	No
1337	Westminster	parliament	3 Mar.–16 Mar.	No	No	No
1337	Westminster	council	26 Sept.–4 Oct.	Yes	No	Yes
1338	Westminster	parliament	3 Feb.–14 Feb.	No	No	No
1338	Northampton	council	26 July–2 Aug.	Yes	No	No
1339	Westminster	parliament	3 Feb.–17 Feb.	No	No	No
1339	Westminster	parliament	13 Oct.–c. 3 Nov.	No	No	No
1340	Westminster	parliament	20 Jan.–19 Feb.	No	No	No
1340	Westminster	parliament	29 Mar.–10 May	Yes	Yes	Yes
1340	Westminster	parliament	12 July–26 July	No	No	No
1341	Westminster	parliament	23 Apr.–27/28 May	Yes	No	Yes
1342	Westminster	council	16 Oct.–?	No	No	No
1343	Westminster	parliament	28 Apr.–20 May	No	Yes	No
1344	Westminster	parliament	7 June–28 June	Yes	No	Yes
1346	Westminster	parliament	11 Sept.–20 Sept.	Yes	No	No
1348	Westminster	parliament	14 Jan.–12 Feb.	No	No	No
1348	Westminster	parliament	31 Mar.–13 Apr.	Yes	Yes	No
1351	Westminster	parliament	9 Feb.–1 Mar.	No	Yes	Yes
1352	Westminster	parliament	13 Jan.–11 Feb.	Yes	No	Yes
1352	Westminster	council	16 Aug.–25 Aug.	No	No	No
1353	Westminster	council	23 Sept.–12 Oct.	No	Yes	Yes

Table 5: Continued

| Year | Place | Designation[1] | Dates of session[2] | Taxes granted | | Statutes |
				Direct	Indirect[3]	enrolled
1354	Westminster	parliament	28 Apr.–20 May	No	No	Yes
1355	Westminster	parliament	23 Nov.–30 Nov.	No	Yes	No
1357	Westminster	parliament	17 Apr.–8/16 May	Yes	No	Yes
1358	Westminster	parliament	5 Feb.–27 Feb.	No	No	No
1360	Westminster	parliament	15 May–?	No	No	No
1361	Westminster	parliament	24 Jan.–18 Feb.	No	No	Yes
1362	Westminster	parliament	13 Oct.–17 Nov.[5]	No	Yes	Yes
1363	Westminster	parliament	6 Oct.–30 Oct.	No	No	Yes
1365	Westminster	parliament	20 Jan.–17 Feb.	No	Yes	Yes
1366	Westminster	parliament	4 May–11 May	No	No	No
1368	Westminster	parliament	1 May–28 May	No	Yes	Yes
1369	Westminster	parliament	3 June–11 June	No	Yes	Yes
1371	Westminster	parliament	24 Feb.–29 Mar.	Yes	No	Yes
1371	Winchester	council	8 June–17 June	No	No	No
1372	Westminster	parliament	3 Nov.–24 Nov.[6]	Yes	Yes	No
1373	Westminster	parliament	21 Nov.–10 Dec.	Yes	Yes	No
1376	Westminster	parliament	28 Apr.–10 July	No	Yes	No
1377	Westminster	parliament	27 Jan.–2 Mar.	Yes	No	Yes

Notes
1. Titles of the assemblies are as given in the writs of summons.
2. The *terminus post quem* is normally that fixed for the day of assembly in the writs of summons, and the *terminus ad quem* is that on which the writs *de expensis* were issued. Days lost because of the non-arrival of members are not accounted for here.
3. With two exceptions, this column relates solely to the wool subsidy. The exceptions are 1372 and 1373, when tunnage and poundage was granted along with the maltolt in parliament (*Rotuli Parliamentorum*, London, 1783, ii. 310, 317).
4. Adjournment of previous session.
5. The lords were asked to stay on after the dismissal of the commons: *Rotuli Parliamentorum*, ii. 273.
6. The burgesses were asked to stay on after the dismissal of the knights: *Rotuli Parliamentorum*, ii. 310.

Sources
H. G. Richardson and G. O. Sayles, *The English Parliament in the Middle Ages* (London, 1981), ch. XXI, pp. 66–7, 68–82; E. B. Fryde, D. E. Greenaway, S. Porter and I. Roy, eds., *Handbook of British Chronology*, 3rd edn (London, 1986), pp. 556–64; *Rotuli Parliamentorum*, ii. *passim*; *Statutes of the Realm*, (London, 1810–28), i. *passim*.

Notes for further reading

Good accounts of Edward III's reign are found in M. McKisack, *The Fourteenth Century* (Oxford, 1959) and M. Prestwich, *The Three Edwards* (London, 1980). P. Johnson, *The Life and Times of Edward III* (London, 1973) and M. Packe, *King Edward III* (London, 1983), are not works of scholarship, but the former has the benefit of being illustrated. The most recent interpretation of this period is R. W. Kaeuper, *War, Justice, and Public Order: England and France in the Later Middle Ages* (Oxford, 1988). A contrary view is put forward in W. M. Ormrod, 'Edward III and the Recovery of Royal Authority in England, 1340–60', *History*, lxxii (1987), 4–19. The most notable biographies relating to this period are R. Barber, *Edward, Prince of Wales and Aquitaine* (London, 1978), and K. Fowler, *The King's Lieutenant: Henry of Grosmont, First Duke of Lancaster, 1310–1361* (London, 1969).

The social and economic background is covered by M. M. Postan, *The Medieval Economy and Society* (Harmondsworth, 1975); J. L. Bolton, *The Medieval English Economy* (London, 1980); E. Miller and J. Hatcher, *Medieval England: Rural Society and Economic Change, 1086–1348* (London, 1918); and J. Hatcher, *Plague, Population and the English Economy, 1348–1520* (London, 1977). An alternative and revealing study is C. Dyer, *Standards of Living in the Later Middle Ages* (Cambridge, 1989).

The artistic achievements of this period are brilliantly summarized in J. Alexander and P. Binski, eds., *Age of Chivalry: Art in Plantagenet England,1200–1400* (London, 1987). Two useful studies setting the literature of the fourteenth century in its political context are J. Barnie, *War in Medieval Society: Social Values and the Hundred Years War, 1337–99* (London, 1974), and J. Coleman, *English Literature in History, 1350–1400: Medieval Readers and Writers* (London, 1981).

On Edward III's wars, E. Perroy, *The Hundred Years War*, trans. W. B. Wells (London, 1951), is still the classic account; but C. Allmand, *The Hundred Years War* (Cambridge, 1988), provides a convenient summary and up-to-date bibliography. J. Le Patourel's important essays on the subject are reprinted in his *Feudal Empires: Norman and Plantagenet* (London, 1984). The two essential works on the Scottish war are R. G. Nicholson, *Edward III and the Scots, 1327–1335* (Oxford, 1965), and J. Campbell, 'England, Scotland and the Hundred Years War in the Fourteenth Century', in J. R. Hale, J. R. L. Highfield and B. Smalley, eds., *Europe in the Later Middle Ages* (London, 1965), pp. 184–216. Also useful is A. Grant, *Independence and Nationhood: Scotland 1306–1469* (London, 1984).

There is no general study of kingship in later medieval England. A. L. Brown, *The Governance of Late Medieval England, 1272–1461* (London, 1989), is the most recent attempt to characterize administration in this period. For the court and its role in politics see C. Given-Wilson, *The Royal Household and the King's Affinity: Service, Politics and Finance in England 1360–1413* (London and New Haven, 1986). The best introductions to the legal system are A. Harding, *The Law Courts of Medieval England* (London, 1973) and E. Powell, *Kingship, Law and Society: Criminal Justice in the Reign of Henry V* (Oxford, 1989). For the tax system M. W. Beresford, *The Lay Subsidies and Poll Taxes* (Canterbury, 1963) is particularly useful. There is an excellent account of the structure of county administration by R. B. Pugh in *The Victoria County History of Wiltshire*, v (Oxford, 1957), pp. 1–43.

On parliament, G. L. Harriss, *King, Parliament and Public Finance in Medieval England to 1369* (Oxford, 1975), is fundamental. Aspects of this book are summarized by the same author in 'War and the Emergence of the English Parliament, 1297–1360', *Journal of Medieval History*, ii (1976), 35–56, and 'The Formation of Parliament, 1272–1377', in R. G. Davies and J. H. Denton, eds., *The English Parliament in the Middle Ages* (Manchester, 1981), pp. 29–60. See also R. Butt, *A History of*

Parliament: The Middle Ages (London, 1989). E. B. Fryde and E. Miller, eds., *Historical Studies of the English Parliament* (Cambridge, 1970), contains a number of important essays. The controversial arguments of H. G. Richardson and G. O. Sayles are summarized in G. O. Sayles, *The King's Parliament of England* (London, 1975).

The standard work on the aristocracy remains K. B. McFarlane, *The Nobility of Later Medieval England* (Oxford, 1973), but more recent and detailed work is summarized in C. Given-Wilson, *The English Nobility in the Late Middle Ages* (London, 1987). J. T. Rosenthal, *Nobles and the Noble Life, 1295–1500* (London, 1976), is interesting; and G. A. Holmes, *The Estates of the Higher Nobility in Fourteenth Century England* (Cambridge, 1957), deals with far more than just estate administration.

P. Heath, *Church and Realm, 1272–1461* (London, 1988), provides a general survey of ecclesiastical politics and an excellent bibliography. R. N. Swanson, *Church and Society in Late Medieval England* (Oxford, 1989), contains a wealth of material, though much of it relates to the fifteenth century. Still very useful are W. A. Pantin, *The English Church in the Fourteenth Century* (Cambridge, 1955), and A. Hamilton Thompson, *The English Clergy and their Organization in the Later Middle Ages* (Oxford, 1941). J. R. L. Highfield, 'The English Hierarchy in the Reign of Edward III', *Transactions of the Royal Historical Society*, 5th ser., vi (1956), 115–38 condenses much essential work on the episcopate.

A useful starting point for the study of the gentry is chapter 3 of Given-Wilson's English Nobility (see above). Otherwise the best case study is N. Saul, *Knights and Esquires: The Gloucestershire Gentry in the Fourteenth Century* (Oxford, 1981). On the shire as a political unit see J. R. Maddicott, 'The County Community and the Making of Public Opinion in Fourteenth-Century England', *Transactions of the Royal Historical Society*, 5th ser., xxviii (1978), 27–43. On links between nobility and gentry, K. B. McFarlane's study of 'Bastard Feudalism', *Bulletin of the Institute of Historical Research*, xx (1945), 161–80, reprinted in his posthumous collection, *England in the Fifteenth Century* (London, 1981), pp. 23–43, remains the classic text, though it has been modified by subsequent research, conveniently summarized by G. L. Harriss in the introduction to the latter work. The most recent studies, providing extensive bibliographies, are J. M. W. Bean, *From Lord to Patron: Lordship in Late Medieval England* (Manchester, 1989), and J. G. Bellamy, *Bastard Feudalism and the Law* (London, 1989).

R. H. Hilton, *The English Peasantry in the Later Middle Ages* (Oxford, 1975), is not quite what the title implies, but it provides a starting point for study of the rural population. The same author's *The Decline of Serfdom in Medieval England*, 2nd edn (London, 1983), *and Bond Men Made Free* (London, 1973), are essential reading. J. R. Maddicott, 'The English Peasantry and the Demands of the Crown', in T. H. Aston, ed., *Landlords, Peasants and Politics in Medieval England* (Cambridge, 1987), pp. 285–359, is very important for the economic situation of the peasantry before the plague. R. H. Hilton and T. H. Aston, eds., *The English Rising of 1381* (Cambridge, 1984), contains a number of important essays.

For urban society see S. Reynolds, *An Introduction to the History of English Medieval Towns* (Oxford, 1977), and C. Platt, *The English Mediaeval Town* (London, 1976). Interesting case studies are G. A. Williams, *Medieval London: From Commune to Capital* (London, 1963); C. Platt, *Medieval Southampton* (London, 1973); J. W. F. Hill, *Medieval Lincoln* (Cambridge, 1948); and R. H. Britnell, *Growth and Decline in Colchester, 1300–1525* (Cambridge, 1986). A wealth of material is also available in the various studies made for the *Victoria County History* and for M. D. Lobel and W. H. Johns, eds., *Atlas of Historic Towns* (London, 1969–75).

On the politics of commerce see T. H. Lloyd, *The English Wool Trade in the Middle Ages* (Cambridge, 1977), and the collected essays of E. B. Fryde, *Studies in Medieval Trade and Finance* (London, 1983). R. Horrox, *The de la Poles of Hull*, East Yorkshire Local History Series, xxxviii (1983), provides a convenient summary of Fryde's work on the credit dealings of William de la Pole.

Abbreviations

AHT	*Atlas of Historic Towns*, ed. M. D. Lobel and W. H. Johns, 2 vols. (London, (1969–75).
Anon. Chron.	*The Anonimalle Chronicle, 1333–1381*, ed. V. H. Galbraith (Manchester, 1927).
Avesbury	*Robertus de Avesbury De Gestis Mirabilibus Regis Edwardi Tertii,* ed. E. M. Thompson, Rolls Series (1889).
Baker	*Chronicon Galfridi le Baker de Swynebroke*, ed. E. M. Thompson (Oxford, 1889).
BIHR	*Bulletin of the Institute of Historical Research.*
BJRL	*Bulletin of the John Rylands Library.*
BL	British Library.
BRUO	A. B. Emden, *A Biographical Register of the University of* Oxford to 1500, 3 vols. (Oxford, 1957–9).
CChR	*Calendar of Charter Rolls.*
CCR	*Calendar of Close Rolls.*
CFR	*Calendar of Fine Rolls.*
CIM	*Calendar of Inquisitions Miscellaneous.*
CIPM	*Calendar of Inquisitions Post Mortem.*
CLBL	*Calendar of Letter Books of the City of London*, ed. R. R. Sharpe, 11 vols. (London, 1899–1912).
Concilia	*Concilia Magna Britanniae et Hiberniae*, ed. D. Wilkins (London, 1737).
CPML	*Calendar of Plea and Memoranda Rolls of the City of London*, ed. A. H. Thomas and P. E. Jones, 6 vols. (Cambridge, 1926–61).
CPR	*Calendar of Patent Rolls.*
CYS	Canterbury and York Society.
DNB	*Dictionary of National Biography*, ed. L. Stephen and S. Lee, 63 vols. (London, 1885–1900) .
EcHR	*Economic History Review.*
EGW	*The English Government at Work, 1327–1336*, ed. J. F. Willard, W. A. Morris, J. R. Strayer and W. H. Dunham, 3 vols. (Cambridge, Mass., 1930–40).
EHR	*English Historical Review.*
Fasti	J. Le Neve, *Fasti Ecclesiae Anglicanae, 1300–1541*, new edn, compiled by H. P. F. King, J. M. Horn and B. Jones, 12 vols. (London, 1962–7).
Foedera	*Foedera, Conventiones, Literae et Cujuscunque Generis Acta*, ed. T. Rymer, Record Commission edn, 3 vols. in 6 parts (1816–30).
Froissart	*Chroniques de Jean Froissart*, ed. S. Luce, G. Raynaud, L. and A. Mirot, Société de l'Histoire de France, 15 vols. (Paris, 1869–1975).
GEC	G. E. Cokayne, *The Complete Peerage of England, Scotland,* Ireland, Great Britain and the United Kingdom, new edn, rev. V. Gibbs et al., 13 vols. (London, 1910–59).

HBC	*Handbook of British Chronology*, ed. E. B. Fryde, D. E. Greenaway, S. Porter and I. Roy, 3rd edn (London, 1986).
HMC	Royal Commission on Historical Manuscripts.
HSEP	*Historical Studies of the English Parliament*, ed. E. B. Fryde and E. Miller, 2 vols. (Cambridge, 1970).
JBS	*Journal of British Studies*.
JEH	*Journal of Ecclesiastical History*.
JMH	*Journal of Medieval History*.
LRDP	*Report from the Lords' Committees . . . for All Matters Touching the Dignity of a Peer*, 4 vols. (London, 1820–9).
P&P	*Past and Present*.
PRO	Public Record Office.
Reading	*Chronicon Johannis de Reading et Anonymi Cantuariensis*, ed. J. Tait (Manchester, 1914).
Return of MPs	*Return of the Name of Every Member of the Lower House of Parliament 1213–1874*, 2 vols. (Parliamentary Papers, 1878).
RP	*Rotuli Parliamentorum*, 6 vols. (London, 1783).
RPHI	*Rotuli Parliamentorum Angliae Hactenus Inediti*, ed. H. G Richardson and G. O. Sayles, Camden Society, 3rd ser., li (1935).
RS	Rolls Series.
SCCKB	*Select Cases in the Court of King's Bench*, ed. G. O. Sayles, 7 vols., Selden Society, lv, lvii, lviii, lxxiv, lxxvi, lxxxii, lxxxviii (1936–71).
SCH	*Studies in Church History*.
SMRH	*Studies in Medieval and Renaissance History*.
SR	*Statutes of the Realm*, 11 vols., Record Commission (1810–28).
SS	Selden Society.
TRHS	*Transactions of the Royal Historical Society*.
VCH	*Victoria County History*.
Walsingham	*Historia Anglicana of Thomas of Walsingham*, ed. H. T. Riley, 2 vols., Rolls Series (1863–4).
WAM	Westminster Abbey Muniments.
YB	Year Book(s).

Unless otherwise stated, all manuscripts cited here are in the Public Record Office.

Notes

INTRODUCTION

1 *Foedera*, II (ii). 683.
2 See especially the eye-witness account in Baker, pp. 26–8, discussed by A. Grandsen, *Historical Writing in England II: c. 1307 to the Early Sixteenth Century* (London, 1982), pp. 37–42.
3 *Political Poems and Songs Relating to English History*, ed. T. Wright, RS (1859–61), i. 219–24.
4 Walsingham, i. 327–8, as translated in J. Barnie, *War in Medieval Society: Social Values and the Hundred Years War* (London, 1974), pp. 140–2.
5 *Ibid.*
6 *The Brut*, ed. F. W. D. Brie, Early English Text Soc. (1906–8), ii. 333.
7 For further discussion and detailed references see pp. 183–5.
8 See the important article by J. R. Maddicott, 'Magna Carta and the Local Community', *P&P*, cii (1984), 25–65.
9 M. Prestwich, *Edward I* (London, 1988), pp.401–35, is the most recent survey.
10 M. V. Clarke, *Medieval Representation and Consent* (London, 1936), pp. 173–95; B. Wilkinson, 'The Deposition of Richard II and the Accession of Henry IV', *HSEP*, i. 337–44; M. McKisack, *The Fourteenth Century* (Oxford, 1959), pp. 88–91.
11 For the evolution of this term see M. Powicke, *The Community of the Realm* (New York, 1973), esp. pp. 68–71.

CHAPTER 1: THE EARLY YEARS, 1327–41

1 For the coronation oath of 1308 see A. L. Brown, *The Governance of Late Medieval England, 1272–1461* (London, 1988), pp. 12–13. For the official record of Edward III's coronation see *CCR, 1327–30*, p. 100; and for the conditions attached, see H. G. Richardson, 'The English Coronation Oath', *Speculum*, xxiv (1949), 65.
2 N. Fryde, *The Tyranny and Fall of Edward II, 1321–1326* (Cambridge, 1979), pp. 207–27,

provides a useful summary of this period.
3 GEC, vii. 399; *RP*, ii. 3–6.
4 *Ibid.*, ii. 10, 12.
5 J. F. Baldwin, 'The King's Council', *EGW*, i. 131–3.
6 *RP*, ii. 7, 11.
7 *Ibid.*, ii. 7; *Foedera*, II (ii). 695, 707, 782, 814.
8 G. A. Holmes, *The Estates of the Higher Nobility in Fourteenth Century England* (Cambridge, 1957), pp. 13–14.
9 For what follows see *idem*, 'The Rebellion of the Earl of Lancaster, 1328–9', *BIHR*, xxviii (1955), 84–9.
10 R. M. Haines, *The Church and Politics in Fourteenth-Century England: The Career of Adam Orleton* (Cambridge, 1978), pp. 161–88; *idem*, *Archbishop John Stratford* (Toronto, 1986), pp. 191–214.
11 G. P. Cuttino and T. W. Lyman, 'Where is Edward II?', *Speculum*, liii (1978), 522–44.
12 *RP*, ii. 52; Baldwin, 'King's Council', p. 136.
13 For what follows see C. G. Crump, 'The Arrest of Roger Mortimer and Queen Isabel', *EHR*, xxvi (1911), 331–2.
14 *Foedera*, II (ii). 799–800, as translated in *CCR, 1330–3*, pp. 158–9.
15 I. Kershaw, 'The Great Famine and Agrarian Crisis in England, 1315–1322', in R. H. Hilton, ed., *Peasants, Knights and Heretics* (Cambridge, 1976), pp. 85–132; J. R. Maddicott, 'The English Peasantry and the Demands of the Crown, 1294–1341', in T. H. Aston, ed., *Landlords, Peasants and Politics in Medieval England* (Cambridge, 1987), pp. 285–359.
16 J. G. Bellamy, *Crime and Public Order in England in the Later Middle Ages* (London, 1973), pp. 69–88.
17 G. L. Harriss, *King, Parliament and Public Finance in Medieval England to 1369* (Oxford, 1975), p. 523.
18 *Foedera*, II (i). 650.
19 The importance of the 'Disinherited' is highlighted by R. G. Nicholson, *Edward III and the Scots, 1327–1335* (Oxford, 1965), on which this account depends.
20 E. Perroy, *The Hundred Years War*, trans. W. B. Wells (London, 1951), pp. 83–5.

21 For the importance of this dispute see G. P. Cuttino, *English Diplomatic Administration, 1259–1339*, 2nd edn (Oxford, 1971), pp. 100–11.

22 C. J. Tyerman, 'Philip VI and the Recovery of the Holy Land', *EHR*, c (1985), 25–52.

23 J. Le Patourel, *Feudal Empires: Norman and Plantagenet* (London, 1984), ch. XII, pp. 179–80.

24 For what follows see W. M. Ormrod, 'The Crown and the English Economy, 1290–1348', in B. M. S. Campbell, ed., *Before the Black Death: Studies in the Crisis of the Early Fourteenth Century* (Manchester, 1991), and the works cited there.

25 E. B. Fryde, *Studies in Medieval Trade and Finance* (London, 1983), ch. V, pp. 250–69; Harriss, *Public Finance*, pp. 231–93; J. R. Maddicott, 'Poems of Social Protest in Early Fourteenth-Century England', in W. M. Ormrod, ed., *England in the Fourteenth Century: Proceedings of the 1985 Harlaxton Symposium* (Woodbridge, Suffolk, 1986), pp. 130–44.

26 T. F. Tout, *Chapters in the Administrative History of Mediaeval England* (Manchester, 1920–33), iii. 31–68.

27 A. Tuck, *Crown and Nobility, 1272–1461* (London, 1985), pp. 103–4, provides a convenient summary.

28 K. B. McFarlane, *The Nobility of Later Medieval England* (Oxford, 1973), pp. 158–61.

29 The text of the ordinances is printed in Tout, *Chapters*, iii. 143–50.

30 Nicholson, *Edward III and the Scots*, p. 115.

31 Harriss, *Public Finance*, pp. 253–4.

32 *Ibid.*, pp. 260–4.

33 Fryde, *Studies*, ch. XIII, p. 83.

34 Harriss, *Public Finance*, p. 285; K. Fowler, *The King's Lieutenant: Henry of Grosmont, First Duke of Lancaster, 1310–1361* (London, 1969), p. 35.

35 The best account of the ensuing crisis is N. M. Fryde, 'Edward III's Removal of his Ministers and Judges, 1340–1', *BIHR*, xlviii (1975), 149–61.

36 *Anglia Sacra*, ed. H. Wharton (London, 1691), i. 21; R. M. Haines, 'Some Sermons at Hereford Attributed to Archbishop John Stratford', *JEH*, xxxiv (1983), 425–37.

37 *Croniques de London*, ed. G. J. Aungier, Camden Soc., orig. ser., xxviii (1844), p. 90, as translated in Tout, *Chapters*, iii. 131.

38 Harriss, *Public Finance*, pp. 298–301.

39 W. M. Ormrod, 'Agenda for Legislation, 1322–*c*.1340', *EHR*, cv (1990), 1–33, and the sources cited there.

CHAPTER 2: THE MIDDLE YEARS, 1341–60

1 This chapter pursues ideas first discussed in W. M. Ormrod, 'Edward III and the Recovery of Royal Authority in England, 1340–60', *History*, lxxii (1987), 4–19.

2 Le Patourel, *Feudal Empires*, ch. XII, p. 186. See also *ibid.*, ch. XV, pp. 155–83.

3 Harriss, *Public Finance*, pp. 304–8.

4 The most recent discussion is J. Vale, *Edward III and Chivalry* (Woodbridge, Suffolk, 1982), pp. 76–94.

5 Ormrod, 'Recovery of Royal Authority', pp.13–17.

6 For details see J. R. L. Highfield, 'The English Hierarchy in the Reign of Edward III', *TRHS*, 5th ser., vi (1956), 115–38.

7 For what follows see Harriss, *Public Finance*, pp. 313–465, *passim*.

8 I follow the cautious orthodoxy of J. Hatcher, *Plague, Population and the English Economy, 1348–1530* (London, 1977), p. 25. However, recent research suggests death rates of around 50% in this first outbreak: R. A. Davies, 'The Effect of the Black Death on the Parish Priests of the Medieval Diocese of Coventry and Lichfield', *Historical Research*, lxii (1989), 85–90; R. Lomas, 'The Black Death in County Durham', *JMH*, xv (1989), 127–40. Specialized studies on particular estates are summarized in J. L. Bolton, *The Medieval English Economy, 1150–1500* (London, 1980), pp. 207–45.

9 For the importance of the money supply in determining economic trends during this period see T. H. Lloyd, 'Overseas Trade and the English Money Supply in the Fourteenth Century', in N. J. Mayhew, ed., *Edwardian Monetary Affairs (1279–1344)*, British Archaeological Reports, xxxvi (1977), 111–2, 121; M. Mate, 'The Role of Gold Coinage in the English Economy, 1338–1400', *Numismatic Chronicle*, 7th ser., xviii (1978), 141.

10 The quotation comes from a painted inscription in Acle church, Norfolk, commemorating the plague of 1348–9 (I owe this reference to Dr Pamela Tudor-Craig). An incised inscription on the same subject is found at Ashwell church, Herts.

11 W. M. Ormrod, 'The English Government and the Black Death of 1348–49', in Ormrod, ed., *England in the Fourteenth Century*, pp. 175–88.

12 A revealing phrase used in the preamble to the ensuing Statute of Labourers: *SR*, i. 311.

13 *SR*, i. 319, 321, 322. For the importance of the concession regarding military assessments, see M. Powicke, *Military Obligation in Medieval England* (Oxford, 1962), pp. 194–9. Contrary to my statement in 'Recovery of Royal Authority', p. 10, this legislation did not allow parliament any actual control over purveyance.

14 *The Eyre of Northamptonshire 3–4 Edward III A. D. 1329–1330*, ed. D. W. Sutherland, SS, xcvii–iii (1983), i, pp. xxii–xxxvi.

15 B. A. Hanawalt, *Crime and Conflict in English Communities, 1300–1348* (Cambridge, Mass., 1979), pp. 229–38. Note particularly the comments in *Chronicles of the Reigns of Edward I and Edward II*, ed. W. Stubbs, RS (1882–3), ii. 138.

16 SC8/208/10360.

17 The following two paragraphs depend on B. H. Putnam, 'The Transformation of the Keepers of the Peace into the Justices of the Peace, 1327–1380', *TRHS*, 4th ser., xii (1929), 19–48, supplemented by personal communications from Anthony Verduyn.

18 *The 1341 Royal Inquest in Lincolnshire*, ed. B. W. McLane, Lincoln Record Soc., lxxviii (1988), pp. ix–xv, provides a summary and full bibliography.

19 J. G. Bellamy, *The Law of Treason in England in the Later Middle Ages* (Cambridge, 1970), pp. 61–74.

20 The following depends on Le Patourel, *Feudal Empires*, ch. XIII, pp. 19–39.

21 There is virtually no contemporary comment on the 1360 settlement. *Anon. Chron.*, pp. 48–9, is critical, as also is the commentary by John Erghome on the prophetic verses ascribed to John of Bridlington (*Political Poems and Songs*, i. 123–215). But the relevant section of the *Anon. Chron.*, even if based on a contemporary lost chronicle, was only written up at a later stage, and the comments on the treaty may therefore reflect the disillusionment of the 1370s or 1380s. Erghome's commentaries, usually ascribed to *c.* 1362–4, could also be as late as 1369 (Barnie, *War in Medieval Society*, pp. 145–7). The parliament roll for 1361, when the treaties of Brétigny and Calais were confirmed, is lost; but it is worth noting the enthusiastic comments of the commons on the peace in the extant parliament roll of 1363: *RP*, ii. 276.

CHAPTER 3: THE LATER YEARS, 1360–77

1 Froissart, vii. 101, as translated by Tout, *Chapters*, iii. 239.

2 *Ibid.*, iii. 245–51, 259; iv. 161–2.

3 *CCR, 1360–4*, pp. 181–2, 197–8; E159/137, *Recorda*, *Pasch*, m. 14; E368/133, *Recorda*, *Pasch*, mm. 14d–15; A. Hamilton Thompson, 'The Pestilences of the Fourteenth Century in the Diocese of York', *Archaeological Journal*, lxxi (1914), 114.

4 *Ibid.*, p. 115. Note, however, the much higher replacement rate in the diocese of Exeter: J. F. D. Shrewbury, *A History of Bubonic Plague in the British Isles* (Cambridge, 1970), p. 129.

5 Sir William Beveridge, 'Wages in the Winchester Manors', *EcHR*, vii (1936–7), 27.

6 J. C. Sainty, *Officers of the Exchequer*, PRO List & Index Soc., special ser., xviii (1983), pp. 40, 59, 69, 78, 86.

7 *VCH Berks.*, iii. 59.

8 Putnam, 'Transformation', pp. 45–7.

9 SR, i. 380–2; F. E. Baldwin, *Sumptuary Legislation and Personal Regulation in England* (Baltimore, 1926), pp. 51–5.

10 The following depends on E. Powell, 'The Administration of Criminal Justice in Late-Medieval England: Peace Sessions and Assizes', in R. Eales and D. Sullivan, eds., *The Political Context of Law: Proceedings of the Seventh British Legal History Conference* (London, 1987), pp. 53–4.

11 *RP*, ii. 276, as translated by McKisack, *Fourteenth Century*, p. 221.

12 As suggested by J. Sherborne, 'John of Gaunt, Edward III's Retinue and the French Campaign of 1369', in R. A. Griffiths and J. Sherborne, eds., *Kings and Nobles in the Later Middle Ages: A Tribute to Charles Ross* (Gloucester, 1986), p. 50.

13 J. W. Sherborne, 'Indentured Retinues and English Expeditions to France, 1369–1380', *EHR*, lxxix (1964), 725.

14 The most detailed account of court politics in this period is C. J. Given-Wilson, 'The Court and Household of Edward III, 1360–1377', University of St Andrews Ph.D. thesis (1976), summarized in *idem, The Royal Household and the King's Affinity: Service, Politics and Finance in England, 1360–1413* (London and New Haven, 1986), pp. 146–60.

15 G. Holmes, *The Good Parliament* (Oxford, 1975), pp. 68–9, provides a summary of Alice's early career. S. Harbison, 'William of

Windsor, the Court Party and the Administration of Ireland', in J. Lydon, ed., *England and Ireland in the Later Middle Ages: Essays in Honour of Jocelyn Otway-Ruthven* (Blackrock, Co. Dublin, 1981), pp. 154–5, shows that it is unlikely that Alice was married to William of Windsor until the early 1370s, and that she was therefore probably not responsible for the latter's controversial appointment as lieutenant of Ireland in 1369.

16 J. W. Sherborne, 'The Costs of English Warfare with France in the Later Fourteen Century', *BIHR*, 1 (1977), 135–50. See also E. B. Fryde, 'Introduction to the New Edition', in C. Oman, *The Great Revolt of 1381*, 2nd edn (Oxford, 1969), pp. xii–xxi.

17 *Anon. Chron.*, p. 85, as translated by Holmes, *Good Parliament*, p. 102.

18 For the precedent of 1325 see p. 66.

19 S. Armitage-Smith, *John of Gaunt* (London, 1904), p. 137. The idea was discredited by J. C. Wedgwood, 'John of Gaunt and the Packing of Parliament', *EHR*, xlv (1930), 623–5; and H. G. Richardson, 'John of Gaunt and the Parliamentary Representation of Lancashire', *BJRL*, xxii (1938), 175–222.

20 Tout, *Chapters*, iii. 308.

21 *RP*, ii. 365.

22 Froissart, viii. 230–1; *Froissart: Chronicles*, trans. G. Brereton (Harmondsworth, 1978), pp. 195–6.

23. *Political Poems and Songs*, i. 215–8, also in *Historical Poems of the XIVth and XVth Centuries*, ed. R. H. Robbins (New York, 1959), pp. 102–6, and in *Medieval English Verse*, trans. B. Stone (Harmondsworth, 1964), pp. 114–17.

CHAPTER 4: THE KING

1 *RP*, ii. 7, 11.

2 *Ibid.*, ii. 330. Richard was finally granted the title in Nov. 1376: *CChR, 1341*–1417, p. 231; *LRDP*, v. 56.

3 M. A. Michael, 'A Manuscript Wedding Gift from Philippa of Hainault to Edward III', *Burlington Magazine*, cxxvii (1985), 582–600. For the tradition of *miroirs* in England, see J. P. Genet, 'Political Theory and Local Communities in Later Medieval France and England', in J. R. L. Highfield and R. Jeffs, eds., *The Crown and Local Communities in England and France in the Fifteenth Century* (Gloucester, 1981), p. 23; and for a list of tracts addressed to Edward III see J. P. Genet, 'Ecclesiastics and Political Theory in Late Medieval England: The End of a Monopoly', in B. Dobson, ed., *The Church, Politics and Patronage in the Fifteenth Century* (Gloucester, 1984), pp. 31–2. For a useful summary of some of the *miroirs* which might have been available to Edward III, see L. K. Born, 'The Perfect Prince: A Study in Thirteenth- and Fourteenth-Century Ideals', *Speculum*, iii (1928), 470–504.

4 *The Treatise of Walter de Milemete, De Nobilitatibus, Sapientiis, et Prudentiis Regum*, ed. M. R. James (Roxburghe Club, Oxford, 1913).

5 *Vita Edwardi Secundi*, ed. N. Denholm-Young (London, 1957), pp. 36–7.

6 J. G. Edwards, 'Ranulph, Monk of Chester', *EHR*, xlvii (1932), 94.

7 W. M. Ormrod, 'Edward III and his Family', *JBS*, xxvi (1987), 407–8; *idem*, 'The Personal Religion of Edward III', *Speculum*, lxiv (1989), 871–2.

8 *Ibid.*, pp. 853–62.

9 M. Bloch, *The Royal Touch: Sacred Monarchy and Scrofula in England and France*, trans. J. E. Anderson (London, 1973).

10 Ormrod, 'Personal Religion of Edward III', p. 863.

11 R. A. Brown, H. M. Colvin and A. J. Taylor, *The History of the King's Works: The Middle Ages* (London, 1963), i. 162, gives an estimate of £90,000; the higher figure (including the cost of works at Westminster) is given by Given-Wilson, 'Court and Household', p. 279. In 1362 the building at Windsor was said to be a 'business... near the king's heart' (*CCR, 1360–4*, p. 397).

12 *Original Letters Illustrative of English History*, ed. Sir Henry Ellis, 3rd ser., i (London, 1866), pp. 33–9.

13 The episode is widely reported in the chronicles: e.g. Baker, pp. 103–8; Reading, pp. 107–8; Avesbury, pp. 408–10; *Anon. Chron.*, pp. 30–1; Walsingham, i. 273–4.

14 A. H. Burne, *The Crecy War* (London, 1955), pp. 340–1, points out that the march into Burgundy also had some tactical significance.

15 Vale, *Edward III and Chivalry, passim*, esp. pp. 2, 67–9, 93–4; J. Taylor, *English Historical Literature in the Fourteenth Century* (Oxford, 1987), pp. 44–5.

16 Ormrod, 'Personal Religion of Edward III', p. 860.

17 Edward was referred to as 'king of the sea'

in 1372 (*RP*, ii. 311), and in the 15th century the *Libelle of Englyshe Polycye* extolled his exploits at sea: V. J. Scattergood, *Politics and Poetry in the Fifteenth Century* (London, 1971), pp. 46–7, 92.

18 The articles (*Foedera*, II (i). 650) are known only from their citation by Adam Orleton in a private dispute of 1333–4. See Haines, *Stratford*, pp. 183–4.

19 *De Speculo Regis Edward III*, ed. J. Moisant (Paris, 1891), esp. p. 116; L. E. Boyle, 'William of Pagula and the Speculum Regis Edwardi III', *Mediaeval Studies*, xxxii (1970), 331–2.

20 Haines, *Orleton*, pp. 189–90; *idem, Stratford*, pp. 289–90, 326–7.

21 The first obvious reference to Edward II's deposition came in the political crisis of 1386–7: see M. H. Keen, *England in the Later Middle Ages* (London, 1973), pp. 278–82.

22 For Henry IV's title see K. B. McFarlane, *Lancastrian Kings and Lollard Knights* (Oxford, 1972), pp. 43–58.

23 *Pace* Cuttino and Lyman, 'Where is Edward II?', pp. 522–44, I accept the more orthodox view of Edward's end. See also the valuable comments of Haines, *Stratford*, pp. 208–13.

24 *RP*, ii. 52.

25 Ormrod, 'Personal Religion of Edward III', pp. 869–71.

26 See p. 183.

27 The distinction is not an historical one, but I hope it reflects the political reality of the 14th century. Part of the problem in dealing with this subject is that there was no contemporary definition of the prerogative. The legal tract *Praerogativa Regis* (*SR*, i. 226–7, early Edward I) is preoccupied with the relationship between the king and his tenants-in-chief, and with the crown's regalian rights over the church. See F. W. Maitland, 'Praerogativa Regis', *EHR*, vi (1891), 367–72.

28 *Foedera*, II (ii). 1091. This is not a piece of legislation, but an instruction to the king's representatives in England in 1339 to bargain away prerogative rights in exchange for more profitable levies. The pardon eventually granted in 1340 was less specific, but was supposedly binding for the king's life: *SR*, i. 290; Harriss, *Public Finance*, p. 412. See also H. M. Chew, 'Scutage in the Fourteenth Century', *EHR*, xxxviii (1923), 19–41; J. F. Hadwin, 'The Last Royal Tallages', *EHR*, xcvi (1981), 344–58.

29 *SR*, i. 322.

30 Hadwin, 'Last Royal Tallages', p. 354; Fryde, *Studies*, ch. V, pp. 260–1; Harriss, *Public Finance*, p. 245.

31 In fact, the feudal aid of 1346 contravened the statute of 1340: Harriss, *Public Finance*, pp.412–13.

32 T. F. T. Plucknett, 'Parliament', *EGW*, i. 117–19; Fryde, *Studies*, ch. V, pp. 258–9; Harriss, *Public Finance*, pp. 376–83.

33 See pp. 107-8.

34 Harriss, *Public Finance*, pp. 261–3.

35 *Ibid.*, p. 263 and n. 3.

36 *RP*, ii. 128, 130; *SR*, i. 296.

37 *Ibid.*, i. 295, 297.

38 Fryde, *Tyranny and Fall*, pp. 65–6; Tuck, *Crown and Nobility*, pp. 197–8.

39 Bellamy, *Law of Treason*, pp. 51, 55, 62–74, 80–5.

40 See pp. 62–5, 154–7, 175-6.

41 Harriss, *Public Finance*, pp. 323–7, 335–40; W. M. Ormrod, 'The English Crown and the Customs, 1349–63', *EcHR*, 2nd ser., xl (1987), 35–6.

42 Harriss, *Public Finance*, pp. 320–3. Harriss's statement (*ibid.*, pp. 322–3) that the maltolt was remitted in 1350 is an error.

43 The grant was made in 1355 (*RP*, ii. 265; not 1356, as stated by Harriss, *Public Finance*, p. 430); but it was intended to dovetail with the current subsidy, due to expire at Michaelmas 1356. For details see J. G. Edwards, *The Second Century of the English Parliament* (Oxford, 1979), p. 21.

44 Given-Wilson, *Royal Household*, pp. 121–3. For the first such request, in 1371, see p. 67.

45 Given-Wilson, *Royal Household*, pp. 123–30.

46 Tout, *Chapters*, iii. 266–82.

47 Edward made a total of six campaigns to Scotland between 1327 and 1336, and two more in 1341–2 and 1355–6. For details see J. Bain, *The Edwards in Scotland, A. D. 1296–1377* (Edinburgh, 1901); H. C. Maxwell–Lyte, *Historical Notes on the Use of the Great Seal of England* (London, 1926), p. 409.

48 I have compiled a detailed itinerary for this period based on the place-dates in published chancery enrolments and unpublished chancery warrants, wardrobe accounts, and other miscellaneous documents. Many of Edward's visits to the midlands and the west seem to have been hunting expeditions.

49 Given-Wilson, *Royal Household*, pp. 28–34.

50 E.g. the meeting of the council at Langley in January 1349: *CCR, 1349–54*, p. 1. The issue rolls furnish numerous examples of correspondence — much of it under the secret seal and signet — sent by the king to

his chief advisers: e.g. *The Issue Roll of Thomas of Brantingham, 44 Edward III*, ed. F. Devon (London, 1835), pp. 385, 389, 456, 237, etc.

51 M. C. Hill, *The King's Messengers, 1199–1377* (London, 1961), *passim*, and esp. the statistics on pp. 141–2.

52 For example, a royal banquet was held at Westminster on 6 June 1353 to entertain a French deputation: E101/392/12, f. 13.

53 For what follows see B. Wilkinson, 'The Authorisation of Chancery Writs under Edward III', *BJRL*, viii (1924), 107–39; W. M. Ormrod, 'Edward III's Government of England, *c.* 1346–1356', University of Oxford D. Phil. thesis (1984), pp. 61–98.

54 Tout, *Chapters*, iii. 78.

55 *Ibid.*, iii. 56–66.

56 *HBC*, p. 39; Tout, *Chapters*, vi, 378, *s.v.* 'Regents'. The instructions for the abortive regency of 1372 (*Foedera*, III (ii). 962) survive in draft form in C49/47/9.

57 SCl/37/170.

58 See p. 128.

59 Ormrod, 'Edward III's Government', pp. 107–8.

60 C81/908/13, 29; C81/1330/20; C81/1334/19; SCl/61/53, etc.

61 C4712129, no. 1; *CLBL, G.* 297.

62 E368/124, m. 301; C81/1333/61. For the convoy system see M. K. James, *Studies in the Medieval Wine Trade*, ed. E. M. Veale (Oxford, 1971), pp. 24–6.

63 *CCR, 1337–9*, p. 291.

64 *Foedera*, III(ii). 657; Tout, *Chapters*, v. 61. For the diplomatic significance see P. Chaplais, *Essays in Medieval Diplomacy and Administration* (London, 1981), ch. XXII, p. 181.

65 Fowler, *King's Lieutenant*, p. 81. The resulting treaty (BL Add. Ch. 59142) is printed in P. Chaplais, *English Medieval Diplomatic Practice: Part I, Documents and Interpretation* (London, 1982), ii. 507–10.

66 'Some Documents Regarding the Fulfilment and Interpretation of the Treaty of Brétigny (1361–1369)', ed. P. Chaplais, *Camden Miscellany XIX*, Camden Soc., lxxx (1952), 7–8; G.P. Cuttino, *English Medieval Diplomacy* (Bloomington, Ind., 1985), p. 94.

67 Nicholson, *Edward III and the Scots*, p.115; Harriss, *Public Finance*, pp.304, 324 and n. 3.

68 Fryde, 'Removal of Ministers', pp. 149–50; *CLBL, F.* 58.

69 *CPR, 1340–3*, pp. 111–13. See also the king's order for the payment of wages to the commissioners: C81/272/13682, printed in

SCCKB, v, p. cxxxviii.

70 SCl/62/85, partly translated by J. R. Maddicott, 'Parliament and the Constituencies, 1272–1377', in R. G. Davies and J. H. Denton, eds., *The English Parliament in the Middle Ages* (Manchester, 1981), p. 85.

71 C81/1560/4; SCl/42/177.

72 C81/1331/31, cited by Harriss, *Public Finance*, p. 182, n. 2; C81/1332/56.

73 SC8/246/12268: see Maxwell-Lyte, *Great Seal*, pp. 147–8; V. H. Galbraith, *The Literacy of the Medieval English Kings* (Oxford, 1957), pl. opp. p. 24, and p. 38, n. 47.

74 E.g. *CCR, 1346–9*, p. 605; *ibid., 1349–54*, p. 275, etc. It was at the king's discretion that charters of pardon requested by members of the nobility for their followers were sealed: *Foedera*, II (ii). 1194, 1236; III (i). 6, etc.

75 Maxwell-Lyte, *Great Seal*, p. 369.

76 C81/1335/17–23.

77 Tout, *Chapters*, iii. 151; J. R. Maddicott, 'Law and Lordship: Royal Justices as Retainers in Thirteenth- and Fourteenth-Century England', *P&P Supplement*, iv (1978), 48–51.

78 C81/1331/21; C81/338/20221.

79 Tout, *Chapters*, iii. 245–51.

80 C81/1331/57.

81 C81/1334/49; C81/1334/37. Earlier, in 1335, when he had granted the sheriffdom of Cambs. to John Kiryell, the king had been content to allow the chancellor and treasurer to decide whether the appointee was fit to take office: C81/224/8821.

82 The king's bench, it may be noted, freely acknowledged the personal influence of the king in its proceedings: *SCCKB*, iii, pp. cxxxiii–iv.

83 E. L. G. Stones, 'The Folvilles of Ashby–Folville, Leicestershire, and their Associates in Crime, 1326–1347', *TRHS*, 5th ser., vii (1957), 125–7.

84 For what follows see H. J. Hewitt, *The Organization of War under Edward III* (Manchester, 1966), pp. 29–30, 174.

85 Plucknett, 'Parliament', pp. 119–20; *SCCKB*, iii, pp. cxviii–xix. Hewitt's figures (*Organization of War*, p. 30) suggest that pardons decreased after 1340; but this is to forget that leaders of military retinues were entitled to ask for pardons for their men, and that many of these, when issued, were not enrolled. See A. E. Prince, 'The Indenture System under Edward III', in J. G. Edwards, V. H. Galbraith and E. F. Jacob, eds., *Historical Essays in Honour of James Tait*

(Manchester, 1933), p. 296; Maxwell-Lyte, *Great Seal*, pp. 320–1.

86 SC1/39/27, printed in B. Wilkinson, *The Chancery under Edward III* (Manchester, 1929), p. 18, n. 7; *SCCKB*, vi. no. 44; *CLBL*, G. 2, 23; SC1/55/86.

87 *CPR, 1340–3*, pp. 111–13.

88 C49/46/13. For Coggeshall see W. R. Jones, 'Rex et Ministri: English Local Government and the Crisis of 1341', *JBS*, xiii, no. 1 (1973), 12–13.

89 *Ancient Petitions Relating to Northumberland*, ed. C. M. Fraser, Surtees Soc., clxxvi (1966), no. 194, with references.

90 C81/1331/40; C81/1336/54–5. For these sessions see B. H. Putnam, *The Place in Legal History of Sir William Shareshull* (Cambridge, 1950), pp. 64–5.

91 E368/121, m. 20; D. Crook, 'The Later Eyres', *EHR*, xcvii (1982), 265–6.

92 E122/189/35.

93 *CCR, 1330–3*, pp. 320–1; *Munimenta Civitatis Oxonie*, ed. H. E. Salter, Oxford Historical Soc., lxxi (1920), pp. 150–1. See in particular the king's frequent interventions in the long-standing dispute between Queen Isabella and the Prior of Coventry: *RPHI*, pp. 240–66; C81/1331/56; C81/1333/58. Note also the case of Lady Wake (see p. 128).

94 SC8/192/9556 (*Calendar of Ancient Petitions Relating to Wales*, ed. W. Rees, University of Wales Board of Celtic Studies, History and Law Ser., xxviii (1975), p. 319), enclosed in C81/1336/62, and resulting in *CCR, 1343–6*, p. 582. Holmes, *Estates*, pp. 16, 39. For the Denbigh case see also the privy seal writ copied on to a schedule sewn to C66/246, m. 27. For the particular significance of Edward's intervention in the marches see R. R. Davies, *Lordship and Society in the March of Wales, 1282–1400* (Oxford, 1978), pp. 257, 269–73.

95 This dispute is discussed briefly in A. Hamilton Thompson, 'William Bateman, Bishop of Norwich, 1344–1355', *Norfolk Archaeology*, xxv (1935), 122–4. The Norwich temporalities were seized into the king's hands as a result of the quarrel in Aug. 1346, and the cognizance of pleas in Lynn was specifically reserved when the rest of the temporalities were restored in Nov. 1347 (E372/192, m. 42d; *CCR, 1346–9*, p. 338). A commission set up in 1346 found that the bishop owed his privilege to a private agreement with the town in 1310, but had no formal rights to

the franchises (*CPR, 1345–8*, p. 170; *CIM*, ii. no. 2001). Consequently, Bateman several times requested a final resolution (SC8/239/11920–1; SC8/246/ 12274, printed in *SCCKB*, ii, pp. cxxvii–viii); but the council continued to prevaricate (C49/7/21, printed in *SCCKB*, v, pp. clii–iii). In June 1348 the council was still divided on the issue (C81/1336/52; the year is uncertain). Consequently, the restoration of the Lynn franchises to the bishop in May 1350 was purely a matter of grace (SC8/246/12212, enclosed in C81/345/20991, and resulting in *CPR, 1348–50*, p. 551, warranted by the king and the privy seal; E372/195, m. 41d). For the concurrent dispute between Bateman and the Abbot of Bury St Edmunds see p. 122.

96 *RP*, ii. 392. Evidently the request went unsatisfied: see the record of the Montagu holdings in Holmes, *Estates*, pp. 28–9.

97 SC8/243/12149–50; C81/1332/34. For the background to the latter case see K. C. Newton, *Thaxted in the Fourteenth Century*, Essex Record Office Publications, xxxiii (1960), p. 4.

98 For the problems experienced by suitors in trying to gain access to the aged king, see pp. 112–13.

99 Tout, *Chapters*, iii. 148.

100 Wilkinson, *Chancery*, pp. 30–1.

101 C81/1331/50.

102 For the situation in Edward's last years see pp. 112–13.

103 I identify three categories of petitions which may be said to have gone directly before the king: (a) those for which an accompanying warrant survives under the secret seal or signet; (b) those which resulted in a chancery instrument warranted *per ipsum regem*; and (c) those which include responses denoting royal intervention.

104 SC8/227/11309 (Maxwell-Lyte, *Great Seal*, p. 145); SC8/227/11343 (*CCR, 1349–54*, p. 411); SC8/246/12284, enclosed in C81/1333/69; SC8/246/12293, enclosed in C81/1334/2 (*CPR, 1354–8*, p. 92).

105 *Foedera*, III(i). 180. Conciliar replies to petitions often reserved matters of grace to the king: e.g. *Northern Petitions*, ed. C. M. Fraser, Surtees Soc., cxciv (1982), nos. 159, 160. It was also common for the special committees set up to receive and hear private petitions in parliament to qualify their decisions with the phrase 'if it please the king': e.g. *RP*, ii. 36, 38–9, 41, 85–6, 93, etc; *RPHI*, pp. 161–2, 183, 229, 284.

106 SC8/246/12269, enclosed in C81/1333/31 (N. Saul, *Knights and Esquires: The Gloucestershire Gentry in the Fourteenth Century*, Oxford, 1981, p. 151); SC8/247/12303, enclosed in C81/1334/33 (*CPR, 1354–8*, pp. 369–70); SC8/226/11300 (*CPR, 1370–4*, p. 471); SC8/239/11918, enclosed in C81/1336/46 (*CPR, 1343–5*, p. 587).

107 SC8/246/12268 (*CPR, 1348–50*, p. 561). The bill of privy seal was developed in 1349–50 specifically to deal with such *de cursu* business: see Ormrod, 'Edward III's Government', pp. 85–7.

108 C81/219/8362; SC8/241/12037; 253/ 12646; SCl/39/6, 7; etc.

109 *RP*, ii. 180.

110 SC8/247/12319, 12321; C81/1335/46, 47; *CPR, 1361–4*, p. 242.

111 SC8/185/9250 (Maxwell-Lyte, *Great Seal*, p. 108); SC8/226/11292 (*CPR, 1374–7*, p. 484); SC8/228/11354 (*CPR, 1374–7*, p. 462).

112 The following two paragraphs depend on B. P. Wolffe, *The Royal Demesne in English History* (London, 1971).

113 Holmes, *Good Parliament*, p. 156.

114 See the grants of such wardships contained in *CFR, 1347–56*, pp. 174–447, *passim*.

115 Holmes, *Good Parliament*, p. 66. See also *CFR, 1369–77*, pp. 171, 214.

116 *RP*, ii. 355–6.

117 B. P. Wolffe, 'Acts of Resumption in the Lancastrian Parliaments, 1399–1456', *HSEP*, ii. 62–8.

118 See pp. 110–14.

119 *Parliamentary Texts of the Later Middle Ages*, ed. N. Pronay and J. Taylor (Oxford, 1980), pp. 72, 85, etc.

120 *RP*, ii. 225, 309.

121 G. L. Harriss, 'The Commons' Petition of 1340', *EHR*, lxxviii (1963), 637. A number of common petitions of 1346 received the reply that the king alone could provide answers: *RP*, ii. 161, 162.

122 Tout, *Chapters*, iii. 304, 318.

123 For a judicious and broad-ranging review, see J. S. Roskell, 'Perspectives in English Parliamentary History', *HSEP*, ii. 296–323.

124 I follow H. G. Richardson and G. O. Sayles, *The English Parliament in the Middle Ages* (London, 1981), ch. XXI. The views of these writers have been much criticized, but they seem to me to fit very well with the known facts. See Ormrod, 'Edward III's Government', pp. 140–84.

125 F. W. Maitland, 'Introduction to Memoranda de Parliamento, 1305', *HSEP*, i. 107–24; Maddicott, 'Parliament and the Constituencies', pp. 61–9.

126 *RP*, ii. 127, 443; Fryde, 'Removal of Ministers', pp. 149–50.

127 Richardson and Sayles, *Parliament*, ch. XXI, p. 73; *RP*, ii. 272.

128 Richardson and Sayles, *Parliament*, ch. XXI, p. 3, n. 6.

129 For what follows see D. Rayner, 'The Forms and Machinery of the "Commune Petition" in the Fourteenth Century', *EHR*, lvi (1941), 198–233, 549–70; Ormrod, 'Agenda for Legislation', pp. 1–33.

130 In 1341 the crown distinguished between petitions from the *grantz* and from the *communes*: *RP*, ii. 130. For the practice of 'intercommuning' between lords and commons, see J. G. Edwards, *The Commons in Medieval English Parliaments* (London, 1957), pp. 5–18; W. N. Bryant, 'Some Earlier Examples of Intercommuning in Parliament, 1340–1348', *EHR*, lxxxv (1970), 54–8.

131 The importance of this precedent is stressed (indeed, probably overstressed) by G. O. Sayles, *The King's Parliament of England* (London, 1975), pp. 115–17.

132 In Richard II's first parliament the commons asked that all those petitions presented in the Good Parliament which had received the reply 'le roi le voet' (the king wishes it) should be made up into statutes. The council's reply was typically evasive, and its action notably selective. See *RP*, iii. 17; *SR*, ii. 1–5.

133 Harriss, *Public Finance*, pp. 27–48.

134 This figure is based on the column of net yields in Ormrod, 'English Economy', table 1. They differ from the tax assessments (i.e. gross yields) used by most historians: e.g. E. Miller, 'War, Taxation and the English Economy in the Late Thirteenth and Early Fourteenth Centuries', in J. M. Winter, ed., *War and Economic Development: Essays in Memory of David Joslin* (Cambridge, 1975), pp. 11–31.

135 J. F. Willard, *Parliamentary Taxes on Personal Property, 1290 to 1334* (Cambridge, Mass., 1934), pp. 13–18.

136 For a fresh analysis of the terminology of these early assemblies, see Brown, *Governance of Late Medieval England*, pp. 169–73.

137 That is, assemblies for which the writs of summons used *consilium* or *tractatus* rather than *parliamentum*. See Richardson and Sayles, *Parliament*, ch. XXI, p. 66.

138 E.g. Harriss, *Public Finance*, p. 234, assumes that the assembly of Sept. 1337 was a parliament; Fryde, *Studies*, ch. V, pp. 253, 260, recognizes that it was a great council, but minimizes the significance of this. The exceptional nature of this assembly is clearly demonstrated by the fact that the government, in addition to issuing the normal writs for election of the commons, also sent out writs summoning named representatives from each shire and elected representatives from certain towns: *Return of MPs*, i. 115, n. (a). I owe this point to Anthony Verduyn.

139 Richardson and Sayles, *Parliament*, ch. XXI, p. 76. It is worth noting that the common petition presented at Lincoln was not answered, but deferred elsewhere: *SCCKB*, v, pp. cxxxii–iii; G. O. Sayles, *The Functions of the Medieval Parliament of England* (London, 1988), p. 48. It is also significant that very few private petitions were presented in these assemblies. For instance, there are only two references on the close rolls to petitions entered at the time of the Westminster council of September 1337: *CCR, 1337–9*, pp. 193, 200. Compare the record of parliaments in the same period: Richardson and Sayles, *Parliament*, ch. XXI, p. 3 and nn.

140 Tout, *Chapters*, iii. 92, 95, n. 1; Fryde, *Studies*, ch. V, pp. 260–1.

141 They are, respectively, Ormrod, 'Agenda for Legislation', pp. 31–3; *RP*, i. 430; *ibid*., ii. 7–11; *RPHI*, pp. 224–30, 232–9, 268–72. See also Rayner, '"Commune Petition"', pp. 553–9. There is some doubt over the date of *RPHI*, pp. 268–72 (see Fryde, 'Parliament and the French War', p. 248, n. 34; Harriss, *Public Finance*, p. 248, n. 2), but this does not affect the argument put forward here.

142 See pp. 173–5.

143 *RP*, ii. 107; Harriss, *Public Finance*, p. 258.

144 Harriss, 'Commons' Petition of 1340', pp. 625–54.

145 Richardson and Sayles referred to the 'series of repetitive and ill-digested statutes that offer such a marked contrast to the legislation of the first Edward' (*Parliament*, ch. XXI, p. 13). In fact, the process had been well under way since the last years of Edward I: G. L. Harriss, 'The Formation of Parliament, 1272–1377', in Davies and Denton, eds., *English Parliament*, pp. 45–7.

146 *Ibid*., p. 40. The *Modus Tenendi Parliamentum* states that the first function of parliament is to discuss war, though it does not actually require the king to call parliament for this reason (*Parliamentary Texts*, pp. 75, 88). A political poem of *c*. 1338–9 comments (sarcastically), 'A king ought not to go forth from his kingdom in manner of war unless the community of his realm consent to it': *Anglo-Norman Political Songs*, ed. I. S. T. Aspin, Anglo-Norman Texts, xi (1953), p. 111.

147 *RP*, ii. 67, 69.

148 For what follows see Harriss, *Public Finance*, pp. 314–20.

149 *RP*, ii. 103, 118.

150 *Ibid*., ii. 158–9; Avesbury, pp. 363–7.

151 E.g. *RP*, ii. 252, 262, 264, etc.

152 Reading, pp. 147–8; Walsingham, i. 294. There is no parliament roll for 1361, but note the statement by the king's agent in 1369 that the peace of 1360 had been accepted 'par l'avys et conseil de ses grantz et comunes': *RP*, ii. 299.

153 *Ibid*., ii. 301.

154 I follow Harriss, *Public Finance*, pp. 3–48, 314–20 (summarized in G. L. Harriss, 'War and the Emergence of the English Parliament, 1297–1360', *JMH*, ii, 1976, 35–56). Some of Harriss's arguments have been challenged, most recently by Prestwich, *Edward I*, pp. 453–8; but these criticisms do not affect his interpretation of the period in question here.

155 W. M. Ormrod, 'Political Theory in Practice: The Forced Loan on English Overseas Trade of 1317–18', *Historical Research*, lxiv (1991), 204–15.

156 M. C. Buck, 'The Reform of the Exchequer, 1316–1326', *EHR*, xcviii (1983), 254.

157 On the management of parliament see also pp. 76–9.

158 Richardson and Sayles, *Parliament*, ch. V, pp. 151–4; ch. XVI, pp. 85–8; ch. XXI, pp. 78–82, summarized in Sayles, *King's Parliament*, pp. 137–41.

159 *RP*, ii. 225, 229, 237.

160 *Ibid*., ii. 271, 355; J. G. Edwards, '"Justice" in Early English Parliaments', *HSEP*, i. 291–2.

161 For what follows see Harriss, *Public Finance*, pp. 356–75.

162 *RP*, ii. 311.

163 *Ibid*., ii. 304; *RPHI*, pp. 279–80.

164 *RP*, ii. 140, 238, 313.

165 E.g. *RP*, i. 285; ii. 265, 295, etc. See also T. F. T. Plucknett, *Statutes and their Interpretation in the First Half of the Fourteenth Century* (Cambridge, 1922), pp. 134–6.

166 W. Holdsworth, *A History of English Law*, ii, 4th edn (London, 1936), p. 435.

167 *RP*, ii. 139–40, 203, 241; Ormrod, 'Recovery of Royal Authority', p. 11.

168 *SR*, i. 293; *RP*, ii. 244. For the interpretation of the 1340 statute see P. C. Saunders, 'Royal Ecclesiastical Patronage in England, 1199–1351', University of Oxford D. Phil. thesis (1978), pp. 361–73. The so-called statute *Pro Clero* of 1352, although responding to clerical petitions entered on the parliament roll (*RP*, ii. 244–5) and itself written up on the dorse of the statute roll (*SR*, i. 324–6), was not in fact issued until some time after the parliament of Jan. 1352 (see p. 133). This legislation restricted retrospective action to vacancies within the king's own reign. The king confirmed this point in 1353: *Foedera*, III (i). 256.

169 *RP*, ii. 368. For the abuse of the Statute of Purveyance in the 1370s see p. 108.

170 *SR*, i. 265, 374.

171 *RP*, ii. 295, 297. It is interesting to note the contrast with 1337, when the king had only entertained selected noble friends at the conclusion of a parliament: Tout, *Chapters*, iii. 63 and n. 1.

172 See G. L. Harriss, 'The Management of Parliament', in *idem*, ed., *Henry V: The Practice of Kingship* (Oxford, 1985), pp. 137–58.

CHAPTER 5: THE MINISTERS

1 The memoranda rolls of the exchequer, for instance, quadrupled in size between c. 1290 and 1307: see J. C. Davies, 'The Memoranda Rolls of the Exchequer to 1307', in *idem*, ed., *Studies Presented to Sir Hilary Jenkinson* (London, 1957), pp. 97–154. For bureaucratic developments in general see M. T. Clanchy, *From Memory to Written Record: England, 1066–1307* (London, 1979).

2 *CPR, 1327–77, passim*; *CCR, 1327–77, passim*.

3 Statistics based on the tables in *SCCKB*, v, pp. c–ci; vi, pp. xlvi–l.

4 For the criteria used by the chancery in deciding whether or not to enroll documents issued under the great seal, see R. F. Hunnisett, 'English Chancery Records: Rolls and Files', *Journal of the Society of Archivists*, v, no. 3 (1975), 158–68.

5 E163/25, file of indentures for Trin. 16 Edw III.

6 *Rolls from the Office of the Sheriff of Beds. and Bucks., 1332–1334*, ed. G. H. Fowler, Quarto Memoirs of the Bedfordshire Historical Record Soc., iii (1929).

7 The amount of Yorks. business undertaken in Michaelmas 1348 can best be judged from the fact that the *Panella* file for this term, the file of bills and writs relating to possessory assizes, had to be split into two (the first and only time this was necessary before the 16th century), with one of the two large files being reserved solely for Yorks. cases: KB146/2/22/4/1–2. For further details see Ormrod, 'Edward III's Government', pp. 189–93.

8 J. L. Grassi, 'Royal Clerks from the Archdiocese of York in the Fourteenth Century', *Northern History*, v (1970), 12–33, provides a convenient summary.

9 *Idem*, 'Clerical Dynasties from Howdenshire, Nottinghamshire and Lindsey in the Royal Administration, 1280–1340', University of Oxford D. Phil. thesis (1960), pp. 177–8, 466–7, 469–70; Wilkinson, *Chancery*, pp. 162–4. One aspect of Sibthorpe's career not previously noted is his regular inclusion on the eastern assize circuit: e.g. C66/203, m. 22d; C66/233, mm. 37d, 36d; etc. It was extremely unusual for a chancery clerk to be appointed as a justice of assize in the mid-14th century.

10 A. Hamilton Thompson, *The English Clergy and their Organization in the Later Middle Ages* (Oxford, 1947), pp. 247–51, 254–77.

11 F. Crooks, 'John de Winwick and his Chantry in Huyton Church', *Transactions of the Historic Society of Lancashire and Cheshire*, lxxvii (1925), 26–38; *VCH Wilts*, iii. 320–4; *The Edington Cartulary*, ed. J. H. Stevenson, Wiltshire Record Soc., xlii (1987), pp. xiii–xxvi.

12 Putnam, *Shareshull*, pp. 22–6.

13 *The Records of the City of Norwich*, ed. W. Hudson and J. C. Tingey (Norwich, 1906–10), ii. 38, 39; *Records of the Borough of Leicester*, II, ed. M. Bateson (London, 1901), p. 77.

14 *Eyre of Northamptonshire*, i, p. xxiv.

15 Maddicott, 'Law and Lordship', esp. pp. 25–40.

16 For the canons of St George's see S. L. Ollard, *Fasti Wyndesorienses* (Windsor, 1950).

17 Ormrod, 'Edward III's Government', pp. 232–3; Brown, Colvin and Taylor, *King's Works*, i. 173.

18 Fryde, *Studies*, ch. VIII, pp. 74–8.

19 E368/125, m. 126.

20 *CCR, 1364–8*, pp. 114–25; E159/141, m. 11; Tout, *Chapters*, iii. 243–51; 'The Ransom of John II, 1360–70', ed. D. M. Broome, *Camden Miscellany XIV*, Camden Soc., 3rd ser., xxxvii (1926), pp. 1–5.

21 The link between the two events is not certain, but the timing is highly suggestive: Ormrod, 'Edward III's Government', pp. 256–9.

22 A. L. Brown, *The Early History of the Clerkship of the Council* (Glasgow, 1960).

23 The following analysis is based on my own reading of the available primary evidence. See also Ormrod, 'Edward III's Government', pp. 99–118.

24 See also Richardson and Sayles, *Parliament*, ch. XXI, pp. 66–7.

25 C47/2/29, nos. 1–5; C47/2/31, nos. 4–6; C47/28/9, no. 8; C81/1538/20; M. Prestwich, 'English Armies in the Early Stages of the Hundred Years War: A Scheme in 1341', *BIHR*, lvi (1983), 103–13.

26 Ormrod, 'Edward III's Government', p. 113; C. Given-Wilson, *The English Nobility in the Late Middle Ages* (London, 1987), p. 184 n. 12, p. 207 n. 51.

27 C256/4/1, no. 18.

28 *SCCKB*, v, pp. clii–iii; *Select Cases before the King's Council, 1243–1482*, ed. I. S. Leadam and J. F. Baldwin, SS, xxxv (1918), pp. 35–7; *CCR, 1364–8*, pp. 60–1, 404.

29 *Ibid., 1349–54*, pp. 28, 34.

30 *Les Reportes del Cases in Camera Stellata*, ed. W. P. Baildon (privately printed, 1894), pp. xliv–lv; J. F. Baldwin, *The King's Council in England during the Middle Ages* (Oxford, 1913), pp. 355–6.

31 Tout, *Chapters*, v. 30–4, 68–74; Ormrod, 'Edward III's Government', pp. 68–97, 132–8.

32 Unlike Tout, I am reluctant to assume that the keeper of the privy seal was 'early in the reign of Edward III, definitely recognised as one of the three chief ministers of state' (*Chapters*, v. 59). The keeper does not appear in the available records of the administrative council with any regularity until the 1360s, and it was not until 1372 that he began to be named in the witness lists to royal charters. See also Ormrod, 'Edward III's Government', p. 133 and n. 3.

33 *Idem*, 'Recovery of Royal Authority', p. 14. For further references see E403/411, 26 July 1362; E403/413, 23 Jan. 1363; *Issue Roll of Brantingham*, p. 446; E403/ 461, 18 Nov. 1376; etc.

34 C81/357/22191, duplicated in E208/4, file 26–27 Edw III, no. 49. For further examples see the chancery warrants printed in *Chronique de Jean le Bel*, ed. J. Viard and E. Deprez, Société de l'Histoire de France (1904–5), ii. 337, 389, etc., although it should be appreciated that letters addressed to the chancellor and treasurer during periods when the king was away from England fall into rather a different category.

35 SC1/42/84; C81/1538/33.

36 Compare the lists of those summoned to this assembly (*LRDP*, iv. 596) with the commissions of 10 July recorded on the roll of the staple (C67/22, m. 25).

37 C81/1538/53. The resulting commissions are in *CPR, 1367–70*, p. 460; *CFR, 1369–77*, pp. 91–2.

38 E.g. C49/6/26, printed in Baldwin, *King's Council*, pp. 475–6; C81/1538/35; etc.

39 C81/1538/36; Putnam, *Shareshull*, pp. 51–2, 68–72.

40 Baldwin, *King's Council*, pp. 262–306, *passim*. Baldwin argued that the council sprouted a number of specialized subcommittees to deal with the increased load of business in the mid-14th century. See also *Select Cases in the Exchequer Chamber*, ed. M. Hemmant, SS, li, lxiv (1933–48), i, pp. xii–xx. However, M. H. Keen has recently questioned the assumption that the court of chivalry (and by extension the court of admiralty) emerged in this way ('The Jurisdiction and Origins of the Constable's Court', in J. Gillingham and J. C. Holt, eds., *War and Government in the Middle Ages*, Woodbridge, Suffolk, 1984, pp. 159–69).

41 *CIM*, iii. no. 50; C49/7/27. For the background, see R. E. Archer, 'The Estates and Finances of Margaret of Brotherton, *c.* 1320–1399', *Historical Research*, lx (1987), 266–7.

42 SC8/228/11397–8; *Liber Assisarum*, 26 Edw III, pl. 60 (printed in *Les Reports del Cases en Ley*, London, 1678–80, v. 131); *CCR, 1349–54*, pp. 567–9; E159/130, *Brev. Bar., Mich.*, m. 13; *CChR, 1341–1417*, p. 142. This is one of many similar cases revolving around the wording of royal charters.

43 For their qualifications and careers see *DNB*, ii. 922–3; xv. 352; xvii. 590–1.

44 See the cases cited in W. M. Ormrod, 'The Origins of the *Sub Pena* Writ', *Historical Research*, lxi (1988), 12–13 and n. 11.

45 *Ibid.*, pp. 11–20. The chancery rolls suggest that specific money penalties were increasingly used as threats in administrative

actions as well as in summonses before the council during the second half of Edward III's reign (*CCR, 1354–60*, pp. 534–5; *ibid., 1360–4*, pp. 115, 116, 118, 120, 268, 397; *ibid., 1374–7*, pp. 432–3; etc). The most dramatic instance, however, is the *sub pena* writ issued under the great seal of the exchequer in July 1372 summoning William of Windsor before the treasurer and barons for unspecified business, and threatening a money penalty of £10,000 (*sic*) for default (E159/148, *Brev. Retorn., Trin.*). For the background to this summons see Harbison, 'William of Windsor', pp. 159–60.

46 For what follows see Richardson and Sayles, *Parliament*, ch. XXII, pp. 377–97.

47 My statistics are based on the summonses printed in *LRDP*, iv. *passim*.

48 The influence of the chancery clerks over the business of parliament is discussed by G. P. Cuttino, 'King's Clerks and the Community of the Realm', *Speculum*, xxix (1954), 404–6.

49 E. L. G. Stones, 'Sir Geoffrey le Scrope (*c.* 1280 to 1340), Chief Justice of the King's Bench', *EHR*, lxix (1954), 3, 10–12.

50 *RP*, ii. 113. For Stonor see *DNB*, liv. 478–9.

51 Note esp. the abolition of presentment of Englishry (an antiquated Norman procedure for the identification of murder victims) and the new forms of action at *nisi prius* (the procedure whereby cases pending in the central courts could be adjourned before the justices of assize or other courts sitting in the localities): *SR*, i. 282, 286–7.

52 B. H. Putnam, 'Chief Justice Shareshull and the Economic and Legal Codes of 1351–1352', *University of Toronto Law Journal*, v (1943–4), 251–83; *idem, Shareshull*, pp. 52–4.

53 *SR*, i. 292–4; and see pp. 132–3.

54 Ormrod, 'Origins of the *Sub Pena* Writ', p. 14, and references.

55 Reading, p. 113; Walsingham, i. 275–6. Putnam, *Shareshull*, p. 70, ascribed this scheme to Shareshull; but the detailed provisions for the collection of the subsidy of 1352 (*SR*, i. 327–8) suggest expert financial assistance.

56 It is also worth noting that Edington personally communicated news of the tax grant, and of the agreed form of collection, to the exchequer: E159/128, *Communia, Hil.*, m. 9d; E368/124, m. 44.

57 Ormrod, 'Agenda for Legislation', pp. 22–3.

58 *SR*, i. 285; *CPR, 1340–3*, pp. 310, 363, 441, 446, 580–1, 587.

59 *RP*, ii. 149, 150; *CLBL, F.* 107.

60 *RP*, ii. 240; *SR*, i. 321; Putnam, *Shareshull*, pp. 72–3; Ormrod, 'Customs', pp. 30– 1; *idem*, 'Edward III's Government', pp. 172–3, 204–5.

61 See pp. 30-1, 51.

62 H. L. Gray, *The Influence of the Commons on Early Legislation* (Cambridge, Mass., 1932), pp. 225–7, 248–9.

63 *RP*, ii. 113.

64 For provisions see p. 120; for treasons see Bellamy, *Law of Treason*, pp. 86–70; for the staple see pp. 178-9. Compare Harriss, 'Formation of Parliament', pp. 47–8.

65 *RP*, ii. 285–7.

66 *Ibid.*, ii. 286; *SR*, i. 383.

67 *RP*, ii. 286; *SR*, i. 383; *RP*, ii. 287.

68 *RP*, ii. 287–8; *SR*, i. 384–7.

69 B. H. Putnam, *The Enforcement of the Statute of Labourers* (New York, 1908).

70 Saul, *Knights and Esquires*, pp. 108–11; Ormrod, 'Recovery of Royal Authority', p. 11.

71 *RP*, ii. 285. This petition may echo the demand and the repealed statute of 1341 (*ibid.*, ii. 128; *SR*, i. 296). It is interesting to note that the oath imposed on judges under the Ordinance of Justices of 1346 made only one vague reference to 'la forme des estatutz' (*ibid.*, i. 305–6). The obligation to uphold the statutes is conspicuously absent from all the oaths of royal councillors known from this period: see Baldwin, *King's Council*, pp. 345–52.

72 M. Buck, *Politics, Finance and the Church in the Reign of Edward II: Walter Stapeldon, Treasurer of England* (Cambridge, 1983), pp. 219–23.

73 The attempt to place all politically active men in one or other of these camps led Tout (*Chapters*, iii. 1–142) into some highly contorted arguments. Haines, *Stratford*, pp. 429–31, argues that even Stratford, the supposed arch-Lancastrian, cannot be neatly categorized in this way.

74 Stones, 'Sir Geoffrey le Scrope', pp. 4–5; *SCCKB*, iv, pp. xiii, xv, xvii–xviii.

75 I rely on the lists in Tout, *Chapters*, vi. 7–13, 20–2.

76 A good account of the early stages of Stratford's political career is to be found in N. M. Fryde, 'John Stratford, Bishop of Winchester, and the Crown, 1323–30', *BIHR*, xliv (1971), 153–61. Otherwise, see Haines, *Stratford*, pp. 124–214.

77 Baker, p. 27.

78 Fryde, 'John Stratford and the Crown', p. 157.

79 Haines, *Stratford*, p. 230.

80 *Ibid.*, p. 281; Fryde, 'Removal of Ministers', p. 154.

81 Buck, *Stapeldon*, p. 163–96.

82 Maxwell-Lyte, *Great Seal*, pp. 17–18.

83 R. L. Baker, *The English Customs Service, 1307–1343: A Study of Medieval Administration* (Philadelphia, 1961), pp. 23–7, 30–1.

84 B. H. Putnam, 'Shire Officials: Keepers of the Peace and Justices of the Peace', *EGW*, iii. 185–217; M. H. Mills, 'The Collectors of Customs', *ibid.*, ii. 189–91.

85 S. T. Gibson, 'The Escheatries, 1327–41', *EHR*, xxxvi (1921), 218–25. The particular interpretation which Gibson attached to this evidence is no longer acceptable.

86 Tout, *Chapters*, iii. 121; Fryde, 'Removal of Ministers', pp. 149, 156–8.

87 *SCCKB*, vi, pp. xvi–xvii; Maddicott, 'Law and Lordship', pp. 43–4. The quotation comes from YB 14 Edw III, Mich. pl. 109 (*Year Books of the Reign of King Edward III, Years XI–XX*, ed. A. J. Horwood and L. O. Pike, RS (1883–1911), Years XIV and XV, p. 258).

88 *SCCKB*, vi, p. xvii.

89 C49/46/11, briefly discussed by D. Hughes, *A Study of Social and Constitutional Tendencies in the Early Years of Edward III* (London, 1915), p. 101.

90 See the important evidence discussed by Fryde, 'Removal of Ministers', pp. 159–60.

91 The *libellus famosus* and Stratford's reply are printed in *Anglia Sacra*, i. 23–36. Most historians have tended to concentrate on the supposed constitutional significance of the Stratford crisis. See Hughes, *Early Years of Edward III*, pp. 100–52; G. T. Lapsley, *Crown, Community and Parliament in the Later Middle Ages* (Oxford, 1951), pp. 231–72; B. Wilkinson, 'The Protest of the Earls of Arundel and Surrey in the Crisis of 1341', *EHR*, xlvi (1931), 177–93. More balanced accounts are to be found in Fryde, 'Removal of Ministers', pp. 149–61; Harriss, *Public Finance*, pp. 282–304.

92 E. B. Fryde, 'Edward III's War Finance, 1337–41: Transactions in Wool and Credit Operations', University of Oxford D. Phil. thesis (1947), i. 523–7.

93 Haines, *Stratford*, pp. 285–7.

94 Fryde, 'Removal of Ministers', p. 158.

95 Haines, *Stratford*, p. 313.

96 Harriss, *Public Finance*, pp. 520–1.

97 C81/1394/53.

98 Wilkinson, *Chancery*, pp. 155–7; *BRUO*, iii.

99 *Foedera*, III (i). 50; *LRDP*, iv. 558.

100 Tout, *Chapters*, iii. 166, n. 5, cited examples from the chancery warrants to indicate that the king corresponded formally with the regency council by addressing letters to the archbishop, chancellor and treasurer. But this was more a matter of protocol than anything else. The king also corresponded with the chancellor alone on what might be called conciliar matters (e.g. SC1/39/198, printed in Wilkinson, *Chancery*, p. 118, n. 1). For a letter from the regency council to the king addressed in the names of the archbishop, treasurer and chancellor, see SC1/56/6. All three Stratfords appeared in the witness lists to royal charters in the 1340s, but it is noticeable that Robert and Ralph dropped out after the death of John in 1348: see C53/135–40, analysed in Ormrod, 'Edward III's Government', pp. 109–11.

101 There is no full-scale biography of Edington. *DNB*, xvi. 386, and McKisack, *Fourteenth Century*, pp. 212–18, provide a brief summary.

102 *HBC*, pp. 105–7.

103 *SCCKB*, vi, pp. liii–lv, lxvi–lxix.

104 Sainty, *Officers of the Exchequer*, pp. 35–6; Wilkinson, *Chancery*, p. 204.

105 Ormrod, 'Black Death', pp. 177–8.

106 Sainty, *Officers of the Exchequer*, pp. 8, 43, 53, 62.

107 J. C. Davies, *The Baronial Opposition to Edward II* (Cambridge, 1918); T. F. Tout, *The Place of Edward II in English History*, 2nd edn (Manchester, 1936).

108 M. Prestwich, 'Exchequer and Wardrobe in the Later Years of Edward I', *BIHR*, xlvi (1973), 1–10; Harriss, *Public Finance*, pp. 208–28; Buck, 'Reform of Exchequer', pp. 241–5.

109 For Kilsby see Tout, *Chapters*, iii. 84–5, 116–18, 120–6, 131–2. The fact that Kilsby remained keeper of the privy seal until June 1342 (when he left to take up a military career) is a striking instance of the king's determination to withstand the political pressure of 1341 and not to yield control of his ministers to the barons or to parliament.

110 *Ibid.*, iii. 170–1; Ormrod, 'Edward III's Government', pp. 74–8.

111 *BRUO*, ii. 1391–2; iii. 1863–4.

112 C81/317/18171 (Wilkinson, *Chancery*, pp. 31, 226); C81/908/5.

113 *BRUO*, ii. 1006–8, 1368–70.

114 Ormrod, 'Edward III's Government', pp. 37–9, 74–84.

115 Chaplais, *Essays*, ch. XXII, pp. 173–4.

116 Tout, *Chapters*, iii. 109, 114–15, 161, 164; iv. 110–12.

117 E. B. Fryde, *William de la Pole, Merchant and King's Banker* (London, 1988), pp. 87–169, provides the most recent detailed guide to the king's credit dealings.

118 Tout, *Chapters*, iv. 118.

119 Fryde, *Studies*, ch. X, pp. 1–17.

120 For what follows see Tout, *Chapters*, iv. 110–35, 304–5; W. M. Ormrod, 'The Protecolla Rolls and English Government Finance, 1353–1364', *EHR*, cii (1987), 622–32; *idem*, 'Edward III's Government', pp. 222–327.

121 T. F. Tout and D. M. Broome, 'A National Balance Sheet for 1362–3', *EHR*, xxxix (1924), 404–19; Harriss, *Public Finance*, pp. 470–502. The only documents surviving from an earlier period and equating with this remarkable series are M. H. Mills, 'Exchequer Agenda and Estimates of Revenue, Easter Term 1284', *EHR*, xl (1925), 229–34; and the fragment of a schedule of 1324 printed in Harriss, *Public Finance*, pp. 523–4, and discussed and corrected by Fryde, *Tyranny and Fall*, pp. 97–8. The document discovered by H. Jenkinson and D. M. Broome, 'An Exchequer Statement of Receipts and Issues, 1339–40', *EHR*, lviii (1943), 210–16, is not of the same type, being merely a transcript of the notional totals of transactions given at the ends of the relevant receipt and issue rolls. The Walton Ordinances of 1338 did not require the compilation of estimates of receipts and issues, but merely the annual audit of warrants received in the lower exchequer and the drawing up of a statement of the king's current obligations to his creditors (Tout, *Chapters*, iii. 144–6, 149). In any case, neither of these orders seems to have been implemented.

122 For the following paragraph see Ormrod, 'Customs', pp. 27–40.

123 Harriss, *Public Finance*, p. 345.

124 *Chronica Monasterii de Melsa Auctore Thoma de Burton*, ed. E. A. Bond, RS (1866–8), iii. 127–42, esp. 135, 141. For the background see M. J. O. Kennedy, 'Resourceful Villeins: The Cellarer Family of Wawne in Holderness', *Yorkshire Archaeological Journal*, xlviii (1976), 107–17.

125 Reading, p. 113.

126 See pp. 37-8. There is no shortage of 18th- and 19th-century biographies of Wykeham, but these inevitably concentrate on his educational and artistic patronage. This side of his career is now usefully summarized in J. Alexander and P. Binski, eds., *Age of Chivalry: Art in Plantagenet England* (London, 1987), pp. 468–75.

127 Brown, Colvin and Taylor, *King's Works*, i. 170–1, 184–5; D. Knoop and G. P. Jones, 'The Impressment of Masons for Windsor Castle, 1360–1363', *Economic Journal*, iii (1934–7), 350–61.

128 Tout, *Chapters*, iii. 237.

129 *Ibid.*, iii. 238–9. It is extremely rare to find petitions addressed to the keeper of the privy seal, but Wykeham was quite clearly seen as a channel through which royal favour might flow: *CPML, 1323–64*, pp. 279–80.

130 C81/1335/47; SC1/56/125.

131 J. R. L. Highfield, 'The Promotion of William of Wickham to the See of Winchester', *JEH*, iv (1953), 37–54.

132 E.g. Reading, pp. 177–8.

133 *BRUO*, i. 112; ii. 1095–7; iii. 1683, provides summaries of their ecclesiastical careers and their principal government offices. Sheppey had earlier worked as a diplomat for Edward III (Highfield, 'English Hierarchy', p. 118), and served on the regency council of 1345 (*Foedera*, III (i). 50). Barnet's first recorded diplomatic missions were in 1361–2, but his summonses to great councils and parliaments in the previous decade suggests that he may well have been involved in diplomacy for some time (*LRDP*, iv. 594, 605, 612, 616, 626; Ormrod, 'Edward III's Government', p. 143).

134 SC8/46/2284.

135 *Anon. Chron.*, p. 97.

136 C. Given-Wilson, 'The Merger of Edward III's and Queen Philippa's Households, 1360–9', *BIHR*, li (1978), 183–7; Ormrod, 'Edward III's Government', pp. 82–3, 324, using evidence derived from Wilkinson, 'Authorisation of Chancery Writs', pp. 134–5; Harriss, *Public Finance*, pp. 470–502.

137 *List of Plea Rolls*, PRO Lists and Indexes, iv (repr. 1963), p. 36 and nn; A. Steel, *The Receipt of the Exchequer, 1377–1485* (Cambridge, 1954), p. 405.

138 *CCR, 1364–8*, p.116.

139 *CLBL, G.* 162–3. For another interesting example see C. G. Crump, 'What Became

of Robert Rag, or Some Chancery Blunders', in A. G. Little and F. M. Powicke, eds., *Essays in Medieval History Presented to T. F. Tout* (Manchester, 1925), pp. 335–47.

140 *Anon. Chron.*, pp. 98, 184. For Kirkton see *The 1341 Royal Inquest in Lincolnshire*, p. xix.

141 For Brantingham's career see Tout, *Chapters*, iii. 225, 233, 261–2.

142 Sherborne, 'Costs of English Warfare', pp. 143–4. For further details see pp. 129, 171.

143 *RP*, ii. 304.

144 Tout, *Chapters*, iii. 270–1; Tuck, *Crown and Nobility*, p. 166.

145 W. Stubbs, *The Constitutional History of England*, 4th edn (Oxford, 1906), ii. 440–3; V. H. Galbraith, 'Articles Laid Before the Parliament of 1371', *EHR*, xxxiv (1919), 579–82; K. B. McFarlane, *John Wycliffe and the Beginnings of English Nonconformity* (London, 1952), pp. 45–6, 59–60; M. Aston, '"Caim's Castles": Poverty, Politics and Patronage', in Dobson, ed., *Church, Politics and Patronage*, pp. 49–52.

146 *Anon. Chron.*, p. 63.

147 Given-Wilson, *Royal Household*, pp. 102–3.

148 E101/509/14 is a list of discharged tallies relating to entries on the receipt rolls between 1369 and 1372, and presumably drawn up as part of an attempt to quantify unpaid assignments issued over the same period. I hope to discuss this more fully elsewhere.

149 W. M. Ormrod, 'An Experiment in Taxation: The English Parish Subsidy of 1371', *Speculum*, lxiii (1988), 59, 80; A. Steel, 'The Practice of Assignment in the Later Fourteenth Century', *EHR*, xliii (1928), 172–80.

150 A. E. Prince, 'The Payment of Army Wages in Edward III's Reign', *Speculum*, xix (1944), 158; Given-Wilson, *Royal Household*, pp. 122–3.

151 Note the comments of Holmes, *Good Parliament*, pp. 64–5.

152 *Anon. Chron.*, p. 93; Holmes, *Good Parliament*, p. 158.

153 There is no official record of the trial, but *Anon. Chron.*, pp. 96–100 provides a detailed account. See also the list of charges given in an *inspeximus* of Wykeham's subsequent pardon issued in December 1377: *RP*, iii. 387–8. For comment on the accusations see V. H. Galbraith's notes in *Anon. Chron.*, p. 184.

154 'Ransom of John II', pp. 4, 11–12.

155 *CPR, 1361–4*, pp. 126, 144, 186; Harriss, *Public Finance*, p. 502.

156 Highfield, 'Promotion of William of Wickham', p. 40 and n. 8.

157 The dates of the confiscation and release of the temporalities are given in Alexander and Binski, eds., *Age of Chivalry*, p. 468. On 6 November the Bishops of Bath and Wells and Salisbury, the Earls of Warwick and Salisbury, the chancellor, treasurer and keeper of the privy seal, and 'other officers of the king' had met at Westminster to discuss 'secret business': E403/461, 18 Nov. 1376. Whether this was the council which actually authorized the seizure of the temporalities is uncertain, but it may be worth noting that Ralph Erghum, the Bishop of Salisbury, was very closely associated with Gaunt (R. G. Davies, 'The Episcopal Appointments in England and Wales of 1375', *Mediaeval Studies*, xliv, 1982, 329–30).

158 *RP*, ii. 373. See also *John Lydford's Book*, ed. D. M. Owen, Devon and Cornwall Record Soc., xix, and HMC Joint Publication, xxii (1974), nos. 178–9.

159 Tout, *Chapters*, iii. 343–5, 352, 380 (n. 2), 396 (nn. 2, 4), 415; vi. 23.

CHAPTER 6: THE MAGNATES

1 J. E. Powell and K. Wallis, *The House of Lords in the Middle Ages* (London, 1968), pp. 282–346.

2 My statistics depend on the lists of summonses in *LRDP*, iv. *passim*. See also the discussion in Powell and Wallis, *House of Lords*, pp. 310–79.

3 P. H. W. Booth, *The Financial Administration of the Lordship and County of Chester, 1272–1377*, Chetham Soc., 3rd ser., xxviii (1981), pp. 173–5; Fowler, *King's Lieutenant*, pp. 225–6; Holmes, *Estates*, p. 5.

4 Fryde, *Tyranny and Fall*, p. 107; GEC, iv. 270–2.

5 Given-Wilson, *English Nobility*, pp. 35–40, provides the most detailed review of these creations.

6 Saul, *Knights and Esquires*, p. 68.

7 J. T. Rosenthal, *Nobles and the Noble Life, 1295–1500* (London, 1976), pp. 59–61.

8 Holmes, *Estates*, pp. 93–4, 97.

9 A full list of those peers who fought for Lancaster in 1322, and details of their fates, may be found in GEC, ii. App. C.

10 *Ibid.*, i. 372; iii. 291; ix. 380.

11 N. Saul, 'The Despensers and the Downfall

of Edward II', *EHR*, xcix (1984), 1–33; S. L. Waugh, 'For King, Country and Patron: The Despensers and Local Administration, 1321–1322', *JBS*, xxii, no. 2 (1983), 23–45.

12 J. C. Davies, 'The Despenser War in Glamorgan', *TRHS*, 3rd ser., ix (1915), 55–7; L. Fox, 'Ministers' Accounts of the Honor of Leicester (1322 to 1324)', *Transactions of the Leicestershire Archaeological Soc.*, xix (1935–7), 209–11; *South Lancashire in the Reign of Edward II*, ed. G. H. Tupling, Chetham Soc., 3rd ser., i (1949), introduction, *passim*; S. L. Waugh, 'The Profits of Violence: The Minor Gentry in the Rebellion of 1321–1322 in Gloucestershire and Herefordshire', *Speculum*, lii (1977), 843–69, esp. pp. 849–52, 863–5.

13 J. M. W. Bean, *From Lord to Patron: Lordship in Late Medieval England* (Manchester, 1989), pp. 200–1. See in particular the charges of maintenance involving Chancellor Baldock and Sir Eble Lestrange in *Eyre of Northamptonshire*, i. 221, 237. For an accusation of maintenance made against Sir Saier Rochford, acting as deputy justice for Lestrange in Lincs. in the early 1330s, see SC8/53/2621.

14 Ormrod, 'Agenda for Legislation', pp. 19–22.

15 *RP*, ii. 62, 446.

16 *Ibid.*, ii. 62, 65; GEC, iv. 270, n. (f).

17 *RP*, ii. 62; GEC, ix. 284.

18 *RPHI*, pp. 232–3, 237; *CPR, 1330–4*, p. 573; Baldwin, 'The Council', p. 152.

19 *CIM*, ii. no. 1469.

20 *CCR, 1337–9*, p. 136.

21 Holmes, *Estates*, pp. 82–3.

22 B. H. Putnam, 'Records of the Keepers of the Peace and their Supervisors', *EHR*, xlv (1930), 435–6.

23 *Idem*, 'Shire Officials: Keepers of the Peace and Justices of the Peace', p. 193; *idem*, 'Transformation', pp. 34–5, 38.

24 *Ibid.*, pp. 30, 38; *RPHI*, pp. 232–3.

25 *CChR, 1327–41*, pp. 348–9, 387, 399, 402; Ormrod, 'Recovery of Royal Authority', p. 6.

26 SC8/97/4826, printed in Saul, *Knights and Esquires*, pp. 266–7.

27 N. Fryde, 'A Medieval Robber Baron: Sir John Molyns of Stoke Poges, Buckinghamshire', in R. F. Hunnisett and J. B. Posts, eds., *Medieval Legal Records* (London, 1978), pp. 198–221. It is interesting to notice that the crown had earlier ordered a general inquiry into the actions of the king's ministers in Beds. and Bucks. as a result of allegations brought, probably by Molyns, against the sub–escheator: C81/181/4520–1; *CPR, 1330–4*, p. 140.

28 SC8/158/7891. For the background see *RP*, ii. 44; *CPR, 1330–4*, p. 199; *CCR, 1330–3*, pp. 360–1.

29 *CPR, 1340–3*, pp. 105–6.

30 *Scalacronica by Sir Thomas Gray of Heton*, ed. J. Stevenson (Edinburgh, 1836), p. 158. This passage has had considerable influence on historical writing: see McKisack, *Fourteenth Century*, p. 154, Tuck, *Crown and Nobility*, pp. 105–6.

31 *RP*, ii. 60–1.

32 Nicholson, *Edward III and the Scots*, pp. 99–102, 107.

33 For an interesting alternative interpretation to what follows, see M. Prestwich, 'Cavalry Service in Early Fourteenth Century England', in Gillingham and Holt, eds., *War and Government*, pp. 147–58.

34 N. B. Lewis, 'The Summons of the English Feudal Levy, 5 April 1327', in T. A. Sandquist and M. R. Powicke, eds., *Essays in Medieval History Presented to Bertie Wilkinson* (Toronto, 1969), pp. 236–49.

35 *Northern Petitions*, no. 111.

36 C. Platt, *Medieval Southampton* (London, 1973), pp. 107–18; E. Searle and R. Burghart, 'The Defense of England and the Peasants' Revolt', *Viator*, iii (1972), 366–75.

37 *CCR, 1333–7*, pp. 679, 701, 723.

38 *Ibid.*, *1337–9*, p. 255; *Foedera*, II (ii). 994.

39 *CPR, 1338–40*, pp. 141–2. These amplified an earlier set of commissions of 7 July (*ibid.*, *1338–40*, p. 134).

40 Harriss, *Public Finance*, pp. 270–302, provides the best statement of the political alignment of the magnates during the Stratford crisis.

41 *Ibid.*, pp. 305–8.

42 *CPR, 1340–3*, pp. 111–13. For Cantilupe, see *The 1341 Royal Inquest in Lincolnshire*, pp. xv–xvii.

43 *Foedera*, II (ii). 1142.

44 Hughes, *Early Years of Edward III*, pp. 216, 222; Fryde, 'Medieval Robber Baron', pp. 202–6. For further examples see Jones, 'Rex et Ministri', pp. 9–14; W. R. Jones, 'Keeping the Peace: English Society, Local Government, and the Commissions of 1341–44', *American Journal of Legal History*, xviii (1974), 310–19; Hughes, *Early Years of Edward III*, pp. 212–36.

45 *CPR, 1343–5*, pp. 393–6.

46 McKisack, *Fourteenth Century*, p. 219.

47 Prince, 'Indenture System', pp. 283–97; K. B. McFarlane, 'Bastard Feudalism', *BIHR*, xx (1945), 163–4; N. B. Lewis, 'The Recruitment and Organization of a Contract Army, May to November 1337', *BIHR*, xxxvii (1964), 1–19; Prestwich, 'English Armies in the Early Stages of the Hundred Years War', pp. 106–7.

48 Henry of Grosmont, for example, refused to raise the siege of Rennes in 1358, despite several royal mandates to this effect: Fowler, *King's Lieutenant*, p. 163.

49 Prince, 'Payment of Army Wages', pp. 137–60.

50 D. Hay, 'The Division of the Spoils of War in Fourteenth-Century England', *TRHS*, 5th ser., iv (1954), 91–109; McKisack, *Fourteenth Century*, pp. 247–8; McFarlane, *Nobility*, pp. 27–31.

51 *Ibid.*, p. 30.

52 *Ibid.*; E403/387, 26 July, 4 Sept. 1357; E403/388, 4 Oct. 1357, 5 Mar. 1358.

53 See respectively: McKisack, *Fourteenth Century*, p. 254; McFarlane, *Nobility*, p. 22 and n. 1; R. K. Morris, 'The Architecture of the Earls of Warwick in the Fourteenth Century', in Ormrod, ed., *England in the Fourteenth Century*, pp. 161–74, esp. 172–4; N. Pevsner and J. Harris, *Lincolnshire* (Harmondsworth, 1964), p. 641; McFarlane, *Nobility*, p. 22. Given-Wilson, *English Nobility*, p. 157 suggests that Bolton Castle may have owed as much to the profits of public office as to the spoils of war. I hope to discuss Umfraville's work at South Kyme in more detail elsewhere.

54 D. Knowles and W. F. Grimes, *Charterhouse* (London, 1954), pp. 5–8; J. Kerr, 'The East Window at Gloucester Cathedral', in *Medieval Art and Architecture at Gloucester and Tewkesbury*, British Archaeological Association Conference Transactions, vii (1985), pp. 116–29.

55 Prince, 'Payment of Army Wages', pp. 152–3; E401/393, 5 July 1348, recording a 'loan' of £16,015 14s. 3d. from the earl, repaid in two instalments on 26 and 28 Oct. 1350. I assume that these are in fact debts left over from the campaign in Aquitaine.

56 E401/391, 17 Jan. 1348; E401/393, 2 Aug. 1348. The exact total, of £4,633 13s. 4d., was repaid in two instalments on 28 Oct. 1349 and 12 Oct. 1353. I am indebted to Roger Axworthy for this information, and for the references in the preceding note.

57 The list of Arundel's loans in McFarlane, *Nobility*, pp. 89–90 contains a number of inaccuracies. The evidence of the chancery rolls is difficult to interpret, and my own calculations depend solely on the receipt rolls. The entries are as follows: E401/501, 24 May 1370: £6,000 (not 1 July as stated in McFarlane, *Nobility*, p. 89, n. 5); E401/501, 28 June 1370: £13,333 6s. 8d. (McFarlane, *Nobility*, p. 89, n. 5; Holmes, *Good Parliament*, p. 76); E401/501, 4 Sept. 1370: £666 13s. 4d. (McFarlane, *Nobility*, p. 89, n. 5); E401/505, 15 Apr. 1371: £5,333 6s. 8d. (not 2,000 marks, as stated by McFarlane, *Nobility*, p. 90, n. 1); E401/508, 16 Aug. 1372: £3,333 6s. 8d. (McFarlane, *Nobility*, p. 90, n. 1); E401/515, 18 Sept. 1374: £10,000 (McFarlane, *Nobility*, p. 90, n. 1). The sum total of these entries is £38,666 6s. 8d.

58 From Tournai on 30 Aug. 1340, Edward III had written to the chancellor and treasurer ordering the swift repayment of debts to the earl: C81/1330/56. For repayment of Arundel's loans in the 1370s, see Holmes, *Good Parliament*, pp. 76–7.

59 M. Prestwich, *The Three Edwards* (London, 1980), pp. 152–4.

60 *CPR, 1345–8*, p. 473.

61 Tout, *Chapters*, iv. 327–8; Given-Wilson, *Royal Household*, p. 88.

62 Haines, *Stratford*, pp. 296, 303–4.

63 GEC, viii. 442–5.

64 *CPR, 1348–50*, p. 145; *CCR, 1349–54*, p. 556; McFarlane, *Nobility*, p. 194 and n. 5, p. 202 and n. 1.

65 The membership of the order, worked out by G. F. Beltz, *Memorials of the Order of the Garter* (London, 1841), is summarized in GEC, ii, App. B.

66 Vale, *Edward III and Chivalry*, pp. 89–91.

67 For what follows see J. S. Roskell, 'The Problem of the Attendance of the Lords in Medieval Parliaments', *BIHR*, xxix (1956), 153–204, esp. 165–9.

68 *RP*, ii. 224, 226–7, 256–7.

69 *Ibid.*, ii. 139. For the background see R. A. Griffiths, 'The English Realm and Dominions and the King's Subjects in the Later Middle Ages', in J. G. Rowe, ed., *Aspects of Late Medieval Government and Society: Essays Presented to J. R. Lander* (Toronto, 1986), pp. 83–105, esp. 92–6.

70 *SR*, i. 310; *CPR, 1350–4*, p. 63; GEC, ii. 61; iv. 97–8.

71 *RP*, ii. 269, 294–5.

72 For outlines of Montagu's career see GEC, xi. 385–8; R. Douch, 'The Career, Lands and Family of William Montague, Earl of Salisbury, 1301–44', *BIHR*, xxiv (1951), 85–8.

73 *CCR, 1330–3*, p. 166; *ibid., 1333–7*, pp. 129–30; *ibid., 1337–9*, pp. 117, 519; etc.

74 C81/1330/11, 24.

75 C81/1538/22; SC1/42/84.

76 SC1/36/105, 139.

77 *Fasti*, iv. 13; GEC, ix. 84–5. A Master William Montagu occurs in the wardrobe accounts of the 1330s (Ormrod, 'Personal Religion of Edward III', p. 868, n. 109). Another of Montagu's kinsmen, William Northwood, was in the service of Queen Philippa, and was personally recommended by the king for membership of the Order of St John of Jerusalem (*CCR, 1343–6*, p. 107; *Calendar of Papal Registers: Letters, 1342–62*, London, 1897, p. 9). For Edward III's involvement in Montagu's foundation of Bisham Abbey (Berks.), see Alexander and Binski, eds., *Age of Chivalry*, no. 679.

78 BL MS Cotton Nero C. VIII, ff. 223–4; *The Wardrobe Book of William de Norwell*, ed. M. Lyon, B. Lyon, H. S. Lucas and J. de Sturler (Brussels, 1983), p. 301.

79 C49/7/7 (printed in Baldwin, *King's Council*, pp. 477–8); Hughes, *Early Years of Edward III*, pp. 68–9; Fryde, *Studies*, ch. V, pp. 261–2; Harriss, *Public Finance*, p. 242, n. 6.

80 See the evidence of the estallment rolls, E101/120/20; BL Add. Rolls 26588–26593, identified and discussed by Ormrod, 'Edward III's Government', pp. 238–9.

81 Fryde, *Studies*, ch. V, p. 262. In fact, it would seem that respites had continued to be granted between Aug. 1338 and Sept. 1339: see *CCR, 1337–9*, pp. 525, 614, 619; *ibid., 1339–41*, pp. 87, 90, 93, 94, 101, 104, 110, 116, 125, 218, 248.

82 For Darcy's role in the crisis of 1340–1 see Tout, *Chapters*, iii. 98, 120 and n. 2, 125, 129 n. 4, 131–2, 135.

83 *Ibid.*, iv. 338–9.

84 For the earl's deputies see *ibid.*, vi. 47. Given-Wilson, *English Nobility*, p. 184, n. 12, suggests on the basis of the witness lists to royal charters that de Vere was regularly at court in the 1360s; but it was common form to include the chamberlain's name in such lists, and I am therefore somewhat doubtful that this evidence proves Oxford to have been in attendance. Note the rarity of his appearances in the memoranda in the dorses of the close rolls in the 1360s (*CCR, 1360–4*, pp. 250–1, 551; *ibid., 1369–74*, pp. 93, 108–9).

85 Given-Wilson, *English Nobility*, pp. 184, 207.

86 *LRDP*, iv. 537–9; Powell and Wallis, *House of Lords*, pp. 348–9.

87 *LRDP*, iv. 562–3.

88 See p. 176.

89 Ormrod, 'Edward III's Government', pp. 136–7. A number of privy seal summonses to the council sent to the Abbot of Westminster survive in WAM 12208, 12220, 12222–3.

90 *LRDP*, iv. 618–19; WAM 12214; *Issue Roll of Brantingham*, pp. 128–30, 239. I do not share the confidence of Brown, *Governance of Late Medieval England*, p. 35, that after 1350 'an average of two or three Great Councils were summoned each year'. On the other hand, it should be noted that great councils were often very shadowy occasions: see, e.g. J. I. Catto, 'An Alleged Great Council of 1374', *EHR*, lxxxii (1967), 764–71.

91 *CCR, 1349–54*, pp. 594–5.

92 *Issues of the Exchequer, Henry III – Henry VI*, ed. F. Devon (London, 1847), p. 166; E403/392, 19 May 1358.

93 SC1/41/49 (Fowler, *King's Lieutenant*, p. 287, n. 115); SC1/41/105 (Saul, *Knights and Esquires*, pp. 79, 160); SC8/297/14836 (*CFR, 1347–56*, p. 423) .

94 *List of Sheriffs for England and Wales*, PRO Lists and Indexes, ix (repr. 1963), pp. 12, 21, 72, 112, 117–18, 127, 157. For the five hereditary sheriffdoms see W. A. Morris, 'The Sheriff', *EGW*, ii. 44–5. It should be noted that Edward III's new grants were not hereditary. Furthermore, John Lisle of Rougemont only enjoyed tenure of the sheriffdom of Cambs. and Hunts. for one year (1351–2), after which it reverted to royal control.

95 *CPR, 1348–50*, pp. 526–7; *ibid., 1350–4*, pp. 85–91.

96 *Ibid., 1367–70*, pp. 191–5; A. Goodman, 'John of Gaunt: Paradigm of the Late Fourteenth-Century Crisis', *TRHS*, 5th ser., xxxvii (1987), 140–3.

97 *RP*, ii. 250.

98 For nomination of under-sheriffs see SC1/43/170 (Wilkinson, *Chancery*, p. 35, n. 5); SC1/50/173–4; Morris, 'The Sheriff', p. 45. For the practice of appointing deputy JPs see *Proceedings Before the Justices of the Peace in the Fourteenth and Fifteenth Centuries*, ed. B. H. Putnam (London, 1938), p. lxxix. For further discussion of this matter see pp. 142–5.

99 Maddicott, 'Law and Lordship', pp. 46–51; *SR*, i. 365, 366; R. W. Kaeuper, 'Law and Order in Fourteenth-Century England: The Evidence of Special Commissions of Oyer and Terminer', *Speculum*, liv (1979), 757–64.

100 SC1/40/4, resulting in the commission in *CPR, 1348–50*, p. 71.

101 *Essex Sessions of the Peace, 1351, 1377–1379*, ed. E. C. Furber, Essex Archaeological Soc. Occasional Publications, iii (1953), pp. 61–5.

102 Tout, *Chapters*, iii. 123, n. 3; iv. 296, n. 2. I owe this and the previous reference to Anthony Verduyn.

103 See pp. 56, 178.

104 The common petitions on prises between 1343 and 1362 are preoccupied with regulations concerning royal purveyors (*RP*, ii. 140, 149, 150, 151, 161, 167, 171, 203, 227, 228, 229, 238, 240, 241, 258, 260). In 1362, however, the commons specifically demanded that lords should not take prises, and asked that penalties be provided against the agents of those magnates who infringed the law (*ibid.*, ii. 269, 270). These suggestions were incorporated in the new Statute of Purveyors (*SR*, i. 371, 373).

105 *Ibid.*, i. 304–5; *RP*, ii. 165. See also B. A. Hanawalt, 'Fur Collar Crime: The Pattern of Crime Among the Fourteenth-Century English Nobility', *Journal of Social History*, viii (1975), 8.

106 Complaints about maintenance in the 1350s and 1360s were few, and general: *RP*, ii. 259, 265, 266.

107 *Ibid.*, ii. 238.

108 *Ibid.*, ii. 141, 166; H. M. Cam, *Liberties and Communities in Medieval England* (London, 1963), pp. 240–2.

109 Harriss, *Public Finance*, pp. 354–5, 516–17.

110 *RP*, ii. 329, 330, 333, 334, 342, 352. The same assembly witnessed the revival of complaints about maintenance by the king's ministers, not heard since 1348 (*ibid.*, ii. 166, 179, 368).

111 SC8/139/6920.

112 *RP*, ii. 334.

113 Ormrod, 'Experiment in Taxation', p. 79; *RP*, ii. 352, 354.

114 R. L. Storey, 'Liveries and Commissions of the Peace, 1388–90', in F. R. H. Du Boulay and C. M. Barron, eds., *The Reign of Richard II: Essays in Honour of May McKisack* (London, 1971), pp. 131–52; Bean, *From Lord to Patron*, pp. 202–5.

115 The following depends on J. M. W. Bean, *The Decline of English Feudalism, 1215–1540* (Manchester, 1968), pp. 104–234, 310–18; McFarlane, *Nobility*, pp. 61–82.

116 McFarlane (*ibid.*, p. 69) stated that 'feoffees were bound in equity to obey his [the lord's] wishes and were answerable in Chancery for any default'. But this has yet to be proved for the period before *c*. 1380. See J. L. Barton, 'The Medieval Use', *Law Quarterly Review*, lxxxi (1965), 562–77; C. J. Given-Wilson, 'Richard II and his Grandfather's Will', *EHR*, xciii (1978), 320–37; *idem*, English Nobility, p. 148.

117 This previously unnoticed case can be pieced together from the references in *CPR, 1348–50*, p. 535; *ibid., 1350–4*, p. 207; *CIM*, iii. nos. 28, 78; *CCR, 1349–54*, p. 550. The fact that it had to be brought before parliament suggests that the chancery alone lacked the authority to deal with such problems.

118 E401/383, 13 March 1346 (which actually records the remission of the fine offered by Warwick); *CFR, 1347–56*, p. 208. In 1353 the Despenser estates were transferred to the dowager Lady Despenser: *ibid., 1347–56*, pp. 378–9.

119 *RP*, ii. 104; C49/8/11; Bean, *Decline of English Feudalism*, p. 195.

120 *Ibid.*, pp. 221–34. As McFarlane also pointed out (*Nobility*, pp. 217–19), it was the nobility who really suffered from the development of enfeoffments to use among their own mesne tenants in the mid-14th century. In this respect see also N. Saul, *Scenes from Provincial Life: Knightly Families in Sussex, 1280–1400* (Oxford, 1986), pp. 23–4.

121 For respites of debts see p. 104. For immunity from assizes see *CCR, 1333–7*, p. 725; *CCR, 1337–9*, pp. 135, 281, 283, 389, 401, 513, 516, 625; *CCR, 1369–74*, p. 466; etc.

122 See, e.g. Keen, *England in the Later Middle Ages*, p. 164.

123 See p. 51. For a full discussion of the importance of these feudal rights before Edward III's reign see S. L. Waugh, *The Lordship of England: Royal Wardships and Marriages in English Society and Politics, 1217–1327* (Princeton, NJ, 1988).

124 Bellamy, *Law of Treason*, pp. 191–5.

125 Note especially Edward I's policy in this respect. McFarlane, *Nobility*, pp. 259–62.

126 *CPR, 1367–70*, p. 223; *Catalogue of Ancient Deeds*, iii. nos. A 4888–9; GEC, x. 396, n. (h). B. P. Wolffe, *The Crown Lands 1461 to 1536* (London, 1970), p. 32, states that the remainder of the lordship of Pembroke was granted to Edward III and his heirs on the marriage of John Hastings with Princess Margaret in 1359, but I can find no record of this.

127 See esp. J. A. Tuck, *Richard II and the English Nobility* (London, 1973), pp. 1–32.

128 Ormrod, 'Edward III and his Family', pp. 410–13.

129 The younger of the two Bohun sisters was originally destined for a nunnery: see Holmes, *Estates*, p. 24.

130 GEC, ii. App. B. For Pembridge, Brian and Buxhull see Given-Wilson, *Royal Household*, pp. 143, 156–7, 160–1, 208, 280–1.

131 Both appear reasonably regularly in witness lists to royal charters during the periods 1369–72 and 1375–6 (C53/152, 154). For Warwick's links with the chamber see Given-Wilson, *Royal Household*, pp. 160, 280–1.

132 For what follows see Ormrod, 'Edward III and his Family', pp. 416–20.

133 Stubbs, *Constitutional History*, ii. 439–53; Tout, *Chapters*, iii. 266–307; Tuck, *Richard II and the English Nobility*, pp. 1–32.

134 C. C. Bayley, 'The Campaign of 1375 and the Good Parliament', *EHR*, lv (1940), 372.

135 Prince, 'Indenture System', pp. 293–4, 295; Sherborne, 'Costs of English Warfare', p. 143.

136 See, e.g. A. Goodman, 'John of Gaunt', in Ormrod, ed., *England in the Fourteenth Century*, pp. 78–9.

137 C81/1336/32–33.

138 C53/154.

139 GEC, ii. App. B.

140 R. I. Jack, 'Entail and Descent: The Hastings Inheritance, 1370 to 1436', *BIHR*, xxxviii (1965), 6.

141 A. McHardy, 'The Effects of War on the Church: The Case of the Alien Priories in the Fourteenth Century', in M. Jones and M. Vale, eds., *England and her Neighbours 1066–1453: Essays in Honour of Pierre Chaplais* (London, 1989), pp. 289–90.

142 SC8/227/11346, 11349. I suggest that the phrase 'le Roi le grande' (or 'le Roy la grantde') used in these petitions is in Latimer's handwriting. This is supported by the endorsement to SC8/227/11349: 'Au chanseler. Fiat carta inde nunc. Willielmo domino de Latyme' (resulting in *CPR, 1374–7*, pp. 72–3). This evidence pre-dates the signed warrants by the chamberlains of Richard II, noted by Maxwell-Lyte, *Great Seal*, pp. 145, 152, and McFarlane, *Nobility*, p. 232.

143 See p. 61.

144 The best introduction to this complicated subject is H. M. Cam, *The Hundred and the Hundred Rolls*, new edn (London, 1963), pp.

137–45. The *Adventus Vicecomitum* sections of the memoranda rolls provide an indication of how many royal hundreds were in private hands. See, e.g. *Calendar of Memoranda Rolls (Exchequer), Michaelmas 1326–Michaelmas 1327* (London, 1968), pp. 1–6, 8–14.

145 *SR*, i. 259; H. M. Cam, *Law-Finders and Law-Makers in Medieval England* (London, 1962), p. 153.

146 *RP*, ii. 305–6, 314, 333, 348, 349, 357.

147 The fine rolls record a fairly steady trickle of leases in the middle years of the reign, a lull between 1363 and 1370, and then a slight increase in the 1370s, though not sufficient to be politically controversial (*CFR, 1347–56*, pp. 40, 101, 106–7, 145, 259, 342, 393–4; *ibid., 1357–68*, pp. 2, 9, 35, 143, 211, 270; *ibid., 1369–77*, pp. 64, 68, 93, 108, 155, 162, 184–5, 219, 248, 357, 369).

148 *Ibid., 1369–77*, p. 248; see also Wolffe, *Royal Demesne*, p. 64.

149 *CFR, 1369–77*, pp. 64, 108, 357.

150 Given-Wilson, *Royal Household*, pp. 151, 201–2; A. Saul, 'Local Politics and the Good Parliament', in A. Pollard, ed., *Property and Politics: Essays in Later Medieval English History* (Gloucester, 1984), pp. 156–71.

151 Holmes, *Good Parliament*, p. 183.

152 *Ibid.*, pp. 156–7.

153 A. Goodman, *The Loyal Conspiracy: The Lords Appellant under Richard II* (London, 1971), pp. 4–6.

154 Holmes, *Good Parliament*, p. 186.

155 Ormrod, 'Edward III and his Family', pp. 418–19 and n. 72.

156 *Issues of the Exchequer*, p. 204.

157 GEC, ii. App. B. The statement in Ormrod, 'Edward III and his Family', p. 419, that Thomas of Woodstock was also made a member of the order on this occasion, is wrong.

158 Tout, *Chapters*, iii. 326.

CHAPTER 7: THE CLERGY

1 J. C. Russell, 'The Clerical Population of Medieval England', *Traditio*, ii (1944), 177–212. Revised figures for 1381 are found in Oman, *Great Revolt*, pp. 163–4.

2 D. Knowles, *The Religious Orders in England* (Cambridge, 1948–59), ii. 255–62.

3 Hatcher, *Plague, Population*, p. 22; A. Hamilton Thompson, 'Registers of John Gynewell, Bishop of Lincoln, for the Years 1347–1350', *Archaeological Journal*, lxviii (1911), 325.

4 B. H. Putnam, 'Maximum Wage–Laws for Priests after the Black Death, 1348–1381', *American Historical Review*, xxi (1915–16), 12–32.

5 J. H. Denton, 'The "Communitas Cleri" in the Early Fourteenth Century', *BIHR*, li (1978), 72–8.

6 See especially the allusions in the poems commemorating the victories of 1346–7: *Political Poems and Songs*, i. 30, 31, 43, 56.

7 Barnie, *War in Medieval Society*, p. 141.

8 For what follows see K. Edwards, 'The Political Importance of the English Bishops during the Reign of Edward II', *EHR*, lix (1944), 311–47; Fryde, *Tyranny and Fall*, pp. 176–277; Tout, *Chapters*, iii. 1–68.

9 *Ibid.*, iii. 116–18. See also John Stratford's quarrel with Adam Orleton in 1333–4, discussed on p. 81.

10 G. Lambrick, 'Abingdon and the Riots of 1327', *Oxoniensia*, xxix/xxx (1964–5), 129–41; *VCH Herts.*, ii. 478–9; M. D. Lobel, 'A Detailed Account of the 1327 Rising at Bury St. Edmund's and the Subsequent Trial', *Proceedings of the Suffolk Institute of Archaeology and Natural History*, xxi (1933), 215–31.

11 *The Peasants' Revolt of 1381*, ed. R. B. Dobson, 2nd edn (London, 1983), pp. 80–3.

12 *The Register of John de Grandisson, Bishop of Exeter*, ed. F. C. Hingeston–Randolph (London, 1894–9), i. 172–3; *The Register of William Melton, Archbishop of York, 1317–1340*, ed. R. M. T. Hill, CYS, lxx, lxxi (1977–8), i. 95.

13 Maddicott, 'Law and Lordship', pp. 25–40; J. G. Bellamy, 'The Coterel Gang: An Anatomy of Fourteenth-Century Criminals', *EHR*, lxxix (1964), 699.

14 Ormrod, 'Agenda for Legislation', p. 20.

15 Haines, *Stratford*, p. 200.

16 M. Mate, 'The Estates of Canterbury Priory before the Black Death, 1315–1348', *SMRH*, new ser., viii (1986), 14, 20.

17 Haines, *Stratford*, p. 289.

18 For the rest of this paragraph see A. Deeley, 'Papal Provision and Royal Rights of Ecclesiastical Patronage in the Early Fourteenth Century', *EHR*, xliii (1928), 497–527; Saunders, 'Royal Ecclesiastical Patronage', *passim*.

19 For detailed studies of procedure under the writ *quare impedit* see F. Cheyette, 'Kings, Courts, Cures and Sinecures: The Statute of Provisors and the Common Law', *Traditio*, xix (1963), 295–349; W. R. Jones, 'Relations of the Two Jurisdictions:

Conflict and Cooperation in England during the Thirteenth and Fourteenth Centuries', *SMRH*, orig. ser., vii (1970), 102–32.

20 YB 17 Edw III, Trin. pl. 17 (*Year Books of the Reign of King Edward the Third, Year* XVII, p. 538), cited by Cheyette, 'Kings, Courts, Cures and Sinecures', p. 322, n. 82.

21 My figures are based on W. E. Lunt, *Financial Relations of the Papacy with England* (Cambridge, Mass., 1939–62), ii. 326–7.

22 These figures derive from J. R. L. Highfield, 'The Relations between Church and the English Crown from the Death of Archbishop Stratford to the Opening of the Great Schism (1349–78)', University of Oxford D. Phil. thesis (1951), p. 407. They differ from those of Lunt, *Financial Relations*, ii. 327, 338, although the annual averages for pontificates work out much the same. See also J. R. Wright, *The Church and the English Crown, 1305–1334* (Toronto, 1980), pp. 27–30.

23 My conclusions are based on a careful reading of the lists of bishops in *Fasti, passim*, and Lunt, *Financial Relations*, ii.724–60.

24 Bangor 1357, 1366, 1375–6; Bath and Wells 1363; Canterbury 1348, 1349, 1374–5; Carlisle 1352–3; Durham 1333; Exeter 1327; Ely 1337, 1345, 1361–2, 1373; Hereford 1360–1, 1369; Llandaff 1347; Norwich 1336–7; Rochester 1372–3; St Asaph 1345–6, 1357; St Davids 1347; Salisbury 1375; Winchester 1345; Worcester 1327, 1349, 1373–5.

25 Carlisle 1352–3; Ely 1373; Exeter 1327; Llandaff 1341; St Davids 1347; Salisbury 1375; Worcester 1327, 1373–5.

26 Canterbury 1374–5; Durham 1333; Ely 1373; St Asaph 1345–6; Winchester 1345.

27 A. K. McHardy, 'The Promotion of John Buckingham to the See of Lincoln', *JEH*, xxvi (1975), 127–35; Highfield, 'Promotion of William of Wickham', pp.37–54. Two other notable rebuffs to royal candidates occurred at Hereford (1369) and St Asaph (1345): *Fasti*, ii. 1; xi. 37.

28 For the increase in royal recoveries see Cheyette, 'Kings, Courts, Cures and Sinecures', pp. 298–318. The number of appeals can best be judged from the commissions and prohibitions issued against those challenging royal recoveries, as recorded on the dorses of the patent rolls. Between 1327 and 1339 there are no such entries; but between 1340 and 1352 there

are a total of 75 separate cases. See Ormrod, 'Edward III's Government', p.171.

29 C. Davies, 'The Statute of Provisors of 1351', *History*, xxxviii (1953), 116–33, is somewhat untrustworthy, but provides a good summary of the parliamentary debates. Another analysis is provided by Lunt, *Financial Relations*, ii. 327–47.

30 *SR*, i. 316–18; *RP*, ii. 232–3.

31 *SR*, i. 329; E. B. Graves, 'The Legal Significance of the Statute of Praemunire of 1353', in C. H. Taylor, ed., *Anniversary Essays* Presented to C. H. Haskins (New York, 1929), pp. 57–80. It may be of some significance that the earliest surviving writ of *praemunire facias* returned into chancery dealing with a contested benefice dates from 1344: C256/2/2, no. 12.

32 *RP*, ii. 244–5.

33 *SR*, i. 325. For the significance of this statute see p. 208, n. 168.

34 *CPR, 1350–4*, pp. 227, 430; *ibid., 1354–8*, pp. 188, 410; *ibid., 1358–61*, pp. 65, 87.

35 Ormrod, 'Edward III's Government', p.171; Highfield, 'Relations', pp. 412–18.

36 For presentations until 1352 see Saunders, 'Royal Ecclesiastical Patronage', App. I. The figures for 1352–9 are my own, taken from the patent rolls.

37 Figures based on *CPR, 1361–4*, pp. 456–525; *CPR, 1364–7*, pp. 1–63.

38 Lunt, *Financial Relations*, ii. 348–51; J. J. N. Palmer and A. P. Wells, 'Ecclesiastical Reform and the Politics of the Hundred Years War during the Pontificate of Urban V (1362–70)', in C. T. Allmand, ed., *War, Literature and Politics in the Late Middle Ages* (Liverpool, 1976), pp. 169–89.

39 C. J. Godfrey, 'Pluralists in the Province of Canterbury in 1366', *JEH*, xi (1960), 23–40.

40 *SR*, i. 385–7. For the implementation of this legislation see the file of writs C255/10/5, discussed in *List of Chancery Files*, PRO List & Index Soc., cxxx (1976), p. 131.

41 Lunt, *Financial Relations*, ii. 351–5; Holmes, *Good Parliament*, pp. 46–7; R. G. Davies, 'The Anglo-Papal Concordat of Bruges, 1375: A Reconsideration', *Archivum Historiae Pontificiae*, xix (1981), 99–146.

42 H. M. Jewell, *English Local Administration in the Middle Ages* (Newton Abbot, 1972), pp. 61–8, provides a convenient summary.

43 J. Scammell, 'The Origins and Limitations of the Liberty of Durham', *EHR*, lxxxi (1966), 473, n. 1; Tout, *Chapters*, iii. 12; J. W. F. Hill, *Medieval Lincoln* (Cambridge, 1948), pp. 121–3.

44 *CChR, 1327–41*, pp. 345–8, arising out of the archbishop's request in SC1/38/142.

45 Ormrod, 'Recovery of Royal Authority', pp. 7–8; *idem*, 'Edward III's Government', pp. 205–13.

46 *Treaty Rolls II: 1337–9* (London, 1972), no. 541; G. T. Lapsley, *The County Palatine of Durham* (Cambridge, Mass.,1924), pp. 272–4; J. Campbell, 'England, Scotland and the Hundred Years War in the Fourteenth Century', in J. R. Hale, J. R. L. Highfield and B. Smalley, eds., *Europe in the Later Middle Ages* (London, 1965), p. 192; Ormrod, 'Experiment in Taxation', pp. 77–8. For 1371 note also the new evidence cited in Table 1.

47 Knowles, *Religious Orders*, i. 39–48, 185–6.

48 *CCR, 1341–3*, pp. 353–4.

49 This dispute is summarized by Hamilton Thompson, 'William Bateman', pp. 118–21. See also *SCCKB*, vi, no. 26; YB 20 Edw III, Pasch pl. 27 (*Year Books of the Reign of King Edward the Third, Year XX (i)*, pp. 214–32); SC8/246/12274 (printed in *SCCKB*, ii, pp. cxxvii–viii).

50 The remainder of this paragraph is based on three main sources: (a) summonses to great councils recorded in *LRDP*, iv, *passim* and in the issue rolls; (b) the conciliar memoranda on the dorses of the close rolls; and (c) the witness lists to royal charters.

51 For Houghton's career as royal diplomat see *BRUO*, ii. 972–3.

52 See respectively G. Williams, 'Henry de Gower (?1278–1347): Bishop and Builder', *Archaeologia Cambrensis*, cxxx (1981), 1–19; Highfield, 'English Hierarchy', p. 120; *BRUO*, iii. 1698–9; Hamilton Thompson, 'William Bateman', pp. 102–37; Tout, *Chapters*, vi. 455, *s.v.* Wyvill.

53 J. H. Denton and J. P. Dooley, *Representatives of the Lower Clergy in Parliament, 1295–1340* (Woodbridge, 1987); A. K. McHardy, 'The Representation of the English Lower Clergy in Parliament during the Later Fourteenth Century', *SCH*, x (1973), 97–107; J. H. Denton, 'The Clergy and Parliament in the Thirteenth and Fourteenth Centuries', in Davies and Denton, eds., *English Parliament*, pp. 88–108.

54 Powell and Wallis, *House of Lords*, pp. 344–6.

55 Roskell, 'Problem of Attendance', pp.165, 166–7.

56 Durham, Prior's Kitchen, Register of Richard Bury, f. vii. For Bradwardine and his connection with Bury see *BRUO*, i. 244–6.

57 SC10/25/1245. For Northborough see *BRUO*, ii. 1368–70.

58 E.g. *Registrum Hamonis de Hethe Diocesis Roffensis,* ed. C. Johnson, CYS, xlviii, xlix (1948), ii. 644–5; *Registrum Johannis de Trillek Episcopi Herefordensis,* ed. J. H. Parry, CYS, viii (1912), pp. 282–3; Cumbria Record Office, DRC/1/2, p.163.

59 *Foedera*, III (i). 275.

60 Tout, *Chapters*, iii. 261, n. 5; iv. 163–4; M. Jones, 'Edward III's Captains in Brittany', in Ormrod, ed., *England in the Fourteenth Century*, p. 118.

61 Chaplais, *Essays*, ch. VIII, pp. 85–6.

62 For Edward III's patronage of civil and canon law at both Oxford and Cambridge see T. H. Aston ed., *The History of the University of Oxford I: The Early Schools* (Oxford, 1984), pp. 237, 239, 572, 586.

63 Mirot and Déprez, 'Les Ambassades Anglaises', *passim*. See also H. S. Lucas, 'The Machinery of Diplomatic Intercourse', *EGW*, i. 312–13, 318–19.

64 Carlton: *BRUO*, i. 355–6. Loughborough: *ibid.*, ii. 1164; *Foedera*, III (i). 284. Chaddesden: Tout, *Chapters*, v. 25 and n. 3; *Foedera*, II (ii). 1228; *Calendar of Papal Registers: Letters,* 1342–62, p. 2; *Calendar of Papal Letters: Petitions,* 1342–1419 (London, 1896), pp. 190, 232. Lecche: *BRUO*, ii. 1118–19. Offord: Baldwin, *King's Council*, p. 82. Branketre, Welwick and Tirrington: Chaplais, 'Master John de Branketre', pp. 169–99.

65 *BRUO*, i. 138–9.

66 E.g. *Historical Papers and Letters from the Northern Registers,* ed. J. Raine, RS (1873), pp. 406–8; Cumbria Record Office, DRC/1/2, pp. 155–6. The bishop was also called upon to supervise the maintenance of Carlisle Castle: HMC, *Ninth Report, Part 1* (London, 1883, repr. 1979), p. 192.

67 *Foedera*, II (ii). 994. In the following year the Bishop of Durham was ordered to set up commissions to provide for arrays, defence and the maintenance of the peace in his palatinate: *Registrum Palatinum Dunelmense,* ed. T. D. Hardy, RS (1873–8), iii. 258–60. This was clearly linked to the commissions of Aug. 1338 discussed on p. 97.

68 Searle and Burghart, 'Defense of England', p. 371.

69 B. McNab, 'Obligations of the Clergy in English Society: Military Arrays of the Clergy, 1369–1418', in W. C. Jordan, B. McNab and T. F. Ruiz, eds., *Order and Innovation in the Middle Ages: Essays in Honor of J. R. Strayer* (Princeton, NJ, 1976), pp. 294, 296. In fact, it should be noted that the clergy's immunity from array had frequently been disregarded by the crown and its local agents before this date: e.g. *Hemingby's Register,* ed. H. M. Chew, Wiltshire Archaeological and Natural History Soc. Records Branch, xviii (1963), nos. 80, 258 (1336–9); HMC, *Ninth Report, Part 1*, p. 189 (1344); WAM 3787 (1347); *The Coucher Book of Selby,* ed. J. T. Fowler, Yorkshire Archaeological and Topographical Association, x, xiii (1891–3), ii. 397 (1355–6).

70 Hewitt, *Organization of War*, pp. 160–5; W. R. Jones, 'The English Church and Royal Propaganda during the Hundred Years War', *JBS*, xix, no. 1 (1979), 18–30.

71 A. K. McHardy, 'Liturgy and Propaganda in the Diocese of Lincoln during the Hundred Years War', *SCH*, xviii (1981), 215–27.

72 J. Coleman, *English Literature in History, 1350–1400: Medieval Readers and Writers* (London, 1981), p. 266.

73 A. Gwynn, 'The Sermon-Diary of Richard Fitzralph, Archbishop of Armagh', *Proceedings of the Royal Irish Academy*, xliv (section C) (1937–8), 24, 50.

74 Maddicott, 'Poems of Social Protest', pp. 130–44.

75 K. Walsh, *A Fourteenth-Century Scholar and Primate: Richard FitzRalph in Oxford, Avignon and Armagh* (Oxford, 1981), pp. 227–9.

76 P. Heath, *Church and Realm, 1272–1461* (London, 1988), pp. 115–16; Cambridge University Library, Ely Diocesan Records, G/1/1 (Register of Thomas Lisle), ff. 82–82v.

77 W. A. Pantin, *The English Church in the Fourteenth Century* (Cambridge, 1955), pp. 182–5, provides a summary.

78 McKisack, *Fourteenth Century*, p. 250; C. Allmand, *The Hundred Years War* (Cambridge, 1988), p. 153.

79 R. Hilton, *Bond Men Made Free: Medieval Peasant Movements and the English Rising of 1381* (London, 1973), pp. 207–13.

80 The extent of the clergy's holdings was a matter of some controversy, but by the 1370s it was widely believed that they controlled a third of the wealth of the country: see, e.g. E. C. Tatnall, 'John Wycliff and *Ecclesia Anglicana*', *JEH*, xx (1969), 24.

81 The definitive study is M. Howell, *Regalian Right in Medieval England* (London, 1962).

82 Information derived from *Fasti, passim*. The

only notable exceptions were at York (Apr. 1340–Sept. 1342) and Lichfield (Nov. 1358–Sept. 1360).

83 *SR*, i. 294. This has an obvious parallel in the promise concerning wardships made to lay tenants-in-chief during the same parliament (*ibid.*, i. 285-6). Note that some monastic and cathedral chapters had won the right to farm temporalities before 1340: e.g. *CFR, 1327–37*, pp. 120–1 (Ely); E. R. Stevenson, 'The Escheator', *EGW*, ii. 138 (Glastonbury).

84 E.g. *Concilia*, ii. 712; *CPR, 1354–8*, pp. 215–16.

85 Fryde, *Tyranny and Fall*, pp. 117–18; Buck, *Stapeldon*, p. 144.

86 *SR*, i. 294.

87 *RP*, ii. 245; *SR*, i. 326.

88 B. Wilkinson, 'A Letter of Edward III to his Chancellor and Treasurer', *EHR*, xlii (1927), 248–51.

89 C49/67/5, printed in Richardson and Sayles, *Parliament*, ch. XXV, p. 32, n. 73; and in *SCCKB*, iii, p. cxxi.

90 KB27/385, Rex, mm. 26–30; KB29/14, m. 3; E403/382, 21 Oct. 1356; E368/129, *Brev. Retorn.*, *Pasch*, m. 3d. I owe thanks to John Aberth for discussing this case with me.

91 *SCCKB*, vi. no. 98; *CPR, 1364–7*, pp.159, 420.

92 See pp. 90–1.

93 Ormrod, 'Edward III's Government', pp. 247–59.

94 E. B. Fryde, 'The Tenants of the Bishops of Coventry and Lichfield and of Worcester after the Plague of 1348–9', in Hunnisett and Post, eds., *Medieval Legal Records*, pp. 223–66.

95 Fryde, *Studies*, ch. IV, pp. 198–211.

96 L. H. Butler, 'Archbishop Melton, his Neighbours, and his Kinsmen, 1317–1340', *JEH*, ii (1951), 61–2.

97 *Foedera*, II (ii). 1039–40; *CPR, 1338–40*, p. 122; *Wardrobe Book of Norwell*, p. 75.

98 *CChR, 1327–41*, pp. 447, 454–5.

99 The Canterbury province in fact granted an extra 10th on the understanding that it would not be required to contribute to the wool grants: *CFR, 1337–47*, pp. 98–9; *CCR, 1337–9*, p. 584; *ibid.*, 1339–41, pp. 56, 80, 94. *Ibid.*, 1337–9, p. 592, draws a clear distinction between the parliamentary prelates, paying wool, and the rest of the clergy, paying the 10th.

100 *Ibid.*, 1346–9, pp. 262, 268; *Foedera*, III (i). 116; *Reg. Trillek*, pp. 298–9; *A Calendar of the Register of Wolstan de Bransford, Bishop of Worcester, 1339–49*, ed. R. M. Haines, HMC Joint Publication ix, for Worcester Historical Soc., new ser., iv (1966), no. 1290.

101 *Reg. Trillek*, pp. 308–9; Reg. Lisle, f. 227.

102 *RP*, ii. 453–4.

103 *CPR, 1345–8*, pp. 337–42. I am indebted to Roger Axworthy for providing figures from the receipt rolls to confirm my arguments.

104 *Concilia*, iii. 87–8; *Original Charters Relating to the City of Worcester*, ed. J. H. Bloom (Oxford, 1909), pp. 185–6.

105 My own calculations from E401/500, 501, 503, 504, 505.

106 E401/501, 18 July 1370 (£2,000), 15 Sept. 1370 (£333 6s. 8d.); E401/503, 7 Dec. 1370 (£666 13s. 4d.). These loans were repaid between 9 Nov. 1370 and 15 Mar. 1371.

107 *Northern Petitions*, no. 162.

108 *Treatise of Walter de Milemete*, p. xix; C. J. Nederman, 'Royal Taxation and the English Church: The Origins of William of Ockham's *An princeps*', *JEH*, xxxvii (1986), 377–88; Tatnall, 'Wyclif and *Ecclesia Anglicana*', pp. 21, 25.

109 *CFR, 1337–47*, pp. 28–36; *CCR, 1337–9*, pp. 333–7, etc.

110 For instances of tax reductions as a result of the plague of 1348–9 see *Taxatio Ecclesiastica Angliae et Walliae Auctoritate Papae Nicholai IV* (London, 1802), pp. 57, 59, 75; Ormrod, 'Black Death', p. 183 and n. 74.

111 For the background see D. B. Weske, *Convocation of the Clergy* (London, 1937), pp. 158–62. For the conditions see SC1/38/82; SC1/56/4. For requests for relief see SC1/38/81; SC1/55/113; SC1/64/24; etc. The same specification was made in 1360 (SC8/235/11706), as a result of which further requests for relief were entered: e.g. SC1/38/144; SC1/40/151; SC1/40/159; SC1/56/33.

112 Harriss, *Public Finance*, p. 525; Holmes, *Good Parliament*, p. 70.

113 The definitive study is J. H. Denton, *Robert Winchelsey and the Crown, 1294–1313* (Cambridge, 1980). My own statistics differ somewhat from those given by Denton.

114 Ormrod, 'English Economy', tables 2, 3 (slightly amended), with the addition of rough estimates for the clerical taxes of 1279, 1280, 1283 and 1286 based on Prestwich, *Edward I*, p. 569. For the figures for Edward II's reign see W. E. Lunt, 'Clerical Tenths Levied in England by Papal Authority During the Reign of Edward II',

in Taylor, ed., *Essays Presented to Haskins*, pp. 178–9, 182.

115 Lunt, *Financial Relations*, ii. 75–114.

116 The notable exceptions are Clarke, *Representation and Consent*, pp. 15–32; and Weske, *Convocation*, pp. 147–79. E. W. Kemp, *Counsel and Consent* (London, 1961), pp. 89–112, also touches on the importance of ecclesiastical taxation.

117 The following is based on a careful reading of the sources cited by Weske, *Convocation*, pp. 244–59, 280–7, supplemented by additional unpublished material on clerical *gravamina* in the PRO.

118 *Concilia*, ii. 622–4.

119 Denton, *Winchelsey*, p. 55 and *passim*.

120 Weske, *Convocation*, pp. 155, 259; W. E. Lunt, 'The Collectors of Clerical Subsidies Granted to the King by the English Clergy', *EGW*, ii. 228–9; Holmes, *Good Parliament*, pp. 147–9.

121 *Concilia*, ii. 625–6; W. Wake, *The State of the Church and Clergy of England in their Councils* (London, 1703), pp. 287, 288. In Dec. 1339 the northern province reiterated its opposition to additional taxes: C270/14, no. 2.

122 For the conditions attached to the 10th of 1327 see Lunt, 'Collectors of Clerical Subsidies', pp. 227–8. In 1334 there is no evidence that the Canterbury clergy made conditions, but the northern province reiterated those of 1327: *ibid.*, pp. 229–30. The conditions attached to the 10th granted in Sept./Oct. 1336 were retrospectively applied to that of Mar./May 1336 (*ibid.*, pp. 230–1).

123 *Ibid.*, pp. 227–8. In Dec. 1327 Archbishop Melton complained that the conditions were not being observed (SC1/38/103); but in Dec. 1327–Feb. 1328 the new evaluation was carried out (Lunt, 'Collectors of Clerical Subsidies', pp. 241–2).

124 *Northern Petitions*, no. 109.

125 Lunt, 'Collectors of Clerical Subsidies', pp. 227–8 (1327); *ibid.*, pp. 230–1 (1336); C270/14, no. 3 (1347); C270/14, no. 5 (1351).

126 C270/14, no. 3.

127 Harriss, *Public Finance*, pp. 348–54, 356–75.

128 For what follows see W. R. Jones, 'Bishops, Politics and the Two Laws: The *Gravamina* of the English Clergy, 1237–1399', *Speculum*, xli (1966), 209–42.

129 See, e.g. the comments of Prestwich, *Edward I*, pp. 252–3, on the *gravamina* of 1280. Contrast the situation with demands

concerning the form of collection, which had been linked directly to the payment of taxes since at least 1294 (Denton, *Winchelsey*, p. 71).

130 See pp. 64–5.

131 SC8/46/2281.

132 *SR*, i. 292–4.

133 *Concilia*, ii. 712.

134 See the judgements of Haines (*Stratford*, pp. 48–101), who regards Stratford as the architect of the ecclesiastical legislation of 1340 (*ibid.*, pp. 264–5), and points out that the archbishop himself communicated this 'charter of liberties' to all the bishops of his province (*ibid.*, p. 266 and n. 309).

135 Jones, 'Gravamina', pp. 227–33.

136 C270/14, no. 3. See also SC1/42/140.

137 Weske, *Convocation*, p. 253; C270/13, no. 1; C270/14, no. 5. It is worth noting that the unspecified petitions of the Canterbury clergy were referred to a special commission set up on 1 Sept. 1351, and it was only at this point that writs were issued for the appointment of collectors of the first year of the tax: *Foedera*, III (i). 230; *CCR, 1349–54*, p. 322.

138 The *gravamina* were included on the parliament roll (*RP*, ii. 244–5), but the king suspended a decision on some of them (*Concilia*, iii. 28–9), and the archbishop's letters communicating the so-called statute *Pro Clero* were only issued in July (*ibid.*, iii. 23–5). The confirmation of the second year of the subsidy is recorded on the memoranda roll in Trinity term 1352 (E159/128, *Recorda, Trin.* m. 2).

139 *Concilia*, iii. 38–9.

140 SC1/56/4.

141 *Concilia*, iii. 39, translated in Weske, *Convocation*, pp. 160–1.

142 *Ibid.*, pp. 255, 285; SC1/38/80; SC1/40/181.

143 Jones, 'Gravamina', pp. 233–4.

144 *SR*, i. 390–8.

145 See p. 90.

146 Ormrod, 'Experiment in Taxation', pp. 64–6.

147 W. L. Warren, 'A Reappraisal of Simon Sudbury, Bishop of London (1361–75) and Archbishop of Canterbury (1375–81)', *JEH*, x (1959), 139–52; Davies, 'Episcopal Appointments of 1375', pp.306–32.

148 C270/14, no. 6.

149 Weske, *Convocation*, pp. 133–5.

150 Holmes, *Good Parliament*, pp. 18–19; J. H. Dahmus, *William Courtenay, Archbishop of Canterbury, 1381–1396* (University Park, PA, 1966), p. 12.

151 Weske, *Convocation*, p. 259; Holmes, *Good Parliament*, pp. 147–9.
152 *RP*, ii. 357–8; Jones, 'Gravamina', pp. 233–4.
153 *RP*, ii. 368.
154 Jones, 'Gravamina', p. 234.
155 Holmes, *Good Parliament*, pp. 187–8.

CHAPTER 8: PROVINCIAL SOCIETY AND THE GENTRY

1 For what follows see Maddicott, 'English Peasantry'; R. H. Hilton, 'Peasant Movement in England before 1381', *EcHR*, 2nd ser., ii (1949), 117–36; *idem, Bond Men Made Free*, pp. 144–85; E. B. Fryde, *The Great Revolt of 1381*, Historical Association Pamphlet, c (1981).
2 E.g. *Peasants' Revolt of 1381*, pp. 78–80.
3 *RP*, ii. 25, 208.
4 *Ibid.*, ii. 175–6, 177, 182, 184, 187, 189, 212.
5 For this matter see M. K. McIntosh, 'The Privileged Villeins of the English Ancient Demesne', *Viator*, vii (1976), 295–328; R. Faith, 'The "Great Rumour" of 1377 and Peasant Ideology', in R. H. Hilton and T. H. Aston, eds., *The English Rising* of 1381 (Cambridge, 1984), pp. 43–52; E. M. Hallam, *Domesday Book through Nine Centuries* (London, 1986), pp.99–105.
6 *RP*, ii. 94.
7 *Peasants' Revolt of 1381*, pp. 80–3.
8 C49/45/26. For other aspects of this case see Maddicott, 'Law and Lordship', pp. 37–9.
9 Faith, '"Great Rumour"', p. 45.
10 Hilton, 'Peasant Movements', pp. 125–30; Hallam, *Domesday Book*, pp. 99–105, 199–209.
11 C81/129/7119.
12 *RP*, ii. 180; R. H. Hilton, *The Decline of Serfdom in Medieval England*, 2nd edn (Cambridge, 1983), pp. 29–30. It is possible that this debate was sparked off by the dispute between the Bishop of Ely and Richard Spink, which came up in the same parliament (*RP*, ii. 192). SC8/134/6668 contains a petition from the 'prelates, lords and peers of the realm and others having villeins in obedience' on the same subject as *RP*, ii. 180.
13 *RP*, ii. 242; *SR*, i. 323; P. R. Hyams, 'The Action of Naifty in the Early Common Law', *Law Quarterly Review*, xc (1974), 331.
14 Faith, '"Great Rumour"', pp. 71–3.
15 Powicke, *Military Obligation*, pp. 174–5.
16 Saul, *Knights and Esquires*, pp. 6–29; D. A. L. Morgan, 'The Individual Style of the English Gentleman', in M. Jones, ed., *Gentry and Lesser Nobility in Late Medieval Europe* (Gloucester, 1986), pp. 15–35, esp. p. 16.
17 Thus in the abortive attempts of 1344 to assess landholders for providing troops: Powicke, *Military Obligation*, pp. 195–9.
18 Figures based on J. Quick, 'The Number and Distribution of Knights in Thirteenth Century England: The Evidence of the Grand Assize Lists', in P. R. Coss and S. D. Lloyd, eds., *Thirteenth Century England* I (Woodbridge, 1986), pp. 114–23, esp. p. 119; and J. A. F. Thomson, *The Transformation of Medieval England, 1370–1529* (London, 1983), p. 113.
19 T. B. Pugh, 'The Magnates, Knights and Gentry', in S. B. Chrimes, C. D. Ross and R. A. Griffiths, eds., *Fifteenth-Century England, 1399–1509: Studies in Politics and Society* (Manchester, 1972), p. 97.
20 Saul, *Knights and Esquires*, pp. 34–5.
21 C. Given-Wilson, 'The King and the Gentry in Fourteenth-Century England', *TRHS*, 5th ser., xxxvii (1987), 99–100, estimates 'a figure of about 2,300 to 2,500 "county families" throughout England in the late middle ages'.
22 J. C. Bridge, 'Two Cheshire Soldiers of Fortune of the Fourteenth Century: Sir Hugh Calveley and Sir Robert Knollys', *Journal of the Chester Archaeological Society,* xiv (1908), 112–231; M. Jones, 'La Mort de Walter Huet (1373)', *Bulletin de la Société d'Études et de Recherches Historiques du Pays de Retz,* iv (1984), 28–34; P. Morgan, *War and Society in Medieval Cheshire, 1277–1403*, Chetham Soc., 3rd ser., xxxiv (1987), pp. 149–84.
23 Unless otherwise stated, the following statistics are based on A. E. Prince, 'The Strength of English Armies in the Reign of Edward III', *EHR*, xlvi (1931), 357; and Sherborne, 'Indentured Retinues', pp. 718–46.
24 Prestwich, 'English Armies in the Early Stages of the Hundred Years War', p. 112.
25 The lists in *Crecy and Calais from the Public Records*, ed. G. Wrottesley, William Salt Archaeological Soc., xviii (2) (1897), pp. 193–203, yield a total of 927 knights. For conscription, see Powicke, *Military Obligation*, pp. 197–8.
26 *Wardrobe Book of Norwell*, pp. xcvi–vii.
27 S. Walker, 'Profit and Loss in the Hundred Years War: The Subcontracts of Sir John Strother, 1374', *BIHR*, lviii (1985), 100–6.

28 McFarlane, *Nobility*, p. 30; *CPR, 1345–8*, p. 226; *List of Sheriffs*, p. 97; *CPR*, 1350–4, p. 89, etc; *Rotuli Scotiae* (London, 1814–19), i. 772, 795, 807, 841, 843, 857.

29 *CIM*, iii. no. 531. It is interesting to notice that, despite his honorary status of banneret, Coupland apparently never took up knighthood. His name appears in the list of non-knights in Westmorland compiled during the distraint of 1356 (C47/1/15).

30 S. E. Rigold, *Nunney Castle* (London, 1957), p. 4; D. J. Turner, 'Bodiam, Sussex: True Castle or Old Soldier's Dream House?', in Ormrod, ed., *England in the Fourteenth Century*, pp. 267–77, esp. 273–4.

31 *CPR, 1345–8*, pp. 306, 535.

32 See p. 109.

33 SC8/227/11328; *CPR, 1374–7*, pp. 68–9.

34 Powicke, *Military Obligation*, pp. 198, 200–1. For the extensive fines collected in 1347 see *CFR, 1337–47*, pp. 497–524, and E401/387, 8 March 1347 (entries totalling £3,115 14s. 7d.).

35 SC1/41/23.

36 SC1/40/191. In the mid-1340s it was necessary to find men 'out of retinue' to serve as commissioners of array in Lincs.: SC1/39/170.

37 Tout, *Chapters*, iii. 95. Wake was a knight of the royal household: BL MS Cotton Nero C. VIII, ff. 223, 224; *Wardrobe Book of Norwell*, pp. 301, 302; E36/204, f. 86. It was this which no doubt helped him retain the sheriffdom during the purge of 1340–1: see Fryde, 'Removal of Ministers', p. 157, n. 1.

38 Jones, 'Edward III's Captains in Brittany', pp. 109–15. For further discussion see Saul, *Knights and Esquires*, pp. 54–9.

39 G. G. Astill, 'The Medieval Gentry: A Study in Leicestershire Society, 1350–1399', University of Birmingham Ph.D. thesis (1977), pp. 258–9.

40 For what follows, see Bean, *From Lord to Patron*, which provides full bibliographical references.

41 See pp. 106–8.

42 Prince, 'Strength of English Armies', p. 366.

43 I follow Bean, *From Lord to Patron*, pp.155–9, 245–6, which revises figures given by J. R. Maddicott, *Thomas of Lancaster* (Oxford, 1970), pp. 44–5, and McFarlane, 'Bastard Feudalism', p. 165.

44 For estimates of the size of peacetime retinues in the mid- and later 14th century see Holmes, *Estates*, pp. 58–84, *passim*; M. Cherry, 'The Courtenay Earls of Devon: The Formation and Disintegration of a Late Medieval Aristocratic Affinity', *Southern History*, i (1979), 72–6; Saul, *Knights and Esquires*, pp.84–5; Given-Wilson, *English Nobility*, p. 79. K. Mertes, *The English Noble Household, 1250–1600* (Oxford, 1988), pp. 183–93, judges that in 1350–80 the average earl's household (including domestic staff) numbered only about 80, and notes a considerable increase in size in the 15th century.

45 S. K. Walker, 'Lordship and Lawlessness in the Palatinate of Lancaster, 1370–1400', *JBS*, xxviii (1989), 325–48, esp.332–3.

46 K. S. Naughton, *The Gentry of Bedfordshire in the Thirteenth and Fourteenth Centuries*, University of Leicester Department of English Local History Occasional papers, 3rd ser., ii (1976), pp. 11, 27–8, 51; B. McLane, 'Changes in the Court of King's Bench, 1291–1430: The Preliminary View from Lincolnshire', in Ormrod, ed., *England in the Fourteenth Century*, p. 158; Astill, 'Medieval Gentry', ch. 5; S. M. Wright, *The Derbyshire Gentry in the Fifteenth Century*, Dugdale Record Soc., viii (1983), 60–2, 144–5. Note also the timely comments on gentry independence in the 14th century by P. R. Coss, 'Bastard Feudalism Revised', *P&P*, cxxv (1989), 57–62.

47 Maddicott, *Thomas of Lancaster*, pp. 59, 62, 295–7, 315. Astill, 'Medieval Gentry', p. 226, notes a permanent reduction in the number of Leics. families associated with the house of Lancaster after the 1320s. For the instability of the Despenser affinity in the same period see Waugh, 'For King, Country and Patron', pp. 23–45.

48 Harriss, *Public Finance*, pp. 255–8.

49 S. Walker, 'Lancaster v. Dallingridge: A Franchisal Dispute in Fourteenth Century Sussex', *Sussex Archaeological Collections*, cxxi (1983), 87–94.

50 R. Somerville, *History of the Duchy of Lancaster, I: 1265–1603* (London, 1953), pp. 360, 367, 382; Fowler, *King's Lieutenant*, p. 178 and p. 284, nn. 40, 43. Cokayn was knight of the shire for Derbs. on at least eight occasions 1338–62, and for Lancs. in 1348: *Return of MPs*, i. 121–69, *passim*. He was also appointed keeper of certain Lancastrian estates after the death of Henry of Grosmont: *CIPM*, xi. no. 118 (p. 101); *John of Gaunt's Register, 1372–6*, ed. S. Armitage-Smith, Camden Soc., 3rd ser., xx–xxi (1911), ii. no. 1799. For his descendants see *DNB*, iv. 682.

51 *List of Sheriffs*, p. 157. For Shakenhurst's

links with the earl see *CPR, 1343–5*, p. 517; *CCR, 1369–74*, p. 108. He was MP for Worcs. on at least four occasions (1339, 1351, 1354, 1360).

52 C49/7/4. For other aspects of Bocking's career see N. Denholm-Young, *The Country Gentry in the Fourteenth Century* (Oxford, 1969), p. 70.

53 Given-Wilson, *Royal Household*, pp.212–16; *idem*, 'The King and the Gentry', pp. 98–9, 100–1.

54 Figures based on BL MS Cotton Nero C. VIII,ff. 225v, 228, 229v, 231; *Wardrobe Book of Norwell*, p. 305; E36/204, f. 87; and Given-Wilson, *Royal Household*, p. 278. Given-Wilson makes little of the political significance of the esquires.

55 BL MS Cotton Nero C. VIII, f. 225v, etc; *Wardrobe Book of Norwell*, p. 305.

56 E101/392/12, f. 41.

57 Saul, *Knights and Esquires*, p. 119.

58 *Issue Roll of Brantingham*, p. 416. This may be an earlier form of the procedure adopted by the 1440s, whereby lists of three nominees for each sheriffdom were compiled by the council and sent to the king to be 'pricked': see J. S. Wilson, 'Sheriffs' Rolls of the Sixteenth and Seventeenth Centuries', *EHR*, xlvii (1932), 31–45, esp. p. 44.

59 For what follows see Saul, *Knights and Esquires*, pp. 106–67, *passim*. For a specific example of the confusion which sometimes arose over the supposed qualifications of officials, see R. F. Hunnisett, *The Medieval Coroner* (Cambridge, 1961), p. 125.

60 SCl/51/11.

61 SCl/41/49; R. H. Hilton, *The English Peasantry in the Later Middle Ages* (Oxford, 1975), p. 218.

62 SCl/40/43 (Wilkinson, *Chancery*, p. 35 and n. 6).

63 C81/312/17617.

64 *SR*, i. 388; *RP*, ii.308; Saul, *Knights and Esquires*, p. 110.

65 *Ibid.*, pp. 110–11.

66 Putnam, 'Transformation', pp. 43–4.

67 Putnam, *Enforcement*, pp. 93–4; SCl/40/161; SCl/42/25.

68 E13/80, m. 7d.

69 *Crecy and Calais from the Public Records*, pp. 31, 93; *List of Sheriffs*, p. 92; *List of Escheators*, p. 94; *CCR, 1349–54*, pp. 413, 625; *CPR, 1350–4*, p. 526.

70 E.g. Saul, *Knights and Esquires*, p. 151.

71 Ormrod, 'Edward III's Government', p. 204; Putnam, *Enforcement*, pp. 44–9.

72 *List of Sheriffs*, p. 12; *Return of MPs*, i. 159,

161, 164, 170, 172, 177, 179, 184. It should be noted, however, that some knights of the shire experienced difficulties in obtaining their wages. See, e.g. the writs *de expensis sicut alias* collected in C219/330, nos. 12–19, and scattered through other files in the same class. Some of the reasons for this problem are explained by L. C. Latham, 'Collection of the Wages of the Knights of the Shire in the Fourteenth and Fifteenth Centuries', *EHR*, xlviii (1933), 455–64; and Cam, *Liberties and Communities*, pp. 236–47.

73 Note, however, the exceptions of Beds. and Bucks. and of Lincs.: Morris, 'The Sheriff', p. 78.

74 *Munimenta Civitatis Oxonie*, pp. 264–5, 271, 273; *Cambridge Borough Documents*, I, ed. W. M. Palmer (Cambridge, 1931), p. 36.

75 *The Knights Hospitallers in England*, ed. L. B. Larking, Camden Soc., old ser., lxv (1857), 205. For further details of Trussell's eventful career see McFarlane, *Lancastrian Kings*, pp. 227–9.

76 *Select Cases Before the King's Council*, pp. 54–60.

77 SC8/32/1555.

78 *Ancient Petitions Relating to Northumberland*, pp. 121–2.

79 SC8/65/3215; *CPR, 1367–70*, p. 202.

80 *RP*, ii. 189; *CPR, 1361–4*, p. 293.

81 SC8/238/11888.

82 JUST 1/639/1, m. 7.

83 SC8/209/10415; SCl/41/148.

84 *RP*, ii. 352. Note also the evidence of the wardrobe accounts: C. J. Given-Wilson, 'Purveyance for the Royal Household, 1362–1413', *BIHR*, lvi (1983), 148–9.

85 *RP*, ii. 352, 354; SC8/14/655. See also SC8/119/5914. C49/8/5, discussed by Rayner, '"Commune Petition"', p. 231, n. 3, provides further evidence of the unpopularity of purveyors in the later 1370s.

86 *CPR, 1354–8*, p. 237.

87 Stones, 'Folvilles', pp. 117–36; Bellamy, 'Coterel Gang', pp. 698

88 Among Alberd's more spectacular crimes see *CPR, 1334–8*, pp. 146, 200; *ibid., 1354–8*, p. 120; *ibid., 1367–70*, p. 51. His administrative career can be pieced together from the printed chancery rolls and the *Return of MPs*.

89 See pp. 31–2, 57.

90 See p. 98.

91 Lestrange was a king's yeoman, who held over £40 of land as Lord of Myddle (E198/3/18). He was much in favour at

court during the first decade of Edward III's reign (*CChR, 1327–41*, pp. 94, 136, 137, 292), and secured a life interest in the post of bailiff errant of Norfolk and Suffolk in 1338 (*CPR, 1338–40*, p. 108). His actions may have provoked disquiet as early as 1335 (*RP*, ii. 93, discussed by Cam, *Hundred and Hundred Rolls*, p. 136). He had in fact already been removed from office in the summer of 1340 (*CPR, 1340–3*, p. 88), but it was not until the commissioners of trailbaston arrived in Norfolk in 1341 that he apparently received a trial, the details of which are in *CPR, 1340–3*, p. 355. Lestrange was in fact subsequently pardoned and readmitted to his old office: *CPR, 1340–3*, p. 383; *CCR, 1341–3*, p. 671. For further complaints about bailiffs errant see *RPHI*, pp. 189–90; H. M. Cam, 'Shire Officials: Coroners, Constables, and Bailiffs', in *EGW*, iii.172, 173.

92 Hughes, *Early Years of Edward III*, pp. 209–11; W. N. Bryant, 'The Financial Dealings of Edward III with the County Communities', *EHR*, lxxxiii (1968), 762–3. Of the 4,000 marks offered by Northants., at least £337 16s. had still not been paid in 1348: E368/121, m. 7, and see also *RP*, ii. 178–9.

93 C81/147/3811; SC8/64/3156; SC8/327/E832. Similar petitions were made by the commons in parliament: e.g. *SCCKB*, v, p. cxliii; E175/2/27. This evidence calls into question some of the assumptions of M. M. Taylor, 'The Justices of Assize', in *EGW*, iii. 235–6.

94 *RP*, ii. 194, 371; SC8/158/7866.

95 Harriss, 'Formation of Parliament', p. 51, n. 53.

96 See in particular the comments of J. B. Post, 'Some Limitations of the Medieval Peace Rolls', *Journal of the Society of Archivists*, iv, no. 8 (1973), 635–8.

97 Putnam, *Proceedings*, p. xcvi.

98 SC8/119/5916; 'Rolls of the Gloucestershire Sessions of the Peace, 1361–1398', ed. E. G. Kimball, *Transactions of the Bristol and Gloucestershire Archaeological Society*, lxii (1940), 32–4. Note, however, the more regular sessions in Yorks., at least during the early 1360s: *Yorkshire Sessions of the Peace, 1361–1364*, ed. B. H. Putnam, Yorkshire Archaeological Soc. Record Ser., c (1939), pp. xx–xxi.

99. *RP*, ii. 333.

100 For the procedure for payment of JPs adopted in 1388 see Putnam, *Proceedings*, pp. lxxxviii–xci. J. R. Maddicott, 'The Birth and Setting of the Ballads of Robin Hood', *EHR*, xciii (1978), 279, considers the JPs to have been 'relatively inconspicuous figures' before the last quarter of the 14th century.

101 The following pursues ideas discussed by E. Powell, *Kingship, Law, and Society: Criminal Justice in the Reign of Henry V* (Oxford, 1989), pp. 9–20.

102 The phrase is that of A. B. White, *Self-Government* at the King's Command (Minneapolis, Minn., 1933).

103 See p. 32.

104 Though note the comments of Powell, *Kingship, Law, and Society*, p. 20.

105 The two crucial studies are W. A. Morris, *The Early English County Court* (Berkeley, Cal., 1926); and R. C. Palmer, *The County Courts of Medieval England* (Princeton, NJ, 1982).

106 C49/7/20.

107 J. R. Maddicott, 'The County Community and the Making of Public Opinion in Fourteenth-Century England', *TRHS*, 5th ser., xxviii (1978), 30.

108 *Ibid*.

109 E.g. in 1344–5 the inquiry into persons failing to take up knighthood in Beds.and Bucks. was taken in full county court: C47/2/58, no. 5.

110 J. F. Willard, 'Edward III's Negotiations for a Grant in 1337', *EHR*, xxi (1906), 727–31; Hilton, *English Peasantry*, pp.215–18.

111 Harriss, *Public Finance*, pp. 396–400.

112 SC1/39/111–20.

113 SC1/42/156.

114 Maddicott, 'County Community', pp.33–6; *idem*, 'Parliament and the Constituencies', p. 81; Harriss, *Public Finance*, p. 365.

115 Maddicott, 'County Community', pp. 36–7; Ormrod, 'Recovery of Royal Authority', p. 11, n. 40. For further examples from this period see *RP*, ii.177; SC8/71/3509; SC8/73/3611; SC8/321/E488.

116 The following is based on an analysis of the petitions (printed and unprinted) collected under county headings in *Index of Ancient Petitions*, PRO Lists and Indexes, i, rev. edn (1966). It needs to be pointed out that not all the petitions addressed in the name of the shire communities were necessarily drawn up in the county courts. In 1390–1, for instance, Simon Elvington petitioned 'for himself and for the profit of the people of Yorkshire' (SC8/110/5473).

117 E.g. *RP*, ii. 40, 177, 380; C81/195/5970; SC8/53/2621.

118 E.g. *RP*, ii. 345; *Northern Petitions*, nos. 67, 113; SC8/141/7039; SC8/164/8175;

SC8/207/10318; SCl/42/19, 21.

119 E.g. *RP*, ii. 176, 194, 401, 417; *Northern Petitions*, no. 169; *Ancient Petitions Relating to Northumberland*, nos. 188, 189, 197; SC8/163/8143 (*CCR, 1327–30*, p. 72).

120 Notts. and Derbs.: SC8/218/*10855 (CPR, 1348–50*, pp. 62–3); SC8/261/13031; SC8/258/12866. Surrey and Sussex: SC8/75/3707; *RP*, ii. 352. See also the cases of Devon (*ibid.*, ii. 190) and Northumberland (*Ancient Petitions Relating to Northumberland*, pp.104–5; *RP*, ii. 349). It is worth noting that from the 1360s the exchequer seems to have begun to preserve more systematically the petitions for allowance put forward by the sheriffs: see *Exchequer (K. R.) Sheriffs' Accounts (E. 199): Class List*, PRO List & Index Soc., cxxvii (1976), passim.

121 *RP*, ii. 349, 370; SC8/109/5405; SC8/342/16132. See also the sheriffs' requests for remissions in E199/10/36, 39, 40, etc. This problem was to become a matter of general concern in the 15th century: see R. Virgoe, 'The Crown, Magnates, and Local Government in Fifteenth-Century East Anglia', in Highfield and Jeffs, eds., *The Crown and Local Communities*, pp.73–4.

122 C49/46/5; *RP*, ii. 348.

123 Maddicott, 'Parliament and the Constituencies', p. 83; *idem*, 'County Community', p. 39.

124 Harriss, *Public Finance*, pp. 405–8.

125 SC8/64/3190.

126 Ormrod, 'Agenda for Legislation', p. 16.

127 Lancs., although raised to palatine status in 1351, continued to send representatives to parliament, and therefore to pay royal taxes. See J. W. Alexander, 'The English Palatinates and Edward I', *JBS*, 22, no. 2 (1983), 11–12.

128 E.g. C219/5, Part 1, file 1 (Cornwall); file 8 (Rutland); C219/5, Part 2, file 19 (Middx); etc. The classic study remains L. Reiss, *The History of the English Electoral Law in the Middle Ages*, trans. K. L. Wood-Legh (Cambridge, 1940).

129 M. M. Taylor, 'Parliamentary Elections in Cambridgeshire, 1332–38', *BIHR*, viii (1940–1), 21–6; K. L. Wood-Legh, 'Sheriffs, Lawyers and Belted Knights in the Parliaments of Edward III', *EHR*, xlvi (1931), 373.

130 Richardson, 'Parliamentary Representation of Lancashire', pp. 178–9, 182.

131 *CLBL*, G. 20. 22 of the 33 knights known to have sat in the great council were actually returned to this parliament: see K. L. Wood-Legh, 'The Knights' Attendance in the Parliaments of Edward III', *EHR*, xlvii (1932), 406.

132 C219/7, Part 1, file 11 (privy seal writ attached to Glos. return).

133 *CLBL*, G. 182.

134 J. G. Edwards, 'The *Plena Potestas* of English Parliamentary Representatives', *HSEP*, i. 136–49.

135 Harriss, *Public Finance*, p. 357.

136 *Ibid.*, p. 256.

137 For what follows see J. F. Willard, 'The Taxes Upon Movables of the Reign of Edward III', *EHR*, xxx (1915), 69–74; *idem*, *Parliamentary Taxes*; C. Johnson, 'The Collectors of Lay Taxes', in *EGW*, ii. 210–26; *The Lay Subsidy of 1334*, ed. R. Glasscock (London, 1975); Fryde, 'Edward III's War Finance', ch. 4, 7; Ormrod, 'English Economy'; *idem*, 'Black Death', pp. 182–5; *idem*, 'Experiment in Taxation', pp. 68–81; Fryde,'Introduction to the New Edition', pp. xii–xvii.

138 See pp. 65–9.

139 The last instalment of this tax was due in Feb. 1340: Fryde, 'Edward III's War Finance', ii. 3–4.

140 The parliament roll explains the refusal in terms of poverty, but it is noticeable that the commons expressed themselves willing to aid the king 'pur aucunes chargeantes bosoignes', meaning, presumably, war. For the truce see 'The Anglo-French Negotiations at Bruges, 1374–1377', ed. E. Perroy, *Camden Mis-cellany XIX*, Camden Soc., 3rd ser., lxxx (1952), 37.

141 Harriss, *Public Finance*, pp. 365–6.

142 *Return of MPs*, i. 98–159, *passim*; GEC, vi. 62–6.

143 Harriss, 'Formation of Parliament', p. 38; Brown, *Governance of Late Medieval England*, pp. 209–11. In fact, the knights long continued to take formal precedence over the burgesses: Richardson and Sayles, *Parliament*, ch. XXIV, p. 38 and n. 2.

144 See p. 94.

145 Harriss, *Public Finance*, pp. 516–17.

146 *RP*, ii. 296, discussed by M. M. Postan, *The Medieval Economy and Society* (Harmondsworth, 1975), p. 170. It was this petition which led to the confirmation of the Ordinance and Statute of Labourers (*SR*, i. 388). J. A. Tuck, 'Nobles, Commons and the Great Revolt of 1381' in Hilton and Aston, eds., *English Rising*, pp. 194–212,

shows that there was a marked difference in the reactions of the lords and the commons to the events of 1381.

147 For some statistics see Gray, *Influence of the Commons*, pp. 248–9. The following is based on an analysis of the statutes of Edward III.

148 *RP*, ii. 62, 105, 113, 127. On the money supply, see N. J. Mayhew, 'Numismatic Evidence and Falling Prices in the Fourteenth Century', *EcHR*, 2nd ser., xxvii (1974), 1–15; J. H. A. Munro, *Wool, Cloth and Gold: The Struggle for Bullion in Anglo-Burgundian Trade,* 1340–1478 (Toronto, 1972), pp. 11–41; and M. Prestwich, 'Currency and the Economy of Early Fourteenth Century England', in N. J. Mayhew, ed., *Edwardian Monetary Affairs (1279–1344)*, British Archaeological Reports, xxxvi (1977), 45–58.

149 Fryde, *Studies*, ch. V, pp. 263–5.

150 *RP*, ii. 137–8. For the subsequent reduction in sterling weights and its consequences, see A. E. Feavearyear, *The Pound Sterling*, 2nd edn (Oxford, 1963), pp. 17–18; M. Prestwich, 'Early Fourteenth Century Exchange Rates', *EcHR*, 2nd ser., xxxii (1979), 480–1.

151 *RP*, ii. 160, 167, 228, 230, 240, 253, 260; P. Spufford, 'Assemblies of Estates, Taxation and Control of Coinage in Medieval Europe', *Studies Presented to the International Commission for the History of Representative and Parliamentary Institutions*, xxxi (1966), 125.

152 Feavearyear, *Pound Sterling*, pp. 17–20.

153 *RP*, ii. 240.

154 Little more was heard on this matter until the late 1370s: see W. M. Ormrod, 'The Peasants' Revolt and the Government of England', *JBS*, xxix (1990), 27–8.

155 C81/248/11261, printed in E. Déprez, *Les Préliminaires de la Guerre de Cent Ans* (Paris, 1902), pp. 418–19.

156 *RP*, ii. 136, 165, 262.

157 *Ibid.*, ii. 299.

158 *Ibid.*, ii. 316–20.

159 *Ibid.*, ii. 322.

160 Note, however, that several of the issues first raised by the commons in the Good Parliament were successfully enacted in the first parliament of Richard II: N. B.Lewis, 'Re-election to Parliament in the Reign of Richard II', *EHR*, xlviii (1933), 380–5.

161 M. J. Bennett, *Community, Class and Careerism: Cheshire and Lancashire Society in the Age of Sir Gawain and the Green Knight* (Cambridge, 1983), argues for a strong sense of regional identity in the 14th

century; but other studies have failed to distinguished much sense of an exclusive 'county society': see Astill, 'Medieval Gentry', ch. 3; Wright, *Derbyshire Gentry,* p. 146; Saul, *Scenes from Provincial Life,* pp. 57–8.

CHAPTER 9: URBAN SOCIETY AND THE MERCHANTS

1 The best survey of this problem is S. Reynolds, *An Introduction to the History of English Medieval Towns* (Oxford, 1977), pp. 52–65.

2 See esp. M. D. Lobel, *The Borough of Bury St. Edmund's* (Oxford, 1935); S. H. Rigby, 'Boston and Grimsby in the Middle Ages: An Administrative Contrast', *JMH*, x (1984), 51–66; and A. G. Rosser, 'The Essence of Medieval Urban Communities: The Vill of Westminster 1200–1540', *TRHS*, 5th ser., xxxiv (1984), 91–112.

3 Hilton, *English Peasantry*, pp. 76–94; R. Hilton, 'Towns in Societies: Medieval England', *Urban History Yearbook 1982*, pp. 7–13.

4 W. G. Hoskins, *Local History in England*, 2nd edn (London, 1972), p. 238; *Peasants' Revolt of 1381*, pp. 54–7.

5 D. Keene, 'Medieval London and its Region', *London Journal*, xiv (1989), 101, and the sources cited there.

6 The York evidence is somewhat ambiguous: compare J. N. Bartlett, 'The Expansion and Decline of York in the Later Middle Ages', *EcHR*, 2nd ser., xii (1959–60), 17–33, and R. B. Dobson, 'Admissions to the Freedom of the City of York in the Later Middle Ages', *EcHR*, 2nd ser., xxvi (1973), 1–21. For Colchester, however, the matter seems clear: see R. H. Britnell, *Growth and Decline in Colchester, 1300–1520* (Cambridge, 1986), pp. 86–97.

7 R. B. Dobson, 'Urban Decline in Late Medieval England', *TRHS*, 5th ser., xxvii (1977), 7–10; J. C. Lancaster, 'Coventry', *AHT*, ii. 8; J. Campbell, 'Norwich', *AHT*, ii. 17; M. D. Lobel and E. M. Carus-Wilson, 'Bristol', *AHT*, ii.11; Britnell, *Colchester*, pp. 120–2.

8 *DNB*, xlvii. 25–6; J. Newman, *West Kent and the Weald*, 2nd edn (Harmondsworth, 1976), pp. 454–5, 457.

9 M. McKisack, 'London and the Succession to the Crown during the Middle Ages', in R. W. Hunt, W. A. Pantin and R. W.

Southern, eds., *Studies in Medieval History Presented to F. M. Powicke* (Oxford, 1948), pp. 81–3.

10 G. A. Williams, *Medieval London: From Commune to Capital* (London, 1963), pp. 298–9. See also H. M. Chew, 'The Office of Escheator in the City of London during the Middle Ages', *EHR*, lviii (1943), 324–5. The city eventually paid for its charter: *CLBL*, E. 216–17.

11 Williams, *Medieval London*, pp. 301–2; *CPML, 1323–64*, pp. 68–9.

12 *SR*, i. 270–1. There is a good summary of this dispute in E. Lipson, *The Economic History of England I: The Middle Ages*, 12th edn (London, 1959), pp. 519–23.

13 SC8/120/5981; *CPR, 1334–8*, p. 460.

14 *SR*, i. 314–15; *CLBL*, F. 229; *ibid.*, G.14–15, 52, 185, 206–7. See also *Foedera*, III (ii). 734.

15 Lipson, *Economic History*, i. 522; *CLBL*, G. 231; *RP*, ii. 347. *CLBL*, H. 53 suggests that the 1376 concession was only temporary.

16 *CLBL*, F. 45–9. See also *CPML, 1323–64*, p. 120.

17 *CPML, 1323–64*, pp. 199–201; *CLBL*, F. 143–52; G. 263, 266. In 1346 the sum of 1,000 marks was also levied by way of a gift to the king: *CCR, 1346–9*, p. 77.

18 *CLBL*, G. 85.

19 *Ibid.*, F. 235, 236–7; *Calendar of Letters from the Mayor and Corporation of the City of London, c. 1350–1370*, ed. R. R. Sharpe (London, 1885), no. I. 29; Holmes, *Good Parliament*, pp. 72–4, 77–9.

20 Crook, 'The Later Eyres', pp. 259–60, 263.

21 For details see R. Bird, *The Turbulent London of Richard II* (London, 1949). London's internal politics in this period has recently been reinterpreted by P. Nightingale, 'Capitalists, Crafts and Constitutional Change in Late Fourteenth-Century London', *P&P*, cxxiv (1989), 3–35.

22 *CChR, 1327–41*, *passim*; *ibid.*, *1341–1417*, pp. 1–233, *passim*.

23 Of these, some 27 (42%) were simple confirmations with or without the nonuser clause.

24 *SCCKB*, v, pp. cxxxiii–iv.

25 C49/6/18; *CChR, 1327–41*, pp. 201–2, 231–2.

26 Of these 31, some 11 (35%) were simple confirmations.

27 For what follows see E. G. Kimball, 'Commissions of the Peace for Urban Jurisdictions in England, 1327–1485', *Proceedings of the American Philosophical Society*, cxxi (1977), 448–74. I owe this

reference to Anthony Verduyn.

28 *RP*, ii. 258–9; *SR*, i. 346–7. For the later use of this statute by the crown see C. M. Barron, 'The Quarrel of Richard II with London', in Du Boulay and Barron, eds., *The Reign of Richard II*, pp. 185–6.

29 Kimball, 'Urban Jurisdictions', pp.471–4. See also Putnam, *Enforcement*, App. p. 139; *Rolls of the Warwickshire and Coventry Sessions of the Peace, 1377–1397*, ed. E. G. Kimball, Dugdale Soc., xvi (1939), pp. lxxxiv–xviii; *Records of Some Sessions of the Peace in the City of Lincoln 1351–1354 and the Borough of Stamford 1351*, ed. E. G. Kimball, Lincoln Record Soc., lxv (1971), pp. x, xii, 52.

30 E.g. *CChR, 1341–1417*, p. 179 (Huntingdon); *VCH Cambs.*, iii. 35 (Cambridge); Ormrod, 'Black Death', p. 181 (Newcastle). In 1381 it was stated, in reference to Lincoln, that sessions of the peace held before city authorities were likely to benefit the cities, not the crown: SC8/60/2957.

31 *Warwickshire Sessions*, pp. xxix, lxxxiv. Bristol won the status of a shire specifically because jurisdictional problems had arisen from the town's position partly in Glos. and partly in Somerset. See *The Little Red Book of Bristol*, ed. F. B. Blickley (Bristol, 1900), i. 115–26.

32 *VCH Warwicks.*, viii. 256–9.

33 In addition to the sources cited in *VCH Yorks: City of York*, pp. 68–9, see SC8/162/8089; SC8/176/8780; C49/7/25; and BL Harl. Ch. 43; D.46.

34 *VCH Herts.*, ii. 478–9.

35 *VCH Hants.*, v. 35. For a similar case at Wells see *HMC Calendar of the Manuscripts of the Dean and Chapter of Wells* (London, 1907–14), pp. 111–12.

36 *VCH Oxon.*, iv. 53–7.

37 In addition to the sources cited on p. 219, n. 10, see McKisack, 'London and the Succession to the Crown', pp. 81–2; *VCH Northants.*, iii. 8 and n. 80; and Hilton, *Bond Men Made Free*, pp. 186–207.

38 T. Wright, 'The Municipal Archives of Exeter', *Journal of the Archaeological Association*, xxviii (1862), 313–14; R. Horrox, 'Urban Patronage and Patrons in the Fifteenth Century', in R. A. Griffiths, ed., *Patronage, the Crown and the Provinces in Later Medieval England* (Gloucester, 1981), p. 154.

39 H. Harrod, *Report on the Deeds and Records of the Borough of King's Lynn* (King's Lynn, 1874), pp. 75, 77, 83; *The Making of King's Lynn: A Documentary Survey*, ed. D. M. Owen (London, 1984), pp. 386–7; B.

Wilkinson, *The Mediaeval Council of Exeter* (Manchester, 1931), p. 36; J. S. Furley, *City Government of Winchester from the Records of the XIV and XV Centuries* (Oxford, 1923), pp. 88–9; *CLBL*, F. 55.

40 *Ibid.*, E. 216–17, 231, 270–1; F. 5–8, 143–52; G. 171–2, 173, 275; H. 63; *CPML, 1323–64*, pp. 116–18, 131, 133–4, 153–4, 154–5.

41 *Memorials of London and London Life in the XIIIth, XIVth, and XVth Centuries,* ed. H. T. Riley (London, 1868), pp. 198–9.

42 *Records of the City of Norwich*, ii. 39; *Cambridge Borough Documents*, i. 36.

43 In addition to the sources cited on p. 208, n. 13, see Furley, *Government of Winchester*, p. 116; *Munimenta Civitatis Oxonie*, pp. 264–5, 273; Wright, 'Municipal Archives of Exeter', pp. 311–12, 313; *The Making of King's Lynn*, pp. 386–7.

44 *CChR, 1327–41*, pp. 219–21.

45 Harrod, *King's Lynn*, pp. 83, 84.

46 For proclamations see Maddicott, 'County Community', pp. 33–6. Towns sometimes acquired special copies of the statutes for preservation in their archives: M. McKisack, *The Parliamentary Representation of the English Boroughs during the Middle Ages* (Oxford, 1932), pp. 144–5. One illuminating case is provided by the statute of 1340 requiring clerks of recognizances under the statute of merchants to hold property in the county where they acted (*SR*, i. 285). At least two cities reacted quickly to this, reporting that their own clerks were not so qualified: SC1/41/58 (Lincoln); SC8/211/10501 (Hereford).

47 *Foedera*, III (i). 89–90.

48 *CLBL*, F. 53–4, 87, 161; G. 71, 108.

49 Furley, *Government of Winchester*, p. 144; *Records of the Borough of Leicester*, ii. 68, 77.

50 Vale, *Edward III and Chivalry*, pp. 62–3, 67.

51 C. L. Kingsford, 'The Feast of the Nine Kings', *Archaeologia*, lxvii (1915–16), 119–26.

52 *SR*, i. 381.

53 S. M. Newton, *Fashion in the Age of the Black Prince* (Woodbridge, Suffolk, 1980), pp. 6–13.

54 J. F. Hadwin, 'The Medieval Lay Subsidies and Economic History', *EcHR*, 2nd ser., xxxvi (1983), 200–17, esp. 210–11.

55 Willard, *Parliamentary Taxes*, p. 177. In the 1370s there was an interesting attempt to tax those trading, but not living in the town of Colchester: *The Red Paper Book of Colchester*, ed. W. G. Benham (Colchester, 1902), p. 7.

56 For what follows see Ormrod, 'English Economy'.

57 *CLBL*, F. 68.

58 I work from the list in Hoskins, *Local History*, p. 238, but use the precise assessments set out in *The Lay Subsidy of 1334.*

59 Fryde, 'Edward III's War Finance', i. 506–7. The contribution made by the towns to this levy was complex. Merchants living only by their merchandise paid a 15th of their movable property, but other urban dwellers were supposed to pay a 9th, again assessed on movables. See *RP*, ii. 112–13; *Calendar of the Records of the Corporation of Gloucester,* ed. W. H. Stevenson (Gloucester, 1893), p. 53, no. 43.

60 *Records of the City of Norwich*, i. 207; Ormrod, 'Experiment in Taxation', pp. 75, 80.

61 *Ibid.*, p. 74.

62 *RP*, ii. 185–6, 189, 190, 213.

63 S. L. Thrupp, *The Merchant Class of Medieval London* (Ann Arbor, 1948), p. 87, n. 138.

64 *CChR, 1327–41*, pp. 12–13.

65 E.g. the case of Cambridge cited on p. 147.

66 *Foedera*, III (i). 71.

67 The quotas were reduced (in most cases by a half) and converted to cash on a scale of 5 marks per armed man (*CFR, 1337–47*, pp. 497, 500–4). A few towns still chose to send troops (*Foedera*, III (i). 96–7; SC1/40/8, 35, 37). The letters commuting the charge were preserved in a number of borough archives, no doubt to be produced in the event of another such levy: *HMC Fifteenth Report, Appendix, Part X: Manuscripts of Shrewsbury and Coventry Corporations...* (London, 1899), p. 113 (Coventry); *A Schedule of the Ancient Charters and Muniments of the Borough of Bedford* (Bedford, 1895), p. 6. In fact, no other demand of this type was attempted for the rest of Edward III's reign. On the other hand, it should be noted that townsmen were made liable to the distraints to knighthood ordered in 1356 and 1366: Saul, *Knights and Esquires*, pp. 41–2.

68 See especially J. W. Sherbome, 'The English Navy: Shipping and Manpower, 1369–1389', *P&P*, xxxvii (1967), 163–75.

69 Harrod, *King's Lynn*, pp. 74, 75; C81/267/13147.

70 SC1/40/96; *RP*, ii. 274.

71 Sherbome, 'English Navy', pp. 168–9. For opposition to the levying of sailors for these barges, see Hill, *Medieval Lincoln*, p. 256.

72 *RP*, ii. 319–20, 345–6.
73 A. Saul, 'Great Yarmouth and the Hundred Years War in the Fourteenth Century', *BIHR*, lii (1979), 105–15.For details of what follows see Ormrod, 'English Economy'.
75 T. H. Lloyd, *The English Wool Trade in the Middle Ages* (Cambridge, 1977), p. 155. The rates of duty set out in E. M. Carus-Wilson and O. Coleman, *England's Export Trade, 1275–1547* (Oxford, 1963), pp. 194–6, include such additional levies, but are not always fully accurate.
76 Fryde, *Studies*, ch. X, pp. 1–17.
77 *Ibid.*, ch. IX, p. 9.
78 T. H. Lloyd, 'The Movement of Wool Prices in Medieval England', *EcHR* Supplement, vi (1973), 10, 18–20, 66.
79 E. M. Carus-Wilson, *English Merchant Adventurers* (London, 1954), p. 243. For the pattern of English cloth exports before 1347 see P. Chorley, 'English Cloth Exports during the Thirteenth and Early Fourteenth Centuries: The Continental Evidence', *Historical Research*, lxi (1988), 1–10.
80 Harriss, *Public Finance*, p. 457.
81 Ormrod, 'Customs', p. 33.
82 Fryde, *William de la Pole*, pp. 44, 46.
83 *CFR, 1327–37*, pp. 54–5; E356/8, m. 1.
84 Fryde, *William de la Pole*, pp. 46–9, 51, 72–3, 75, 83, 87–90, 99, 101, 107, 120, 124–6, 136, 139–40, 142–4, 153–4, 182, 210, 223.
85 *Ibid.*, *passim*, provides the most detailed study of Pole's credit dealings, on which the following is based. For the rest of this paragraph see also *idem*, *Studies*, ch. VI, pp. 8–24.
86 *Idem*, *William de la Pole*, p. 122, sets the known total at £111,156.
87 Pole's involvement in the syndicate was first established by G. O. Sayles, 'The English Company" of 1343 and a Merchant's Oath', *Speculum*, vi (1931), 177–205. For what follows see Fryde, *Studies*, ch. X, pp. 1–17.
88 See the evidence of the merchant assembly of Apr. 1347 discussed by F. R. Barnes, 'The Taxation of Wool 1327–1348', in G. Unwin, ed., *Finance and Trade under Edward III* (Manchester, 1918), p. 169.
89 My own calculations based on E401/388, excluding the sums loaned by active members of the farming syndicate, but including the £1,333 6s. 8d. advanced by William de la Pole.
90 The estimate of £5,000 made from the chancery rolls by G. Unwin, 'The Estate of Merchants', in *idem*, ed., *Finance and Trade*,

p. 225, is too conservative; my own figures derive from the receipt rolls, E401/407, 410.
91 C81/1710/53 (?1347/1351) states that Robert Bumpstead, Jr, was refusing to contribute to a loan being raised by the city of Norwich. Bumpstead's reluctance presumably arose from his earlier involvement in the king's wool dealings, which had left him out of pocket: see *CPR, 1338–40*, p. 293; *CCR, 1339–41*, p. 168; *ibid., 1343–6*, p. 145.
92 See pp. 178–9.
93 Ormrod, 'Customs', pp. 35–6 and n. 50; the names of the creditors are recorded on the receipt rolls, E401/443, 446. For outline careers of Not, Aubrey, Bury and Pecche, see A. B. Beaven, *The Aldermen Of the City of London* (London, 1908–13), i. 387, 388, 389.
94 Sherborne, 'Costs of English Warfare', p. 144.
95 E401/500, 501. *VCH Yorks: City of York*, p. 67, gives a lower figure of £300.
96 E401/501; *CLBL*, G. 275–6.
97 E401/501, 28 June 1370.
98 Lloyd, *Wool Trade*, p. 217.
99 For later complaints about non-payment of the loans raised in this period see *RP*, ii. 347; C49/43/10; *RP*, iii. 64, 96; SC8/123/6117.
100 SC1/55/84.
101 For what follows see Holmes, *Good Parliament*, pp. 65–7, 71–4, 78–9, 89, 101–4, 108–26.
102 McKisack, *Parliamentary Representation*, pp. 134–5.
103 Thus Unwin, 'Estate of Merchants', pp. 227–32, followed by E. Power, *The Wool Trade in English Medieval History* (Oxford, 1941), pp. 98–101; Fryde, *Studies*, ch. X, p. 17; and Harriss, *Public Finance*, p. 447.For a contrary viewpoint see Lloyd, *Wool Trade*, pp. 203–7; Ormrod, 'Customs', pp. 27–9.
104 *HBC*, p. 558, nn. 1, 3.
105 The essential study is McKisack, *Parliamentary Representation*.
106 *VCH Warwicks*, viii. 248.
107 *CPR, 1348–50*, p. 306; Beaven, *Aldermen of London*, i. 266–7, 407.
108 *Register of the Freemen of the City of York I: 1272–1558*, ed. F. Collins, Surtees Soc., xcvi (1897), 42; *Return of MPs*, i. 149, 158; *CPR, 1343–5*, p. 107; *ibid., 1348–50*, p. 470; *CCR, 1354–60*, p. 4.
109 McKisack, *Parliamentary Representation*, pp. 83–6, 87, 89. It is only fair to add that some burgesses had problems in securing payment of their wages. The MPs for

Chipping Torrington in 1351, for instance, were still involved in a legal dispute three years later over non-payment of wages: KB27/377, *Rex*, m. 2.

110 See p. 173. For what follows see Barnes, 'Taxation of Wool', pp. 137–77; Power, *Wool Trade*, pp. 63–85; B. Wilkinson, *Studies in the Constitutional History of the Thirteenth and Fourteenth Centuries*, 2nd edn (Manchester, 1952), pp. 55–81; Harriss, *Public Finance*, pp. 420–49; Lloyd, *Wool Trade*, pp. 144–224.

111 *HBC*, p. 557; Harriss, *Public Finance*, pp. 428–9.

112 Fryde, *William de la Pole*, pp. 142–3; *SR*, i. 291–2; Wilkinson, *Studies*, pp. 71–2.

113 Unwin, 'Estate of Merchants', pp. 209–10.

114 *RP*, ii. 138; Barnes, 'Taxation of Wool', p. 166.

115 Fryde, *Studies*, ch. X, pp. 3, 7–8.

116 *LRDP*, iv. 556–7. The subsequent debate in parliament suggests that merchants may have been present in this meeting (Barnes, 'Taxation of Wool', p. 168; Fryde, *William de la Pole*, p. 201), but there is no evidence to prove this (*HBC*, p. 561).

117 Harriss, *Public Finance*, pp. 431, 457, 460.

118 It is possible that merchants may have consented to the subsidy on wine and merchandise (otherwise known as tunnage and poundage), since this was not announced until 15 Mar. (Unwin, 'Estate of Merchants', p. 218), and a group of merchants had been summoned to meet with the council on 7 Mar. (*HBC*, p. 561, n. 2). According to the enrolled account of this subsidy, it was granted 'by the prelates, magnates [and] other men of the sea (*homines de marina*) of the kingdom of England' (E356/5, m. 10). Compare the cloth custom, officially granted on 3 Mar. and authorized, according to the enrolled account, 'by the common assent of the prelates, earls, barons, magnates and others' (E356/7, m. 7). It is just possible that merchants were consulted on the grant of the maltolt, but the debate in parliament in Jan. 1348 suggests not (*RP*, ii. 168; Harriss, *Public Finance*, p. 431) 119. *RP*, ii. 200–1.

120 Harriss, *Public Finance*, p. 429, n. 6, pp. 450–5.

121 Edwards, *Second Century*, pp. 19–22. Edwards and others tend to treat the great council of Sept. 1353 as a parliament.

122 *RP*, ii. 271; *SR*, i. 374; Wilkinson, *Studies*, pp. 77–8.

123 See pp. 178–9.

124 Ormrod, 'Edward III's Government', pp. 178–9.

125 *RP*, ii. 252–3.

126 *SR*, i. 329–31. The Ordinance of the Staple was treated quite differently, being written up on the new roll of the staple (C67/22) and on the roll of proceedings of the great council. The distinction was maintained when it came to proclamation in the shires, for while the staple ordinance was advertised in the usual way (C255/3/3, nos. 62–66), the legislation recorded on the statute roll was apparently not proclaimed at all (see the case printed in R. Steele, *A Bibliography of Royal Proclamations of the Tudor and Stuart Sovereigns I: England and Wales*, Oxford, 1910, p. ix, n. 2). Ironically enough, parliament never queried the validity of the statutes of 1353, whereas it was extremely anxious to ensure proper status for the Ordinance of the Staple: see p. 179.

127 *RP*, ii. 168, 169, 171–2.

128 There are petitions from the merchants on the dorse of the parliament roll for 1343, but this is to be explained by the fact that a merchant assembly was meeting at the same time (*RP*, ii. 143; Lloyd, *Wool Trade*, p. 193).

129 R. L. Baker, 'The Establishment of the English Wool Staple in 1313', *Speculum*, xxxi (1956), 444–53; Lloyd, *Wool Trade*, pp. 115–18.

130 *Ibid.*, p. 118; Mills, 'Collectors of Customs', pp. 190–1. It was apparently on this occasion that the county communities of Hants., Wilts., Berks., Dorset, Glos., and the Isle of Wight, together with the towns of Southampton, Portsmouth and Romsey, all complained about the inconvenience of the Winchester staple and asked that it be transferred to Southampton (SC8/73/3618–19; SC8/78/3900; SC8/146/7291; SC8/155/7725; SC8/160/7979; SC8/164/8170). These petitions are all very similar, and indicate a concerted campaign. All, however, received a negative response.

131 SC8/64/3196 (Norwich); *CLBL*, F. 52–3 (London).

132 Lloyd, *Wool Trade*, pp. 121, 193–4, 202–3.

133 C67/22, m. 25d. The fact that the first draft of this ordinance was already complete by 6 June 1353 was noted long ago by Richardson and Sayles (*Parliament*, ch. XXI, p. 13, n. 4) but has been almost completely missed by historians until Lloyd, *Wool Trade*, pp. 205–7. For evidence of the staples functioning before Michaelmas 1353 see

Reading, pp. 298–9; Avesbury, p. 419; C67/22, mm. 25, 23; C255/4/13, no. 1D. The council called on 1 July (*LRDP*, iv. 596–7) was clearly associated with the implementation of the staples.

134 *RP*, ii. 246–51.

135 Ormrod, 'Agenda for Legislation', pp. 10–11; Lipson, *Economic History*, i. 455, n. 6; Lloyd, *Wool Trade*, pp. 116, 121.

136 *RP*, ii. 85–6; *VCH Northants.*, iii. 24.

137 *SR*, i. 280–1; A. R. Bridbury, *Medieval English Clothmaking* (London, 1982), p. 108.

138 *RP*, ii. 28, 409; SC8/268/13364, 13369; *CPR, 1327–30*, pp. 297–8; *Records of the City of Norwich*, ii, pp. lxv–xvi; Chorley; 'English Cloth Exports', p. 10.

139 *Foedera*, III (i). 58; C16/26, m. 16d. This staple was abandoned by Apr. 1349: C81/333/19733; D. Greaves, 'Calais under Edward III', in Unwin, ed., *Finance and Trade*, p. 340.

140 *RP*, ii. 231; *SR*, i. 314; *CLBL*, F. 229–30; A. H. Johnson, *The History of the Worshipful Company of the Drapers of London* (London, 1914–22), i. 81–5, 93.

141 Harriss, *Public Finance*, pp. 458–9. In 1376 there was a brief attempt to make worsted exports subject to the Calais staple, but this was abandoned after 1377: *Foedera*, III (ii). 1057–8; SC8/85/4243; *CPR, 1377–81*, p. 75; *ibid., 1388–92*, p. 248.

142 H. L. Gray, 'The Production and Exportation of English Woollens in the Fourteenth Century', *EHR*, xxxix (1924), 13–35; Bridbury, *Clothmaking*, pp. 47–59, 88–9.

143 Fryde, *Studies*, ch. XII, pp. 17–30.

144 I have examined the personnel of the commissions in C67/22, m. 25, and find that the case of London, cited by Lloyd, *Wool Trade*, p. 206, is exceptional.

145 *Ibid.*, pp. 203–7.

146 *RP*, ii. 253, 254.

147 *SR*, i. 348–9. Note that the ordinance was not copied out in full on the statute roll, and that the definitive text remained that on the roll of the staple. This helps to explain why the government later found it so easy to override the legislation.

148 Lloyd, *Wool Trade*, pp. 208–9.

149 For the election of the governor of this new staple by the mayors of the existing English staples see SC1/42/130; and note also SC1/62/68.

150 Lloyd, *Wool Trade*, p. 210.

151 R. L. Baker, 'The Government of Calais in 1363', in Jordan, McNab and Ruiz, eds.,

Order and Innovation, pp. 205–14.

152 A. L. Jenckes, *The Origin, the Organization and the Location of the Staple of England* (Philadelphia, 1908), p. 27. Returns to elections of staple officials survive in C47/33, *passim*. For lists of mayors of particular staples see E. E. Rich, 'The Mayors of the Staples', *Cambridge Historical Journal*, iv (1932–4), 192–3 (Westminster); Hill, *Medieval Lincoln*, pp. 249–51 (Lincoln and Boston).

153 The exceptions were Southampton and London. In fact, it was later agreed that merchants of these ports should not be required to take wool to the staples at Winchester and Westminster (Lloyd, *Wool Trade*, pp. 217–18 and n. 77, where the reference should be SC1/41/200). For the resulting decline in rents at the Westminster staple see the references cited in Ormrod, 'Personal Religion of Edward III', p. 875, n. 149.

154 Some time after the resumption of the Calais staple, the merchants of York complained of the illegal levy of 4d. per sack in the staple at Newcastle upon Tyne: SC8/216/10774.

155 *RP*, ii. 332–3. There was also a successful campaign to restore the port and staple of Lynn: *RP*, ii. 396; C67/22, m. 2.

156 Lloyd, *Wool Trade*, pp. 220–2.

157 Holmes, *Good Parliament*, p. 110.

158 For the status of the legislation see p. 233, n. 126.

159 This may in fact be an illusion caused by the change to privy seal summonses (see p. 105), but I have found virtually nothing in the issue rolls to suggest that merchants were summoned by such means in the second half of Edward III's reign.

160 *HBC*, p. 562, n. 2; Unwin, 'Estate of Merchants', p. 242.

161 *Foedera*, III (ii). 617–18; C49/47/5; Lloyd, *Wool Trade*, p. 210.

162 E.g. *Foedera*, III (ii). 88–1; *CLBL*, G. 256. Note that the writ of summons to the parliament of Nov. 1373 also asked for representatives of towns to be experienced in naval affairs: *LRDP*, iv. 661; *CLBL*, G. 312–13.

163 *RPHI*, p. 281.

164 *RP*, ii. 230, 241–2, 372; *RPHI*, p. 281. See also SC8/127/6305, an undatable petition addressed in the name of the merchants, and, judging from its endorsement, presented in parliament. It complains of a new levy of 1d. per cloth taken by the

alnagers on foreign cloth imported into England.

165 Ormrod, 'Customs', p. 31 and n. 24; *RP*, ii. 262.

166 *Ibid.*, ii. 364. Events in the parliament of 1382 suggest that the term 'merchants' was applied not to some other group present in the assembly, but to a subsection of the burgesses in the commons.See M. McKisack, 'Borough Representation in Richard II's Reign', *EHR*, xxxix (1924), 516.

167 *Idem, Parliamentary Representation*, p. 40.

168 Statistics derived from *ibid.*, pp. 11, 22, 26–8.

169 *SR*, i. 315–16, 353–5, 368.

170 *RP*, ii. 231, 232, 249, 261, 270, 276, 279, 282, etc.

171 *Ibid.*, ii. 366.

172 *Records of the City of Norwich*, ii. 44. In 1372 the burgesses had been asked to stay on after parliament was dismissed (see Table 5, n. 5). It is interesting to notice that in this case they presented a separate list of petitions: *RP*, ii. 314–15.

CONCLUSION

1 Stubbs, *Constitutional History*, ii. 393.

2 See, e.g. T. F. Tout, *The History of England from the Accession of Henry III to the Death of Edward III, 1216–1377* (London, 1905), p. 441.

3 G. Holmes, *The Later Middle Ages, 1272–1485* (London, 1962), p. 117.

4 McKisack, *Fourteenth Century*, pp. 270–1. See also *idem*, 'Edward III and the Historians', pp. 1–15.

5 McFarlane, *Nobility*, esp. pp. 156–61; Harriss, *Public Finance*, esp. pp. 313–75.

6 Prestwich, *Three Edwards*, p. 244.

7 B. Wilkinson, *The Later Middle Ages in England, 1216–1485* (London, 1969), pp. 155–6: Keen, *England in the Later Middle Ages*, pp. 163–5.

8 R. W. Kaeuper, *War, Justice, and Public Order: England and France in the Later Middle Ages* (Oxford, 1988), pp. 290–1.

9 See, e.g. Harriss, 'Formation of Parliament', pp. 45–6.

10 Powell, 'Administration of Criminal Justice', pp. 53–7; Storey, 'Liveries and Commissions of the Peace', pp. 131–52; Ormrod, 'Peasants' Revolt', pp. 25–6.

11 Powell, *Kingship, Law, and Society*, pp.168–228; C. Ross, *Edward IV* (London, 1974), pp. 395–404.

12 The anti-war literature of the late 14th century, discussed by Coleman, *English Literature in History*, pp. 84–92, does not seem to have had much lasting impact on Edward's reputation, judging from the references in M. Aston, 'Richard II and the Wars of the Roses', in Du Boulay and Barron, eds., *The Reign of Richard II*, pp.280–317, and Scattergood, *Politics and Poetry*, pp. 46–7, 49–50, 92, 309. I owe some of the ideas in this paragraph to D. A. L. Morgan.

13 S. H. Thomson, 'Walter Burley's Commentary on the Politics of Aristotle', in *Mélanges Auguste Pelzer* (Louvain, 1947), pp. 577–8. For the popularity of Burley's work see J.-P. Genet, 'The Dissemination of Manuscripts Relating to English Political Thought in the Fourteenth Century', in Jones and Vale, eds., *England and her Neighbours*, pp. 218–19, 232.

14 *Political Poems and Songs*, i. 211; *Piers Plowman: the B Version*, ed. G. Kane and E. T. Donaldson (London, 1975), p. 233, l. 113. Note the significant change made to this line in the C-text, possibly as a result of the Peasants' Revolt: *Piers Plowman* by William Langland: *An Edition of the C-Text*, ed. D. Pearsall (London, 1978), p. 37, n. to l. 140.

15 Barnes, *The History of that Most Victorious Monarch Edward III.* (Cambridge, 1688).

16 *Dialogus de Scaccario by Richard, Fitz* Nigel, ed. C. Johnson, F. E. L. Carter and D. E. Greenaway (Oxford, 1983), p. 1.

17 Ormrod, 'Edward III and his Family', p. 398, and the references cited there.

18 Froissart, i. 214.

Select bibliography

1. MANUSCRIPT SOURCES

Cambridge University Library
Ely Diocesan Records, G/l/l (Register of Thomas Lisle)

Carlisle: Cumbria Record Office
DRC/l/2 (Register of Thomas Appleby)

Durham: Prior's Kitchen
Register of Richard Bury

London: British Library
Additional Rolls 26588–26593
MS Cotton Nero C. VIII
Harleian Charter 43.D.46

London: Public Record Office

C47	Chancery Miscellanea
C49	Chancery: Parliament and Council Proceedings
C53	Chancery: Charter Rolls
C66	Chancery: Patent Rolls
C67	Chancery: Patent Rolls (Supplementary)
C76	Chancery: Treaty Rolls
C81	Chancery: Warrants for the Great Seal (Series 1)
C219	Chancery: Writs and Returns of Members of Parliament
C255	Chancery: Miscellaneous Files and Writs
C256	Chancery: Various Summonses
C270	Chancery: Ecclesiastical Miscellanea
E13	Exchequer of Pleas: Plea Rolls
E36	Exchequer, Treasury of Receipt: Miscellaneous Books
E101	Exchequer, King's Remembrancer: Various Accounts
E122	Exchequer, King's Remembrancer: Customers' Accounts
E159	Exchequer, King's Remembrancer: Memoranda Rolls
E163	Exchequer, King's Remembrancer: Miscellanea
E175	Exchequer, King's Remembrancer: Parliament and Council Proceedings
E198	Exchequer, King's Remembrancer: Documents Relating to Serjeanties, Knights' Fees, etc.
E199	Exchequer, King's Remembrancer: Sheriffs' Accounts
E208	Exchequer, King's Remembrancer: Brevia Baronibus
E356	Exchequer, Lord Treasurer's Remembrancer: Enrolled Customs Accounts
E359	Exchequer, Lord Treasurer's Remembrancer: Enrolled Accounts of Subsidies
E368	Exchequer, Lord Treasurer's Remembrancer: Memoranda Rolls
E372	Exchequer, Lord Treasurer's Remembrancer: Pipe Rolls
E401	Exchequer of Receipt: Receipt Rolls
E403	Exchequer of Receipt: Issue Rolls
JUST 1	Justices Itinerant: Assize Rolls, etc.
KB27	King's Bench: Coram Rege Rolls
KB29	King's Bench: Controlment Rolls
KB146	King's Bench: Panella Files

SC1   Special Collections: Ancient Correspondence
SC8   Special Collections: Ancient Petitions
SC10   Special Collections: Parliamentary Proxies

London: Westminster Abbey Muniments
Muniments 3787, 12208, 12214, 12220, 12222, 12223

2. SELECTED PRINTED SOURCES

Only those works cited more than once are listed here.

A. Primary Sources

Ancient Petitions Relating to Northumberland, ed. C. M. Fraser, Surtees Soc., clxxvi (1966)
Anglia Sacra, ed. H. Wharton, 2 vols. (London, 1691)
Anglo-Norman Political Songs, ed. I. S. T. Aspin, Anglo-Norman Texts, xi (1953)
The Anonimalle Chronicle, ed. V. H. Galbraith (Manchester, 1927)
Calendar of Charter Rolls
Calendar of Close Rolls
Calendar of Fine Rolls
Calendar of Inquisitions Miscellaneous
Calendar of Inquisitions Post Mortem
Calendar of Letter Books of the City of London, ed. R. R. Sharpe, 11 vols. (London, 1899–1912)
Calendar of Papal Registers: Letters
Calendar of Papal Registers: Petitions
Calendar of Patent Rolls
Calendar of Plea and Memoranda Rolls of the City of London, ed. A. H. Thomas and P. E. Jones, 6 vols.
    (Cambridge, 1926–61)
Cambridge Borough Documents I, ed. W. M. Palmer (Cambridge, 1931)
Chronica Johannis de Reading et Anonymi Cantuariensis, ed. J. Tait (Manchester, 1914)
Chronicon Galfridi le Baker de Swynebroke, ed. E. M. Thompson (Oxford, 1889)
Chroniques de Jean Froissart, ed. S. Luce, G. Raynaud, L. Mirot and A. Mirot, 15 vols., Société de
    l'Histoire de France (1869–1975)
Concilia Magna Britanniae et Hiberniae, ed. D. Wilkins, 4 vols. (London, 1737)
Crecy and Calais from the Public Records, ed. G. Wrottesley, William Salt Archaeological Soc., xviii (2)
    (1897)
The Eyre of Northamptonshire 3-4 Edward III A. D. 1329–30, ed. D. W. Sutherland, 2 vols., SS, xcvii–viii
    (1983)
Foedera, Conventiones, Literae et Cujuscunque Generis Acta Publica, ed. T. Rymer, Record Commission
    edn, 3 vols. in 6 parts (London, 1816–30)
Historia Anglicana of Thomas of Walsingham, ed. H. T. Riley, 2 vols., RS (1863–4)
The Issue Roll of Thomas de Brantingham, 44 Edward III, ed. F. Devon (London, 1835)
Issues of the Exchequer, Henry III — Henry VI, ed. F. Devon (London, 1847)
The Lay Subsidy of 1334, ed. R. Glasscock (London, 1975)
The Making of King's Lynn: A Documentary Survey, ed. D. M. Owen (London, 1984)
Munimenta Civitatis Oxonie, ed. H. E. Salter, Oxford Historical Soc., lxxi (1920)
Northern Petitions, ed. C. M. Fraser, Surtees Soc., cxciv (1982)
Parliamentary Texts of the Later Middle Ages, ed. N. Pronay and J. Taylor (Oxford, 1980)
The Peasants' Revolt of 1381, ed. R. B. Dobson, 2nd edn (London, 1983)
Political Poems and Songs Relating to English History, ed. T. Wright, 2 vols., RS (1859–61)
Proceedings before the Justices of the Peace in the Fourteenth and Fifteenth Centuries, ed. B. H. Putnam
    (London, 1938)
Records of the Borough of Leicester II, ed. M. Bateson (London, 1901)
The Records of the City of Norwich, ed. W. H. Hudson and J. C. Tingey, 2 vols. (Norwich, 1906–10)
Registrum Hamonis Hethe Diocesis Roffensis, ed. C. Johnson, 2 vols., CYS, xlviii–ix (1948)
Registrum Johannis de Trillek Episcopi Herefordensis, ed. J. H. Parry, CYS, viii (1912)

Report from the Lords' Committees … for All Matters Touching the Dignity of a Peer, 4 vols. (London, 1820–9)

Return of the Name of Every Member of the Lower House of Parliament…1213–1874, 2 vols. (Parliamentary Papers, 1878)

Robertus de Avesbury De Gestis Mirabilibus Regis Edwardi Tertii, ed. E. M. Thompson, RS (1889)

Rolls of the Warwickshire and Coventry Sessions of the Peace, 1377–1397, ed. E.G. Kimball, Dugdale Soc., xvi (1939)

Rotuli Parliamentorum, 6 vols. (London, 1783)

Rotuli Parliamentorum Angliae Hactenus Inediti, ed. H. G. Richardson and G. O. Sayles, Camden Soc., 3rd ser., li (1935)

Select Cases before the King's Council, 1243–1482, ed. I. S. Leadam and J. F. Baldwin, SS, xxxv (1918)

Select Cases in the Court of King's Bench, ed. G. O. Sayles, 7 vols., SS, lv, lvii, lviii, lxxiv, lxxvi, lxxxii, lxxxviii (1936–71)

Statutes of the Realm, 11 vols. (1810–28)

The 1341 Royal Inquest in Lincolnshire, ed. B. W. McLane, Lincoln Record Soc., lxxviii (1988)

The Treatise of Walter de Milemete, De Nobilitatibus, Sapientiis, et Prudentiis Regum, ed. M. R. James (Roxburghe Club, Oxford, 1913)

The Wardrobe Book of William de Norwell, ed. M. Lyon, B. Lyon, H. S. Lucas and J. de Sturler (Brussels, 1983)

Year Books of the Reign of King Edward the Third, Years XI–XX, ed. A. J. Horwood and L. O. Pike, 15 vols. RS (1883–1911)

B. Secondary Sources

ALEXANDER, J., and BINSKI, P., eds., *Age of Chivalry: Art in Plantagenet* England, 1200–1400 (London, 1987)

ASTILL, G. G., 'The Medieval Gentry: A Study in Leicestershire Society, 1350–1399', University of Birmingham Ph.D. thesis (1977)

BAKER, R. L., *The English Customs Service, 1307–1343: A Study of Medieval Administration* (Philadelphia, 1961)

BALDWIN, J. F., 'The King's Council', *EGW*, i. 129–61

— *The King's Council in England during the Middle Ages* (Oxford, 1913)

BARNES, F. R., 'The Taxation of Wool, 1321–1348', in Unwin, ed., *Finance and Trade*, pp. 137–77

BARNIE, J., *War in Medieval Society: Social Values and the Hundred Years War, 1337–99* (London, 1974)

BEAN, J. M. W., *The Decline of English Feudalism, 1215–1540* (Manchester, 1968)

— *From Lord to Patron: Lordship in Late Medieval England* (Manchester, 1989)

BEAVEN, A. B., *The Aldermen of the City of London*, 2 vols. (London, 1908–13)

BELLAMY, J. G., 'The Coterel Gang: An Anatomy of Fourteenth-Century Criminals', *EHR*, lxxix (1964), 698–717

— *The Law of Treason in England in the Later Middle Ages* (Cambridge, 1970)

BRIDBURY, A. R., *Medieval English Clothmaking* (London, 1982)

BRITNELL, R. H., *Growth and Decline in Colchester, 1300–1525* (Cambridge, 1986)

BROWN, A. L., *The Governance of Late Medieval England, 1272–1461* (London, 1989)

BROWN, R. A., COLVIN, H. M., and TAYLOR, A. J., *The History of the King's Works: The Middle Ages*, 2 vols. (London, 1963)

BUCK, M. [C.], *Politics, Finance and the Church in the Reign of Edward II: Walter Stapeldon, Treasurer of England* (Cambridge, 1983)

— 'The Reform of the Exchequer, 1316–1326', *EHR*, xcviii (1983), 241–60

CAM, H. M., *The Hundred and the Hundred Rolls*, new edn (London, 1963)

— *Law-Finders and Law-Makers in Medieval England* (London, 1962)

— *Liberties and Communities in Medieval England* (London, 1963)

CHAPLAIS, P., *Essays in Medieval Diplomacy and Admini*stration (London, 1981)

CHEYETTE, F., 'Kings, Courts, Cures and Sinecures: The Statute of Provisors and the Common Law', *Traditio*, xix (1963), 295–349

CHORLEY, P., 'English Cloth Exports during the Thirteenth and Early Fourteenth Centuries: The Continental Evidence', *Historical Research*, lxi (1988), 1–10

CLARKE, M. V., *Medieval Representation and Consent* (London, 1936)

COKAYNE, G. E., *The Complete Peerage*, new edn, rev. V. Gibbs et al., 13 vols. (London, 1910–57)

COLEMAN, J., *English Literature in History, 1350–1400: Medieval Readers and* Writers (London, 1981)

CROOK, D., 'The Later Eyres', *EHR*, xcvii (1982), 241–68

CUTTINO, G. P., and LYMAN, T. W., 'Where is Edward II?', *Speculum*, liii (1978), 522–44

DAVIES, R. G., 'The Episcopal Appointments in England and Wales of 1375', *Mediaeval Studies*, xliv (1982), 306–32

— and DENTON, J. H., eds., *The English Parliament in the Middle Ages* (Manchester, 1981)

DENTON, J. H., *Robert Winchelsey and the Crown, 1294–1313* (Cambridge, 1980)

DOBSON, [R.] B., ed., *The Church, Politics and Patronage in the Fifteenth Century* (Gloucester, 1984)

DU BOULAY, F. R. H., and BARRON, C. M., eds., *The Reign of Richard II: Essays in Honour of May McKisack* (London, 1971)

EDWARDS, J. G., *The Second Century of the English Parliament* (Oxford, 1979)

EMDEN, A. B., *A Biographical Register of the University of Oxford to 1500*, 3 vols. (Oxford, 1957–9)

FAITH, R., 'The "Great Rumour" of 1377 and Peasant Ideology', in Hilton and Aston, eds., *English Rising of 1381*, pp. 43–73

FEAVEARYEAR, A., *The Pound Sterling*, 2nd edn (Oxford, 1963)

FOWLER, K., *The King's Lieutenant: Henry of Grosmont, First Duke of Lancaster, 1310–1361* (London, 1969)

FRYDE, E. B., 'Edward III's War Finance 1331–41: Transactions in Wool and Credit Operations', University of Oxford D.Phil. thesis (1947)

— 'Introduction to the New Edition', in Oman, *Great Revolt*, pp. xi–xxxii

— *Studies in Medieval Trade and Finance* (London, 1983)

— *William de la Pole, Merchant and King's Banker* (London, 1988)

GREENAWAY, D. E., PORTER, S., and ROY, I., eds., *Handbook of British Chronology*, 3rd edn (London, 1986) and MILLER, E., eds.,

— *Historical Studies of the English Parliament*, 2 vols. (Cambridge, 1970)

FRYDE, N. [M.], 'Edward III's Removal of his Ministers and Judges, 1340–1', *BIHR*, xlviii (1975), 149–61

— 'John Stratford, Bishop of Winchester, and the Crown, 1323–30', *BIHR*, xliv (1971), 153–61 'A Medieval Robber Baron: Sir John Molyns of Stoke Poges, Buckinghamshire', in Hunnisett and Post, eds., *Medieval Legal Records*, pp. 198–221

— *The Tyranny and Fall of Edward II, 1321–1326* (Cambridge, 1979)

FURLEY, J. S., *City Government of Winchester from the Records of the XIV and XV Centuries* (Oxford, 1923)

GILLINGHAM, J., and HOLT, J. C., eds., *War and Government in the Middle Ages: Essays in Honour of J. O. Prestwich* (Woodbridge, Suffolk, 1984)

GIVEN-WILSON, C. [J.], 'The Court and Household of Edward III, 1360–1377', University of St Andrews Ph.D. thesis (1976)

— *The English Nobility in the Late Middle Ages* (London, 1987)

— *The Royal Household and the King's Affinity: Service, Politics and Finance in England 1360–1413* (London and New Haven, 1986)

GRAY, H. L., *The Influence of the Commons on Early Legislation* (Cambridge, Mass., 1932)

HAINES, R. M., *Archbishop John Stratford* (Toronto, 1986)

— *The Church and Politics in Fourteenth-Century England: The Career of Adam Orleton* (Cambridge, 1978)

HALLAM, E. M., *Domesday Book through Nine Centuries* (London, 1986)

HARBISON, S., 'William of Windsor, the Court Party and the Administration of Ireland', in J. Lydon, ed., *England and Ireland in the Later Middle Ages: Essays in Honour of Jocelyn Otway-Ruthven* (Blackrock, Co. Dublin, 1981), pp. 153–14

HARRISS, G. L., 'The Commons' Petition of 1340', *EHR*, lxxviii (1963), 625–54

— 'The Formation of Parliament, 272–1377', in Davies and Denton, eds., *English Parliament*, pp. 29–60

— *King, Parliament and Public Finance in Medieval England to 1369* (Oxford, 1975)

HARROD, H., *Report of the Deeds and Records of the Borough of King's Lynn* (King's Lynn, 1874)

HATCHER, J., *Plague, Population and the English Economy, 1348–1530* (London, 1977)

HEWITT, H. J., *The Organization of War under Edward III* (Manchester, 1966)

HIGHFIELD, J. R. L., 'The English Hierarchy in the Reign of Edward III', *TRHS*, 5th ser., vi

(1956), 115–38

— 'The Promotion of William of Wickham to the See of Winchester', *JEH*, iv (1953), 37–54

— 'The Relations between the Church and the English Crown from the Death of Archbishop Stratford to the Opening of the Great Schism (1349–78)', University of Oxford D.Phil. thesis (1951)

— and JEFFS, R., eds., *The Crown and Local Communities in England and France in the Fifteenth Century* (Gloucester, 1981)

HILL, J. W. F., *Medieval Lincoln* (Cambridge, 1948)

HILTON, R. [H.], *Bond Men Made Free: Medieval Peasant Movements and the English Rising of 1381* (London, 1973)

— *The English Peasantry in the Later Middle Ages* (Oxford, 1975)

— 'Peasant Movements in England before 1381', *EcHR*, 2nd ser., ii (1949), 111–36

— and ASTON, T. H., eds., *The English Rising of 1381* (Cambridge, 1984)

HOLMES, G. [A.], *The Estates of the Higher Nobility in Fourteenth Century England* (Cambridge, 1957)

— *The Good Parliament* (Oxford, 1975)

HOSKINS, W. G., *Local History in England*, 2nd edn (London, 1972)

HUGHES, D., *A Study of Social and Constitutional Tendencies in the Early Years of Edward III* (London, 1915)

HUNNISETT, R. F., and POST, J. B., eds., *Medieval Legal Records* (London, 1978)

JONES, M., and VALE, M., eds., *England and her Neighbours: Essays in Honour of Pierre Chaplais* (London, 1989)

JONES, W. R., 'Bishops, Politics and the Two Laws: The *Gravamina* of the English Clergy, 1237–1399', *Speculum*, xli (1966), 209–45

— '*Rex et Ministri*: English Local Government and the Crisis of 1341', *JBS*, xiii, no. 1 (1973), 1–20

JORDAN, W. C., McNAB, B., and RUIZ, T. F., eds., *Order and Innovation in the Middle Ages: Essays in Honor of J. R. Strayer* (Princeton, NJ, 1976)

KEEN, M. H., *England in the Later Middle Ages* (London, 1973)

KNOWLES, D., *The Religious Orders in England*, 3 vols. (Cambridge, 1948–59)

LE NEVE, J., *Fasti Ecclesiae Anglicanae, 1300–1541*, new edn, compiled by H. P. F. King, J. M. Horn and B. Jones, 12 vols. (London, 1962–7)

LE PATOUREL, J., *Feudal Empires: Norman and Plantagenet*, ed. M. Jones (London, 1984)

LIPSON, E., *The Economic History of England I: The Middle Ages*, 12th edn (London, 1959)

— *List of Sheriffs for England and Wales*, PRO Lists and Indexes, ix (repr. with amendments, 1963)

LLOYD, T. H., *The English Wool Trade in the Middle Ages* (Cambridge, 1971)

LOBEL, M. D., and JOHNS, W. H., eds., *Atlas of Historic Towns*, 2 vols. (London, 1969–75)

LUNT, W. E., 'The Collectors of Clerical Subsidies Granted to the King by the English Clergy', *EGW*, ii. 227–80

— *Financial Relations of the Papacy with England*, 2 vols. (Cambridge, Mass., 1939–62)

McFARLANE, K. B., 'Bastard Feudalism', *BIHR*, xx (1945), 161–80, repr. in K. B. McFarlane, *England in the Fifteenth Century* (London, 1981), pp. 23–43

— *Lancastrian Kings and Lollard Knights* (Oxford, 1972)

— *The Nobility of Later Medieval England* (Oxford, 1973)

McKISACK, M., *The Fourteenth Century* (Oxford, 1959)

— 'London and the Succession to the Crown during the Middle Ages', in R. W. Hunt, W. A. Pantin and R. W. Southern, eds., *Studies in Medieval History Presented to F. M. Powicke* (Oxford, 1948), pp. 76–89

— *The Parliamentary Representation of the English Boroughs during the Middle Ages* (Oxford, 1932)

MADDICOTT, J. R., 'The County Community and the Making of Public Opinion in Fourteenth-Century England', *TRHS*, 5th ser., xxviii (1978), 27–3

— 'The English Peasantry and the Demands of the Crown, 1294–1341', *P&P Supplement*, i (1975), repr. in T. H. Aston, ed., *Landlords, Peasants and Politics in Medieval England* (Cambridge,1987), pp. 285–359

— 'Law and Lordship: Royal Justices as Retainers in Thirteenth- and Fourteenth-Century England', *P&P Supplement*, iv (1978)

— 'Parliament and the Constituencies, 1272–1377', in Davies and Denton, eds., *English Parliament*, pp. 61–87

— 'Poems of Social Protest in Early Fourteenth-Century England', in Ormrod, ed., *England in the*

Fourteenth Century, pp. 130–44

MAXWELL-LYTE, H. C., *Historical Notes on the Use of the Great Seal of England* (London, 1926)

MAYHEW, N. J., ed., *Edwardian Monetary Affairs (1279– 1344)*, British Archaeological Reports, xxxvi (1977)

MIROT, L., and DÉPREZ, E., 'Les Ambassades Anglaises pendant la Guerre de Cent Ans', *Bibliothèque de l'École des Chartes*, lix (1898), 550–77; lx (1899), 171–214; lxi (1900), 20–58

MORRIS, W. A., 'The Sheriff', *EGW*, ii. 41–108

NEWTON, S. M., *Fashion in the Age of the Black Prince* (Woodbridge, 1980)

NICHOLSON, R. G., *Edward III and the Scots, 1327–1335* (Oxford, 1965)

OMAN, C., *The Great Revolt of 1381*, 2nd edn (Oxford, 1969)

ORMROD, W. M., 'Agenda for Legislation, 1322–c.1340', *EHR*, cv (1990), 1–33

— 'The Crown and the English Economy, 1290–1348', in B. M. S. Campbell, ed., *Before the Black Death: Essays in the Crisis of the Early Fourteenth Century* (Manchester, 1991)

— 'Edward III and his Family', *JBS*, xxvi (1987), 398–442

— 'Edward III and the Recovery of Royal Authority in England, 1340–60', *History*, lxxii (1987), 4–19

— 'Edward III's Government of England, c. 1346–1356', University of Oxford D.Phil. thesis (1984)

— 'The English Crown and the Customs, 1349–63', *EcHR*, 2nd ser., xl (1981), 21–40

— The English Government and the Black Death of 1348–49', in Ormrod, ed., *England in the Fourteenth Century*, pp. 175–88

— 'An Experiment in Taxation: The English Parish Subsidy of 1371', *Speculum*, lxiii (1988), 59–82

— 'The Origins of the *Sub Pena* Writ', *Historical Research*, lxi (1988), 11–20

— 'The Peasants' Revolt and the Government of England', *JBS*, xxix (1990), 1–30

— 'The Personal Religion of Edward III', *Speculum*, lxiv (1989), 849–11

— ed., *England in the Fourteenth Century: Proceedings of the 1985 Harlaxton Symposium* (Woodbridge, 1986)

PLUCKNETT, T. F. T., 'Parliament', *EGW*, i. 82–128

POWELL, E., 'The Administration of Criminal Justice in Late-Medieval England: Peace Sessions and Assizes', in R. Eales and D. Sullivan, eds., *The Political Context of Law: Proceedings of the Seventh British Legal History Conference* (London, 1987), pp. 48–59

— *Kingship, Law, and Society: Criminal Justice in the Reign of Henry V* (Oxford, 1989)

POWELL, J. E., and WALLIS, K., *The House of Lords in the Middle Ages* (London, 1968)

POWICKE, M., *Military Obligation in Medieval England* (Oxford, 1962)

PRESTWICH, M., *Edward I* (London, 1988)

— 'English Armies in the Early Stages of the Hundred Years War: A Scheme in 1341', *BIHR*, lvi (1983), 102–13

PRINCE, A. E., 'The Indenture System under Edward III', in J. G. Edwards, V. H. Galbraith and E. F. Jacob, eds., *Historical Essays in Honour of James Tait* (Manchester, 1933), pp. 283–9l

— 'The Payment of Army Wages in Edward III's Reign', *Speculum*, xix (1944), 137–60

PUTNAM, B. H., *The Enforcement of the Statute of Labourers* (New York, 1908)

— *The Place in Legal History of Sir William Shareshull* (Cambridge, 1950)

— 'The Transformation of the Keepers of the Peace into the Justices of the Peace, 1327–1380', *TRHS*, 4th ser., xii (1929), 19–48

RAYNER, D., 'The Forms and Machinery of the "Commune Petition" in the Fourteenth Century', *EHR*, lvi (1941), 198–233, 549–70

REYNOLDS, S., *An Introduction to the History of English Medieval Towns* (Oxford, 1977)

RICHARDSON, H. G., 'John of Gaunt and the Parliamentary Representation of Lancashire', *BJRL*, xxii (1938), 175–222

— and SAYLES, G. O., *The English Parliament in the Middle Ages* (London, 1981)

ROSKELL, J. S. 'The Problem of the Attendance of the Lords in Medieval Parliaments', *BIHR*, xxix (1956), 153–204

SAINTY, J. C., *Officers of the Exchequer*, PRO List & Index Soc., special ser., xviii (1983)

SAUL, N., 'The Despensers and the Downfall of Edward II', *EHR*, xcix (1984), 1–33

— *Knights and Esquires: The Gloucestershire Gentry in the Fourteenth Century* (Oxford, 1981)

— *Scenes from Provincial Life: Knightly Families in Sussex, 1280–1400* (Oxford, 1986)

SAUNDERS, P. C., 'Royal Ecclesiastical Patronage in England, 1199–1351', University of Oxford D.Phil. thesis (1978)

SAYLES, G. O., *The King's Parliament of England* (London, 1975)

SCATTERGOOD, V. J., *Politics and Poetry in the Fifteenth Century* (London, 1971)

SEARLE, E., and BURGHART, R., 'The Defense of England and the Peasants' Revolt', *Viator*, iii (1912), 365–88

SHERBORNE, J. [W.], 'The Costs of English Warfare with France in the Later Fourteenth Century', *BIHR*, l (1977), 135–50

— 'Indentured Retinues and English Expeditions to France, 1369–1380', *EHR*, lxxix (1964), 718–46

— 'John of Gaunt, Edward III's Retinue and the French Campaign of 1369', in R. A. Griffiths and J. Sherborne, eds., *Kings and Nobles in the Later Middle Ages: A Tribute to Charles Ross* (Gloucester, 1986), pp. 41–61

STEEL, A., *The Receipt of the Exchequer, 1377–1485* (Cambridge, 1954)

STEPHEN, L., and LEE, S., eds., *The Dictionary of National Biography*, 63 vols. (London, 1885–1900)

STONES, E. L. G., 'The Folvilles of Ashby-Folville, Leicestershire and their Associates in Crime, 1326–1347', *TRHS*, 5th ser., vii (1951), 117–36

— 'Sir Geoffrey le Scrope (c. 1280 to 1340), Chief Justice of the King's Bench', *EHR*, lxix (1954), 1–17

STOREY, R. L., 'Liveries and Commissions of the Peace, 1388–90', in Du Boulay and Barron, eds., *The Reign of Richard II*, pp. 131–52

STUBBS, W., *The Constitutional History of England*, 3 vols., 4th edn (Oxford, 1906)

TATNALL, E. C., 'John Wyclif and *Ecclesia Anglicana*', *JEH*, xx (1969), 19–43

TAYLOR, C. H., ed., *Anniversary Essays in Medieval History Presented to C. H. Haskins* (New York, 1929)

THOMPSON, A. HAMILTON, 'William Bateman, Bishop of Norwich, 1344–1355', *Norfolk Archaeology*, xxv (1935), 102–31

TOUT, T. F., *Chapters in the Administrative History of Mediaeval England*, 6 vols. (Manchester, 1920–33)

TUCK, A., *Crown and Nobility, 1272–1461* (London, 1985)

— *Richard II and the English Nobility* (London, 1973)

UNWIN, G., 'The Estate of Merchants, 1336–1365', in Unwin, ed., *Finance and Trade*, pp. 179–255

— ed., *Finance and Trade under Edward III* (Manchester, 1918)

VALE, J., *Edward III and Chivalry* (Woodbridge, 1982)

WAUGH, S. L., 'For King, Country and Patron: The Despensers and Local Administration, 1321–1322', *JBS*, xxii, no. 2 (1983), 23–45

WESKE, D. B., *Convocation of the Clergy* (London, 1937)

WILKINSON, B., 'The Authorisation of Chancery Writs under Edward III', *BJRL*, viii (1924), 107–39

— *The Chancery under Edward III* (Manchester, 1929)

— *Studies in the Constitutional History of the Thirteenth and Fourteenth Centuries*, 2nd edn (Manchester, 1952)

WILLARD, J. F., *Parliamentary Taxes on Personal Property, 1290 to 1334* (Cambridge, Mass., 1934)

— W. A. MORRIS, J. R. STRAYER and W. H. DUNHAM, eds., *The English Government at Work, 1327–1336*, 3 vols. (Cambridge, Mass., 1940–50)

WILLIAMS, G. A., *Medieval London: From Commune to Capital* (London, 1963)

WOLFFE, B. P., *The Royal Demesne in English History* (London, 1971)

WRIGHT, S. M., *The Derbyshire Gentry in the Fifteenth Century*, Derbyshire Record Soc., viii (1983)

WRIGHT, T., 'The Municipal Archives of Exeter', *Journal of the Archaeological Association*, xxviii (1862), 306–19

Index

Note: Kings and their immediate families are indexed under their first names; members of the nobility are indexed under the titles they held up to 1377. British placenames are categorized under their modern counties, but in the text appear under the relevant medieval shire names.